PRIVATIZATION AND ITS ALTERNATIVES

LA FOLLETTE PUBLIC POLICY SERIES

The Robert M. La Follette Institute of Public Affairs

Robert H. Haveman, *Director*

State Policy Choices: The Wisconsin Experience
Sheldon Danziger and John F. Witte, editors

The Rise of the Entrepreneurial State: State and Local Development Policy in the United States
Peter K. Eisinger

The Midwest Response to the New Federalism
Peter K. Eisinger and William Gormley, editors

Privatization and Its Alternatives
William T. Gormley, Jr., editor

Unemployment Insurance: The Second Half-Century
W. Lee Hansen and James F. Byers, editors

Race, Class, and Education: The Politics of Second-Generation Discrimination
Kenneth J. Meier, Joseph Stewart, Jr., and Robert E. England

to deliver services. For the sake of clarity, it is useful to differentiate them from both classic, marketplace solutions and reforms that take place within government itself.

Alternatives to Privatization

Supporters of privatization claim that the private sector can do a better job than the public sector. More specifically, they argue that public bureaucracies are prone to failure. Many opponents of privatization concede the failures of public bureaucracies but they argue that the performance of public bureaucracies can be improved through institutional redesign. Some leading proposals for reform include the following:

Greater Accountability to Consumers. If public bureaucracies were made more accountable to the people whose interests they are supposed to serve, their performance might improve dramatically. Imagine an educational system in which all students attend public schools but parents are free to send their children to the public school of their choice. Or imagine a welfare system in which social workers are routinely evaluated by their clients for their courtesy, knowledgeability, and helpfulness. The basic idea is to improve the performance of public agencies through greater consumer choice or clientele feedback.

Greater Accountability to Politicians. If public bureaucracies were made more accountable to politicians, who in turn are accountable to the electorate, similar results might be achieved. Elected by the voters, chief executives often lack control over important executive branch officials. The Senior Executive Service (SES), created by Congress in 1978, addressed this problem and strengthened executive control by authorizing the president to reassign approximately 8,000 upper-level federal employees. In a similar fashion, at the local level mayors could be given greater authority to hire and fire top city officials. Alternatively, public bureaucracies could be made more accountable to the legislative branch through more vigorous legislative oversight.

Listening to Workers. In many public bureaucracies, workers are brimming with ideas on how to improve their agency's performance. In private industry in Japan and elsewhere, workers have been encouraged to offer suggestions and to participate in the corporate planning process. The same approach could yield substantial benefits to public agencies accustomed to a more hierarchical approach.

Decentralization. In some instances, more radical solutions may be warranted. Instead of abandoning hierarchical thinking, one could abandon hierarchical structures. In education, for example, decentralization could unleash the creative potential of principals and teachers. In law enforcement, decentralization could enable police officers to experiment with law enforcement strategies or techniques appropriate to their neighborhood.

ment of Housing and Urban Development in the 1970s and the 1980s. As yet, education vouchers have been widely discussed but seldom tried.

A third form of privatization, far more popular in other countries, is the sale of assets. In Great Britain, asset sales have been an integral part of the Thatcher administration's privatization program (Hennessy 1989:501). According to Touche Ross, only 24 percent of local governments in the United States have sold some assets to private buyers over the past five years, and only 21 percent expect to do so in the next two years. At the federal level, Conrail and some government loan portfolios have been sold but proposals to sell Amtrak, the Naval Petroleum Reserves, and other assets have not gone very far.

A fourth form of privatization is load-shedding, which involves the government's abandoning some activity, which may or may not be picked up by the private sector. Thus when the federal government cuts back welfare benefits, public service employment programs, or support for the arts, the private sector must decide whether to take up the slack.

Contracting out, vouchers, asset sales, and load-shedding are widely recognized forms of privatization. However, they do not exhaust the full range of experiments at the public-private boundary. In a number of instances, public and private roles have been redefined to permit creative partnerships between the government and private citizens. For example, the federal government has turned the management of some public housing units over to tenants, who are authorized to make a wide variety of decisions concerning entry (who may join the community), exit (who must leave the community), and conduct (how residents must behave). The Kenilworth-Parkside Public Housing Project in Washington, D.C., with 464 units, is an example of a tenant-run public housing project.

In some states, land trusts have been authorized to purchase and preserve environmentally sensitive tracts of land. These nonprofit organizations act in lieu of the government to preserve wildlife habitats, rural landscapes, and open spaces. In some instances, they also offer recreational opportunities.

At the local level, many police departments have encouraged the formation of neighborhood crime watch programs staffed by ordinary citizens who monitor neighborhood activity and report suspicious behavior to the police. To be sure, neighborhood crime watch programs merely supplement services provided by public police officers, but in a very real sense, law enforcement services are being provided by private citizens.

These initiatives, and others like them, are perhaps best thought of as institutional hybrids. They are forms of privatization since they involve the transfer of government functions to the private sector; on the other hand, they preserve a strong role for government and they do not rely upon private, for-profit firms

In this book, a number of distinguished scholars wrestle with the controversy by examining privatization and its alternatives from several different vantage points. In most instances, they evaluate recent evidence on privatization and express a point of view on the relative merits of privatization and other strategies to improve the delivery of public services.

There are several premises behind this undertaking that should be made explicit at the outset:

Theoretical arguments and empirical research both deserve attention and debate. A rich body of literature tells us when we should prefer the market and when we should prefer the government (Bator 1958; Coase 1960; Baumol 1965; Wolf 1979; Weimer and Vining 1989:29–178). We need to be attentive to positive and normative theories. At the same time, we need to test these theories in a variety of different settings, in the hope of specifying circumstances when privatization does and does not make sense.

An inquiry into privatization should be multidisciplinary in nature. Much of the privatization debate has focused on cost containment—the province of economics. But many other values are at stake—values that political scientists, sociologists, lawyers, and planners can best address.

A study of privatization should be an exercise in comparative analysis. We need to compare privatization in different policy arenas, at different levels of government, and in different countries. Above all, we need to compare privatization with its alternatives, including some that have been tried and others that have merely been proposed. The debate will remain artificially constrained if the privatization option is the only interesting option on the table.

The Many Faces of Privatization

In the United States, the principal form of privatization is contracting out. According to a 1987 survey by Touche Ross, 99 percent of all local governments have contracted out services over the past five years; 96 percent expect to contract out services in the next two years. Contracts are awarded to for-profit firms in some instances, nonprofit organizations in others. Contracting out is also widespread at the state level. In New Jersey for example, building maintenance, data management, advertising, drug treatment, educational testing, and other services are contracted out by the state (The Eagleton Institute 1987).

Another form of privatization is the voucher, whereby certain consumers are authorized to purchase earmarked goods or services from the private market. The government specifies who is eligible to purchase the services and who is eligible to provide them. The leading example of vouchers in this country is the food stamps program. Housing vouchers have also become more common in recent years as a result of experimental programs adopted by the Depart-

1   *William T. Gormley, Jr.*

The Privatization Controversy

In recent years, many governments have decided to transfer responsibility for a variety of public services, in whole or in part, to the private sector. Governments have opted for privatization, as it is called, in an effort to reduce burdens on the public purse, maximize consumer choice, and promote other goals. The movement towards privatization has been especially striking in Great Britain, where the Thatcher government has privatized everything from airlines to oil companies to public housing. In the United States most local governments have embraced privatization to some degree, while the federal government and state governments have proceeded more cautiously.

To supporters, privatization conjures up visions of a lean, streamlined public sector more reliant on the private marketplace for the delivery of public services. To critics, privatization conjures up visions of a beleaguered government bureaucracy ceding responsibility for vital public services to unreliable private entrepreneurs. To other observers, privatization inspires neither rapture nor alarm but rather cautious interest. At its best, privatization can reduce the costs of government and introduce new possibilities for better service delivery. At its worst, privatization can raise costs and has the potential to undermine other important values, such as equity, quality, and accountability.

William T. Gormley, Jr., is Professor of Political Science and Public Affairs at the University of Wisconsin–Madison.

PART 1
THE IDEA OF PRIVATIZATION

Acknowledgments

This book grew out of a conference on "Privatization in a Federal System" that took place at Wingspread in Racine, Wisconsin, November 5–7, 1987. Although almost all of the articles were written afterwards, the conference itself stimulated a spirited dialogue which helped to focus the book on explicit comparisons between privatization and its alternatives. I would like to thank the Robert M. La Follette Institute, the Johnson Foundation, the Bradley Foundation, and Waste Management, Inc. for making the conference possible.

I am grateful to Dennis Dresang, the founding director of the La Follette Institute, for his early support and to Bob Haveman, the current director, for holding my feet to the fire and insisting that I complete this project. I would also like to thank Alice Honeywell, Publications Director of the La Follette Institute, for copy-editing this book with her usual professionalism and enthusiasm. Finally, I appreciate the thoughtful comments of Marc Bendick, Jr., B. Guy Peters, and David Weimer, who read all or part of the manuscript and offered helpful advice. Though they bear no responsibility for the final outcome, the book is better, thanks to their comments.

In this book, we have tried to approach a timely public policy controversy from a multidisciplinary and comparative perspective. Whether one studies privatization, or federalism, or some other topic, it is important to harvest the best available insights from several disciplines. It is equally important to consider the context in which policy choices are made. The case for privatization may be stronger in some policy domains than others and more compelling in some countries than others. In selecting contributors to this book, I have tried to identify scholars with rather different perspectives. The result, I hope, is a volume which will continue the debate that we began at Wingspread.

Tables

Contents

The University of Wisconsin Press
114 North Murray Street
Madison, Wisconsin 53715

3 Henrietta Street
London WC2E 8LU, England

5 4 3 2 1

Printed in the United States of America

Library of Congress Cataloging-in-Publication Data
Privatization and its alternatives / edited by William T. Gormley, Jr.
    342 pp.   cm.—(La Follette public policy series)
    Includes bibliographical references and index.
    1. Privatization—Case studies.   2. Education and state.
   3. Housing policy.   4. Law enforcement.   I. Gormley, William T.,
   1950–   .   II. Series.
   HD3845.P73   1990
   338.9—dc20
   ISBN 0-299-11700-6   90-13042
   ISBN 0-299-11704-9 (pbk.)   CIP

Privatization and Its Alternatives

Edited by

William T. Gormley, Jr.

THE UNIVERSITY OF WISCONSIN PRESS

Policy Analysis. In highly complex issue areas, better data may enable public agencies to save money, improve their performance, or both. Since the early 1970s, the White House has sought to do this by requiring federal agencies to assess the costs and benefits of proposed rules and regulations before adopting them. A number of states also require agencies to issue economic impact statements (e.g., before adopting new environmental protection standards).

Audits. Where large amounts of money are being spent, there is always the danger that some funds will be misspent. In recent years, legislative audit bureaus have become more sophisticated and more important. The General Accounting Office has become a more vigorous and aggressive watchdog of federal agencies. At the same time, the number of inspectors general has increased to the point where virtually all of the cabinet-level departments in the federal government have an inspector general charged with ferreting out waste and corruption.

Criteria for Choice

In order to evaluate privatization and its alternatives, it is necessary to specify criteria for choice. Some criteria refer to outcomes, while others refer to the process by which decisions are made or by which services are delivered. The choice of criteria is a personal matter, and the contributors to this book differ in their value priorities. However, most would agree that the following criteria are important:

Efficiency. The standard benchmark for economists, efficiency is widely used as a criterion by other policy analysts as well. An efficient allocation of resources is one from which no person can be made better off without making another person worse off. A variation on this theme is that efficiency is realized when a new policy makes everyone better off if one assumes that winners compensate losers and still come out ahead. Efficiency is more than just cost containment. The idea is not merely to cut costs but to do so without reducing benefits by a commensurate amount.

Effectiveness. Some goals are sufficiently important that we believe in achieving them even if the costs of doing so are high. Thus in some instances, the key question is not whether benefits exceed costs but how a particular set of benefits or goals can best be achieved. Effectiveness, then, is the achievement of desired goals.

Equity. There are many different ways to interpret equity. One useful distinction is between horizontal equity, which means those in similar circumstances should be treated alike, and vertical equity wherein income disparities are reduced or eliminated. Another popular distinction is between equal opportunity and equal results. Equal opportunity means that persons have the same life chances regardless of race, sex, creed, or color. Equality of results means that persons enjoy the same income or the same standard of living. In general, horizontal equity and equal opportunity are less controversial than vertical equity and equal results.

Reliability. Many public services are sufficiently vital that their interruption would cause a major inconvenience. Thus reliability, or the continuous provision of satisfactory services, is often important. Some services (e.g., trash pickup, bus service) are essential enough that everyone wants the assurance that they will be provided steadily.

Quality. The production of goods and services is not an either-or phenomenon. There are fine gradations in the quality of service, whether the services involve park maintenance, data processing, or nursing home care. In some instances, modest variations in service quality may not concern us a great deal. In others, however, quality will be a key consideration.

Accountability. According to political scientists, accountability is an indispensable ingredient of a representative democracy. Accountability may take a variety of forms (e.g., a bureaucracy may be accountable to politicians, judges, or citizens). However, the common denominator is the opportunity for periodic review (of an agency or firm) by voters or customers or their surrogates.

Empowerment. A number of sociologists, planners, and political scientists have preached the virtues of empowerment, especially at the local level, where government is small enough to permit something resembling self-governance. Empowerment means that citizens have the opportunity to control their own destiny by making decisions that affect their lives. Empowerment differs from accountability in that it is more intensive, more direct, and more immediate.

Legitimacy. Whatever the decision-making process employed by government, it is important that people believe the process to be fair. If citizens have confidence in the marketplace, then substantial privatization may well be legitimate. If citizens have confidence in the government and more limited confidence in the fairness of the open market, then privatization may well lack legitimacy. In short, citizen perceptions matter.

Choice. A final criterion for choice is choice itself. There is much to be said for policy options that preserve options for consumers and producers alike. The advantages of diversity are considerable. Choice promotes innovation and experimentation. In addition, it offers the prospect of greater satisfaction with services freely chosen by those who will receive them.

The New Battleground

Privatization has proceeded at a rapid pace in some service areas, far slower in others. Table 1.1 reveals the extent of contracting out by local governments for a variety of services. In some instances, contracting out is widespread. For example, 59 percent of local governments have contracted out for solid waste collection or disposal, 45 percent have contracted out for vehicle towing

Table 1.1. Contracting of Services by Local Governments

Service	Percentage of Cities/Counties Contracting Each Service
Administration	36%
Airports	11
Buildings or Grounds	43
Child care or day care	5
Data processing	31
Elderly or handicapped	12
Fleet or vehicle maintenance	21
Hospitals, health care or emergency services	16
Housing or shelters	5
Parking lots or garages	7
Public safety or corrections	7
Recreation, parks, convention halls, stadiums, or cultural activities	19
Solid-waste collection or disposal	59
Streets and roads	29
Traffic signals or street lighting	32
Transit or transportation	17
Utilities	10
Vehicle towing or storage	45

Source: Touche Ross. 1987. "Privatization in America," p. 10. Washington, D.C.: Touche Ross.

or storage, and 43 percent have contracted out for buildings or grounds. In other areas, contracting out is less prevalent. For example, only five percent of local governments have contracted out for child care or day care, and only 12 percent have contracted out for services for the elderly or the handicapped.

These figures should be placed in perspective. When only five percent of all local governments report that they contract out for day care, that does not mean that 95 percent provide these services themselves. Rather, most local governments do not yet provide these services at all. Similarly, we may safely assume that large numbers of local governments—especially smaller jurisdictions—do not provide special services for the elderly, on their own or through contractors. Nevertheless, Table 1.1 does indicate sharp differences in the extent of privatization across service areas.

One way to understand differences in the extent of privatization is to distinguish, as Savas (1987:121) does, between "physical and commercial services" and "protective and human services." Privatization has advanced much more rapidly in the former area than in the latter. Janet Pack (1987:524–25), offers another useful distinction: between the production of intermediate goods and services (desks, laundry services, highway maintenance) and the production of final goods and services (education, health care, transportation, etc.). According to Pack, privatization to date has been concentrated in the area of intermediate goods or services.

Many local governments have discovered that they can save money by privatizing "physical and commercial services" or "intermediate goods and services." Thus local governments cite cost containment as the principal reason for contracting out services for buildings or grounds, fleet or vehicle maintenance, parking lots or garages, solid waste collection or disposal, streets and roads, transportation, utilities, and other hard services. In a number of instances, cost savings have been substantial. However, the new wave of privatization opportunities does not lend itself to an exclusive focus on cost containment. Where human services are involved, other values—equity, quality, accountability, legitimacy—come into play.

The new battleground over privatization differs from the old battleground in four respects. First, the debate now focuses sharply on human services, or social services, such as care for the sick, the poor, the mentally ill, children, and the elderly. These services involve not the manipulation of equipment but interactions with people. As Bendick (1984) has noted, success is more difficult to measure and to achieve in such issue areas, which involve complex, long-range goals. Thus empirical research, though vital, is likely to be more treacherous and less definitive than in other issue areas.

Second, the new debate involves issues that intersect several levels of government, raising complex questions of shared responsibility and coordination in a federal system. In contrast to street sweeping and trash collection, where local governments are more or less on their own, the provision of social services is usually a multigovernmental task, with federal, state, and local governments all playing a role. This increases the number of opportunities for creative experimentation and helpful consultation but it also increases occasions for delay and even paralysis if governments cannot resolve their differences over funding or program direction.

Third, the new debate requires us to think more carefully about the role of nonprofit organizations in our society. Whereas for-profit firms have taken the lead in offering a variety of "hard" services, nonprofit groups have specialized more in "human" services, where the current controversy is focused. Are nonprofits, which rely to a substantial extent on highly motivated volunteers, better able to maintain high quality at low costs? Do nonprofits deserve the special advantages conferred upon them by the federal tax code? These are questions that thoughtful commentators are just beginning to address (Weisbrod 1988).

Fourth, the new debate raises questions that transcend the value of efficiency. In deciding whether to privatize prisons, we must consider the legal and ethical implications of doing so. In deciding whether to privatize public

Table 1.2. Privatization and Its Alternatives

Policy Area	Privatization Proposals	Public Sector Alternatives	Hybrid Proposals
Education	vouchers, tuition tax credits	open enrollment, decentralization, magnet schools	public subsidies to private schools
Housing	vouchers, sale of public housing units, contracting out	improved management, regulatory federalism	tenant management
Law and Order	private prisons, private security systems	community-oriented policing	moonlighting by public law enforcement officers

housing, we must consider the psychological and sociological ramifications of new opportunities for home ownership or tenant management. In deciding whether to privatize education, we must consider the organizational and political dynamics of local schools and local school boards.

Some of the most innovative and controversial proposals for privatization in the future involve three vital policy domains: education, housing, and law enforcement. All three of these policy domains, to varying degrees, involve human services, multiple levels of government, nonprofit organizations, and values that transcend efficiency. In education, for example, the services are primarily people-oriented; all three levels of government provide some funding and impose some regulations; most service providers are nonprofit organizations; and political, philosophical, legal, and sociological questions frequently intrude into the debate.

A wide variety of proposals have been offered to improve the quality of education, housing, and law enforcement through privatization. In addition, many alternatives to privatization have been proposed (see Table 1.2). By focusing on these three policy domains, we can better understand the dilemmas that policy makers confront on the new privatization battleground. At the same time, more general commentary—at the beginning and the end of this book—will help to place these three policy domains in perspective.

Privatization in Theory and Practice: A Preview

The Idea of Privatization

Stuart Butler begins the debate on privatization by arguing that the private sector can discharge public responsibilities more effectively and more efficiently than the public sector. Among the public responsibilities he mentions are education, transportation, garbage pickup, and environmental protection. Butler notes that there are many different forms of privatization, each of which must be evaluated separately. Although he generally supports privatization, Butler expresses reservations about contracting out, which he fears may create new constituencies favoring increased levels of government spending. He also worries that private firms heavily dependent on vouchers may develop a powerful lobby on behalf of increased government spending. Thus he warns that privatization does not automatically reduce the size or cost of government.

 Paul Starr takes a much more critical view of privatization, which he believes encourages a narrow, inward-looking perspective. Starr contrasts the marketplace, where individuals pursue their individual self-interest, with the polity, where citizens deliberate together in an effort to identify the common good. There is choice in both settings, Starr argues, but democratic political choice offers better prospects for civic discovery. Starr further contends that privatization is self-defeating, that sharp reductions in the public sector's role will trigger a counter-cyclical resurgence of the public sector, that privatization will undermine the competition it claims to promote, and that privatization will invite greater public regulation of the private sector, ultimately making the private sector less distinctive than it is today.

Education Policy

Dwight Lee fires the opening salvo in the education policy debate by arguing in favor of education vouchers, which parents could use to defray educational expenses at the public or private school of their choice. According to Lee, vouchers would improve the quality of elementary and secondary education while lowering costs. Equipped with greater control over their children's education, parents would inform themselves about options and purchase educational services with their children's best interests in mind. Schools, forced to compete for students, would provide educational experiences preferred by parents while cutting unnecessary administrative costs. Although empirical research on education vouchers is limited, Lee cites evidence on the relative performance of public and private school students to support his claim that private schooling is superior.

 Like Lee, Richard Elmore favors greater choice in education. Unlike Lee, Elmore prefers experiments in choice that work within the existing public school system. Examples include public school choice programs in Minnesota, New York, and Washington that widen parental options within a public school setting. Elmore analyzes these experiments and concludes that they have succeeded to some degree. However, he emphasizes that it is not enough to increase choices for education consumers. Equally important, educators (or producers) must have greater freedom and flexibility in the programs they design so that they can increase the variety of options available to parents.

In most developed countries, public funding of education predominates.

However, many countries have used some of these funds to subsidize private schools. Usually this is done by providing a uniform grant per student, but in theory differentiated amounts can be paid. This was Australia's policy when, in 1974, it introduced a large need-based subsidy to private schools. Estelle James examines Australia's system, which she characterizes as a policy of limited privatization with redistributive goals. The program constitutes privatization in that it pumps substantial funds into the private sector and increases parental choice. The program is redistributive in the sense that the neediest schools receive higher government subsidies than wealthier schools. Based on data from the 1970s and the 1980s, James finds that private school expenditures on students did increase and that the private school share of total enrollments also increased, following the government's new policy. However, the effects of that policy on private schools were muted by the simultaneous strengthening of public schools, by a reduction in the pool of cheap labor available to private schools, and by a trend towards unionization that diverted much of the new money into teacher salaries.

Housing Policy

The U.S. government has been roundly criticized for failing to address the housing needs of the poor. Public housing in particular has come under fire. As a response to these criticisms, the federal Department of Housing and Urban Development launched an experimental housing voucher program in the 1970s. Under this program, tenants could use government subsidies to rent housing on the open market. G. Thomas Kingsley reviews the evidence on housing vouchers and concludes that they have generally lived up to expectations. However, he notes a sharp distinction between the successful experiments of the 1970s and the poorly-funded experiments of the 1980s, which worked well in some local markets but not so well in others. His overall assessment of vouchers is favorable but he warns that voucher programs must be adequately funded to succeed.

Although housing vouchers have received considerable attention, the U.S. government has utilized other techniques to attempt to improve housing for the poor. In several instances, the federal government has sought to improve imperfections in the current public housing system by borrowing techniques or purchasing services from private management. Richard Hula discusses several such approaches, including the application of private sector management techniques by public housing administrators, the contracting out of services to private firms, and experiments in tenant management of public housing projects. After reviewing the evidence, he concludes that these approaches have had modest positive impacts at best. Still, the tenant-management experiments do appear to have enhanced the self-esteem and self-respect of poor people by "empowering" them and giving them greater control over their destiny.

One of the most dramatic examples of privatization in recent years has been the sale of approximately one million Council Housing (or public housing) units in Great Britain. Inaugurated by the Thatcher administration in 1980, the sale of public housing units to tenants at discounted rates has been extremely popular. Hilary Silver discusses the origins, implementation, and consequences of the Conservative government's "right to buy" program. In addition to examining economic costs and benefits, she discusses the social consequences of the government's privatization program. Silver concludes that the social costs of the privatization program are considerable and that alternatives to Council Housing Sales, such as local cooperatives, deserve further consideration.

Law Enforcement Policy

In recent years, prison costs have risen more rapidly than any other item in state budgets. Frustrated by this growing drain on scarce resources, state policy makers have turned to for-profit firms to provide a variety of prison services, including, in some instances, the management of state prisons. The federal government has also contracted out corrections services to the private sector. Malcolm Feeley places these developments in historical perspective by examining the implications of earlier movements towards the privatization of corrections policy. In particular, he notes that privatization in the 18th and 19th centuries enabled the British and American governments to expand the range and severity of criminal sanctions while lowering costs. Today, as earlier, Feeley argues that privatization is likely to transform the outputs of our criminal justice system.

The role of the private sector in deterring crime and apprehending criminals also continues to grow. In fact, at the moment, 1.1 million people are employed by private security agencies, in comparison to only 600,000 public law enforcement officers. Moreover, a number of public law enforcement officers "moonlight" for the private sector. Albert Reiss discusses the legal and ethical problems that arise when public police officers work off-duty for private employers. As public police officers continue to provide these services through the private sector, questions arise as to how these employment opportunities should be arranged—through the police department, through the police union, or through individual officers themselves. Reiss analyzes each of these options, discussing their advantages and disadvantages. He also raises troublesome questions about supplementary law enforcement services, whether provided by public or private employees.

The United States is not alone in developing new initiatives to prevent crime, apprehend criminals, and reduce the costs of caring for prisoners. Japanese approaches to these tasks range from privatization to semi-privatization to more traditional public sector alternatives. Setsuo Miyazawa analyzes a number of these approaches, including the supply of materials for prison factories by private industries, the private provision of security services, the mobilization of local residents by public police officers, and reliance on part-time nominally paid individuals to serve as probation officers.

Privatization in Practice

Although the theoretical rationale for privatization rests primarily on the expectation of greater efficiency, state and local officials cite other reasons for privatizing. Drawing upon an extensive survey of New Jersey public officials, Carl Van Horn discusses their reasons for and experiences with privatization. He focuses on the most common form of privatization—contracting out—and explains how corruption has crept into the contracting process, with unfortunate results for the political system.

Like Van Horn, Janet Rothenberg Pack is critical of contracts, especially where competitive bidding is absent or limited, but her critique extends to other forms of privatization as well. With efficiency as her criterion, Pack critically examines a wide variety of privatization initiatives, ranging from asset sales to vouchers to contracts. Based on her own research and others', she concludes that we should approach privatization with considerable caution.

In a concluding chapter, I summarize some of the key empirical findings of the book. I then attempt to specify the conditions under which privatization is most and least appropriate. In addition, I examine different forms of privatization, highlighting their strengths and weaknesses. Finally, I evaluate public-private hybrids and public sector alternatives to privatization.

The privatization debate, as an exercise in institutional policy analysis, is part of a larger debate on how we should redesign our political, economic, and social institutions (March and Olsen 1989). It is a particularly important debate because it encompasses a wide variety of public services that affect the quality of our daily life and because it increasingly concerns the toughest policy dilemmas that we face—in such areas as health, education, welfare, and criminal justice. It is also a particularly instructive debate because it focuses on a critical nexus—namely, that between the public and the private sectors. Whether we view that nexus from an ideological, philosophical, or practical perspective, the choice between public and private service delivery reveals a great deal about who we are and the kind of society we would create.

REFERENCES

Bator, Francis. 1958. "The Anatomy of Market Failure." *Quarterly Journal of Economics* 72 (August): 351–79.

Baumol, William. 1965. *Welfare Economics and the Theory of the State*. 2d ed. Cambridge, Mass.: Harvard University Press.

Bendick, Marc, Jr. 1984. "Privatization of Public Services: Recent Experience." In *Public-Private Partnership*, ed. Harvey Brooks et al., 153–71. Cambridge, Mass.: Ballinger.

Coase, Ronald. 1960. "The Problem of Social Cost." *Journal of Law and Economics* 3 (October): 1–44.

Eagleton Institute of Politics. 1987. "Alternative Methods for Delivering Public Services in New Jersey." New Brunswick, N.J.: Rutgers University.

Hennessy, Peter. 1989. *Whitehall*. New York: Free Press.

March, James, and Johan Olsen. 1989. *Rediscovering Institutions: The Organizational Basis of Politics*. New York: Free Press.

Pack, Janet Rothenberg. 1987. "Privatization of Public-Sector Services in Theory and Practice." *Journal of Policy Analysis and Management* 6 (Summer): 523–40.

Savas, E. S. 1987. *Privatization: The Key to Better Government*. Chatham, N.J.: Chatham House.

Touche Ross. 1987. "Privatization in America." Washington, D.C.: Touche Ross.

Weimer, David, and Aidan Vining. 1989. *Policy Analysis: Concepts and Practice*. Englewood Cliffs, N.J.: Prentice Hall.

Weisbrod, Burton. 1988. *The Nonprofit Economy*. Cambridge, Mass.: Harvard University Press.

Wolf, Charles. 1979. "A Theory of Non-Market Failures." *The Public Interest* 55 (Spring): 114–33.

2 *Stuart Butler*

Privatization for Public Purposes

Privatization is the shifting of a function, either in whole or in part, from the public sector to the private sector. Increasingly, privatization is being examined by government officials as a strategy for improving public policy. Through some combination of changing ownership of functions in society, introducing competition from the private sector, and allowing consumer choice through vouchers and other approaches privatization may be able to achieve some public purpose more effectively, more efficiently, and more accurately. That is the basic argument for privatization.

The provision of services by the public sector is a very complex issue, and the factors affecting it also are very complicated. That is just as true of privatization. For this reason, privatization comes in various forms to achieve various purposes. A form of privatization that works effectively in one situation may not work effectively in another. When we look at privatization, we have to ask what kind of private sector approach might be most effective in each situation. We are learning that some private sector approaches may not work in certain circumstances, while other forms of privatization may be successful.

Whether one is for or against privatization does not mean one has, in principle, to be for or against government responsibility for providing particular

Stuart Butler is Director of Domestic Policy Studies at The Heritage Foundation, Washington, D.C.

services. There are some people who support privatization because they want to see, as an end in itself, a reduction of scale of government activity and its influence in our lives and economy. There are other people, however, who support privatization because they feel that the private sector can be more effective at attaining a governmental goal that previous public policies have also tried to achieve. In education, for example, some people advocate the wholesale abandonment of public education and its replacement by the private sector while others support education vouchers to fulfill the public purpose of universally available good education more effectively through the use of the market. That's another form of privatization with a different purpose. Being for or against privatization does not mean being for or against a particular goal of public policy.

Asset Sales

Forms of privatization range from the most complete to the least complete. The most complete form of privatization is the wholesale selling of a government asset or the shifting of a function entirely out of government, such that government ceases to be the provider or controller of that function. Outside the United States, that is the principal form of privatization. In Britain, promoting that form of privatization has achieved almost the level of a crusade. It is a very fundamental part of the quiet social and political revolution occurring within Britain. The United States has seen less of that form of privatization, primarily because many of the functions now being privatized in other countries have traditionally been in the private sector in this country.

The benefits available from this most complete form of privatization depend on the particular type of asset involved. In some cases—and this has been generally true in Europe—this form of privatization is being adopted as a means of restoring market forces to a commercial activity that previously had been in the government domain. Most common in Britain and elsewhere in Europe, the idea behind this denationalization is that by changing the ownership and management dynamics, the enterprise will operate more efficiently, and so they will provide goods and services to the customer more efficiently. Management decisions will not be distorted by the kinds of influences, particularly political influences, that attend government ownership. Moving high performance sports car companies, such as Britain's Jaguar Motors, back into the private sector is an example of this kind of thinking.

Second, there is the goal, and a very strong political force behind this first form of privatization, of simply raising cash. If you sell an asset owned by government, it is often a way of raising a good deal of money. Clearly, this has been a major reason for privatization of this type in recent years in Europe, and also a major factor in the Reagan administration's interest. The argument is that by offering such basically commercial concerns for sale, the government may achieve not only a one-shot benefit through the inflow of cash but also it can secure a long-run benefit to public finances generally. This is a controversial argument, but one that rests on the premise that if government offers a commercial asset for sale in the market, a potential buyer will expect to obtain greater revenue from that asset than the government can expect. Therefore the buyer is willing to pay a higher price for it than it is actually worth to the government. This, of course, is the economic reason why buyers and sellers of any asset usually feel they have gained. In cases where the government is running a loss on that asset, even if it gives it away it may well be ahead of the game. But also profitable assets may well be worth selling, if the bid price reflects the buyer's expectation that he can manage the asset more efficiently than the government can. So the argument for selling assets also carries a secondary argument that it actually will, in the long run, benefit government.

A third argument put forward for asset sales and divestment of government activities is that in some cases merely changing ownership may achieve public purposes more effectively than maintaining public ownership. The drive toward nationalization in Britain and many other countries after the Second World War rested on the premise that public ownership of key elements of the economy meant they could be run in the public interest, free of the need to obtain profits. Thus, it was said, there would be a beneficial influence in the economy, that would assure availability of essential services. Any Englishman who has spent many hours waiting at a train station for a train that didn't arrive because of strikes by public sector workers would smile wryly at that kind of argument today. Supporters of privatization claim that because of the sensitivity of the private sector to its customers, as opposed to the insensitivity of many publicly held operations to their customers, the private sector can assure more dependable services than can public ownership.

In addition, some asset transfers involve more specific goals than assurance of service. For example, the sale of public housing rests on the contention that private, resident ownership of a housing unit leads residents to take a personal interest in the maintenance, improvement, and quality of that asset, keeping the quality of the stock at a higher level than with public ownership. In Britain the government has transferred more than a million units of public housing to private citizens. One of the strongest arguments for that is that it actually improves the public housing projects. Indeed, by walking through a public housing project where sales have taken place it is possible to pick out units sold to residents: doors are freshly painted, gardens better tended, and structural improvements are evident.

There are other areas where this debate still rages. In public lands management, for example, some people argue that public ownership of certain lands, in practice, means no ownership, to the detriment of the environment. In fact, the innovative use of private ownership—not just selling land to the largest available corporations but rather creative forms of private ownership—may reach environmental and conservation objectives much more effectively than keeping that land in public ownership. The reason for this is that allowing, say, environmental organizations to own and management public land would depoliticize and "debureaucratize" land management decisions.

Similarly, in the debate over the air traffic control system, the privatizer's argument is that when an industry consists of two conflicting elements (a privately held market-based element, namely airlines, and a bureaucratic element, the air traffic control system), they do not work together well. They do not mix any better than oil and water. Thus the transference of ownership of air traffic control in some form to private owners may in fact achieve the objective of an efficient and universal system more effectively, by mixing oil with oil, so to speak.

Needless to say, a number of concerns arise over this form of privatization. There is a growing concern in Britain, for instance, about the ramifications of transferring a huge public monopoly into the private sector as a private monopoly. A number of the large utilities privatized in Britain in the last few years, such as the telephone system, have been transferred as regulated monopolies. There is now increasing concern that a lack of competition may erode the potential benefits of privatization. The view in Britain now is that there is a need to introduce greater competition as functions move to the private sector. A private monopoly may move the economy forward, but not as fast or as extensively as if competition occurred at the same time.

There is also the concern that with government divestiture, opportunities to pursue public objectives are lost. Experience in the European countries with nationalized industries shows that there is little confidence that simply retaining a function in the public sector assures the public interest. But Europeans have also determined that regulation or covenants must be built into sales to assure that the private owner continues to provide certain services to less advantaged economic groups after the divestiture.

Deregulation

The second most complete form of privatization is a combination of deregulation and tax incentives. That could be anything from such radical ideas as moving government pension or insurance programs such as social security and Medicare to the private sector, to more mundane ideas such as deregulation of mass transit systems at the municipal level in order to allow other forms of mass transit in the private sector to compete for customers.

The arguments for this are several. The most general argument for deregulation applies in this instance—improving efficiency and economic benefits through competition. The case for tax incentives as an added boost is that by encouraging individuals to behave in a way that meets a particular public objective, such as providing incentives for private medical coverage and private pension programs, these services can be provided more efficiently than through publicly provided systems.

Of course, Paul Starr (1987:134) and others have argued that a tax incentive system inevitably must involve a net subsidy to the private sector. Starr and other critics allege that tax incentives to spur some kind of private activity means that the rest of society is subsidizing a private activity, and this is somehow unfair. In a narrow sense he is right. A tax incentive does mean a corresponding burden on other taxpayers who are not eligible. But of course a direct-expenditure program to achieve a public purpose also imposes burdens on taxpayers. The question is whether an incentive is a way of encouraging private activity that meets public goals; it can be a very efficient method compared with a spending program. Consider, for example, somebody who gets some relief from property taxes for choosing private garbage collection at a condominium rather than using city services. Even if one assumes that a tax incentive is a tax expenditure (a loss of revenue equivalent to sending a check in the mail), the degree of that subsidy may be very much less than the reduced cost to government by that person opting out of the public sector and choosing a private provider instead. If the government saves a hundred dollars a month by a group of individuals choosing private garbage collection for a tax incentive of twenty-five dollars a month, then one could argue that the individual is actually subsidizing the rest of society rather than vice versa since the tax relief is unlikely to cover the full cost of the private service. So tax incentives are not subsidies to the private sector except in very specific cases where the degree of tax loss is actually greater than the cost avoided by that person's choosing private as opposed to public provision.

Other concerns are raised against this kind of privatization. One is that it may reduce the degree of scrutiny that the public sector has over more sensitive types of services. That is a legitimate concern in principle, but more pertinent to some types of activities than to others. Allowing individuals to choose private rather than public transportation, there may be less concern about deregulation than if Americans could opt out of social security in favor of potentially less sound private pensions. But in practice, concerns about deregulation to achieve privatization really are not much different from the well debated issues about economic deregulation generally.

Contracting Out

The third form of privatization, and the most common one in this country, especially at the state and local level, is the contracting out of functions, where the government finances a service but hires contractors to provide it, on behalf of government, to certain individuals or groups. This includes not only commercial services, but also basic human services.

One benefit claimed for this type of privatization is that it gives greater flexibility to government by not having to keep a costly function in-house. Government thus has the opportunity to shop around for vendors, and choose the quality and quantity of services it wishes. It is also said that contracting out invites competition and therefore enables a public manager to have a greater opportunity of finding a more innovative or less expensive service.

Contracting out is not confined to profit-making, commercial vendors; it can also be with nonprofits or even with individuals in low-income communities (e.g., public housing management by tenants).

A number of concerns arise over contracting out. In fact, of all the forms of privatization, it is the form with which I am least comfortable. In some cases, for instance, the logic of contracting out is undermined because competition is very limited or even doesn't exist. For example, proponents of privatization always have a difficult time dealing with weapons procurement from the private sector largely because there may not be effective competition. Not many people make B1 bombers. There are limits on information in such sensitive areas so we do not usually see a normal competitive market. In contrast, more commercial services like janitorial services are fairly easy to measure. A lot of firms are providing them, and a lot of information is exchanged, so a high degree of competition is available. The best argument for contracting out is in these latter, more routine services.

A second concern is bad contracts. I do not see this as a particularly big problem, but the public sector unions are forever dragging up various contracts where the service was not quite what they expected even though it conformed to the fine print. This is not a fundamental flaw of privatization itself, but is simply part of the learning process. When you move from one form of service provision to another, you have to learn the way in which contracts operate. The quality of contracts at the state and local level is steadily improving, so bad contracts should not be an obstacle, but a reason for prudence and caution when considering contracting.

A third concern is the danger of excessive dependence on a particular provider. Many municipalities have entered into a contract with a vendor of a particular service, fired everybody in the public sector, and then discovered six months later that the vendor is having financial difficulties and becomes delinquent in providing service. These municipalities were stuck in a rather difficult situation. But various steps are being taken to deal with that, such as splitting up a function geographically. Some cities, such as Phoenix, now have different contractors for different parts of the cities, so they are not dependent on any particular one citywide. Standard procedures that are quite routine in private sector "sourcing out" are now being adopted in the public sector to reduce this concern with contracting.

Finally, there is probably the most difficult issue for those conservatives who see privatization as way of curbing growth in government. Contracting out seems to go hand-in-hand with private sector pressures to expand government. If one is in favor of limited government, one should remember that defense contractors and human services professionals are not known for their eagerness to reduce the level of government spending. Indeed, some years ago Marc Bendick (1984) wrote an article advocating privatization as a way of defending and indeed expanding the human services budget. He argued that if private sector people who are very efficient at delivering a service are brought in, they also will be very efficient at lobbying. Thus money is more likely to keep flowing than if only the public sector were involved. I think Bendick is essentially correct. Contracting out may be a way, in fact, of securing and expanding government expenditure. That is a very real concern to me as a conservative.

Vouchers

The final form of privatization is vouchers. Government provides recipients of services with funding, in an earmarked form to use to shop around for services in the market. Vouchers can achieve various objectives. Where a market does exist, and the only real problem is that certain individuals do not have the income to buy enough of the service, vouchers allow that market to continue to operate with minimal government involvement while catering to low-income segments of the population. The Food Stamp program is a good example of this use of vouchers. In addition it is argued that vouchers may, in many instances, be more beneficial and more effective than contracting out, because instead of contractors being able to exploit or ignore clients (because they have a direct link to government) they must be more sensitive to the individuals to whom they are providing services.

In addition, there are strong arguments that vouchers may be the only way of insuring quality of service to certain groups. The argument for education vouchers, for example, centers on the proposition that the public school system is not serving low-income individuals adequately, and that vouchers would give low-income parents the economic power either to force changes in the public school system or to opt for private education. Basically the same argument applies in housing: vouchers would be an advance over public housing or even subsidized private projects, because tenants would have the chance to shop around.

A number of concerns arise concerning vouchers. One is that recipients of vouchers may not be adequately informed to make wise choices as to how to dispose of their income to obtain services. In some cases, this may be a legitimate argument. I'm not a great advocate of Medicaid vouchers for the mentally ill homeless, for example. But in other cases, such as education vouchers, the concern about the good sense of the recipient seems to be a rearguard argument by those providers who are gaining from the present system and who wish to prevent real competition and block a challenge to their unique position to take advantage of a market captive.

The political dynamics of vouchers, like those of contracting out, also are sometimes troubling. For example, constant political efforts to extend the Food Stamp program, not so much from the low-income beneficiaries of services as from those who provide the services. In fact, the agriculture industry is one of the strongest supporters of food stamps. Farmers are always shedding crocodile tears for the poor and the hungry, and demanding that more of their crops be purchased with food stamps. For those who wish to contain government activity, vouchers may be slightly more attractive politically than contracting out because the providers tend to be less organized. But they are not a simple solution to the problems of contracting.

Conclusion

In conclusion, privatization is a highly varied concept. One approach may be more appropriate in one case than another. Certain types of privatization may be a step backward from direct government control of services, but in other cases, privatization gives government the flexibility to exercise greater control. In fact, all we are really talking about with privatization is making the private sector available, in some form, for achieving public objectives. As New York Governor Mario Cuomo has put it, "The purpose of government is to make sure services are provided, not necessarily to provide services." Privatization is a tool to make sure those services are provided as effectively and as efficiently as possible.

REFERENCES

Bendick, Marc, Jr. 1984. "Privatization of Public Services: Recent Experience." In *Public-Private Partnership*, ed. Harvey Brooks et al., 153–71. Cambridge, Mass.: Ballinger.

Starr, Paul. 1987. "The Limits of Privatization." In *Prospects for Privatization*, ed. Steven Hanke, 124–37. New York: Academy of Political Science.

3 *Paul Starr*

The Case for Skepticism

As a policy movement in the United States, privatization has a double identity. At one level, it proposes some specific ideas for reorganizing public services. But at another level, it promises to change our view of what responsibilities ought to be public. The methods of reorganization attract attention from management-minded reformers interested in improving the efficiency and effectiveness of public services. However, the privatization movement as a whole gains its most devoted support from ideologically minded conservatives hostile to many of the purposes of public services. Some analysts would like to evaluate privatization solely as a management technique, but that restricted view misses the overarching purposes of privatization as a strategy for reconstructing the liberal democratic state. To accept privatization as a framework for reform in our society is to accept a deeper set of assumptions about the capacities of democratic government and the appropriate sphere of common obligation. I believe we ought not to accept those premises and should accordingly be wary of what privatization represents and promises.

Paul Starr is Professor of Sociology at Princeton University and Co-Editor of *The American Prospect*.

The Privatization Package

The concept of privatization has a multitude of uses and definitions. In public policy discussion, it usually refers to a shift from public to private in the production of goods and services. The term covers a heterogeneous package of measures, including: 1) governmental disengagement from a function, as in the cessation of a program; 2) the sale or lease of assets, such as land, infrastructure, or state-owned enterprises; 3) the replacement of publicly produced services with public payments for private services, through contracts, vouchers, or cost-plus reimbursement; or 4) some forms of deregulation that open up an industry to private competition, where previously public institutions were the only legal providers.[1]

The various types of privatization policy differ sharply in their impact on government functions and finance. The effects range from radical reductions in the government's role to the maintenance of public fiscal responsibility while privatizing the means of implementation. These diverse policies do not logically entail one another, and it is entirely possible to support some but oppose others. However, privatization policies come to us in a political bundle, not logically, but ideologically connected.

√ This bundling of policies was crucial in turning privatization from a notion into a movement; the bundling is what gives privatization a sense of novelty and importance. After all, the individual policies are not new. The federal government has been contracting out services and selling assets ever since the early years of the Republic, when it contracted out postal operations and sold off public lands. At least to Americans, privatization includes much, like contracting, that is commonplace—and that makes it seem reasonable. Yet it also includes some ideas, like privatizing prisons, parks, and money,[2] that are unusual—and they make privatization seem bold. By combining the prosaic and the unfamiliar, the practical and the ideological, the right-wing advocates of privatization have created a stew with an aroma that some find tantalizing and others repugnant. As they hoped, they have assembled a more extensive coalition of supporters than previously existed. By the same token, they have engendered a wide coalition of committed opponents. The idea of privatization polarizes political debate more than many of the individual policies it describes. Those who like polarization ought to like the idea of privatization.

Ideas matter. It is not possible to discuss privatization as if it consisted only of techniques and not of ideas. What I oppose most strongly about privatization is the message that privatization policies and their advocates convey about the possibilities of democratic government and public services. The message is that government usually fails, and whenever it fails the answer is not to try to correct its failings, but to turn to the private sector. The literature of privatization depicts all political decision making, regardless of public participation or governmental checks and balances, as systematically distorted, inefficient, and undesirable. Privatization proponents tell us that we are uniformly better off when we turn away from politics and exercise choices as consumers rather than as citizens. Indeed, the advocates of privatization scarcely recognize that voters and public officials can ever act as responsible citizens at all. Finally, the illusion promoted by advocates of privatization is that they possess a wholesale remedy to a great variety of problems, as if we could clear the air and deal with all the complexities of public life by moving in one direction alone.

Free Markets, Free Citizens, and Free Choice

The preeminent question in the debate over privatization concerns the values that privatization promotes. Advocates of privatization usually present the choices made in the market as realizing the ideal of free choice. The title of Milton and Rose Friedman's book *Free to Choose* (1980) captures this conception of choice, as a choice exercised by individuals directly in the marketplace. But there are other mechanisms of choice, most crucially the political alternative of public discussion and democratic government. That alternative, while scarcely perfect, has some signal virtues, contrary to the purely negative conception of politics advanced by those who conceive of the market as the ideal choice mechanism.

The market and the polity represent two different moral frameworks for choice. The conventional view of political economy regards markets and governments as two methods of aggregating preferences, as if neither had any role in shaping them. However, a democratic polity is designed to do more than convey the individual preferences of the electorate to the state. Democracy, after all, is "government by discussion." The point of elections and legislative deliberations is not simply to count votes, but to discuss alternative paths of choice. Politics confronts us with the interests and problems of other people, which is one reason some find it boring. It obliges us to explain the connection that our ideals and interests have to some larger public good, no doubt a rich source of hypocrisy but still a useful exercise. At its best, public discussion generates new ideas and possibilities for satisfying diverse interests. Often it fails or is intensely frustrating, but even the frustrations sometimes are instructive. The critics of democratic politics have a point: it is not an efficient means of securing private goods individuals already know they want. However, through the conflicts, compromises, and inventions of politics, we learn to want different things for ourselves and our world. The value of this process is missed entirely by those devoted single-mindedly to the market.

Moreover, are not the publicly formulated preferences of the political process as worthy of respect as private preferences, indeed often more worthy because they are subject to criticism and open discussion? If the members of a community consistently vote themselves public schools, ought we not to re-spect those preferences? Ought we not to consider that while private actions in the marketplace generally have limited time horizons, public discussion highlights interests of future generations?

In a recent collection of essays, Robert Reich and others (1987) argue that politics is not simply a battleground of self-interest (the model of the misnamed "public choice" school). It is also a field of conflict over different conceptions of the public good. In evaluating policies, Reich suggests, we need to take into account the effects not only on efficiency and income distribution, but also on competing visions of our common life and its purposes. This is one of the things that ought to concern us about privatization: the desiccated vision of democratic politics that the privatization movement implicitly promotes.

In a public debate at the October 1987 meeting of the Association of Public Policy and Management, Mancur Olson, long an advocate of the economic ap-proach to understanding politics, remarked that voters are often easily conned by crackpot ideas and fads because they do not pay much attention to public affairs. He argued that the value to the rational individual of public affairs knowledge is the product of the personal benefit of a public policy and the potential influence that the individual voter might have, which in a large democracy is vanishingly small. According to Olson, because most people do not derive enough value from their knowledge of public affairs, they pay little attention and can be easily seduced.

I suggested in reply that the same argument could be used to oppose democ-racy altogether. Moreover, if Olson were correct, people would never vote because voting makes no sense from a strictly individualistic, rational, interest-maximizing point of view. In fact, according to Olson's logic, the more rational people are, the less likely they would be to vote. To conceive of alternatives to his approach, you need to begin, not with some presocial individual acting in a political void, but with societies and states that have the institutional capaci-ties to shape personal identities and motivations, including the sense of loyalty and citizenship.

All of this is pertinent to the debate over privatization. In the market, some people have more "votes" because they have more money, and they need concern themselves with no one's benefit except their own. That is a kind of freedom, but a society that provided only the freedom of the market would not be free. A free people must also have the freedom to place some decisions outside the market, in part to avoid making all the conditions of life contingent on individual economic capacities. In the polity, votes are distributed equally, without regard to purchasing power, but just as important, the act of voting is, as we tell our children, a responsibility. It involves obligations to learn, to understand, and to do what we think is right. This is a matter not simply of civics lessons in schools, but of what Reich (1987) calls "civic discovery," the political learning that takes place when groups encounter each other in the public arena.

Privatization shrinks that arena. In certain societies, that may well be desirable. Some issues, like religion, elicit deep and unbridgeable disagreements. Under those circumstances, if questions of eternal salvation become political choices, the norms of civility and requirements of constitutional democracy may become impossible to maintain. Better that religion should be privatized and politics kept free of theological controversy. In general, the sphere of moral belief and personal conduct ought to be not only free from political control, but also outside political contention, to protect both political life and moral communities from becoming excessively entangled with each other.

However, the privatization of moral choice is not what the privatization movement is pursuing. Indeed, many of the same people who advocate privatization want to impose greater state control on moral life. The privatization movement in the United States is chiefly focused on privatizing services that the state provides. The forerunners of the movement were opposed to instituting many of these services in the first place. Having lost that fight, conservatives now return to the battle, assuming the mantle of pragmatic reformers concerned about cost effectiveness and ferreting out hidden subsidies to the undeserving. Since there are plenty of inefficiencies in public management and inequities in public expenditure, the criticisms often have merit. But the question is what the examples illustrate and where the criticisms lead. Do the examples of inefficient public programs prove an endemic sickness in the public sector, curable only by privatization? Or do we already suffer from too much privatization, not too little?

Privatization and Efficiency

The privatization movement in the United States takes some of its inspiration from developments abroad. The recent liberalization programs of communist countries and the privatization of nationalized industries in Great Britain and elsewhere in the West suggest to some that privatization is sweeping the world. However, those developments are of little relevance in the United States, which thankfully never socialized the means of production or nationalized the "commanding heights" of industry. The problems of the communist countries are systemic. In suppressing both private firms in the market and the independent social and political organizations of civil society, the communists shut down both of the signal-producing systems that help generate productive innovation and peaceful change. By contrast, public enterprises in the capitalist world operate in an environment rich with market signals. Consequently, the structural position of state-owned firms in the two systems is not equivalent. Many public enterprises in the capitalist world are actually more market-driven than are the private enterprises permitted in the Soviet Union and China.

In fact, some of the major public enterprises in capitalist countries have a positive record. The Italian state investment companies, for example, have played a key role in Italy's economic development since World War II by modernizing its business management, telecommunications systems, and transportation infrastructure and by building large industrial enterprises that have competed successfully on the world market. There is no comparative evidence to prove that, within the capitalist world, countries with relatively higher public spending or relatively larger public enterprise sectors have slower rates of economic growth. Public enterprise performance seems to depend, not simply on ownership, but on the relation between political authority and management. I am not suggesting public ownership is widely to be recommended, but it is not the uniform disaster that the privatization movement makes it out to be.

In general, it seems useful to distinguish, as I have elsewhere, between three types of privatization programs being pursued in different contexts (Starr, forthcoming). In Eastern Europe, the Soviet Union, and some developing countries, privatization involves institution-building—that is, constructing a basic enabling framework for the market and civil society. This is a healthy development, though there is no guarantee it will work if the basic apparatus of state planning is kept in place. In the capitalist countries with large public sectors, privatization involves balance-shifting—that is, changing the public-private balance primarily by moving state-owned enterprises into private ownership. This also may be a healthy development, though the jury is still out on whether it significantly improves productivity and growth.

In the United States, we already have a framework of private institutions, and we have no large public enterprise sector. Privatization here primarily takes a third form—that is, relying on private firms for the provision of public services. While that does involve a shifting of the public-private balance, it also brings about a blurring of the public-private boundary. Contracting out, vouchers, the privatization of prisons, and the privatization of infrastructure are all examples of the boundary-blurring privatization program.

Even those who approve privatizing state-owned industrial enterprise may have reason to doubt the rationale behind privatizing public institutions like schools and prisons. The big difference is that education, corrections, and many other programs targeted for privatization will generally continue to receive public funds. Rather than being dependent on the market, the private firms receiving contracts and vouchers will still be dependent on public appropriations, and they have every reason to try to milk the public treasury for all it is worth. Some will honestly press for higher spending levels; others will try to gain political favor through campaign contributions and outright bribery. Since large amounts of money pivot on contracting decisions, corruption is predictable. To expect otherwise is naive.

Under certain conditions, contracting out or voucher plans may be more efficient than direct public services, but there is no reason to expect that the privatization options will be uniformly superior. When government chooses between producing a service or contracting for it, it is confronting a make-buy decision. If it were always more efficient to buy rather than to make, no large, multi-unit private corporations would exist: there would only be small firms and "hollow corporations" contracting for goods and services with other small firms. When private companies decide to employ people directly, they are making a decision for bureaucracy over the market, perhaps to ensure more direct control or better information. For the same reasons, direct public employment may be more advantageous to a government than contracting out.

One particular danger in contracting out is that governments may become captive of particular contractors, especially as the contractors acquire inside knowledge, including information about costs that potential competitors may be unable to get. Even if governments can take advantage of multiple suppliers at the initiation of contracting out, they may find little or no competition at times of contract renewal. As a result, the contractors may be able to raise prices dramatically, and the initial advantages of contracting out may vanish like a mirage.

Unlike private companies' decisions about out-sourcing, governments also have to consider the peculiar characteristics of certain public functions, such as the control of deadly force, and the demands of accountability to public officials and the electorate at large. The proponents of privatization seem to believe the old notion that it is possible to achieve a clean separation of politics and administration. However, because the separation is not so neat, privatization necessarily conveys a degree of political authority to private firms. Since the advocates of privatization do not think much of democratic government in the first place, they are not much inclined to worry about any loss of public control. But the rest of us may see privatization as transferring more power to private companies than we think they should have.

The Monetization of Hidden Subsidies

Many of the proponents of privatization, such as the President's Commission on Privatization (1988), say their proposals are aimed to bring into the full light of day subsidies to particular groups that are now concealed or at least not explicitly measured or accounted for in the budget. Two kinds of subsidies stand out:

Subsidies from below-market prices. For example, federal information programs provide statistical data and a variety of other programs at prices well
below cost. Federal loan programs provide mortgage and other financing at
below-market interest rates. Military commissaries provide groceries at a 25
percent discount, and Amtrak passengers pay less for tickets than would be
necessary to recover costs.

Cross-subsidies within programs. Some services are priced higher than cost,
others lower, with the result that a tax is effectively levied on one group while
benefits flow to others. For example, urban residents pay more while rural
populations pay less for postal services than each would pay in a competitive
private postal market.

   The President's Commission repeatedly claimed not to be recommending
the elimination of such subsidies. Like many other advocates of privatization,
the commission said that if Congress wished to subsidize the beneficiaries of
these programs, it could do so directly through transfer payments. A shift to
direct payments would achieve, first of all, fiscal clarification, and second, the
elimination of allocative inefficiencies that arise from having some services
priced too high and others too low. Privatization, in short, would help get
prices right.
   There is much merit to these claims, but the monetization of subsidies has
some political effects that need to be plainly understood. It is impossible (and
even if possible, undesirable) to monetize fully all the subsidies and transfers
in fiscal systems. Every exception to general income tax rates can be considered a tax expenditure (a form of fiscal clarification about which conservatives
are distinctly unenthusiastic). Every choice of location for a federal facility can
be considered a regional rather than a national benefit. Every age-related program, from education to Social Security, can be considered a transfer between
generations. If we were to attempt to determine the full picture of resource
flows through the fiscal system by income class, region, age, and other relevant
groupings, the process would never end—and we would never agree.
   Second, and more important, the process would intensify conflicts and make
us less of a nation. In the nineteenth century, the eastern states financed the
development of the West through the construction of roads and waterways,
provision of military defense, extension of the postal system, and later the
construction of dams and electric power plants. That effort was understood not
exclusively as a regional transfer, but as the building of the United States. In
some respects, we must regard ourselves as constituting a national household.
In a family the parents do not consider the bread they put on the table as a subsidy to their children. They are not counting their children's nutrition as a cost
to themselves, but as their very own nourishment. Inasmuch as we have a

future as a nation, we cannot regard every program as a subsidy to particular interests. We must regard much of what government does as an investment in our common future and evaluate policies and programs for what they will do to strengthen—or weaken—the bonds of membership in the nation.

Monetizing subsidies, therefore, is more than an act of fiscal clarification. It says that we will count a program as a subsidy, and in doing so it erodes the legitimacy of that program. The President's Commission says that if we were to privatize postal services, we could subsidize rural families that might lose postal service in a freely competitive market. But surely to monetize that subsidy is to put it at the jeopardy of the annual budgetary process, where it is less likely to survive than if it represents part of the mission of the Postal Service in preserving universal mail service.

For many other programs, such as governmental information programs, direct subsidies would be difficult and expensive to administer. Subsidies would require an increase in means testing, which diminishes privacy. Moreover, direct subsidies to consumers, instead of indirect subsidies through lower-priced services, potentially mean an extension of government control over those consumers who receive subsidies. For that reason, direct subsidies can actually mean a loss of individual liberty.

Privatization as a Self-Limiting Process

In certain respects, privatization is likely to be self-limiting and self-defeating. Although the advocates of privatization intend to diminish public spending and the sphere of governmental action, some privatization policies would likely generate responses leading back to a greater public role.

First, consider the political feedback effects of contracting out and vouchers. Advocates of privatization say that achieving public purposes through private providers will reduce spending pressure on government, but this seems highly unlikely. As Stuart Butler has conceded, the firms receiving contracts and vouchers are no less likely than public employees to agitate for greater appropriations. Defense, health care, and construction are examples of publicly financed but privately produced services. The private producers are among the most active spending lobbies in the nation. Not only do they lobby for higher appropriations; they use their influence to secure favorable terms under government contracts and reimbursement systems. So to expect that privatization in other areas will yield budgetary relief seems entirely illusory. Educational vouchers, in particular, bear a great resemblance to third-party payment in health insurance and would likely have a highly inflationary impact on school expenditures.

Privatization may also be self-limiting because programs intended to promote private services may end up socializing them. One reason why many private firms dislike working under government contracts is that they subject themselves to more government regulation in the form of audits, legislative scrutiny, and judicial review. These controls are not the result of blind and misguided regulation, but the predictable side-effect of periodical scandals. Under new privatization programs, the same sequence of scandal and regulation would be certain to unfold. Many private school administrators are wary of educational vouchers precisely because they fear that once they receive governmental funds they will become subject to an increasing amount of public regulation. Inevitably, that is exactly what will happen. If a community's tax dollars are going to support phony or poorly organized private schools, the citizens are going to demand greater accountability—and that means audits, legislative scrutiny, and judicial review. Perversely enough, the effort to move from public to private risks making private institutions more public and diminishing some advantages of the contrasting alternatives in the public and private sectors that we now have.

Yet another reason why privatization might be self-limiting is the potential for instability in the economy. In periods of instability or severe downturns in growth, the public expects the federal government to take effective remedial measures. In this respect, the changes wrought by the New Deal are still in effect. The recent examples of federal intervention to save failing financial institutions illustrate the continued expectations of government action. The greater the magnitude of economic tremors, the more likely is the state to assume a direct role, even in those areas where in recent years it has appeared to be winding it down. The withering away of the state was long a Marxist illusion about communist societies. If some exponents of privatization believe the state in capitalist societies will wither away, they are likely to prove just as wrong.

Reframing the Debate

The advocates of privatization have succeeded in focusing attention on some serious problems of public expenditure and public management. Those problems need our attention, but privatization is not a general solution to them. Privatization may seem attractive often because of the procedures we have established for managing public organizations; we can change the procedures. We may need to reduce the regulatory controls on the public sector, monitoring results rather than prescribing detailed procedures, thereby encouraging managers—and employees—to develop new approaches to their tasks.

What we cannot afford is the preconception that government is destined to fail at whatever it does. We need the distinctive capacities of government to meet a variety of problems poorly handled by the market and private charity. The AIDS epidemic is a current example. Private insurance carriers want nothing to do with the carriers of the virus, much less those sick with the disease; commercial insurers will rationally seek to avoid paying the costs of AIDS by restricting coverage. Charitable and volunteer work has been immensely valuable in responding to the epidemic, but as the philanthropies and voluntary agencies know best of all, our society depends on government for the bulk of funds for research, prevention, and treatment to cope with the epidemic.

Health care is generally an example where our devotion to private provision has proved both costly and inequitable. Canada, with a public system of health insurance, spends 8.6 percent of its gross national product on health care, while we spend more than 11 percent. Yet the Canadians provide universal coverage, whereas the United States has some 38 million people without any insurance. One study estimates that half the difference between the two countries consists of higher administrative costs of health insurance and health care in the United States (Evans 1989). Recent public opinion evidence indicates far higher levels of public satisfaction with health care in Canada than in the United States (Blendon 1989). So do we need more privatization of health services—or less?

I am not suggesting that we need a uniformly stronger governmental role or that we ought to oppose every policy described as privatization. It would be foolish and wrong-headed to object to contracting out as a matter of principle. Similarly, no one could reasonably reject, on principle, all conceivable sales of government assets. Disposing of some assets (as well as investing in others) may represent a rational redeployment of resources. Governments ought periodically to review the assets under public ownership to ensure that they are being put to best use. But the privatization movement is not asking for an unprejudiced review of government operations and assets. Its advocates want us to think about government as irredeemably incompetent, to empty out the portfolio of public responsibilities, and to avoid entertaining any new ideas about affirmative uses of public authority. Privatization is an effort to channel political debate. The intent is not just to improve the efficiency of particular services, but to change aspirations in our society, to direct them into the market and out of the arena of politics and the sphere of common responsibility. The validity of that effort is the basis on which privatization ought ultimately to be judged.

NOTES

1 For further discussion, see Starr (1988).
2 The privatization of money would involve ending the government's monopoly on the creation of legal tender. For example, competing banks might issue competing dollar bills. Or they might construct entirely new currencies backed by varying reserves. For a proposal, see Rahn.

REFERENCES

Blendon, Robert J. 1989. "Three Systems: A Comparative Survey." *Health Management Quarterly* 11:2–10.

Evans, Robert G., et al. 1989. "Controlling Health Expenditures—The Canadian Reality." *New England Journal of Medicine* 320:571–77.

Friedman, Milton, and Rose Friedman. 1980. *Free to Choose: A Personal Statement.* New York: Harcourt Brace Jovanovich.

President's Commission on Privatization. 1988. *Privatization: Toward More Effective Government.* Washington, D.C.: GPO.

Rahn, Richard W. 1986. "Time to Privatize Money?" *Policy Review* 36 (Spring):55–57.

Reich, Robert, ed. 1987. *The Power of Public Ideas.* Cambridge, Mass.: Ballinger.

Starr, Paul. 1988. "The Meaning of Privatization." *Yale Law and Policy Review* 6:6–41.

Starr, Paul. Forthcoming. "The New Life of the Liberal State: Privatization and the Restructuring of State-Society Relations." In *The Political Economy of Public Sector Reform and Privatization*, ed. Ezra Suleiman and John Waterbury. Boulder, Colo.: Westview.

PART 2
EDUCATION POLICY

4 *Dwight R. Lee*

Vouchers—The Key to
Meaningful Reform

The education of our citizens is of overriding importance in maintaining a free and productive society. And there are widely accepted reasons for government to play a role in the educational process. The important question is not whether government should be involved in education, but how government should be involved. The importance of education makes it imperative that we examine government's role with an eye to maximizing its contribution. The central thesis of this chapter is that government can best improve the educational process in the United States by reducing its direct role in the provision of education. Educational reform that relies on extending government control over educational decisions will be far more costly, and far less effective, than reform that shifts more control to those who consume educational services. The argument here is that educational vouchers would make educational decisions more responsive to the public's desire for efficiently provided quality education than can be the case with the existing structure of public education.

In order to proceed, it is useful first to consider the benefits provided by basic education (K-12) and the justification for a government role in making that education available. Following is a brief intellectual and political history of educational vouchers from the writings of Adam Smith to the recent politics of voucher experiments. This history provides a general overview of the

Dwight Lee is Ramsey Professor of Economics at the University of Georgia.

advantages of educational vouchers, advantages that are discussed in detail in the next section. The final section outlines some of the standard objections to the voucher approach to education and a brief summary concludes the paper.

Education and the Role of Government

The case for a role for government comes from considering the benefits provided by education. When people acquire an education, the benefits that result extend beyond those individuals. By becoming more literate and more informed about the world in which they live, individuals become better able to perform both as workers and citizens. The benefits that result when workers increase their productive skills are benefits which those workers are able, to a large extent, to capture for themselves through higher pay and better prospects for promotion. But most education is aimed not at narrowly improving people's job skills, but rather at providing them with an understanding, in common with their fellow citizens, of the social order in which they live and of the traditions and norms upon which that order is based. More succinctly, most education is aimed at producing informed and responsible citizens.

The benefits that result when individual citizens make more informed public choices are, in the lexicon of economists, public benefits; that is, benefits that, once generated, are equally available to all citizens (see Tullock 1971). Therefore, individuals recognize that they receive only some small portion of the benefits generated by making informed public choices and, also, that they can free-ride on the informed choices of others. Although everyone is better off when a diligent effort to become broadly informed is made by all, from the perspective of each individual there is little motivation to make such an effort. It is certainly the case that most individuals will invest less in general education than is socially desirable, if each is faced with the full cost of acquiring that education. So the case for government involvement in education is clear. By making education freely available, or available with a significant subsidy, government is able to motivate people to acquire more education than they otherwise would to the general advantage of all.[1]

There exists another argument for a government role in education which goes beyond, although it relates to, the standard public good argument. It has been argued that the productivity of free market institutions depends, at least over the long run, on the public perception that these institutions are not only efficient but also fair. A key consideration in the public's perception of market fairness is that, to the extent possible, individuals have an equal opportunity to compete for the wealth generated by the productivity of the market place. A basic education exerts a significant influence on a person's ability to enter meaningfully into the competitive market game, and by making education universally available government makes an important contribution to the fairness of the market.[2]

Not all scholars who have examined education find the case for government involvement persuasive. Some have argued that public schooling does little to increase the public's willingness to acquire a basic education. Studies by West (1967) and Fishlow (1966) conclude that the percentage of children receiving a basic education in 19th-century New York and New England before the public school movement abolished fees for schooling was not significantly lower than after the fees were abolished.[3]

If that is indeed the case, that government has done little to increase the number who acquire a basic education, then the standard justifications for government support of basic education are obviously weakened. It is not the purpose of this paper, however, to attempt to resolve, or even enter into, the debate over whether government should play a role in education. The fact is, the governments of every nation are involved in the education of its citizens and so it makes sense to concentrate on how to make this involvement as productive as possible (see Lott 1987). So for the purpose of this paper it is accepted that the benefits generated by education, particularly basic education, are such that in the absence of government involvement they will be undersupplied.

It is important to distinguish between two different types of government involvement in the provision of education. Government can be actively involved in the provision of education, using tax dollars to construct the schools, to hire the teachers and administrators, and to organize these factors in supplying education services. Or government can finance education without involving itself in its supply. For example, government could provide parents of school-age children with vouchers that could be used to purchase education from schools that were privately owned and controlled, with the owners of these schools able to redeem the vouchers with the government for cash. Of course, between government-supplied education and government-financed education is the possibility of a voucher system with government imposing certain eligibility requirements and standards on the schools receiving the vouchers.

Even when the consumption is financed by government, there are advantages to having a good or service provided by private producers, especially when it can be provided directly to the individual consumer. A greater motivation among private producers to supply a service that consumers desire comes from prospects for profit and the discipline of competition. For example, it is federal government policy to make adequate nutrition available to all, regardless of income. Few would argue that the best way of implementing this policy is by having the federal government nationalize food production and distribution. There can be no doubt that nationalization would significantly reduce our ability to produce and distribute food. A far more effective approach is the one we now observe, which is a policy of food vouchers, better known as food stamps. Those who qualify receive vouchers for food which they use to purchase food from private suppliers. The ability of government to make food available to a target group is achieved without reducing the efficiency of food production.

So the desirability of having government play an important role in education is consistent with the desire to have education provided by private producers. Indeed, the above discussion suggests that the objectives of government educational policy (quality education, universally available, and efficiently provided) would best be achieved if government were not directly involved in supplying education. There are compelling arguments to be made that a move to a policy of educational vouchers would greatly improve the quality and lower the cost of the basic education provided in this country. Before considering these arguments in detail, however, it will be useful to look at a brief intellectual and political history of educational vouchers.

A Brief Intellectual and Political History

Although Adam Smith did not explicitly recommend a voucher system for education, his views on education pointed in the direction of such a system. Smith's reputation as the founder of economics is based on his clear articulation of the advantages realized from organizing economic activity through private markets, but he was not opposed to a role for government in many sectors of the economy. In particular, Smith ([1776] 1937: 768) argued that "education . . . is . . . beneficial to the whole society, and may, therefore, without injustice, be defrayed by the general contribution of the whole society." At the same time, however, Smith had little confidence in the ability of public agencies to provide quality education. According to Smith ([1776] 1937: 721), "These parts of education (private instruction), it is to be observed, for the teaching of which there are no public institutions are generally the best taught." Smith believed that better teaching would result only when the payment teachers received came from their pupils, and therefore depended on providing the student with quality instruction.[4]

So Smith saw the justification for at least some public financing of education, but at the same time recognized that education is best supplied in response to the incentives generated by private arrangements. It was Milton Friedman (1955) who first argued for tying the desirability of publicly financed education to the advantages of privately supplied education with a policy of educational vouchers. Friedman gave educational vouchers public prominence by advocating them in his widely read *Capitalism and Freedom* in 1962.

Since 1962 the concept of educational vouchers has received wide attention and broad support in the academic community. Literally hundreds of articles and books have been written on the economics and politics of educational vouchers. Support for educational vouchers has spanned the ideological spectrum from Milton Friedman on the right to Christopher Jencks, a democratic socialist on the left, who has put forth specific proposals for testing and implementing vouchers (Jencks, et al. 1970).

Political interest in educational vouchers has been far less than academic interest. Vouchers received some political attention at the federal level in the early 1970s when the Office of Management and Budget spent several million dollars for voucher demonstrations. At the beginning of the Reagan Administration, renewed political attention was directed at the possibility of providing parents with more choice in the educational decisions affecting their children. Although vouchers received some discussion, most of the focus was on tax credits whereby parents who sent their children to private schools were compensated, at least partially, with a reduction in their tax burdens. With the publication of the report, *A Nation at Risk*, by the National Commission on Excellence in Education, a tremendous amount of public and political attention has been directed at educational reform. However, despite some occasional remarks by former Secretary of Education William Bennett in favor of a voucher approach to educational reform, there has been little effective political interest in educational vouchers.

The lack of political interest in vouchers, while disappointing, is not surprising even though public sympathy for reform in public education is clearly widespread. For the very reason that a policy of educational vouchers would constitute meaningful reform, such a policy motivates little support and plenty of opposition. The advantages of vouchers, which are discussed in more detail in the next section, derive from the fact that they transfer control over educational decisions out of the political arena and into the marketplace. But this is equivalent to reducing the control of the producers of education and increasing the control of the consumers. And this is a shift in control that educational producers can be expected to oppose, and oppose effectively, since when decisions are being made in the political arena the interests of producers' groups tend to dominate those of consumer groups.

The benefits from educational vouchers are spread among all consumers of education, and indeed, over all of society. While in the aggregate these benefits are potentially enormous, from the perspective of each individual they are comparatively modest. Furthermore, each individual's motivation as a consumer to take the type of political action needed to change public policy is small. Because of the sheer number of consumers, each knows both that he can benefit as a free rider if others work effectively for improvements in educational policy, and that if others do not work for policy improvements, then any efforts he makes will surely be ineffective. On the other hand, the public-school professionals who oppose educational vouchers see significant individual costs associated with a move to vouchers, are well organized politically, and as a result, are able to exert strong political influence in opposition to the voucher approach. The same political influence that has allowed the public school lobby to realize advantages from its control over educational decisions can be expected to be used in an effort to frustrate meaningful reform, since meaningful reform would threaten those advantages.

Even when educational vouchers overcome political opposition to the point of being considered experimentally, the effects of special interest political influence is clearly visible. The federally funded voucher experiment that ran the longest and which has been considered most successful was conducted in Alum Rock, California. As one would predict, however, restrictions were placed on the use of these experimental vouchers that diluted the competitive pressures imposed on public school professionals. For example, public school teachers did not face loss of income if, in response to parental choice, enrollment in their classes declined. Loss of enrollment meant that teachers were given priority for teaching jobs at other schools and makeshift work at full pay until such jobs were available. At the same time, those teachers who succeeded in attracting additional students were not rewarded with higher salaries. The schools which were providing superior education, as indicated by extra demand from parents, were not able to expand in order to accommodate that demand. Students who were not able to get their first choice were assigned to available schools. In addition, for a private school to become eligible to receive vouchers, it had to satisfy a host of requirements on such issues as teacher certification, pay and fringe benefits, and faculty-student ratios (requirements which have little, if any influence on the quality of education). These requirements made it effectively impossible for a private school to compete against the public schools for the vouchers.

The current level of political interest suggest that the time has not come for educational vouchers. For the most part, public desire for reform has not focused on proposals that require fundamental changes in existing arrangements and practices. Unfortunately, though predictably, it has been possible to satisfy public concern over educational quality with cosmetic changes and platitudes about political commitment to educational excellence. But despite the difficulty of engaging the political process to embrace the voucher approach to education, this approach has the potential of improving the quality while lowering the cost of education. We now turn to a more detailed discussion of the economics behind this conclusion and the evidence which supports it.

The Economic Case for Educational Vouchers

Vouchers would motivate parents to become more informed on the effectiveness of the teaching their children receive by increasing the control their decisions have on that teaching. At the same time the use of vouchers would provide educators with information on the type of educational approaches that work best, and with the motivation to employ those approaches. In order to understand best how vouchers would achieve these objectives, it is useful to consider why these objectives are not being achieved by the public schools under current arrangements.

Public schooling, K-12, is currently supplied by local governments, made available with no direct charge to all school-age children, and financed through general taxation. The amount of tax paid by parents of school-age children is independent of whether or not they send their children to public schools. Parents have the option of choosing private schools for their children, but doing so obliges them to pay twice for their children's education—once for the public schools with their tax payments, and again for the private schools with their tuition payments. When parents send their children to public schools, which most of them do, given the high additional cost of sending them to private school, they typically have little control over the school their children attend or the type of instruction they receive. In order for parents to send their children to a public school other than the one assigned, they have to move, and even then may not get the school of their choice. In order for parents to influence the type of instruction their children receive in the absence of moving, they have to become involved in school politics. A predictable consequence is that parents have little motivation to be informed on the quality of their children's education since it is difficult for them to act decisively on such information.

Turning to the supply side, under the current arrangement, producers of public education are not paid directly by the consumers of education. The connection between how well producers respond to the desires of consumers and the rewards producers receive is therefore rather tenuous. Public school professionals find that they have a wide range of latitude and can put personal concerns ahead of the concerns of consumers of education without suffering adverse financial consequences. If, for whatever reason, the quality of education declines at a particular school, there is unlikely to be a noticeable decline in enrollment as a consequence, or a reduction in the funding the school receives. Indeed, it is quite possible that schools in which the performance of students is declining will be able to justify additional funding in order to address the problem. Conversely, making a diligent effort to improve the quality of education, and to do so at less cost, will not likely result in additional financial rewards for those responsible, or additional funding for the schools where they work.[5] Indeed, the public school principal who improved educational quality and was able to reduce cost in the process would more likely find his budget reduced than his efforts financially rewarded.

Under a voucher policy, parents of school-age children would receive vouchers which could be spent for education at the school of their choice. Parents could, if they chose to do so, supplement the vouchers in order to send their children to a more expensive school than the voucher alone would allow, but the vouchers they receive can be used only for education.[6] Government-run schools can still exist under the voucher approach, but their funding would depend entirely on their ability to compete for vouchers (i.e., the patronage of parents of school-age children) against schools owned and operated by private proprietors. Government could impose some broad requirements on eligible schools with respect to basic subject matter, but would have little control over the details of a school's curriculum or be allowed to impose specific course requirements on the education of the school's teachers. Within the broad rules that apply to all private businesses, school owners would be allowed to hire, fire, and set salaries in response to market forces and the desire for profits. Under such a policy of educational vouchers, incentives on both the demand side and the supply side of the education market would be altered dramatically, and for the better.

The ability of parents to choose their children's school would increase their desire to determine which educational approach works best for their children, a desire that tends to be weak under present public school arrangements. Economists have long pointed out that people are reluctant to become actively involved in issues that are decided politically. When decisions on issues are made politically in response to majority voting and legislative lobbying, each individual realizes that his or her vote, or even his or her participation in a lobbying effort, is not likely to determine the outcome. Indeed, in most elections the probability that the individual will be killed in an accident on the way to the polls is greater than the probability that his vote will break what would otherwise be a tie, and therefore be decisive. So becoming informed on political issues does little to affect the well-being of the individual who goes to the trouble to do so, and the tendency to remain rationally ignorant on political issues is a strong one.[7]

Parents surely feel, for example, that the education of their children is more important than the purchase of a used car. Yet it should not be surprising that parents of school-age children commonly spend more time informing themselves about used cars than they do about the public schools their children attend. In the used car market there are many alternatives, and the choice the individual makes is a decisive choice. Consumers get what they choose, and they get it because of the choice they made. Information on educational alternatives in the public school system is less valuable because choices based on this information are not decisive. The parents who, because they have become informed on the type of education their children are receiving in the public schools, desire an alternative within the public school system are unlikely to be able to exercise much influence toward the realization of that alternative. Even though the education of their children is far more important than the used car they drive, parents whose children are in the public schools will find information on education less valuable than information on used cars.

The advantage of the voucher approach to education in this regard is clear. With parents being able, under the voucher approach, to send their children to any one of a number of schools, they would have far more control over the type of education their children received than most have now. Giving parents the same meaningful choice in education that they now have in nutrition, housing, clothing, and used cars would certainly increase their motivation to make informed decisions on the schools their children attend and the type of instruction they receive.

Directly related to the additional motivation the voucher approach would provide parents to make informed educational choices for their children is the motivation educators would have to respond to these choices under a voucher policy. Those schools that did not provide the quality of education that parents desire for their children would not receive as many vouchers, and therefore revenue, as those schools that did. This does not mean that competition will push schools toward uniformity. To the extent that diverse preferences exist among parents for the type of educational experiences they would like their children to have, diverse educational experiences will be offered. Some parents will desire sex education for their children, while others will not. Some parents will desire avant-garde teaching methods, while others will not. Some parents will desire that their children be allowed to say prayers in the classroom, while others will not. And some parents will desire that their children be exposed to reading material that other parents will consider too risqué. In an educational market created by vouchers, there is no reason why differences in educational preferences would lead to the acrimonious social divisions that now result as people find no way to resolve their differences except through political combat over public school policy that applies to all.

Not only will proprietors of schools be motivated to respond to the preferences of parents, they will be motivated to do so as cost effectively as possible. Strong incentives will exist to eliminate unproductive administrative functions, unnecessary specialists, professional growth activities that result in no professional growth, and salary schedules tied to taking teaching courses rather than demonstrating teaching competence. This motivation will exist because with schools privately owned and operated, those with the authority to create cost saving through greater efficiency are the direct recipients of the benefits of those savings. Savings realized from more efficient provision of education allows some combination of greater profits for owners, higher salaries for competent teachers, and a stronger competitive position through lower tuition for students. Certainly the incentive would no longer exist, as it does in all public agencies (including the public schools), to be panicked into a spending spree if it appears that some of the budget will be unspent at the end of the budget year.

It is possible to get a measure of the cost efficiency advantage that could be realized with the voucher approach to education by examining the per pupil

cost differences between existing private and public schools. According to
statistics compiled by the U. S. Department of Health, Education, and Welfare
(now broken up into the Department of Health and Human Services, and the
Department of Education), it cost 2.12 times as much in the United States to
educate a pupil in a public school than in a private school during the 1977–
78 school year (U. S. Department of Health, Education, and Welfare 1979).
This figure no doubt overstates the cost advantage of private school since most
private schools are church-affiliated and the salaries of the religious staff fail
to reflect the market value of services they provide. However, after adjusting the salary figures to account for this private school "subsidy," Bredeweg
(1982:38–56) found that public schools still spent 1.91 times as much to educate a pupil as did private schools over the 1977–78 school year. Similar results
are found in other studies for other school years (Lott 1987).

The incentives private schools face, and that all schools would face under
the voucher system, do more than provide a motivation to keep costs down.
Parents not only want low tuition, they also demand quality education for
their children, and when forced to compete for the patronage of these parents,
schools would have to provide both. So one would not expect that the lower
costs of the private schools comes at the expense of educational quality, and the
evidence bears this out. After statistically controlling for family background
variables that affect academic performance, Coleman, Hoffer, and Hilgore
(1982) found that students progress faster in private schools than in public
schools.

It does not seem to be the case, as some have argued, that private schools
do better than public schools because private schools can admit only the better
students while public schools are required to take everyone. Private schools,
as with any business, are anxious to increase their clientele and are not dis-
posed to turning away students. Indeed, in recent years private schools have
actively and effectively recruited minority students. While enrollment of whites
in private high schools increased 0.3 percent from 1972 to 1983, over the
same period it increased 59 percent for blacks and 54 percent for Hispanics
(Feistritzer 1987). And according to a recent article, 60 percent of parochial
private schools do not expel a single student during a given academic year
(Keisling 1982:27).

A better explanation for the superior performance of private schools is contained in considerations such as the following: private school students are 50
percent more likely to put in an hour's worth of homework each night than are
public school students; 70 percent of all private school students are enrolled in
an academic program compared to 34 percent of public school students; a third
year of language is taken by 14 percent of private school students compared to
6 percent of public school students; chemistry is taken by 53 percent of private
school students but by only 37 percent of public school students; geometry is

taken by 84 percent of private school students and by only 53 percent of public school students (Keisling 1982).

Going to the heart of the matter, private schools do better because they operate in a competitive environment in which their survival depends on doing better. The advantage of educational vouchers is that they would create an environment in which all schools are subjected to the discipline of competition.

Objections and Responses

Several objections that are not directly related to the efficiency advantages of a voucher system have been raised. These objections are based on the view that our system of public education serves more important purposes than providing instruction in basic academic skills. Therefore, even if our existing public schools are not teaching these basic skills as effectively and economically as they would be taught under a voucher approach, it is still better to stay with the existing system.

A major objection to educational vouchers is that they would undermine efforts to achieve racial balance in our schools. It is feared that parents would exercise the power of choice provided by vouchers to avoid sending their children to schools with minority enrollments and schools would become segregated by race. Another, and somewhat related, objection to vouchers is that they would discriminate against the poor who lack the ability to supplement their vouchers in order to send their children to better, and more expensive schools. Economic as well as racial segregation is therefore seen to be the consequence of educational vouchers. There are also those who worry that a voucher policy would violate the constitutional separation between church and state because government-financed vouchers would be used by some to send their children to church-affiliated schools. Finally, there are those who object to educational vouchers because they believe that as long as government funding is involved, government control will also be involved, and involved to a degree that will reduce, if not negate altogether, the advantages that can be realized only from vouchers unencumbered by government regulation.

This is not an exhaustive list of the objections to educational vouchers, but it does include the most substantive objections. But there are reasons for believing that even these objections are misplaced. The argument is not that the objections are misplaced because they center on unimportant problems. Rather, it will be argued that educational vouchers either moderate, or do nothing to aggravate, these problems while motivating the provision of better education at lower cost.

Consider the problem of racial segregation in our schools. It cannot be denied that, whether for reasons of discrimination or a desire for ethnic identity, many parents place a positive value on their children attending school primarily with other children of the same ethnic background. For most parents, however, the overriding concern is that their children receive a good education. Schools that offer quality instruction in a setting that is safe and conducive to learning are, regardless of the ethnic composition of the classroom, desired by almost all parents. And under a voucher system, schools that fail to offer quality instruction in a setting conducive to learning will be unable to remain viable with coerced attendance. When required to compete for vouchers, schools will realize the advantage in providing the type of educational opportunities that appeal across ethnic divisions. This is the same advantage that motivated 39.2 percent of church-affiliated private schools to have minority enrollments of 25 percent or more, and 29.8 percent of them to have minority enrollments or 50 percent or more, in the 1985–86 school year. Catholic schools had a 21.8 percent minority enrollment in 1986 (Feistritzer 1987).

The argument here is not that perfect racial integration would be achieved under an educational voucher policy. Obviously, it would not. But compared to the degree of segregation that continues to exist in public schools, and the socially divisive attempts to reduce this segregation through forced busing, the voucher approach has much to recommend it. Vouchers would create incentives for schools and parents to accommodate racial differences and accentuate the common desire for quality education, incentives that simply do not exist under current public school arrangements. These incentives will, of course, not be compelling to everyone, but residual discrimination under the voucher approach can be addressed by refusing to redeem vouchers from schools that engage in overt racial discrimination.

The concern that educational vouchers will discriminate against the poor is completely unfounded. It is true, of course, that the wealthy can more easily supplement their vouchers in order to send their children to more expensive schools than can the poor. But to argue this is to do no more than recognize the obvious fact that the wealthy have more money than the poor, a fact that public policy on educational vouchers can do nothing about. Vouchers would, however, make it easier for a poor family to send its children to a more expensive school than is currently the case. Under current arrangements, public school students usually go to a neighborhood school. If poor people feel that their neighborhood public school is inadquate and want to send their children to a better school, they now have one of two options. They can either move into the neighborhood served by the preferred public school, or send their children to private school. The first option likely will require moving into a far more expensive house and the second will definitely require paying twice for their children's schooling. Either of these options will be more expensive than marginally supplementing their education vouchers in order to send their children to a better school.

It is also important to emphasize that vouchers, by making it easier for poor parents to transfer their children to what they believe are better schools, will pose a competitive threat that can only result in better schools for those children who do not transfer. The choices that can be exercised with vouchers will improve the level of instruction in all schools since those that do not improve cannot long remain viable. Of course rich parents will be able to spend more on their children's education than poor parents under a voucher approach to education, just as they are able to under the current approach. But that is beside the point. The important point is that under a voucher system the education for all would improve. And furthermore, the education received by poor children would improve most since vouchers would put the schools they attend under the same competitive pressures that the private schools attended by so many of the wealthy are already subject to.

If a voucher system were ultimately to become policy, their constitutionality would of course, have to be determined by the courts. There are, however, reasons to believe that the Supreme Court would rule that educational vouchers are consistent with the constitutional separation of church and state. In a 1984 Supreme Court decision (*Mueller v. Allen*), the Court considered the constitutionality of programs designed to reduce the tax burden of parents who send their children to non-public schools. The ruling was that such programs are constitutional if they help defray expense at both public and non-public schools; the programs have neither the intention nor the effect of inhibiting or advancing any particular religion; and the government funding (or tax relief) goes first to the parents rather than directly to the schools. Certainly these conditions are all satisfied by educational vouchers as a voucher policy would normally be implemented. The vouchers would be redeemable at any school, public or private, and by being widely redeemable, there is no reason to believe that vouchers would inhibit or advance any particular religion, or religion in general. Furthermore, the primary purpose of vouchers is to provide educational choice by channeling the funding of schools through parents rather than giving it directly to schools.

Finally, consider the concern that educational vouchers will come with so many governmental restrictions that they will be no better, and possibly worse, than what we have now. This is a genuine concern as evidenced by the restrictions imposed on the vouchers used in the Alum Rock experiment. Indeed, there has been reluctance on the part of Catholic clergy to embrace vouchers because of their concern that they will come with extensive public control (Doyle 1977). But even though political reality suggests that vouchers will be more encumbered with regulations than is ideal, it is hard to imagine them providing parents with less choice and public schools with more protection against competition than exists today. The strongest evidence that educational vouchers would be an improvement over the current approach to public education is the intense political opposition to vouchers by public school professionals.

Conclusion

While there are sound reasons for the public financing of basic education, there is no justification for the public provision of that education. Public financing of education through the public provision of education has resulted in a public school system in which parents have little direct control over where their children attend school or the type of education they receive. It is not surprising that our public school professionals have viewed their students as captives and have paid more attention to the prerequisites of their professions than to the concerns of their clients.

The most effective thing we could do to improve the quality of education in the United States is to make educators compete for the consumer's dollar. This can be done in a way that maintains public financing of education through a policy of educational vouchers. Educational vouchers are not a panacea. They would not work perfectly and problems would remain over which there would be legitimate concern. But without the tonic of genuine competition, which educational vouchers would provide, educational reform will remain little more than political rhetoric to cover up and perpetuate the failures of our existing public school system.

NOTES

1 As every economist knows, and wants everyone else to know, everything has a cost and education cannot literally be made freely available. More precisely, the marginal cost of educational facilities and instruction can be made zero to the user by supporting education with a tax whose burden is independent of one's consumption of education. This leaves, of course, the opportunity cost of the student's time, which can be significant. For this reason, governments typically encourage educational attainment with both the carrot of subsidies and the stick of mandatory attendance requirements.

2 This case for a government role in education has been forcefully made by James Buchanan as part of a larger argument for the importance of justice in a viable social order. In making the case for government involvement in education, Buchanan states, "A conceptually different justification (different from the public good justification) for publicly financed education emerges when we look at potential adjustments in starting positions, at handicaps aimed at making the game 'fair'" (Buchanan 1986:135).

3 West (1970) reached the same conclusion after studying school attendance figures and literacy rates in 19th- and early 20th-century England.

4 Again quoting from Smith, "In other universities the teacher is prohibited from receiving any honorary or fee from his pupils, and his salary constitutes the whole of the revenue which he derives from his office. His interest is, in this case, set as directly in opposition to his duty as it is possible to set it. It is the interest of every man to live as much at ease as he can; and if his emoluments are to be precisely the same, whether he does, or does not perform some very laborious duty, it is

certainly his interest, at least interest as vulgarly understood, either to neglect it all together, or, if he is subject to some authority which will not suffer him to do this, to perform it in as careless and slovenly a manner as that authority will permit" (Smith [1776] 1937:717–18).

5   Merit pay for superior teachers has received recent attention as a means of motivating better teaching. While possibly a step in the right direction, under current public school arrangements parental evaluation of educational quality will have less to do with identifying superior teachers than would be the case if parents could reward or punish particular schools by being allowed to choose which schools their children attend. It should also be pointed out that the National Education Association has consistently opposed merit pay proposals.

6   The determination of the value of each educational voucher is a detail that will vary somewhat from one school district to another and which is not of major concern here. One possibility is to have each voucher redeemable for the per student cost of education in the current public school system. This would increase government expenditures on education since the vouchers would cover all school-age children in the community, including those who were attending private, rather than public, schools before the switch to voucher. However, for reasons that will become clear, the per student cost of education will surely decline under a voucher policy, and so the value of each voucher can, without loss of educational quality, be less than the average cost of education under current arrangements.

7   The argument that remaining ignorant on political issues is a rational response to the fact that one's individual vote is unlikely to determine the outcome of an election was first made by Downs (1957: chapter 13). Many polls measuring the general public knowledge of political issues lend empirical support to the rational ignorance argument. Of course, many people do become politically informed, not necessarily because they feel they have a decisive say in political outcomes, but because they perceive acquiring political information as a benefit rather than a cost (Hirschman 1982).

REFERENCES

Bredeweg, Frank H. 1982. *United States Catholic Elementary Schools: 1981–82*. Washington, D.C.: National Catholic Education Association.

Buchanan, James M. 1986. "Rules for a Fair Game: Contractarian Notes on Distributive Justice." Chap. 12 in *Liberty, Market and the State: Political Economy in the 1980's*, 123–39. New York: New York University Press.

Coleman, James S., Thomas Hoffer, and Sally Hilgore. 1982. *High School Achievement: Public, Catholic and Private Schools Compared*. New York: Basic Books.

Downs, Anthony. 1957. *An Economic Theory of Democracy*. New York: Harper and Row.

Doyle, Denis P. 1977. "The Politics of Choice: A View From the Bridge." In *Parents, Teachers and Children: Prospects for Choice in American Education*, James S. Coleman et al., 227–55. San Francisco: Institute for Contemporary Studies.

Feistritzer, Emily. 1987. "Public Versus Private: Biggest Difference Is Not the Students." *Wall Street Journal* December, 15.

Fishlow, Albert. 1966. "The American Common School Revival: Fact or Fancy?" In

Industrialization in Two Systems: Essays in Honor of Alexander Gerscheenkron,
     ed. Henry Rossovsky, 40–67. New York: John Wiley and Sons.
Friedman, Milton. 1962. *Capitalism and Freedom*. Chicago: University of Chicago
     Press.
Friedman, Milton. 1955. "The Role of Government in Education," In *Economics and
     the Public Interest*, ed. Robert A. Solo, 123–53. New Brunswick, N.J.: Rutgers
     University Press.
Hirschman, Albert O. 1982. *Shifting Involvements: Private Interest and Public Action*.
     Princeton: Princeton University Press.
Jencks, Christopher, et al. 1970. *Educational Vouchers: A Report on Financing Ele-
     mentary Education by Grant to Parents*. Cambridge, Mass.: Center for the Study
     of Public Policy.
Keisling, Phil. 1982. "How to Save the Public Schools." *New Republic*, 1 November,
     27–82.
Lott, John R., Jr. 1987. "Why is Education Publicly Provided? A Critical Survey."
     CATO Journal 7 (Fall): 475–501.
Smith, Adam. [1776] 1937. *An Inquiry into the Nature and Causes of the Wealth of
     Nations*. Cannon Edition. New York: Modern Library.
Tullock, Gordon. 1971. "Public Decisions as Public goods." *Journal of Political Econ-
     omy* 79 (July–August): 913–18.
U.S. Department of Health, Education and Welfare. 1979. *NCES Bulletin*, October 23.
West, E. G. 1970. *Education and the State*. 2d ed. London: Institute of Economic
     Affairs.
West, E. G. 1967. "The Political Economy of the American Public School Legisla-
     tion." *Journal of Law and Economics* 10 (April): 101–28.
West, E. G. 1982. "The Prospects for Educational Vouchers: An Economic Analysis."
     In *The Public School Monopoly: A Critical Analysis of Education and the State
     in American Society*, ed. Robert B. Everhart, 369–91. San Francisco: Pacific
     Institute for Public Policy Research.

5   *Richard F. Elmore*

Public School Choice as a Policy Issue

The idea that parents, students, and teachers should have greater latitude to choose among public schools is gaining currency with state and local policy makers. The National Governors' Association signaled that public school choice had achieved a new political legitimacy in its 1986 report on education reform, *Time for Results*. The report called attention to a number of recent state and local choice initiatives, including interdistrict transfer schemes, open enrollment systems in desegregating school districts, and "second chance" programs that allow school dropouts to return to the educational program of their choice. By the most current count (Nathan 1989), 25 states have programs that encourage choice among schools. Ten states have laws establishing magnet schools, either statewide residential magnets or within-district magnets. Eleven states have laws that permit students to transfer within and between districts, or that allow secondary students to take courses at postsecondary institutions. Four states have second-chance programs that permit students who have failed in secondary school, or dropped out, to enter alternative high school completion programs at state expense. A number of leading figures in education policy making, including the President of the United States, governors, and leaders of both major teachers' unions, have endorsed some form

Richard Elmore is Research Fellow at the Center for Policy Research in Education and Professor of Education at Harvard University.

of increased state and local experimentation with choice. Controlled choice, usually defined as choice limited to the public schools and regulated for public purposes, including racial balance, appears to be entering the mainstream of education policy making.

The appeal of choice as an instrument of education policy stems from the expectation that it will make the public schools more responsive to clients. The NGA report sets the problem this way:

> Today, the public school system controls both production and consumption of education. The system tells the students what they will learn, at what speed and what quality. Students and their parents have little to say about it. A more responsive system would incorporate what students and their parents say they need with the education services necessary to meet those needs. (p. 67)

 Choice is seen by its advocates as a remedy for a public school bureaucracy grown increasingly unresponsive and complacent in its virtual monopoly over a fundamental public service. Choice advocates envision public schools populated with teachers and students who willingly associate around common means and ends.

 Opponents and skeptics argue that choice will provide little incentive to improve teaching and learning in schools if it is not accompanied by significant improvements in working conditions, teaching practices, and curriculum in schools. In the absence of well-designed limits on choice, skeptics further argue, it will simply reinforce and legitimate segregation by race and class and further entrench unenlightened teaching and curricula that appeal to cohesive groups of parents (for example, see Levin 1987).

Public policy issues are often distinguished as much by what they are *not* about as by what they are. Public policy making about educational choice is not, at least for the moment, primarily about privatization. Policies directed at school choice are presently confined to choices among publicly financed educational institutions, rather than choice between public and private institutions. One can read policy makers' avoidance of pure privatization in either of two ways. Opponents and skeptics fear that policies designed to enhance public school choice are the opening wedge for a more ambitious privatization agenda. Advocates, on the other hand, see public school choice as a way of avoiding privatization by making public schools more responsive, hence more competitive with their private alternatives (for example, see Raywid 1987). Indeed, most uses of public school choice in local districts—magnet schools, open enrollment plans, and controlled choice desegregation plans, for example—are explicitly designed to make public schools more attractive to "active choosers" within the public schools who might otherwise migrate to private schools. In an important sense, then, public policy making on educational choice is about alternatives to privatization, rather than about the introduction of privatization. Some alternatives, however, do rely on the private sector to perform limited services for the public sector, as discussed in the Washington state example below.

Policy Issues

Advocates argue that public school choice will improve responsiveness of the public school bureaucracy to differences among children and introduce incentives for improvements in performance. Achieving these results, however, requires consideration of several issues of design.[1]

Supply and Demand

Most public school choice advocates refer to choice as an issue of client control—from the demand side—because they are essentially anti-bureaucratic in their posture toward public education. Hence, most public school choice policies are advocated primarily as a way for parents to choose their children's school. But providing increased demand-side choice without also providing increased supply-side choice—for educators, in what they teach and with which schools they affiliate—will result in predictable problems. If parents and students are encouraged to choose among alternatives that are similar in content and pedagogy, and over which educators exercise little influence, the result is likely to be increased client dissatisfaction rather than increased responsiveness. Likewise, if educational alternatives are crafted from the immediate experience of educators, without substantial infusions of new knowledge, then the programs that are offered are likely to be more similar than different. Any consideration of public school choice, therefore, must include both the demand and the supply sides.

Public vs. Private Good

Choice affects those who actively choose, but it also affects those who, for one reason or another, do not choose. Choice policies are typically designed with more attention to their effects on active choosers than on inactive choosers.[2]

But public education combines elements of both a private and a public good (Levin 1987). That is, education provides private benefits to specific individuals, such as enhanced appreciation of literature and enhanced income, and it provides collective benefits to society as a whole, such as a literate voting citizenry. Different individuals have different preferences and interests in education, but the welfare of every individual in society depends on each person having a certain level of knowledge and skill. The fact that educational choice may be beneficial to those who actively choose, then, is only one criterion against which choice schemes should be evaluated. The other criterion is the effect of active choice by some on those who do not choose and on certain collective ends that society decides are worth valuing in their own right. Racial equality and access by each citizen to the basic prerequisites of democratic participation are two such collective values. Advocates of public school choice focus mainly on the predicted and actual benefits to active choosers, assuming that a system which is more responsive to active choosers will benefit everyone. In fact, choice policies may have negative effects on inactive choosers and on society as a whole; for example, by siphoning off talented students and concentrating low-achieving students in a few schools, or by allowing low-quality programs to persist because they have a loyal following, educational levels may decline.

Alteration of Existing Structures

Policy decisions on choice are almost never decisions about whether to allow choice or not to allow it, but rather are about how existing structures of choice can be altered for certain purposes.

The education choice issue is ordinarily stated thus: "Should parents, students, and educators be allowed to choose schools?" In fact, even in the most heavily centralized education systems, parents, students, and teachers already exercise some degree of choice. Some of these choices, such as choosing a residence or a private school, are costly to make and difficult to reverse and are highly sensitive to differences in income, race, and social class. Others are less costly and difficult, such as pressuring the school principal to change a child's assigned teacher, or choosing science fiction instead of English literature as a high school elective. These choices are influenced more by whether people see themselves as active or passive choosers in the organizations that provide them services.

Policy debate usually focuses more on the predicted benefits of new choice proposals, rather than on the relationship between existing systems of choice and proposed changes in those systems. Choice policies often make certain options, which were previously available to only a small number of active choosers, more explicit and available to a wider clientele. In addition, choice policies often alter the structure of opportunities and the costs of choice, sometimes intentionally, sometimes inadvertently. In order to understand the effects of choice policies, then, one must understand how they alter the existing regime of choice, not simply what new choices they offer.

The success of public school choice policies, then, depends in large part on how well policy makers and implementors grapple with these inherent problems. One way to observe this problem solving is to examine actual working models of choice.

Three Working Models of Public School Choice

This analysis focuses on three working models of choice: the Minnesota Post-Secondary Options Program, the alternative school choice program in New York City's Community District 4, and the Education Clinics Program in the State of Washington. These examples were chosen for a number of reasons. They represent a range of uses of choice, so they allow for a consideration of how choice works under different circumstances and for different purposes. They exist in very different social, political, and fiscal circumstances, which allows for an analysis of the interaction between those proposing choice and the political actors involved. All three models are reasonably well known and widely cited as examples of how choice might work as an instrument of public policy. These cases are discussed around a relatively simple scheme: a brief description of each model followed by an outline of the social, political, and economic context within which the model developed, the operating characteristics of the model, and the results of implementation.[3] The chapter concludes with an examination of how the models confront the three inherent policy design problems discussed above—demand-side vs. supply-side choice, public vs. private good, and alterations of existing choice structures.

The Minnesota Postsecondary Enrollment Options Program (PEO)

Passed by the Minnesota legislature in the summer of 1985, the PEO program provides that eleventh and twelfth graders in public schools may enroll for courses in postsecondary institutions, including community colleges, public universities, postsecondary vocational-technical schools, and private colleges. Students may elect to take either secondary or postsecondary credit for their coursework. The law provides for the transfer of funds from the student's school district to the receiving postsecondary institution according to a formula based on the district's per pupil expenditure and the portion of the student's academic program taken in the postsecondary institution.

The Community District 4 Alternative School Choice Program

Community District 4 is located in East Harlem, on the upper east side of New York City, one of the poorest neighborhoods in the country. The District 4 model began to emerge in 1973 with the formation of an alternative school, later called Central Park East Elementary School. Between 1973 and the present, the district has formed more than twenty alternative programs which offer parents a wide choice of educational options. At the elementary level, most students attend their neighborhood school, although a substantial number voluntarily choose to attend an alternative school. At the junior high level, all students and their parents participate in a formal process of choosing their school. While the community district is not formally authorized to run high schools, which are administered by the city-wide Board of Education, District 4 runs two high school alternative programs under an agreement with the board.

The Washington State Education Clinics Program
    The education clinics program was passed by the Washington legislature in 1978. The clinics program is designed to serve young people between the ages of 13 and 19 who have dropped out of school. The law permits organizations, including private, for-profit firms, to run remedial programs that provide short-term, intensive, individualized education to drop-outs to prepare them either for re-entry to school or to take the Test of General Educational Development (GED) for a high-school equivalency certificate. Eight clinics are currently in operation, serving about 1800 students. They are run by a variety of organizations, including community-based human services groups, employment training organizations, and American Indian organizations. The two largest clinics, serving nearly one-third of the total participants in the program, are run by Education Clinics, Incorporated, a private, for-profit firm which was instrumental in securing the passage of the clinics legislation and which developed the prototype on which the legislation was based.

The Process of Enactment
    Each of the three models of choice owed its existence to the work of a handful of determined political entrepreneurs with strong anti-establishment views about public school bureaucracy. In the Minnesota case, PEO was one of a number of proposals advanced by Governor Rudy Perpich, legislative reformers, and citizen groups. Minnesota reformers did not deny that the state's education system was one of the best in the nation, by such objective measures as graduation rates and college entrance examination scores. Their concern was that public education had grown complacent, resistant to thinking creatively about improvement, and, above all, demanding of increased financial support during a time of austerity. According to legislative sources, the idea of using choice to light a fire under public school bureaucrats had been discussed frequently in the 1970s. In 1982, the Citizens League, a Minnesota good government group, issued a report containing a number of education reform proposals, including one which would have given education vouchers to low-income families. The low-income voucher was introduced by state legislator John Brandl, a public policy professor from the University of Minnesota's Hubert Humphrey Institute. It garnered support from a variety of sources beyond the Citizens League, including organizations representing private schools. The low-income voucher proposal did not come to a vote in the 1984 session of the legislature but it mobilized strong opposition from estab-

lishment education groups, including teacher, administrator, and school board organizations.

The Minnesota Business Partnership announced a reform agenda in late 1984 that included state-funded "stipends" for 11th and 12th graders to attend either public or private schools. In early 1985, Governor Perpich announced a broad education reform plan that included an open enrollment proposal for all of the state's 11th and 12th graders. The Governor's proposal shifted the debate away from vouchers to open enrollment. The Perpich open enrollment proposal galvanized political opposition of establishment education groups and was defeated after an extended and divisive political debate.

At the same time the open enrollment proposal was defeated, the legislature passed what many considered to be a modest expansion of an existing 1982 law allowing 11th and 12th grade students to enroll in postsecondary institutions. The 1982 law, sponsored by House Majority Leader Connie Levi, was weak and permissive; it gave school districts the authority to make agreements with postsecondary institutions and gave districts and postsecondary institutions the authority to decide whether academic credit would be awarded for courses taken. Levi's 1984 expansion provided, among other things, that the postsecondary choice could be initiated by the student and that public money would follow the student. When the legislature defeated the Perpich open enrollment option, Levi's postsecondary enrollment proposal was revived. Political insiders speculate that Levi's proposal was seen both by legislators and education interest groups as a relatively minor adjustment to an existing law and that education groups were reluctant to upset their generally smooth relationship with the House Majority Leader by opposing her bill. In June of 1985, Democrat Farm Labor Party Governor Rudy Perpich, joined Independent Republican House Majority Leader Connie Levi, in announcing that the post-secondary options proposal put Minnesota in the vanguard of educational reform.[4]

The Washington State Education Clinics Law was no less clear a case of political entrepreneurship. Rex Crossen and Charles Davis, the principal officers of a small for-profit firm called Education Clinics, Incorporated (ECI), decided to capitalize on their experience running job training programs for difficult-to-employ adults by expanding their business to include young people who were having trouble in school. They initially ran summer and school-year tutoring programs and that seemed to be successful with troubled students.

In the mid-1970s, ECI made a series of proposals to local school districts, including the Seattle Public Schools, for public support to run clinic programs for high school dropouts. These proposals were uniformly rebuffed. They took their case to the state legislature, but the office of the state Superintendent of Public Instruction (SPI) and established education groups opposed their proposal. They formed a network of supporters from the state's corporate and civic elite and found a key legislative supporter in the House Majority Leader,

John Bagnariol, whose daughter had been rescued from academic failure by an ECI summer program. On a first attempt, an ECI-initiated proposal passed the legislature but was vetoed by then Governor Dixy Lee Ray, on the advice of established education interests. The following year, 1979, the proposal passed with funding of about $400,000. In its early years the clinic's program weathered political opposition from the superintendent and local school districts and a high level of legislative scrutiny. By 1987, the program had grown to about 1800 students in eight clinics, two of which are run by ECI and the remainder by nonprofit organizations, with an annual appropriation of over two million dollars.

The District 4 choice plan emerged more gradually, but also bears the imprint of political entrepreneurship. New York City's present system of 33 community school districts emerged in the late 1960s out of a political battle over community control of the schools that ended in significant decentralization. Soon after the creation of District 4 two leaders in that community— Community Board President Robert Rodriguez and Community Superintendent Anthony Alavardo, began to press for changes in the schools. Alvarado, a native of East Harlem and a former teacher there, was ambitious and determined to raise the quality of education for children in one of the city's poorest neighborhoods. His early attempts to elicit initiatives from principals and teachers in the district failed. In 1974, he recruited Deborah Meier, a practitioner of open classroom education and member of a citywide network of teachers with similar interests, and invited her to form her own school. Also in 1974, Alvarado recruited Seymour Fliegel, a veteran New York City educator who shared Alvarado's ambitions for innovation, and charged him with the development of alternative programs.

Central Park East Elementary School, started by Meier and her colleagues, was joined in 1974 by two other alternative programs—BETA, a program for 7th and 8th graders with serious emotional and behavioral problems, and East Harlem Performing Arts, a 4th through 9th grade program. These three programs became the nucleus of more than twenty alternative programs developed in District 4 over the next fifteen years. Fliegel says that he and Alvarado had no overarching strategy in the early stages of developing alternative programs other than demonstrating that it was possible to offer high quality education to poor, minority, inner-city children. As the number of alternative programs increased, District 4 developed a philosophy of public-school choice in which an array of alternative programs would be made available to community members, in addition to "regular" schools, and in which teachers were encouraged to form alternatives if they had a coherent plan and a group of colleagues willing to collaborate in that plan.

District 4 personnel observe that the establishment of the alternative programs was accompanied by significant problems. Alternative programs, because they were small, were typically housed in "regular" school buildings, under the nominal authority of the principals in those buildings. This situation produced friction between the schools and the alternative programs which over time was resolved by both personnel shifts and program relocations. At various points in the development of the alternative programs, opposition has emerged from a number of quarters—dissident faculty within and outside alternative programs, unhappy parents and community activists, and suspicious teacher and administrator union representatives. District 4 administrators dealt with this opposition on a piecemeal, non-confrontational level, adjusting political interests by moving personnel, offering inducements to unhappy teachers and administrators, and adopting an accommodating posture toward community opponents. On the whole, alternative programs have developed and thrived out of the persistence of district administrators and program personnel who feel strongly about the basic principle of high quality education for inner-city children.

District 4's alternative school choice program has never been accorded anything more than token support by the citywide school administration. Initially, the district benefitted from the indifference of the central administration. According to early participants, the attitude of central administrators was that the situation couldn't get any worse in District 4, so anything District 4 wanted to do was alright as long as it didn't generate controversy outside the district. As the alternative programs expanded and as the District 4 administration began to tread in areas that were the traditional prerogatives of the central administration—like the establishment of alternative high schools—frictions developed between District 4 and the citywide administration.

In each case, the public school choice initiatives emerged from outside the established political and organizational structures of American education, and owed their existence to the persistence of political entrepreneurs. In Minnesota, the entrepreneurs were political leaders who were dissatisfied with the complacency of established educational interest groups. In Washington, the entrepreneurs were critics from outside the public school establishment who had a proposal about how to reach a particular group of students who were ill served by the public schools. In District 4, the entrepreneurs were renegades within the system who seized the opportunities offered by decentralization in New York City to promote a different approach to the education of inner city children.

Making the Unworkable Work

The conditions under which these public school choice initiatives emerged did not bode well for their success as operating programs. The Minnesota Postsecondary Options program was passed without the active political support of education interest groups whose constituencies would be important to its implementation. The Washington Education Clinics program was seen by mainstream education interest groups as a marginal, special interest issue that distracted attention from the main issue of school finance reform. The District 4 alternative schools program was born in large part out of the frustration of community district administrators over the failure of existing school personnel to offer good ideas for the improvement of education. In no case was there much cause for optimism about the success of the initiatives.

The early implementation of the Minnesota PEO program was accompanied by predictable implementation problems. High school counselors, already overburdened by large case loads and recent state minimum competency requirements, were informed of their responsibilities under the PEO law on the first day of school in the fall of 1985. A large share of the start-up costs of the program were borne by these counselors, who had to understand the terms of the law, handle parent and student inquiries, assist in placing students in post-secondary courses, and adjust the high school schedules and academic programs of students who took postsecondary courses. Some local school administrators engaged in public posturing designed to discourage postsecondary transfers, such as accusing postsecondary institutions of recruiting, arguing the superiority of high school courses over community college courses, and suggesting that students who took postsecondary courses lacked loyalty to their schools. Local school personnel developed a litany of horror stories about students who would lose high school credit, and fail to graduate on schedule because they might enroll in postsecondary courses and drop them.

The Minnesota Education Association, the state's largest teacher organization, proposed an amendment to the PEO law in 1986 which would have limited postsecondary courses to those for which there was no equivalent high school course. The amendment proposed a "comparability review" to determine equivalency between high school and college courses, which would have effectively shifted the control of access from students and parents to educators. The amendment was defeated.

Despite these political and administrative problems, the implementation of PEO proceeded with remarkable smoothness. By the end of the first year, the majority of districts (272 of 434) had students enrolled in postsecondary classes. A substantial minority of principals and teachers remained unconvinced of PEO's merit. Fewer than half the teachers surveyed in the first year classified themselves as supportive of PEO and almost 40 percent of principals reported that PEO had adversely affected staff morale. On the other hand, counselors, who shouldered most of the initial implementation costs of the program, were reported by their principals to be overwhelmingly supportive of PEO.

The Washington State Educational Clinics program was characterized by greater resistance and slower implementation. Responsibility for the program was lodged in the Office of the State Superintendent of Public Instruction, one of the program's strongest opponents during the legislative debate. Start-up was slow; the legislature had to prod SPI to spend the appropriation for clinics in the first two years of the program. Superintendent Frank Brouillett eventually responded to the prodding and certified a diverse collection of clinics. At the local level, clinics met severe resistance from local school administrators, who regarded them as interlopers, as purveyors of inferior education, and as drawing attention to the failures of the public schools. Over time, this adversarial relationship has softened to the point where the majority of students in some clinics are referred by their local school systems.

In its mature form, the program serves about 1800 of the state's estimated 11,000 dropouts in eight clinics located in seven of the state's 39 counties. The program is administered through SPI's Office of Private Education, where its complex certification, reimbursement, and evaluation functions have been thoroughly routinized. The budget for the program has steadily increased, but not enough to expand significantly the scale of the program. The state has recently begun to focus political attention on the dropout problem, but clinics are seen as a small part of the state's overall strategy.

From its beginnings in 1976, the clinics program has operated under stringent controls. The legislation stresses cost control and performance by establishing a well specified reimbursement schedule based on levels of service and group size, strict limits on the length of time a student can spend in the program, and evaluations based on clear output measures, such as GED completion, return to school, or entry into the workplace. The legislation also required clinics to hire only state-certified teachers. These operating controls have meant that clinics have achieved a relatively high degree of success at per-student costs of $600–700 per student per year, while alternative programs for high-risk students administered through the public schools have per-pupil costs of over $2000. The per-student costs of clinics are tightly constrained by a funding formula that reimburses clinics at a set rate for specific activities.

It is also clear that these efficiencies have been achieved at some cost to program quality. One clinic manager observed, for example, that the curriculum in his clinic had not been revised since it was created in the mid-1970s and that teaching had not kept pace with developments in the field. While teachers and students attach high value to the individual attention students receive in clinics, the facilities, materials, and conditions of work in clinics are well below the standards of the public schools. An incentive structure based on strict standards of performance and efficiency, in other words, has resulted in a lack of resources for continued development of new techniques and materials and for amenities comparable to the public schools. Over time, these conditions could seriously limit the capacities of clinics. Since clinics must hire only certified teachers, they must compete for staff by offering either comparable compensation or superior working conditions. The existing incentive structure does not allow clinics to be competitive on compensation. For the most part clinics have relied on the commitment of staff to high-risk students and on the opportunity for more flexible interaction between students and teachers to retain teachers. The absence of resources for curriculum development and improvement of working conditions undermines the ability of clinics to compete for talented staff.

A final irony in the implementation and operations of the clinics program has been that ECI, the for-profit firm that initiated the program, has never made a profit and has, in fact, been in and out of financial insolvency throughout its involvement in the program. Established educational interests saw the introduction of public payments to for-profit firms as a dangerous precedent. But what began as a venture in doing well by doing good has in the end turned out to be a venture in the use of private enterprise to subsidize the public interest. ECI's continued commitment to educational clinics is more a testimonial to its dogged persistence in its initial idea than to the power of the profit motive. Whatever the usefulness of the education clinics program, it does not provide a particularly significant case of privatization.

The District 4 alternative schools program represents an incremental approach to the introduction of public school choice. Seymour Fliegel, a major actor in the development of the District 4 program, argues that the district had no global strategy at the outset of the program. He argues, instead, that the district simply wanted to create some examples of how education could work for inner-city children and use those examples to spawn other examples. The array of alternative programs and the idea of using parental choice to encourage better performance came later. About 10 percent of the district's elementary students are enrolled in alternative programs. All junior-high students are enrolled in alternative programs.

Serious problems arose in the initial implementation of alternative programs. Central Park East Elementary School weathered a series of challenges, first from the principal in the building where it was initially housed and then from a faction of dissident teachers and parents. Throughout the history of the program, the alternative schools have been challenged by community groups and educators within the district as exclusive, elitist, and too highly specialized. The incremental approach used by District 4 administrators was well adapted to anticipating problems and opposition and accomodating them. The alternative schools program has never been directly confronted as a policy decision, either in District 4 or in the broader New York City school system. The program has instead been worked out as a series of specific decisions about specific alternative programs and specific accommodations to specific objections by specific teachers, principals, and parents. The philosophy of

District 4 administrators has been that most opposition can be handled without provoking major political disagreements that would draw the entire alternative program structure into question. Objections by principals to having alternative programs in their buildings, for example, have been accommodated either by negotiating transfers or by providing compensating benefits. Objections by dissident teachers and parents have been met by providing access to other programs or by negotiating over differences of opinion within existing programs. Tensions with the citywide Board of Education have been resolved largely by adroit tactical maneuvers that allow downtown administrators to take credit for District 4 successes.

The pace of development in District 4 has been slow by the standards of those who would implement public school choice with a single comprehensive policy decision. The initial three alternative programs were established in 1973. Thereafter, no more than three alternative programs were established per year. In some years none were established, and in some only one. Twenty-three programs have been started in 16 years. One program—The Sports School, designed to motivate academic learning through involvement in athletics—was "refocused" when district administrators determined it did not meet quality standards. It is now called New York Prep, and it has a primarily academic focus. Another program—BETA, one of the original three alternatives established in 1973, which focused on problems of students with serious emotional and behavioral problems—was closed at the end of the 1989 school year. Its students will be offered positions at other schools. District administrators cited problems with quality as the main reason for this decision also.

District administrators have made clear that there is an open invitation to establish new programs. Development of new programs is encouraged by allowing them to grow at one grade level per year and by accommodating staff size to low enrollments during initial start-up years. But the message is also clear from district administrators to potential program developers that the core ideas of new programs have to be educationally sound and the programs have to be able to sustain faculty and parent support in order to survive. Choice without quality, the argument goes, is no choice at all.

Choice operates differently at the elementary and secondary levels. Of the 23 existing programs, five serve elementary children. The remaining programs serve mainly junior high students. Two high school alternative programs are available in District 4, but most District 4 high school students enroll in the citywide system of high schools. Overall, the majority of District 4 students participate in alternative programs, about one-fifth of the elementary students and all of the junior high students.

The choice system itself in District 4 poses few, if any, operating problems. Parents are notified of their options by a variety of means, including native-language brochures, school meetings, and neighborhood outreach efforts. All parents of junior high students receive information, since all are expected to choose a program. Information on elementary alternatives is readily available, but parents must initiate the process. In winter and spring of each year, parents and students are encouraged to visit alternative programs and then parents are asked to state a preference for six programs. Applications are collected in the district's central office and are circulated to programs by first preferences. Initial selections are made. Then applications are circulated by second preferences, and so forth. District administrators estimate that about 90 percent of parents and students receive one of their first three preferences. The process may be initiated by parents at the end of any term, but turnover within the school year is modest. Administrators and school personnel report no significant operating problems with the choice system, and community complaints seem to be minimal.

District and school-level personnel in District 4 have actively changed organizational constraints that most educators regard as beyond their influence. Alternative programs have demonstrated that many of the "realities" of urban schools that most people take for granted can be changed. Alternative programs, for example, have broken the correspondence between buildings and schools. Several programs, usually embodying different educational approaches and different age groups, are located in the same school building. Uses of staff time and grouping practices within alternative programs are often highly flexible. Alternative programs are typically administered by "directors" rather than principals, because the scale of the programs is smaller and the director's role permits a blurring of the distinction between teacher and administrator. The result of these and other changes in the traditional structure of schools is that the alternative programs offer greater adult-student interaction, more attention to individual student learning, and a higher level of agreement among instructional staff, parents, and students over the expectations and academic content of the program.

The Minnesota PEO initiative, the Washington Education Clinics Program, and the District 4 alternative schools program embody different approaches to the implementation and operation of choice programs. The Minnesota PEO initiative was intended to be available to all 11th and 12th grade students in the state and was implemented state-wide immediately after it passed. After initial start-up problems, the program became routinized within its first year of operation. The Washington Education Clinics Program was intended to permit a small number of organizations to operate clinics. Its initial development was constrained both by budget and by the limited support of state agency personnel. After initial state and local resistance, clinics established a modest presence in the state serving a small proportion of the dropout population. The District 4 alternative schools program grew at a slow rate by design, because district administrators subscribed to the belief that choice was meaningless in the absence of quality. Implementation problems were resolved on a case-by-case basis over a long period of time. The system of alternative programs and parent choice is now fully functioning for all junior high students and for about one-fifth of elementary students.

While the policies grew from different implementation and operating strategies, they embody common experiences. Initial political resistance was overcome in each case by persistence and skill. Key operating problems in implementing choice were either surmounted early in the development of the programs or were dealt with on a piecemeal basis over time. In no case has the choice raised insurmountable operational problems. In all cases, the implementation and operating problems were simplified by the deliberately limited scale of the programs.

Evidence and Questions

Evidence exists on the effects of each of the choice programs. The Minnesota Department of Education, at the request of the legislature, maintains data on students' use of the Post-Secondary Enrollment Options program. In the first year of the program, a little over 3 percent of 11th and 12th graders, in about two-thirds of the state's school districts, participated in the PEO option. Seven school districts had participation rates of 15 percent or more. The largest share of the students (49 percent) enrolled in community colleges, with smaller proportions of students enrolled in state universities (34 percent), private colleges (6 percent), and vocational-technical schools (10 percent). Most students took between one and three courses during the year. And most students (87 percent) completed the courses with passing grades. Participants reported being highly satisfied with their choices and reported that the content was more difficult and that they learned more from post-secondary courses than from secondary courses.

Evaluations of the Washington Education Clinics program have been conducted regularly by the Legislative Budget Committee, an independent audit arm of the legislature. The most recent studies indicate that incoming clinic students have become increasingly disadvantaged each year, as measured by grade-level achievement lags, and proportion of students from families on welfare. The most recent data available (1984) indicate that the average clinic student was about three years behind in grade-level achievement measures, and had been out of school for about five months when entering the program. For those students tested (about two-thirds of the total participants), the average length of participation was 30 days and the average gain on standardized achievement measures was about one grade level. The ECI clinics, which are the only for-profit clinics in the program, consistently perform in the top two or three in all performance measures. Somewhere between one-half and two-thirds of clinics participants leave clinics for work, military service, or further schooling. These results compare favorably with results from conventional school dropout prevention programs, which typically cost more than three times as much. Overall, the evidence suggests that the program has significant positive effects on its intended clients, that for-profit clinics perform as well or better than nonprofits and that clinics are able to hold the majority of dropouts long enough to significantly improve their learning. The evidence also suggests that clinics are cost effective relative to other dropout programs, but there is insufficient evidence to determine whether there is a difference on cost effectiveness between for-profit and not-for-profit clinics.

District 4 administrators calculate their successes in terms of citywide achievement measures. In 1973, when the alternative schools program was established, District 4 ranked 32nd, or last, among community districts on the citywide reading test, with 16 percent of its students scoring at or above grade level. By 1982 the district's ranking had risen to 18th, with almost half of its students scoring at or above grade level. And by 1987, the district had risen to the middle of the distribution of districts, with almost two-thirds of its students reading at or above grade level. The number of students accepted at citywide competitive high schools has risen from 10 in 1973 to over 250 in 1987. School-level personnel in alternative programs report significant gains in retention of talented teachers, staff morale, and teachers' perceptions of the quality of their work lives.

This evidence paints a generally positive picture of the effects of choice programs, and it reinforces a growing consensus among policy makers that the introduction of choice can improve both the conditions of teaching and learning and performance of students. At the same time, the evidence is insufficient to support a general proposition that choice works, or to describe the conditions under which choice might contribute to positive effects on teachers and students. In the case of the Minnesota PEO program, the evidence deals with the exercise of choice (i.e., how many students used the option with what kinds of institutions for what kinds of courses), but not with the educational effects of choice on choosers and nonchoosers. The most one can say from the evidence is that a small, but significant, proportion of students successfully exercised their option to choose postsecondary courses, with undetermined effects on their learning. In the case of Washington State Education Clinics program, there is direct evidence of participants' achievement and relative costs of clinics and other institutions serving similar clients. But there is no direct evidence on the relative educational effects of clinics versus other possible options. Nor is there any direct evidence on the exercise of choice, per se (e.g., comparisons of the educational experience and achievement of students with similar risk profiles who did and did not choose to enter clinics). In the District 4 alternative schools program, the aggregate data on student reading achievement and high school entrance are adequate to demonstrate that the district has managed a general improvement of its educational program relative to other community districts in New York. But the data do not support any specific conclusions about the role that choice has played in that improvement. We don't know, for example, how much of the gain in reading scores at the elementary level is explained by the proportion of students participating in alternative schools versus those in regular schools. Nor do we know whether gains in regular schools can be explained as spillover effects from alternative programs, or as effects of program improvement independent of choice. At the junior high level, we have no profile of achievement in alternative and regular schools as the district moved to full implementation of choice, so we have no way of knowing whether increases in alternative school enrollment pulled achievement up or whether achievement was tending up in all schools independent of alternative school enrollment.

As circumstantial evidence, data on the effects of choice programs are intriguing. As evidence of the dynamics of choice and the role that choice plays in teaching and learning, the data do not support any specific conclusions.[5] This result does not reflect negatively on either the evidence or the programs. In each case, the evidence was gathered to answer specific questions that did not necessarily bear on the more general dynamics and effects of choice. Likewise, the programs themselves should not be judged on the basis of whether they improve our general knowledge of how choice operates, since they were undertaken for other reasons. The conclusion is only that the evidence does not support general claims about the effectiveness of choice. Such claims would have to be based on a more systematic understanding, and on more specific evidence, of how choice operates. The practical experience embodied in working models of choice has much to contribute to this understanding.

First, these cases demonstrate that any systematic understanding of the effects of choice has to take its point of departure from a clear understanding of the demand-side conditions of choice. The effects we expect to find are, in part, a function of how people select themselves into programs. At least two distinctive sets of demand-side conditions are apparent in the models we have examined. One set might be called *option demand,* where clients have the option to choose, and the other *universal choice,* where everyone in a particular set of clients is required to choose. The Minnesota PEO is predicated on the assumption that a specific population, 11th and 12th grade students, should have the option to choose postsecondary courses, but not that all eligible students should have to choose between secondary and postsecondary courses. The Washington State Clinics program likewise stresses option demand for a particular population, 13- to 19-year-old dropouts, rather than universal choice. The District 4 alternative program, on the other hand, is an option demand program at the elementary level and a universal choice program at the junior high level.

Option demand and universal choice set very different conditions for access. Option demand systems have at least two levels of self-selection—choosing to exercise the option and choosing among alternative programs—while universal choice systems have only one level of self-selection—choosing among alternative programs. In effect, option demand systems say to the client, "If you are interested in choosing, you have the following alternatives." Universal choice systems say to the client, "You must choose among the following alternatives."

Because option demand systems involve two levels of self-selection, one would expect them to produce more homogeneity of preferences among the people who choose any given alternative. If group homogeneity of preferences promotes engagement in learning, then option demand systems should produce greater effects for active choosers, other things being equal, than universal choice systems. But differences between active and inactive choosers in option demand systems should also grow over time. If there is no universal requirement to choose, and if choice promotes effects, then active choosers should gain relative to inactive choosers.

By this logic, universal choice systems should have an equalizing effect, relative to option demand systems. If everyone is required to choose, then distinctions between active and inactive choosers become less important; they are simply translated into differences in preference among alternatives.

Second, the cases demonstrate that effects can be influenced by supply-side conditions on choice. The cases embody at least two different approaches to supply-side design. The Minnesota PEO program is a relatively unregulated system of supply within well defined institutional structures. That is, the PEO program does not attempt to regulate what is taught within the post-secondary courses that PEO students take; it only stipulates the set of institutions within which students may choose courses. By contrast, both the Washington State Clinics program and the District 4 alternative schools program involve relatively explicit supply-side regulation. The state bureaucracy, for example, regulates the duration of the program, the qualifications of clinic staff, and the nature of the expected outcomes. District 4 administrators have exercised extensive controls over the number and content of alternative programs in the name of academic quality.

What students learn, and how learning differs among students with different attributes, is a function of what and how students are taught. If supply is relatively unregulated, one would have to know a great deal about the range of available educational offerings and what clients are actually choosing in order to predict what effect choice would have on specific types of learning. One would not expect choice to have a large effect on knowledge of science, for example, if relatively few students were choosing science courses, or if parents were choosing educational programs for their children with little or no science content. With a more heavily regulated supply, the expected effects become easier to predict, but the possibilities for matching clients' preferences with educational programs become more limited. So for example, as in District 4, where alternative programs were allowed to develop around distinctive themes but were still required to cover basic academic subjects, then one would expect all alternative programs to meet some level of performance on science, but some might exceed that level because of special attention to the subject. The point is that one cannot say how choice will improve student learning without some knowledge of how choice systems influence what is taught to whom.

Furthermore, the cases demonstrate that the incentives embedded in choice systems can have a considerable effect on the quality of educational experience for students. This is especially true where quality is defined, for example, according to the nature and duration of adult-student interaction, expectations for student learning, the content of materials, and teaching practices. The Minnesota PEO system assumes that if there are significant quality differences between secondary and post-secondary institutions, students possess adequate information to make those judgments and to choose accordingly. In other words, the PEO program assumes that program quality is adequately handled by self-regulation within educational institutions. The Washington State Clinics program embodies significant controls on eligibility, on teacher–student interaction, and on duration of contact, as well as significant financial incentives for clinics to produce gains on standardized educational outcome measures. While these controls and incentives seem to produce significant results with students, clinic staff report that curriculum and instruction in clinics are not keeping pace with changes in the field. In District 4, teacher initiative provides the supply of ideas on which alternative programs are based, but district-level standards of quality significantly influence the range of programs available. Whether choice systems explicitly regulate quality or not, then, they introduce incentives that affect quality, and quality is presumably a key supply-side determinant of the educational effects of choice.

Whether choice generally improves teaching and learning, then, is not a question that can be fully answered simply by citing positive evidence from evaluations of existing models. The issue requires a much more systematic understanding of the demand- and supply-side conditions that determine what gets taught to whom. While existing models of choice have much to teach us about these conditions, the evidence on program effects does not support a general conclusion that choice by itself is associated with positive effects on student and learning.

Conclusion

As noted at the outset, the success of public school choice policies, in political, administrative, and educational terms, depends on how well these policies grapple with certain inherent problems. These problems are: 1) how demand-side and supply-side choice interact to affect conditions of teaching and learning; 2) how differences among active and inactive choosers affect the public purposes of education; and 3) how new policies affect existing structures of choice. While the three working models analyzed here do not represent the full range of possible uses of choice as an instrument of educational policy, they do provide some useful conclusions about how policy makers and practitioners have grappled with these inherent problems.

The three cases demonstrate the interdependence of supply-side and demand-side policies and the need for a more complete understanding of this interdependence. The Minnesota PEO program is primarily a demand-side policy which, in effect, delegates supply-side issues of what gets taught to whom to existing institutions on the assumption that these institutions are well equipped to make judgments of content and quality. Hence, it is not surprising that evaluations of PEO stress how many students choose to take courses in postsecondary institutions rather than what students actually learn in those courses. The policy is well equipped to influence the former, and not equipped at all to influence the latter. The Washington State clinics program and the District 4 alternative schools program are examples of policies that are designed to actively influence both the demand and supply sides. In the clinics program, demand is regulated by restricting student eligibility and supply is regulated by personnel and content controls as well as financial incentives. In the District 4 program, demand is regulated by using option demand at the elementary level and universal choice at the junior high level, while supply is regulated by teacher initiative and central decision making about program quality.

Educational choice policies are frequently touted by their advocates as a means of "deregulating" education—that is, substituting the discipline of market incentives for external regulation. These working models of choice demonstrate that the introduction of choice is not really deregulation, but a change in the regulatory regime, or incentive structure, within which schools operate. The Minnesota case demonstrates that the decision not to regulate the supply side, except by specifying institutions from which students might choose, is, in effect, a decision to let the internal structures of those institutions control content. It is, in other words, a form of supply-side self-regulation. The Washington State and District 4 programs involve significant regulation of both the supply and demand sides, but the resulting incentive structure under which schools operate in those programs is very different from that under which most schools operate. In other words, choice policies are less about deregulation than they are about changing the regulatory regime of schools to allow more demand- and supply-side influence over who gets access to what types of education.

The three working models also demonstrate the influence of public school choice programs over active and inactive choosers. The Minnesota PEO and Washington Clinics programs, as noted above, operate on the principle of option demand. Option demand policies provide access to alternative programs, but do not require all eligible clients to choose. The major consequence of this approach is that the programs can be considered successful even if they serve only a relatively small proportion of the total pool of eligible clients. The Minnesota PEO program serves about three percent of the state's 11th and 12th graders; the Washington Clinics program serves about 12 percent of the state's total estimated dropout population, and about 16 percent of the estimated dropout population in the seven counties in which clinics are located. Yet evaluations of these programs regard them as a success, because these evaluations focus on the clients served, rather than on the larger system or the total pool of potential clients. Option demand systems should demonstrate significant effects with their clients, since they are well designed to capitalize on the motivations of active choosers, and only those who are motivated to choose are served.

But one would not expect option demand systems that serve a small proportion of the total client pool to exert great influence on the overall quality of the educational system or on the educational opportunities and performance of the remainder of the client pool. If option demand systems stabilize at levels like those of the Minnesota PEO program and Washington Clinics program, then institutions and clients can adapt quite easily to the existence of choice by making relatively minor changes in their standard ways of doing business. One would not expect the Minnesota PEO program, for example, to result in major changes in high school curricula that would benefit all students. One would predict only relatively small changes on the margins of the curriculum designed to retain the small proportion of active choosers. Likewise, one would not expect establishment of education clinics to result in major changes in high school curricula or significant reductions in dropouts. Given the difficulties that most potential dropouts pose for public schools, one would predict what, in fact, has happened, which is that high schools have learned to use clinics as referral agencies rather than to compete with them.

Universal choice policies, such as the junior high alternative programs in District 4, present a much different set of incentives to clients and institutions. If all clients are required to choose among programs upon entry to the system, and if there are effective supply-side incentives and regulations to induce quality, then one would expect client choice to have relatively broad effects on clients and institutions. It is more difficult for schools to adapt to universal choice systems with minor changes, since all clients and all institutions are required to choose.

While universal choice policies attempt to eliminate the distinction between active and inactive choosers at the entry level, the distinction may reappear again in the daily operation of schools. Universal choice policies require all parents to choose which program their children will attend, but they cannot then coerce parents into exercising active engagement in their children's schooling after the choice is made. Hence, whether clients stay engaged in schooling after they choose is as much a function of program design and supply-side regulation as it is of initial choice. In fact, District 4 demonstrates this principle quite clearly. It combines a strong emphasis on demand-side client choice with teacher-initiated alternative programs shaped by strong supply-side regulation.

Whether public school choice policies operate to the benefit of active and inactive choosers, then, seems to be heavily dependent on whether choices are defined in option demand or universal terms and whether supply-side incentives induce quality improvements. In any case, it seems implausible to argue, as some advocates of public school choice do, that choice benefits all clients because it introduces strong incentives for school improvement. Who benefits from choice and what those benefits are depends not just on whether choice exists, but also on how it is structured.

Finally, the three working models demonstrate how the introduction of new choice policies might affect existing systems of choice. Active choosers exercise some degree of choice in all public school systems, whether in the selection of a residence, in influencing the assignment of students to teachers, in the choice of courses at the secondary level, or in the assignment of students to special programs within or between schools. The underlying policy issue in these examples, then, is not whether choice exists, but how extensively the introduction of new policies changes the ground rules under which choices are made.

The enactment and implementation of the Minnesota PEO and Washington Clinics programs seem to be exercises in the domestication of new choice policies by existing political interests and organizational structures. In principle, both programs could have had potentially far-reaching positive effects on students and educational institutions. In practice, the programs have been easily accommodated by the existing systems without serious disruption of the operating routines of high schools, or major changes in most students' educational experience. Shifts in enrollment under the two programs have been small and high schools seem neither to have been seriously inconvenienced nor to have substantially changed their usual way of doing business. While established educational groups feared these proposals prior to their enactment, their fears seem to be largely unfounded. By the same token, the programs have not had the galvanizing effect on public education that their sponsors hoped they would have.

The District 4 alternative school program is a rather different case. The evidence is strong that the program has significantly changed the terms of public school choice for students and parents, at least at the junior high level, and the operating routines of the community district and schools. On a number of dimensions—the size of schools, the nature of teachers' work in schools, the way individual schools' missions are defined, the assignment of students and teachers to schools, and the relationship of the community district to schools—District 4 operates differently from other community districts in New York and from other school districts generally. These changes, one must hasten to add, are the result of dogged persistence over a period of 16 years, a much longer period than most school systems are willing to devote to an educational innovation. So for students, parents, and educators in East Harlem, the alternative school program has changed the structure of choice that existed before the program was introduced, and those changes have been largely in the direction of equalizing choices between active and inactive choosers and putting choice in the service of educational quality.

From the perspective of the whole school system of the City of New York, however, District 4 seems to have had little effect. None of the other 30-plus community districts has undertaken anything like District 4's system of alternative programs. While the citywide administration's posture toward District 4 has evolved from oblique disregard to uneasy support, it has scrupulously avoided any suggestion that District 4's experience might be generalized to other community districts. From the citywide perspective, then, District 4 looks like another case of the domestication of choice to the existing system, even though its effects are much more extensive when viewed from within.

Overall, then, this analysis of working models of choice has demonstrated, first, that significant changes in the structure of public school choice are feasible, politically and administratively; second, that the effects of these new systems of choice on students and schools are highly sensitive to the details of their design; and third, that changes in the structure of public school choice are easily domesticated by the existing structure. If changes in public school choice are to have the dramatic effects that their advocates suggest are possible, then there will have to be a good bit more attention to the design of new structures and to implementation strategies.

NOTES

1 The information in this section is drawn largely from Elmore, "Choice in Public Education." In Boyd and Kirchner.

2 The distinction between active and inactive choosers is developed in Elmore, "Choice in Public Education," 83. In any given structure at any given time, some clients actively exercise the options available to them while others acquiesce in what the structure deals them. Clients cannot, however, be neatly divided into choosers and nonchoosers, because any client is a potential chooser under the right set of circumstances. Hence, the underlying policy issue is not who chooses and who

doesn't, but what incentives a given structure offers for some people to be active choosers and some to be inactive.

3   See Doug Archbald, "The Origins, Effects, and Political Significance of a State Legislated Program of Choice in Education: The Minnesota Postsecondary Enrollment Options Law," Center for Policy Research in Education, July 14, 1988; Richard Elmore, "Community District 4, New York City," Center for Policy Research in Education, October 1988; and Richard Elmore, "The Washington State Education Clinics Program," Center for Policy Research in Education, February 1989. These cases are also designed to be used for teaching purposes to introduce students and practitioners to the study of policy and organization in education. Unless otherwise noted, all evidence in the following analyses is drawn from these cases.

4   Parts of this account are drawn from Tim Mazzoni, "The Politics of Educational Choice in Minnesota." In Boyd and Kirchner.

5   For a fuller treatment of the effects of choice, see Richard F. Elmore, "Choice as an Instrument of Public Policy: Evidence from Education and Health Care," paper prepared for the Conference on Choice and Control in American Education, sponsored by the Robert M. La Follette Institute of Public Affairs, University of Wisconsin–Madison, May 1989.

REFERENCES

Boyd, William, and Charles Kirchner, eds. 1988. *The Politics of Excellence and Choice in Education*. 1987 Yearbook of the Politics of Education Association. New York and London: Falmer Press.

Levin, Henry. 1987. "Education as a Public and Private Good." *Journal of Policy Analysis and Management* 6 (4): 628–41.

Nathan, Joe. 1989. "Progress, Problems, and Prospects with State Choice Plans." In *Public Schools by Choice*, ed. Joe Nathan, 204–7. St. Paul, Minn.: Institute for Learning and Teaching.

National Governors Association (NGA), Center for Policy Research and Analysis. 1986. *Time for Results: The Governors' 1991 Report on Education*. Washington, D.C., 66–93.

Raywid, Mary Ann. 1987. "Public Choice, Yes; Vouchers, No!" *Phi Delta Kappan* 68 (10): 762–69.

6 *Estelle James*

Private Education and Redistributive Subsidies in Australia

Australia is probably the only country to experiment with a large need-based private educational subsidy at the primary and secondary levels. Interestingly, it is the need of the school, rather than the individual student, which is assessed. A per capita payment is made from both the state and the central government, at higher rates for public schools and for "poor" private schools. Private schools receive assistance, but not as much as public schools; choice is facilitated, but more so for the lower than the upper classes. We might call this a policy of limited privatization with redistributive subsidies. It is also very much like a voucher system, in which the voucher value varies depending on the school attended.

Why was this system adopted and how does it work? Does it foster economic efficiency—competition, diversity, and satisfaction of diverse tastes at minimum cost? Or does it raise total costs and diminish support for a strong public school system? Is the need-based criterion desirable because it enhances quality and equity or undesirable because it increases the burden on the public treasury and encourages the withdrawal of private resources? These issues will be analyzed in this chapter, both from a positive and normative vantage point. That is, I ask what forces led to redistributive school subsidies, what problems

Estelle James is Professor of Economics at the State University of New York–Stony Brook.

were encountered and solutions attempted, who were the winners and losers, and are the results good or bad for society as a whole?

The Australian case is of particular interest to Americans, because Australia has many characteristics in common with the United States, including a federal system where education is largely financed and controlled at the state level and a constitution which prohibits an established church.[1] Furthermore, their system of limited privatization was adopted to deal with the problem of educational quality for disadvantaged schools, a problem which is also of great concern here. Since the consequences of their subsidy program were largely consistent with a priori predictions based on economic theory, this suggests that they may have more general applicability, beyond the Australian context.

The first part of this chapter briefly describes the cost configuration that motivated this policy in Australia and examines the criteria for aid. Which schools qualify and for how much aid? How is "need" defined and how are "rich" schools treated? The following section outlines the growth of private enrollments and the increasing restrictions on the entry of new schools to subsidized status. The next two parts describe the various consequences of limited privatization and the policy responses to these consequences, some of which were unintended. Included here are changes in the use of private resources; in quality, costs, and salaries in private schools; and in regulation and bureaucracy, all of which make the private sector more like the public sector. The fifth section examines the impact on government support for public schools. Finally, the conclusion assesses the overall efficiency and equity of a system of redistributive subsidies or limited educational privatization.

Privatization through Subsidization

Although privatization often involves a reduction in government spending for public goods, alternatively it may involve increased government spending in order to maintain a robust private sector in a market dominated by public institutions. Some forms of privatization strengthen the private sector, while increasing its dependence on government subsidies. This was the approach taken in Australia in the last two decades.

In 1963, before the subsidy program began, 24 percent of all Australian students were in private schools, most of them in Catholic schools (See Table 6.1a). The subsidies were instituted by the Liberal Party in 1963 and vastly enlarged by the Labor Party in 1973–74 in a political competition for the votes of these families, particularly the large Catholic bloc.

The Cost-Quality Rationale for Subsidies

The ostensible rationale for the subsidies was the low quality in many private schools, presumably generating external diseconomies for society as a

Table 6.1a. Public and Private Enrollments in
Primary and Secondary Schools (in hundreds)

Year	Public	Private	Total	% PVT
1905	622	145	767	18.9
1915	733	173	905	19.1
1925	873	229	1101	20.8
1935	913	230	1142	20.1
1945	875	273	1148	23.8
1955	1287	408	1695	24.1
1965	1855	580	2435	23.8
1975	2290	620	2910	21.3
1980	2318	667	2985	22.3
1982				23.7
1984	2261	760	3020	25.2

Source: 1905–1980 figures from Commonwealth
Schools Commission, 1981, *Report for the Triennium, 1982–84*, Canberra, p. 27. 1982 figure
from A.C.T., Vol. I, p. 17. 1984 figure taken
from Tables 6.1b and 6.1c.

whole, and public funding was designed to improve the situation. This belief—that quality was low in private schools, which were run by nonprofit
organizations—conflicts with the theoretical argument that such organizations
can be counted on to produce high quality, even in situations where consumer
information is limited (Hansmann 1981; James and Rose-Ackerman 1986). It
also conflicts with recent empirical evidence on the quality of private school
outputs in Australia. At the time of adoption, however, this evidence was not
available to policy makers. Instead, they observed that most private schools,
especially the Catholic schools, operated with low inputs per student, and from
that inferred that their quality was also low. Tables 6.2a and 6.2b show that
in 1974, even after partial subsidies had been introduced, the large Catholic
subsector had a monetary expenditure per student less than half that of public
schools.

As in other countries with large unsubsidized private sectors, student/fac-
ulty ratios, student/staff ratios, and class size were very high in these schools,
40–50 percent higher than in public schools (see Tables 6.3 and 6.4). In addition, teachers in private schools were paid much less than those in public
schools. This is partially because religious personnel donated their time as
teachers, lay teachers were not unionized, and working conditions were considered more desirable, compensating for the lower wages. Moreover, their
teachers had lower credentials and qualifications, were more likely to be part
time or women, and had higher work loads than those in public schools. All of
these input indices were used as evidence of low private school quality in the

1960s and early 1970s and became the normative justification for need-based public subsidies (For supporting data see Commonwealth Schools Commission, *Australian Students and Their Schools* 1979: 113–22; *Report for the Triennium 1979–81*: 29).

Alternative Criteria for Aid

What are the key issues that must be decided when a system of subsidies to private schools is adopted? The first question is simply, how much aid should be given and according to what criteria? If the aid is based on need, how is need defined? A closely related question is, should the use of private resources be encouraged or discouraged and if so, how? A third set of questions concerns the entry problem: Should existing schools be permitted to expand? Should new schools be permitted to enter the market? And if so, should they be eligible for aid on equal terms with the older schools? It is also necessary to determine what measures of accountability and responsibility accompany the aid and to analyze how this changes the behavior of the private schools. A Schools Commission was set up to deal with these issues and run the complex subsidy program. Their responses will be discussed in this and the following sections.

Many different criteria may be used for allocating subsidies in a system of limited privatization. For example, aid may be targeted for particular programs, such as those for disadvantaged groups; narrow programs of this sort have been used in the United States. The underlying philosophy is that government is primarily responsible for funding public schools but certain critical outputs, often of a redistributive nature, will be publicly financed in private schools also. At the opposite end of the spectrum is Holland, where equal payments are made by the government to fund public and private schools fully. The basic idea here is that government is responsible for financing the education of all children, but parents have the right to choose the type of school that they prefer.

In between are systems such as that in Australia, where private schools are partially subsidized. Whereas some in-between systems, such as Japan's, are set up to reward the better schools, the Australian system was set up to help the needier schools that suffered from low quality because they could not raise their own resources. In this sense it may be termed a redistributive subsidy system.

How is Need Defined?

Redistributive subsidies can be based on the need of the individual or the school. Australia opted for the latter, probably because it was administratively simpler, particularly in a federal system, less disruptive to the public school system, and could be targeted toward low quality schools and politically powerful groups. To be eligible for subsidy, schools had to be nonprofit organizations; that is, they were prohibited from distributing their net earnings as dividends or capital gains, and instead had to reinvest all revenues internally. Nonprofit status is a requirement for subsidy in most countries, a requirement that may stem from politicians' belief that this will minimize the probability of misappropriation and political scandal (a chronic fear in situations where direct monitoring is difficult), or may stem from the political power of the religious organizations for whom the subsidies were intended (see James 1991).

In any need-based subsidy program one must evaluate need, and this is difficult whether the unit of analysis is the individual or the school. Besides the conceptual difficulties in defining need, any definition tied to subsidies may distort behavior in unintended ways, leading schools to decrease and conceal activities that make them look affluent while increasing those that make them look needy. Ironically, the end result may be both inefficient and inequitable.

How was school need measured in Australia and how were these problems handled? An index of private resources, variously called the school recurrent resources index (SRRI) or the educational resources index (ERI) was calculated; schools were placed into different categories depending on the size of this index relative to a public school or community standard; and those in lower categories received larger per capita subsidies. The number of categories, the differential subsidy between them, and the method of calculating the government standard have changed repeatedly over the last twenty years, but both the Liberal and the Labour governments have retained the basic formula.

By the mid 1980s, schools were slotted into 12 different categories, whose private resources ranged from zero to over 100 percent of the community standard. The government (state plus central) paid from 30 percent to 50 percent of these standard costs (see Tables 6.6a and 6.6b). Most private schools, including the large Catholic diocesean schools, were clustered in the four high-subsidy categories, in which expenditures per student were far lower than the target and government provided over 70 percent of their total revenues.

How are Rich Schools Treated?

One of the first questions that arose in 1974 was how to treat schools—mainly the elite secondary schools—whose actual private resources exceeded the target level. After much political wrangling, the wealthiest schools were assured that they would receive at least 30 percent of standard costs from state and Commonwealth sources. With a hint of quid pro quo, they were urged to use these funds to widen access, not to raise their real resource levels. This same issue arose again exactly ten years later, with very similar results (Commonwealth Schools Commission, *Report for the Triennium, 1976–78*: 154–57; *Funding Policies for Australian Schools* 1984: 51–52).

Such a subsidy can be justified only as a move toward a pure voucher system—on grounds that it will give people greater choice and generate competition, thereby creating an incentive for efficiency, both in public and private schools. But to achieve this goal, subsidies must be accompanied by free entry for schools that meet minimum quality constraints. Otherwise excess demand is likely to result, as existing schools benefit from public resources and either raise their fees or use nonprice rationing so that the subsidies constitute a transfer payment to those who are fortunate enough to get into the limited number of places. It is paradoxical, therefore, that, while granting subsidies to rich schools, the Australian government restricts what might be a major beneficial consequence, the entry of new high quality schools. This combination of subsidies to existing rich schools, limitations on entry, and absence of regulations over price and other rationing criteria suggests that the subsidies to rich schools were not motivated either by efficiency or equity grounds, but simply by a political economy rationale—a desire to expand the circle of influential "winners," in order to build a broad coalition in favor of the redistributive subsidy system.

Enrollment Trends and Entry Problems

In 1963, before subsidies began, private schools enrolled 23 percent of all primary students, 27 percent of all secondary and 36 percent of upper secondary students in Australia (see Tables 6.1b and 6.1c). Most of the private primary students were in Catholic schools but about one-third of the secondary students were in elite independent, mostly Anglican, schools. The private share of enrollments fell throughout the 1960s, as the school-age cohort increased and parents were unwilling to pay the high fees needed for an expansion of private sector places. By 1972, despite the modest government subsidies then in effect, private enrollments had fallen to 20, 24 and 32 percent of the total, respectively, at each level, 21 percent overall. Private schools feared further declines.

However, public inputs grew rapidly during the 1970s, and with that we would expect to observe a shift of enrollments from the public to the private sector. Indeed, the private sector share started to climb after 1974, and by 1984 was 25 percent of the total.[2] This enrollment gain shows that a not insignificant number of people will choose private schools when they are subsidized, so if the goal of the government is to boost private school enrollments, that goal can be achieved. Nevertheless, most students remain in the public sector.

The growth in private enrollments brought to the fore questions regarding entry conditions, eligibility of new private schools for subsidy, and rules regarding expansion of old schools. Different countries have adopted very different policies on these issues, policies which ultimately determine the degree of privatization.

Table 6.1b. Public and Private Enrollments in Primary Schools
(in hundreds)

	Public	Private	Total	% PVT	% Cath	% Other
1963	1264	371	1635	22.7	NA	
1965	1287	377	1664	22.7	20.4	2.3
1966	1325	376	1701	22.1	NA	
1968	1391	375	1766	21.2	NA	
1969	1420	372	1792	20.8	NA	
1970	1441	371	1812	20.5	18.3	2.2
1972	1455	364	1819	20.0	NA	
1975	1456	354	1810	19.6	17.3	2.3
1978	1517	360	1877	19.2	NA	
1980	1508	376	1884	20.0	17.1	2.9
1982	1455	394	1849	21.3	17.9	3.4
1984	1359	406	1764	23.0	19.0	4.0

Source: 1963–72 figures from Report of the Interim Committee for the Australian Schools Commission, 1973, *Schools in Australia*, Canberra, p. 27.
1972–82 figures and % Catholic 1965–70 from Commonwealth Schools Commission, 1984, *Australian School Statistics*, Canberra, pp. 6–9.
1984 figures from Report of the Review Committee, 1985, *Quality of Education in Australia*, Canberra, p. 17 and imputed from Planning and Funding Policies for New Non-Government Schools, 1985, Canberra, p. 4.

Table 6.1c. Public and Private Enrollments in Secondary Schools
(in hundreds)

Year	Public	Private	Total	% Pvt	% Cath	% Other	% Pvt Upper Sec.
1963	491	181	672	26.9	NA	NA	NA
1965	568	203	771	26.3	17.7	8.7	36.2
1966	593	208	801	26.0	NA	NA	NA
1968	664	226	890	25.4	NA	NA	NA
1969	694	231	925	25.0	NA	NA	NA
1970	719	237	956	24.8	16.9	7.9	32.4
1972	773	247	1020	24.2	NA	NA	NA
1975	834	266	1100	24.1	16.6	7.5	31.0
1978	837	278	1115	24.9	NA	NA	NA
1980	810	290	1101	26.3	18.2	8.2	32.2
1982	828	318	1146	27.7	18.8	8.9	33.9
1984	902	354	1256	28.2	19.0	9.2	33.2

Source: See Table 6.1b.

Initial Australian Policy: Easy Entry and Enrollment Growth

During the first decade of the subsidy program, Australian policy on entry was liberal. Government documents proudly announced that there was no limit on the number of students for whom per capita payments could be made, interest subsidies and capital grants were available for starting new schools or expanding old ones, small schools (which included many new ones) were put into a higher need category, and additional start-up bonuses were awarded to help during the difficult early years. As a result, between 1974 and 1980, 237 new schools opened, of which one-third were Catholic, one-third were affiliated with some other religious community, and one-third were nondenominational or secular. More than half of the total, including practically all the Catholic schools, received capital grants from the government (which in turn meant that only one-third of the non-Catholic schools got such grants) (Schools Commission, *Report for the Triennium 1982–84*, pp. 337–46).

The predominance of religious entrepreneurship is consistent with observations about the origins of private schools in other countries. Since the government generally supplies only two-thirds of a building's cost, schools that have the backing of religious organizations can more easily come up with the matching funds and get the grant. At the same time, it is interesting to note that the secular and nondenominational schools were the fastest growing group, constituting 35 percent of the new schools although they comprised only 5 percent of the old schools. This trend accelerated after 1980 (Schools Commission, *Australian Students and Their Schools* 1979: 104; Australian Teachers Federation, *Background Notes* 1985: No. 35).

Entry Problems

But by the 1980s several problems began to emerge. One was the fact that some of the small sects did not have the stable membership or financial capacity to sustain the schools they had started. Thus, they operated at small size, far below the cost levels in government schools and, after imposing heavy costs on the public treasury, some eventually went out of business. Another problem concerned timing: Some new private schools took a long period to plan and build, resulting in temporary overcrowding followed by eventual excess capacity in the neighborhood public school.

A third and more significant problem stemmed from the fact that private schools had, in fact, expanded much further and faster than initially envisaged. When the system of need-based subsidies was planned in 1973, private enrollments were declining, and the subsidies were supposedly intended to stabilize them at 1972 levels (Report of the Interim Committee 1973: 68). But in fact, by 1975 private enrollments had surpassed their 1972 levels. Moreover, after 1978, with the passing of the baby boom, the total number of students stabilized, so further increases in private enrollments were at the expense of public.

If there are economies of scale in education, smaller public schools mean higher per capita costs, especially in the short run when many factors are fixed. A diversion of students to the private sector may then impose real resource costs on society, particularly if accompanied by the birth of many small private schools. The possible existence of economies of scale, which might justify restrictions on entry for private schools, is examined at length elsewhere (James 1988). Here I simply point to the facts that schools seem able to operate efficiently over a wide range of sizes, the natural monopoly argument does not seem relevant in urban areas, and, in any event, the subsidy per student received by most private schools is less than the marginal cost of a public school place. Thus, the public treasury saves resources when a shift from public to private sector takes place, even if there are economies of scale, and the willingness of people to pay fees signifies that to them the benefit of variety exceeds its cost.

While there may not be strong economic efficiency reasons for limiting entry, there were strong political economy reasons, including pressure from the Australian Federation of (Public School) Teachers, when private jobs threatened to replace public jobs. Also significant was the outcry from parents when faced by the possible closure of their neighborhood public schools. Such closures imply heavy political costs and, if these costs prevent closure, the result is heavy economic costs of keeping many small schools alive (Report of the Committee of Review 1983). Therefore, with the return to power of the Labour Party in 1983 came a new and less welcoming policy toward entry.

New Policies: Restricted Entry

Under the rules now in effect, before a new private school can obtain capital or subsidies it is required to give 24 months' notice to the government, to demonstrate that it can meet minimum enrollment guidelines and to show that it has reasonable prospects of financial viability. These requirements can easily be justified, in terms of society's desire to avoid high risk ventures.

In addition, an impact study must be made of the new school's educational and financial effect on existing public and private schools. A separate (limited) capital and current budget was set for new schools, and those in developing areas (e.g., new suburbs), which would not adversely affect existing schools, were given priority within this budgetary constraint (Report of the Panel of the Commonwealth School Commissioners, *Planning and Funding Policies for New Non-Governmental Schools*, 1985). This restriction on market competition is less easy to justify on efficiency grounds.

Clearly these criteria are designed to protect the public schools, the large private school systems, and the existing independent private schools, which were not anxious for competition from newcomers. Not surprisingly, these were the very interest groups that were represented on and consulted by the commission that formulated the new guidelines. On the other hand, these criteria limit the ability of the system to accommodate minority groups and changing tastes. For example, fundamentalist Christians, Moslems or those espousing a secular Rudolph Steiner pedagogy will now face obstacles if they try to get government support for new schools, particularly if they live in old established neighborhoods. So too will more conventional, high quality schools. With entry restricted, existing subsidized schools enjoy a quasi-monopoly position which reduces their competitive pressures for efficiency and increases their potential profits.

Ironically, while restricted entry reduces the likelihood of public school closure, and therefore seems designed to satisfy public school users, it also has the opposite effect of insulating the public school bureaucracy from consumer pressure, thereby giving them discretionary power over matters such as curriculum and teaching methods. In the revamping of the high school curriculum which took place in Australia in the mid-1980s, administrators, teachers, and academics played a much more active role than parents or students. This consolidation of producer power is one of the consequences of a system where existing schools, whether public or private, enjoy preferential access to subsidies, where entry of new schools and therefore exit of consumers, is restricted. It may also be one of the political economy reasons why, in most societies, entry to subsidized status is limited and public schools are given preferential access to funds.

Costs and Quality

What is the expected impact on quantity, quality and costs when a percapita government subsidy is instituted? If the underlying demand and supply conditions remain unchanged and free entry of new subsidized schools is permitted, the subsidy will be passed along to the consumer in the form of lower price, quantity will increase, and quality (as measured by cost per student) will be unchanged in the new long-run equilibrium. In this sense, public funds crowd out equivalent private funds per student for ex ante enrollment levels, but aggregate private funding increases if the demand curve is elastic.

In the short run, however, or in the long run with limited entry, price does not fall by the full extent of the subsidy and "potential profits" are generated. If the schools are for-profit, they might choose to distribute these profits as dividends to their owners. If nonprofit, they must use their surplus in other ways. For example, academic inputs per student may be raised for quality-maximizers, enrollments may be expanded for quantity-maximizers, salaries and perks may be enhanced for disguised profit-maximizers, athletic facilities may be enlarged for sports-maximizers or price may be lowered together with nonprice rationing for ideology-maximizers, etc. The Australia situation fits this nonprofit limited-entry case, where the outcome is not uniquely determined.

There are several additional complications in the Australian case. First of all, as we have seen, their subsidy system was need-based, inversely related to private resources. That is, over a wide range any reduction in private revenues would be replaced largely by public revenues, obviously increasing the incentive to keep price low, draw on the public treasury, and raise quantity instead of quality. We would also expect to find private resources diverted to uses that do not enter into the need index (e.g., using private resources for a school swimming pool, which does not detract from government subsidies, rather than for current inputs, which are covered by subsidies). Along similar lines, if religious organizations were previously subsidizing their schools (e.g., by donating the services of priests and nuns), they may choose to divert these private subsidies to other uses once public subsidies are available.

Counteracting these forces was the rapid rise in costs per student in the public sector during this period. To the extent that private schools are in competition with public schools, they too will have a positive incentive for raising their spending. The degree to which each of these effects was operative, and the government's attempts to contain them, are documented in this section.

Empirical Data on Costs

Tables 6.2a and 6.2b show that current expenditure per student, in constant dollars, did indeed rise, in all school types, between 1974 and 1981. But if we look at current real (monetary plus inputed) inputs per student (used by the Schools Commission as a measure of quality) or at other indices of real current inputs, such as faculty/student or staff/student ratios (Tables 6.3 and 6.4), we find that these did not rise nearly so fast as monetary expenditures in the private sector. Moreover, public subsidies per student rose faster than any of these measures (Tables 6.5a and 6.5b). Specifically, subsidies rose 110 percent, current monetary expenditures 65 percent, and current real inputs about 33 percent, between 1974 and 1981. All figures are expressed in constant dollars, per student, averaged over primary and secondary levels (see Tables 6.2a, 6.2b, 6.5a, and 6.5b). Ironically, the net impact of all these changes was to widen the current real expenditure gap between public and private schools, which the subsidies had been designed to erase.

Part of the explanation for this widening gap lies in the rapid rise in public school spending during this period. Another part lies in the diversion of private resources for capital expansion and debt service, particularly in the independent (non-Catholic) private schools. But more important, particularly

Table 6.2a. Expenditures per Primary School Student (XPS) (in 1982 $)

	1974	% tot	1976	% tot	1981	% tot	1981/1974
Public XPS	1184		1468		1754		1.48
Catholic							
Teacher salaries	445	44	591	52	796	58	1.79
Other oper. exp.	112	11	149	13	186	14	1.66
Curr. monetary XPS	557	55	740	65	982	72	1.76
Contrib. services	287	29	218	19	176	13	.61
Current real XPS	844	84	958	84	1158	85	1.36
Debt service	45	4	53	5	63	5	1.40
Capital	114	11	133	12	146	11	1.28
Total XPS	1003	100	1144	100	1367	100	1.35
Current real XPS/							
Pub. school XPS	.72		.65		.66		.92
Pub. inc. per student/							
Curr. real XPS	.56		.73		.83		1.48
Tuition/Current							
real XPS	.11		.11		.11		1.0
Other Private							
Teacher salaries	759	47	822	45	949	41	1.25
Other oper. exp.	280	18	333	18	408	18	1.46
Curr. mon. XPS	1039	65	1155	63	1357	59	1.31
Contrib. services	193	12	224	12	245	11	1.24
Current real XPS	1237	78	1380	76	1602	70	1.30
Debt service	70	4	67	4	115	5	1.64
Capital	291	18	362	20	584	25	2.00
Total XPS	1594	100	1809	100	2301	100	1.44
Curr. real XPS/							
Pub. school XPS	1.04		.94		.91		.88
Pub. inc. per student/							
Curr. real XPS	.29		.40		.52		1.79
Tuition/Current							
real XPS	.56		.52		.46		.82

Source: 1974 data are from Schools Commission, 1979, *Australian Students and Their Schools*, Canberra, pp. 140, 151 updated to 1982 prices. 1986 and 1981 data are from *Australian School Statistics*, 1984. Canberra, pp. 50–52. Public data are for 1974–5, 1976–7, 1981–2. Public expenditure per student for 1981 is estimated on basis of 1980–81 + 1.5%; for 1976 is estimated on the basis of 1977–78 minus 6.5%, taking account of the rate of growth in public expenditures during these periods. See Tables 6.5a and b for data on income from public and private sources. Current real XPS = monetary + imputed XPS. XPS = expenditures per student.

Table 6.2b. Expenditures per Secondary School Student (XPS) (in 1982 prices)

	1974	%	1976	%	1981	%	1981/1974
Public XPS	2038		2346		2844		1.40
Catholic							
Teacher salaries	728	41	912	49	1255	55	1.72
Other oper. exp.	234	13	289	15	425	19	1.82
Curr. monetary XPS	962	54	1201	64	1680	74	1.75
Contrib. services	386	22	298	16	194	8	.5
Current real XPS	1348	76	1499	80	1874	82	1.38
Debt service	104	6	116	6	107	5	1.03
Capital	309	17	262	14	307	13	.99
Total XPS	1761	100	1878	100	2288	100	1.29
Current real XPS/							
Pub. school XPS	.67		.64		.66		.99
Pub. inc. per student/							
Curr. real XPS	.53		.74		.79		1.49
Tuition/Current							
real XPS	.24		.22		.20		.83
Other Private							
Teacher salaries	1531	53	1443	48	1625	47	1.06
Other oper. exp.	667	23	726	24	788	23	1.18
Curr. monetary XPS	2198	76	2169	72	2413	70	1.10
Contrib. services	0	0	104	3	0	0	0
Current real XPS	2198	76	2273	75	2413	70	1.10
Debt service	122	4	124	4	173	5	1.42
Capital	554	19	590	20	879	25	1.59
Total XPS	2874	100	2986	100	3465	100	1.21
Curr. real XPS/							
Pub. school XPS	1.08		.97		.85		.79
Pub. inc. per student/							
Curr. real XPS	.25		.36		.54		2.16
Tuition/Current							
real XPS	.77		.71		.70		.91

Source: See Table 6.2a.

Table 6.3. Student/Faculty Ratios

	Public	Catholic	Other	All Private	Private/Public
Primary and Secondary					
1952	27.4			29.0	1.2
1955	27.5			31.8	
1960	26.5			33.5	1.3
1963	26.2	38.3	17.4	30.7	1.2
1966	24.5	35.7	16.3	29.2	1.2
1969	23.0	31.9	16.0	27.4	1.2
Primary					
1970	27.3	34.3	18.2	31.2	
1972	25.7	31.2	17.1	28.2	1.1
1974	24.2	28.4	17.7	26.5	1.1
1976	22.0	26.7	17.8	25.2	1.1
1978	21.1	25.4	17.6	24.0	1.1
1980	20.2			22.1	1.1
1982	19.4			21.9	1.1
1982/72	.8			.8	1.0
Secondary					
1970	16.9	23.5	14.4	20.5	1.2
1972	16.2	22.2	14.2	19.6	1.2
1974	14.8	20.3	14.3	18.3	1.2
1976	13.7	19.2	14.1	17.3	1.3
1978	12.8	17.6	13.6	16.4	1.3
1980	12.2			15.3	1.3
1982	12.4			15.1	1.2
1982/72	.8			.8	1.0

Source: 1952–60 figures from Ross Williams, 1984, "The Economic Determinants of Private Schooling in Australia," Appendix B, Discussion Paper
#94, Australian National University. 1963–69 figures from Report of the
Interim Committee for the Australian Schools Commission, 1973, *Schools
in Australia*, Canberra, p. 32. 1970–74 figures from Schools Commission,
Report for the Triennium 1976–78, p. 36. 1976–78 figures from Schools
Commission, *Report for the Triennium 1982–84*, p. 250. 1980–82 figures
calculated from Schools Commission, 1984, *Australian Schools Statistics*,
pp. 7, 24.

in the Catholic schools, was the decline in volunteer services and the rise in
teacher salaries, which meant that more money was now needed to purchase
the same number of teachers and other staff. Each of these developments will
be discussed below.

Private Resources: Decline and Polarization
    A need-based system, which places a heavy tax on marginal private income,
provides a strong incentive to become more needy. The greater the number
of categories the greater the responsiveness to need but also the more schools

Table 6.4. Student/Staff Ratios[a]

	Public	Private	Private/Public
Primary			
1974	159	249	1.57
1978	122	170	1.39
1982	100	138	1.38
Secondary			
1978	68	57	.84
1982	63	55	.87

Source: 1974 figures are from Schools Commission, 1975, *Report for the Triennium 1976–78*, Canberra, p. 39. 1978 figures are from Schools Commission, 1979, *Australian Students and Their Schools*, Canberra, pp. 128–36. The data given in this source for private schools is for 1977. To approximate 1978 data I took the average of 1977 and 1979 figures; the latter is from Schools Commission, 1981, *Report for the Triennium 1982–84*, Canberra, pp. 226–254. 1982 is from Schools Commission, 1984, *Australian School Statistics* Canberra, pp. 28–30.

[a] Staff includes ancillary and administrative staff. Professional staff are not included because some of these are classified as teaching staff, particularly in the government system. The data for 1974 include primary and secondary; these are not given separately. The primary ratio would be higher than the number given. Most of the primary staff are in Catholic schools while more than half of the secondary staff are in non-Catholic schools.

will be at the boundaries where they will face this incentive to reduce private revenues in order to increase public subsidies.

For example, if we look at the 12-category scheme in effect in Australia in 1985, we find it would be foolish for a school to operate at the bottom of category 3; by reducing its private fees it can move into category 4 and actually increase its total resources. Even more striking, a school in category 5 (with a private income, say, of $950) can move into category 8 (by reducing its private income to $680), thereby saving $270 in private resources while almost maintaining its total resources (see Table 6.6a). We would expect, therefore, to find a decline in the average level of private funding and a polarization between rich and poor schools, with very few operating in categories 3, 5, 6, and 7.

To counter the problem of declining private resources, the subsidy guidelines have always required maintenance of effort; initially this was interpreted to mean that all private inputs should rise at the same rate as average Australian income (Report of the Interim Committee 1973: 8, 73). But there was

Table 6.5a. Income per Primary School Student (in 1982 $)

	1974	% tot	1976	% tot	1981	% tot	1981/1974
Catholic							
Tuition	91	10%	102	9%	125	9	1.37
Other cash income	77	8	94	8	120	9	1.56
Total private mon. income	168	18	196	17	245	18	1.46
Contrib. service	287	31	218	20	176	13	.61
Total private income	455	49	415	37	421	30	.93
Commonwealth curr. grant	264	28	442	40	587	43	2.22
State current grant	166	18	209	19	298	22	1.80
Commonwealth capital grant	44	5	49	4	72	5	1.64
Total public income	474	51	700	63	957	70	2.02
Total income	929	100	1115	100	1378	100	1.49
Other							
Tuition	690	46	715	41	742	35	1.08
Other cash income	262	18	233	13	305	14	1.16
Total private mon. income	952	64	948	54	1047	49	1.10
Contrib. service	193	13	224	13	245	11	1.27
Total private income	1144	77	1172	68	1292	61	1.13
Commonwealth curr. grant	163	11	284	16	418	20	2.56
State current grant	150	10	211	12	313	15	2.09
Commonwealth capital grant	40	3	62	4	110	5	2.75
Total public income	353	23	557	32	841	39	2.38
Total income	1497	100	1729	100	2133	100	1.42

Source: Schools for the A.C.T., 1983, Vol. 2, Canberra: Australian Government Printing Service, pp. 70–74; Schools Commission and Australian Bureau of Statistics, 1979, *Australian Students and Their Schools*, Canberra, p. 151; Schools Commission, 1984, *Australian School Statistics* Canberra, pp. 51–53.

Table 6.5b. Income per Secondary School Student (in 1982 $)

	1974	% tot	1976	% tot	1981	% tot	1981/1974
Catholic							
Tuition	326	21%	331	18%	373	17%	1.15
Other cash income	126	8	100	5	174	8	1.38
Total private mon. income	452	29	431	23	547	25	1.21
Contrib. service	386	25	298	16	194	9	.5
Total private income	838	54	730	40	741	33	.88
Commonwealth curr. grant	351	23	659	36	902	41	2.57
State current grant	226	15	366	20	498	22	2.20
Commonwealth capital grant	138	9	80	4	84	4	.61
Total public income	715	46	1105	60	1484	67	2.08
Total income	1553	100	1834	100	2225	100	1.43
Other							
Tuition	1683	65	1625	56	1688	50	0
Other cash income	368	14	364	13	393	12	1.07
Total private mon. income	2052	79	1989	69	2081	62	1.01
Contrib. service	0	0	104	4	0		0
Total private income	2052	79	2092	72	2081	62	1.01
Commonwealth curr. grant	256	10	377	13	645	19	2.52
State current grant	215	8	369	13	501	15	2.33
Commonwealth capital grant	85	3	66	2	150	4	1.76
Total public income	556	21	812	28	1296	38	2.33
Total income	2608	100	2904	100	3378	100	1.30

Source: See Table 6.5a.

Table 6.6a. 12 Category Subsidy Scheme, Primary Schools, 1985 (in 1984 prices)

	% of Standard from Pvt. Srcs.[a]	Private $	Cmnwlth $	State $	Total $	% Rev. from Gvt.
1	≥ 88	≥ 2022	277	345	≥ 2644	≤ 23%
2	76–87	1746–1999	370	345	2461–2714	26–29%
3	51–75	1172–1724	378	345	1895–2447	30–38
4	46–50	1057–1149	559	345	1961–2053	44–46
5	41–45	942–1034	565	345	1852–1944	47–49
6	36–40	827–919	571	345	1743–1835	50–52
7	31–35	712–804	576	345	1633–1725	53–56
8	26–30	597–689	768	345	1710–1802	62–65
9	21–25	483–575	771	345	1599–1691	66–70
10	16–20	368–460	774	345	1487–1579	71–75
11	11–15	253–345	777	345	1375–1467	76–82
12	0–10	0–230	781	345	1126–1356	83–100

Source: Calculated from data in Commonwealth Schools Commission, 1985, *Recommendations for 1986*, Canberra, p. 12. State subsidies estimated based on data in Commonwealth Schools Commission, 1984, *Australian School Statistics*, Canberra, p. 51. 1985 subsidies were assumed to be 15% greater than those given for 1981. State subsidies were not broken down by category of need and are much more uniform than Commonwealth subsidies.
[a] The Community Standard in 1985 was $2298.

no enforcement mechanism other than moral suasion to ensure that this would happen.

In fact, fees and other monetary revenues, which could easily be monitored, did rise at the expected rate. However, non-monetary resources (i.e., contributed services) declined so that, on balance, total private income also declined, particularly within the Catholic system (see Tables 6.5a and 6.5b). At the same time, the non-Catholic schools, many of which were in the more affluent categories to begin with, held their real private income constant or increased it slightly.

Thus, most schools moved into the highest subsidy categories, while a few remain in the lowest subsidy category, operating above standard levels largely on the basis of their own resources. Table 6.7 shows that the proportion of students eligible for the highest subsidies increased steadily after the need-based system was introduced in 1974, particularly at the secondary level, and by 1982 (when a three-category system was used) about 80 percent of all private students were in the "most needy" category, another 17 percent were in the "most affluent" category and only 3 percent were in-between. (*Report for the Triennium 1982–84*: 330–31). The increasing proportion in the bottom resource category, combined with the rising levels of subsidies across the board, meant that the government's share of private school income rose from 0 in 1962 to 30 percent in 1972 to over 60 percent in 1982.[3]

Table 6.6b. 12 Category Subsidy Scheme, Secondary Schools, 1985 (in 1984 prices)

	% of Standard from Pvt. Srcs.[a]	Private $	Cmnwlth $	State $	Total $	% Rev. from Gvt.
1	≥ 88	≥ 2985	440	574	≥ 3999	≤ 25%
2	76–87	2578–2951	586	574	3738–4111	28–31
3	51–75	1730–2544	594	574	2898–3712	32–40
4	46–50	1560–1696	889	574	3023–3159	46–48
5	41–45	1391–1526	893	574	2858–2993	49–51
6	36–40	1221–1357	901	574	2696–2832	52–55
7	31–35	1052–1187	909	574	2535–2670	56–59
8	26–30	882–1018	1211	574	2667–2803	64–67
9	21–25	712–848	1216	574	2502–2638	68–72
10	16–20	543–680	1222	574	2339–2476	73–77
11	11–15	373–510	1227	574	2174–2311	78–83
12	0–10	0–339	1232	574	1806–2145	84–100

Source: Same as Table 6.6a.
[a] The Community Standard in 1985 was $3392.

The Shift from Current to Capital Funds

If one activity is penalized while another is not, we would expect to see a distortion in the pattern of resource use, a shift of resources from the former to the latter; that is exactly what took place in Australia in the decade following the introduction of need-based subsidies. Since private funds used for debt service and capital expenditures were considered unavailable for current expenditures and therefore were not included in the SRRI, schools had an incentive to divert their private revenues in this direction in order to maximize their subsidy. The elite schools, which had been warned not to raise their current spending, had an additional reason for doing so. Consistent with these expectations, capital expenditures rose rapidly in the private sector, particularly among non-Catholic schools, where it grew almost five times as fast as current expenditures (see Tables 6.2a and 6.2b).

If the presubsidy capital-current ratio was efficient, the new higher ratio was clearly inefficient. To discourage this undesired diversion of funds, in 1985 the Schools Commission changed its measure of need to take account of the total private disposable income of a school. Only a standard allowance for capital expenditures was thenceforth permitted in calculating the index of need, even if actual expenditures were greater. However, this change came at the cost of a more complicated administrative procedure as schools were permitted to appeal on the basis of special circumstances.

Contributed Services

I have referred above to the critical role played by contributed services and its decline after subsidies were introduced, a decline which was "far greater

Table 6.7. Enrollments in Highest and Lowest Subsidy Category

	1974	1978	1982
Primary			
Lowest subsidy level	9,412	12,050	39,438
Highest subsidy level	283,958	303,700	345,423
Total students	356,600	360,100	392,192
% in highest subsidy level	80%	84%	88%
Secondary			
Lowest subsidy level	22,005	26,300	83,382
Highest subsidy level	87,449	173,300	221,730
Total students	261,100	278,100	316,611
% in highest subsidy level	33%	62%	70%
Primary & Secondary			
% in highest subsidy level	60%	75%	80%
% in lowest level	5%	6%	17%

Source: Schools Commission, 1978, *Report of the Triennium, 1979–81*, Canberra, p. 66; and *Australian School Statistics*, 1984, Canberra, pp. 6, 39.

and of a different make-up from that anticipated." (Schools Commission, *Report for the Triennium 1979–81*: 67).

Contributed service is defined by Australian data collectors to be the difference between actual outlays on teacher salaries in private schools and outlays that would have been required if the same number of teachers were paid average public school wages. The implication is that the latter usually exceeds the former. Subsumed in this definition are wage differences due to age or qualifications, or compensating for nonwage job advantages (such as a more desirable teaching environment), or stemming from above-market rates in the public sector, or volunteer labor in the private sector.

A major component in contributed services and a major factor enabling the survival of private schools historically has been their use of volunteer labor, particularly of religious personnel. For example, about half of the teachers in Catholic schools in Victoria and New South Wales in 1970 were religious and this percentage was not very different in the other Australian states. These religious personnel were paid only a small fraction of a regular salary, often at the discretion of the parish priest. However, the number of religious personnel was declining before government subsidies were introduced and the decline continued thereafter. By 1974 religious personnel comprised only 36 percent of the Catholic sector; by 1979 they were only 20 percent (Commonwealth Schools Commission, *Australian Students and Their Schools* 1979: 114; Praetz 1982: 11, 36 and 70; Faulkner: 1–10).

Did the availability of public funds accelerate the withdrawal of volunteer labor, a crowding out by public of nonpecuniary private inputs? In support of this hypothesis for Australia we observe that the decline of religious labor was faster in education than in other social services, such as work with the disabled or aboriginals, that were not subsidized. While this shift may have been a function of changing age and preferences, public subsidies enabled it to take place without a rise in tuition fees, a decline in enrollments and, consequently, pressure from church authorities to keep these personnel in the schools.

Along similar lines, the enrollment expansion that was fostered by the subsidies meant that any total amount of services contributed by religious personnel had to be spread thinner. In all these ways, the government's privatization policy probably contributed to the decline in contributed service per student.

Reports of the Schools Commission repeatedly point to the need to increase public funding in order to offset the decline in contributed service and accomplish the original objective of raising quality. Thus, besides being accelerated by the subsidies, the decline in religious personnel also had the effect of raising subsidy levels.

Teacher Salaries

The biggest loss in contributed services did not come from the decline in religious personnel but from the increased salaries of lay teachers, and this too was both an effect of the subsidy policy and a cause of larger subsidy outlays. We saw above that before subsidies private schools in Australia, as in many other countries, economized by paying low salaries to their teachers, often only two-thirds as much as in public schools. And conversely, when large subsidies come, teacher salaries usually rise. In Australia, the subsidies did not have the stated purpose of raising salaries but had that effect, and the major mechanism was not market or regulation but unionization.

Private school teachers had not effectively unionized before 1970, in part because the Australian Federation of Teachers was not interested. Contrary to membership-maximizing theories, the AFT did not want to admit a group that would favor policies, such as increased subsidies to private schools, that were contrary to the ideology of the union and the perceived interests of its original members, the public school teachers. The knowledge that private schools, particularly the nonelite ones, were in a financially precarious position further inhibited unionization. But with the advent of public subsidies, this barrier was removed and unionization proceeded rapidly.

The system of arbitration and industrial commissions that settles collective bargaining disputes in Australia uses comparability across firms and sectors as one major criterion for wage determination, so wage parity with public school teachers was a foreseeable goal. In addition, private schools had little incentive to oppose such wage increases, and could not argue inability to pay, given the expectation that grants would rise along with salaries. In fact, the Labour government adopted early the policy of "retrospective cost supplementation" which required it to raise subsidy levels if wages went up during the year. Salary increases were an inevitable consequence of this privatization policy, they could occur without necessitating price increases, and as contributed services went down, subsidies went up.

Although precise data are not available, Schools Commission reports estimate that parity between public and private school teachers was achieved by the late 1970s (*Report for the Triennium 1979–81*: 17). Information provided by various unions indicates that most states achieved awards with parity in the 1970s and the rest by 1984. The Schools Commission estimated that 80 percent of the decline in contributed services during the 1970s was due to the rising salaries of lay teachers. (*Report for the Triennium 1979–81*: 69). As a result monetary outlays rose much faster than real outlays—a cost escalation which frequently occurs when subsidies are introduced. When we break the 75 percent increase in real teacher payments per student, which occurred between 1974 and 1981, into its component parts, we find that roughly one-third was due to an increase in the real faculty input per student and the remaining two-thirds were due to higher real salaries.

Teacher qualifications also rose during the 1970s, in both public and private sectors, as government financed more pre-service and in-service training and schools provided released time for this purpose (Report of the Review Committee 1985; and Bassett 1980. Unfortunately, precise data are not available on ex ante and ex post qualifications of teachers in private versus public schools.) In the long run, these higher wages may attract a more able and better prepared staff and therefore represent an addition to real inputs which can be maintained only by higher remuneration. But in the short run, large salary increases go to existing teachers, including those whose qualifications are unchanged, and those whose training is specific, fully financed by others and who therefore do not require a higher market return to keep them in school.

Output-Based Measures of Quality

We have seen that private school inputs rose when subsidies were introduced, albeit not by the full amount of the subsidies. The reduction in private inputs, diversion of private resources to other uses, and rise in teacher salaries were all important offsetting forces. Thus, expenditure per student in the private sector continued to lag behind that in the public sector.

What happened to output-based measures of quality? When subsidies to private schools were introduced, the presumption was that quality was lower in private than in public schools. This presumption was based on costs, since practically no systematic data on outcomes were available. Since that time, some evidence on outcomes has become available, throwing the initial assumption into question.

For example, in a test of literacy and numeracy skills given to a large sample of 10- and 14-year-olds (in primary and secondary schools, respectively) in 1975, students in independent schools performed best, in public schools performed worst, and Catholic school students were in between. Moreover, the advantage was generally greater, and statistically significant, at the 14-year level, in comparison to the 10-year level, suggesting a greater value added in private secondary schools. Since these results were obtained shortly after need-based subsidies began, they may be taken as some indication of educational achievement in the ex ante period. Closely related is the finding that in the early 1970s the retention rate from first to final year of secondary school was much higher in Catholic than in public schools and, by far, the highest of all in independent schools (Keeves and Bourke 1976; Bourke and Keeves 1977; *Report for the Triennium 1982–84*: 89).

Private school students, particularly in independent schools, had fathers with markedly higher occupational status and family income than public school students, which undoubtedly accounts for part of the observed difference (see Tables 6.8 and 6.9). Indeed, when family background and geographic location are controlled, the advantage of private primary schools disappears. However, literacy, numeracy, and retention rates remain significantly higher in private secondary schools (Williams, Clancy, Batten and Girling-Butcher 1980 and 1981). Thus, direct measures of educational outputs and educational aspirations as well as indirect measures via school choices by higher socioeconomic (and presumably better informed) groups cast serious doubt on the presubsidy argument that quality was lower in the private sector, including the Catholic subsector.

The evidence about postsubsidy outputs is even sketchier. It appears that the private school advantage in retention rates increased further after 1972, with the greatest gains made in the Catholic system (Report of the Review Committee 1985: 40). Similarly, secondary school graduation rates are higher in private schools, particularly independent schools. Specifically, 40 percent of public school students graduate from secondary school and fewer than half of these enter higher education; more than 50 percent of Catholic school students graduate and half of them continue; more than 90 percent of independent school students finish and two-thirds go on to university. While these differentials decline when socioeconomic background characteristics and parental expectations are controlled, significant differences remain across the public and private sectors (Williams et al. 1980; Williams 1987; Williams and Carpenter 1991).

In 1970 private school students also were more likely than public school stu-

Table 6.8. Father's Occupation, Public versus Private Schools, 1975

	Public	Catholic	Other
Prof. & mgrl.	21	34	64
Small bus. & clerical	21	24	18
Craft workers	25	17	11
Manual & serv. workers	34	25	7

Source: Report of the Committee of Review into the Impact of Radford College, 1983, *Schools for the A.C.T.*, Vol. I, Canberra, p. 21. Information based on sample of 14-year olds in 1975.

Table 6.9. Family Income by School Type, 1976
(Percentage distribution)

	Public	Catholic	Other	Total
Over $18,000	10	16	46	12
$15–18,000	26	30	26	27
$12–15,000	22	23	11	22
$9–12,000	18	15	7	17
Under $9,000	24	17	10	22
	100	100	100	100

Source: Catholic Education Office, 1981, Canberra.

dents to get into prestigious universities (such as Melbourne) and prestigious fields (such as medicine); by 1980 this advantage seemed to have increased (Anderson and Vervoon 1983: 68–69). Unfortunately, we don't know how much of this gain was due to improved value added by private schools and how much to increased selectivity of their student inputs during this period. The increased selectivity, however, may well have been a function of the government's subsidy policy combined with limited entry. In any event, output-based measures of quality appear to confirm the "trustworthiness" of private nonprofit schools as well as their comparative efficiency, relative to public schools, and undermine the initial quality rationale for subsidies.

Regulations, Bureaucratic Systems, and Accountability

Regulations often accompany subsidies in other countries; these usually control inputs such as hiring and firing criteria, teacher qualifications, and salaries, and also strongly influence the distribution of outputs by setting criteria for selecting and excluding students, ceilings or floors on fees, and the composition of decision-making boards. Together the subsidies and regulations make private schools more like public schools than they were ex ante. Is this convergence taking place in Australia? So far there have been very few regulations of existing schools, suggesting that this may be a classic case of the regulatory body being captured by those who are regulated. For example, representatives from the private schools regularly sit on, and for several years headed, the Schools Commission. Nevertheless, I argue that convergence is slowly taking place but that unions and private systemic bureaucracies, rather than regulatory authorities, are playing a major role in this process. (For a longer discussion on regulation, including the impact of unions, see James 1988).

Regulations and Accountability

Information is a necessary condition for regulation and accountability. From the beginning, the Schools Commission made a strong statement that information had to flow to the government about the use of Commonwealth funds by private organizations and by states. However, in its triennial reports, the Commission frequently complained about the difficulties it was encountering in securing this information. In 1984 the Commission tried to remedy this situation by announcing that in the future, information would be required on the objectives and governance of all subsidized schools, the ownership of all assets used by them, their income and expenditures both from public and private sources, their enrollments, staff levels, fees, and criteria for selection and exclusion. Moreover, the Commission recommended that methods of monitoring outcomes should be developed, including the reporting of achievement test scores and university entrance rates, by socioeconomic group. Schools were asked to provide a statement each year about how they intended to use Commonwealth funds and school systems were expected to negotiate formal resource agreements identifying priority areas for spending that were consistent both with private and public objectives, such as assisting students from poverty or non-English speaking backgrounds, or those with physical disabilities, etc. (Commonwealth Schools Commission, *Funding Policies for Australian Schools 1984*; *Program Guidelines 1985*; *Recommendations for 1986*. Also see Report of the Review Committee 1985). It would not be surprising to find requirements about expenditure patterns imposed, making private schools more like public in the future, but so far this has not happened.

Systemic Bureaucracies

Meanwhile, another source of convergence has involved self-regulation via the growth of large private bureaucracies. Systems were developed first for the Catholic schools on the statewide and national levels, and later for the Lutheran and Seventh Day Adventist Schools. Thus, about 80 percent of Australian private schools today are parts of bureaucratic systems.

From the beginning, the Schools Commission realized that its task would be greatly facilitated if it could deal with a few large systems rather than a multitude of independent schools. Therefore, the Commission took several steps

Table 6.10. Number and Size Distribution of Schools, 1972–1982 (% in each size category)

	1–35	36–100	100–400	400–800	800 & over	Total
Primary						
1972-Public	31	20	23	22	5	5851
Private	9	23	57	11	1	1439
1982-Public	21	19	37	21	2	5662[a]
Private	11	20	57	12	1	1513
Secondary						
1972-Public	1	1	17	36	46	989
Private	2	7	57	29	5	326
1982-Public	<1	1	17	48	34	1162
Private	3	5	36	46	10	391

Source: Commonwealth Schools Commission, 1984, *Australian School Statistics*, Canberra, p. 33.

[a] Excludes 334 special schools that were included in 1972.

to bring about the development of systems. First of all, systemic administrative costs were built into the subsidy rate (*Report for the Triennium 1976–78*: 151). Second, some systems, particularly the large Catholic system, were represented on the Schools Commission and on State Planning and Finance Committees which recommended priorities for capital grants. Third, block grants made on the basis of total enrollments and average need of member schools were awarded to systems, which then had the authority to suballocate. This discretionary allocation authority naturally gave the bureaucratic system considerable power over individual schools.

Schools also had reasons to join systems. System authorities helped with the paperwork required by the government, advised new schools that wanted to enter the subsidized market, and provided access to loans and matching funds (and indirect access to public capital grants). In other words, just as systems make it easier for government to deal with schools, so they make it easier for schools to deal with government; to that extent, they were a rational response to the subsidies. Later, when industry-wide collective bargaining took place, they also made it easier for schools to deal with unions.

In return, of course, the schools lost some of their autonomy. For example, the system office set priorities for capital grants, thereby limiting the authority of schools to determine their own expansion rate. Parishes that might have wanted to start a building campaign on their own did not do so if they knew they would not get system support. Schools that might have wanted to raise fees were discouraged if this would endanger the system's subsidy category. Since systems develop curriculum and impart this to teachers in in-service training courses, they influence the academic content of schools. They also play an important and increasing role vis-à-vis labor—appointing principals and other key staff members in schools, negotiating with the union, and dealing with other personnel problems that may arise.

The private systems, like public systems, simplified their job by standardizing certain decisions and discouraging diversity; this may be a method that large organizations, whether public or private, use to reduce their internal transactions costs. School or parental interests do not always share the values of system headquarters, in which case frustration develops, just as it does in public bureaucratic systems. Thus the private schools get help from the "experts" as the public schools do, but they also lose some of their flexibility, individuality and variety, as the public schools do.

Nevertheless, private schools still have considerable autonomy, stemming mainly from the fact that teachers and students are not assigned to them. Instead, each school is able to establish an identity, to label itself and, through a process of selection and self-selection, to attract students and staff who agree with its orientation. Each private school thus ends up as a more homogeneous community along some dimension, usually religious or ideological, that it values.

Support for Public Schools

One important question that always arises about limited privatization is: Will the growth of the private sector diminish support for the public sector? Does public funding for private schools reduce the funds that are available for public schools? On the one hand, withdrawal of large segments of the population from public schools, particularly those with a preference for high quality education, may reduce consumer pressure for spending on the public schools. On the other hand, increased competition from the private sector and pressure from producer groups such as the teachers union may induce states to improve quality in order to keep students in public schools. On a priori grounds we cannot predict which of these divergent forces will dominate.

Some countries, such as Holland, have avoided the problem of political support by tying public spending in both sectors together and limiting private spending. Then the only way expenditures per student in the private schools can rise is if they rise in the public schools as well.

In Australia the subsidies received by private schools were also tied, albeit loosely, to public school spending. The percentage nexus differed across categories, changed from year to year, and was complicated by a federal system in which most spending on public education was determined by the states, with some central transfers, while most subsidies for private education came from the Commonwealth. The teachers union argued that more aid from the Commonwealth would have gone to public schools if private schools had not been eligible for subsidies.

In the short run with total budgets fixed, this may indeed be the case, as the two sectors are competitors in a zero-sum game. For example, in 1976 Commonwealth funds to public schools decreased so that private schools subsidies could increase (Commonwealth Schools Commission, *Report for the Triennium 1977–79*: 16; *Australian School Statistics* 1984: 35–36). But in the longer run the decision to subsidize the private sector coincided with, and may have helped to form a broader coalition favoring, an increase in the total educational budget. Commonwealth grants to public and private schools began at the same time, in the 1960s, and the program for both greatly expanded when the need-based subsidy scheme was adopted in 1973–74. In fact, state-plus-central expenditures on education made a quantum long-term leap, from 5 to 6 percent of GNP.[4] Apparently the political quid pro quo for more private school aid was more public school aid; the major losers were those who would have preferred to cut taxes or shift governmental expenditures to noneducational services. As we have seen, since 1974 expenditures per student in public schools have gone up faster than expenditures per student in private schools, lending some support to the theory that competition will spur such spending.

Thus, while the Australian case does not give us a definitive answer and, indeed, the answer may vary across countries and periods, it does provide some evidence that support for public schools need not decrease and may, in fact, increase under a policy of limited privatization.

Efficiency and Equity: Institutional Design in the Education Industry

Is this policy of limited privatization through redistributive vouchers efficient? Is it equitable? To explore these issues I compare the Australian situation with two polar cases: a pure public system, in which there are only public schools and all students are assigned their places in it (i.e., there are no private schools and no choice within the public sector) and a pure voucher system, where all students are given an equivalent sum to be spent in any school they please, whether founded by public or private entrepreneurs.

If schools are natural monopolies, or if consumers are unable to evaluate school quality, a pure public system can be justified on efficiency grounds (i.e., everyone will be better off if government plans and produces education). In the absence of these two conditions, however, a pure public system introduces several inefficiencies, giving public authorities a tax-financed monopoly with little incentive to respond to consumer preferences, minimize costs, or maximize quality.[5]

At the opposite extreme is a pure voucher system, a market-oriented system that avoids the inefficiencies of the pure public system but which also has very different distributional consequences, consequences which some people would consider undesirable. A pure voucher system does not allow for the mandated distribution of human capital and real income through the tax mechanism or through peer group interactions, as a pure public model does. And it may result in separate schools for people with different religious and pedagogical beliefs, making those who want this segregation better off while those who prefer integration are worse off. (See James 1988 for a fuller development of the differences between a pure public and pure voucher system.)

Of course, many in-between systems exist and, in fact, most real world systems are in between. For example, redistributions of human capital are limited in public systems through mechanisms such as local control, residential segregation, selective schools, magnet schools, internal tracking and curriculum choice. At the opposite extreme, some of the undesired effects of pure voucher systems can be offset by regulations—constraining price, student selection criteria, teacher qualifications and salaries—thereby ruling out the extreme quality differences and segregationist tendencies that might otherwise result. In this paper I have described the mixed system adopted by Australia in 1973–74 in which subsidies are awarded to private schools on the basis of their need, and termed it a redistributive subsidy system.

The Australian system still maintains a preferred position for government schools, which receive public funding at a higher rate than private schools. This means that the public schools continue to enjoy a competitive edge. However, the inefficiencies and divergences from consumer tastes of a pure public system are now limited; that is, beyond a certain point people will opt out, and that point is lower than it would have been before subsidies. The enhanced possibility of opting out also limits the amount of redistribution that can take place through the public system. At the same time, making the subsidy smaller for private than for public schools, larger for poor than for rich schools, and restricting entry to subsidized status allows more redistribution than a pure voucher system would. Indeed, this case study makes it clear that alternative distributional goals can generally be accommodated by varying the size of and eligibility criteria for subsidies; but many of these variations involve trade-offs between choice and redistribution, both in limited amounts. Australia provides some choice and some redistribution at the same time.

This policy of limited privatization encountered several unexpected problems and higher costs than were initially anticipated. For example, it created an incentive for existing schools to become more needy or to give the appearance of need by reducing their private resources or diverting them to other uses; it led to lower contributed services and higher teacher prices, hence higher costs than expected; and it encouraged the entry of many new needy schools that could survive only on the basis of large subsidies. The religious segregated basis for schooling was strengthened and extended to small sects that could not afford to maintain schools on their own. At the same time, with entry limited, elite secondary schools were able to use the subsidies to improve their facilities without expanding access. Another consequence was the increasing regulation and centralization of decisions and the loss of private school autonomy which limited the feasible range of options and will probably continue to do so in the future. I have argued above that most of these consequences were generic and would probably follow if this system were adopted in other countries. Are the benefits of limited privatization great enough to justify these costs?

The Australian system illustrates a central problem in answering this question—the difficulty in separating efficiency from equity considerations and sometimes the irrelevance of efficiency in evaluating alternative institutional designs in the education industry. This difficulty stems from the fact that many people care about how children from other families are educated; that is, the nature of student A's education may enter into family B's utility function, often in a way which conflicts with A's preferences, and if these preferences are very strong, a price may not exist at which one group could compensate the other for acquiescing. Part of the reason why family B may feel this way is that schools shape values, values shape votes and, in a democracy, votes shape policies. This connection between schools and values is strengthened by the nonprofit status of subsidized schools, hence their ideological origin and motivation, in Australia as in most other countries. Thus, the kind of political environment that B lives in, and the laws which govern B's life, depend in part on the nature of A's education—and vice-versa. In this sense, privatization in education is more basic and to some, more threatening, than privatization in health or housing.

In situations where B cares strongly about A's education, an objective assessment of educational subsidy or voucher schemes cannot be made. Unavoidably, the assessment depends on distributional considerations and subjective value judgments, on whether you want to favor B or A. If you believe that consumers can evaluate school quality reasonably well, if you do not fear ideological segregation and the resulting taste formation within the educational system, you will favor subsidies or vouchers which will give people the opportunity to attend the school of their choice. This will probably have the additional consequence of raising the wages of low-paid private school teachers. It will also place limits on the redistribution of income and human capital to low ability, low SES students—but not necessarily greater limits than the mixed public systems which now predominate. A need-based subsidy, as in Australia, may actually bring about a more equitable distribution of educational opportunities than exists in many impure public systems.

On the other hand, those who strongly fear the segregation (on religious or other grounds) and the values that may result from privatization, and do not want government subsidies to be captured by private school employees, will oppose policies that make it easier for people to opt out of the ideologically "neutral" public schools.

While an objective normative assessment of a redistributive subsidy scheme is therefore difficult, a positive assessment of the Australian case is much easier. The benefits clearly exceed the costs for large groups of politically potent people—private school students, teachers, and religious organizations. Their numbers, and their political clout, have been growing as a result of the subsidies. At the same time, their opponents—the AFT, some socialists, and secularists—have had enough power to impose moderate constraints and the unforeseen problems just described together with the growth in private enrollments have stimulated further efforts to increase these controls. The dynamics of this situation suggest that the Australian policy of limited privatization is entrenched but its shape will continue to evolve as a result of the tension between those who want subsidized choice for themselves versus those who believe that limiting this choice is better for society as a whole.

NOTES

This paper was written while I was supported by a grant from the Spencer Foundation, whose assistance I gratefully acknowledge. An earlier version was written while I was a Scholar in Residence at the Rockefeller Foundation Study Center at Bellagio; I appreciate the gift of undisturbed time this provided. This paper is part of a broader project on the public-private division of responsibility for education in international perspective. I wish to thank the other organizations that have generously supported various parts of this study, including the Exxon Education Foundation, the National Endowment for the Humanities, the Social Science Research Council, the Indo-U.S. Subcommission, the American Association of University Women, the Netherlands Institute for Advanced Study, the U.S. Department of Education, the U.S. Agency for International Development, the World Bank and the Program on Nonprofit Organizations at Yale University.

1   The Australian Constitution, like the American, contains a clause prohibiting the establishment of any religion. This clause has set the long-run rules of the game, making it difficult for governments in both countries to respond to short-run changes in taste regarding issues such as state aid to private religious schools. However, when taste changes are sufficiently basic, the long-run rules of the game can change through constitutional amendments or judicial interpretation. Thus, in 1981, the Australian Supreme Court, in response to a legal challenge of the subsidy program, held that it was consistent with the constitution providing that aid was given to all religions on an equal basis.

2   This is consistent with a conclusion, based on a time series regression analysis, that the increase in government's share of total funding raised enrollments in private schools after 1974. See Williams, 1984. The assumption in this analysis is that government did not limit entry to subsidized private schools, an assumption that may no longer be valid.

3 The 1972 figure is based on Report of the Interim Committee, p. 42, plus my
   imputation for "contributed services" in 1972. The 1982 figure is derived from
   Tables 6.5a and b.
4 For comparison: In the U.S. the government spent 6% of GNP on education at
   the beginning of this period but currently spends only 5%, while private sources
   have contributed 1.7% of the GNP throughout. Thus the public share of spending
   is smaller here while the private share is much greater, hence the total % is also
   greater. See U.S. Department of Education, 1985, pp. 24–26.
5 In a pure public system the consumer's recourse is through voice rather than exit.
   Voice is very difficult to exercise, uncertain and long term in its effects, and subject
   both to problems of free-riderism and domination by articulate nonrepresentative
   groups.

REFERENCES

ACT Schools Authority. 1985. *Choice of Schools in the ACT: Parents Have Their Say.*
    Canberra: Australian National University Press.
Anderson, D. S. and A. E. Vervoorn, 1983. *Access to Privilege: Patterns of Partici-
    pation in Australian Post-Secondary Education.* Canberra: Australian National
    University Press.
Anderson, Dan. 1985. "Values, Religious Commitment, Social Class and the Choice
    of Private School." Mimeo.
Australian Federation of Teachers. 1988. *Background Notes.* No. 35.
Bassett, G. W. 1980. *Teachers in Australian Schools, 1979.* Melbourne: Australian
    College of Education.
Batten, Margaret. 1983. *Issues of the Eighties.* Hawthorn, Victoria: Australian Council
    for Educational Research.
Bourke, S. F., and J. P. Keeves. 1977. *Australian Studies in School Performance.*
    Vol. 3, *The Mastery of Literacy and Numeracy.* Canberra: Australian Govern-
    ment Publishing Service.
Chapman, Judith. 1984. *A Descriptive Profile of Australian School Principals.* Can-
    berra: Commonwealth Schools Commission.
Chapman, Judith. 1984. *The Selection and Appointment of Australian School Principals.*
    Canberra: Commonwealth Schools Commission.
Commonwealth Schools Commission. 1984. *Australian School Statistics.* Canberra.
Commonwealth Schools Commission. 1984. *Commonwealth Standards for Australian
    Schools.* Canberra.
Commonwealth Schools Commission. 1984. *Funding Policies for Australian Schools.*
    Canberra.
Commonwealth Schools Commission. 1985. *Program Guidelines 1985.* Canberra.
Commonwealth Schools Commission. 1985. *Recommendations for 1986.* Canberra.
Commonwealth Schools Commission. *Report for the Triennium 1976–78, 1977–79,
    1979–81, 1982–84.* Canberra: Australian Government Publishing Service.
Commonwealth Schools Commission and Australian Bureau of Statistics. 1979. *Aus-
    tralian Students and Their Schools.* Canberra.
Education Department of Victoria, Planning Report. 1983. *Parental Choice of School,*
    Planning Report. Melbourne.

Faulkner, J. V. 1980. "Sociological Changes in the Staffing of Catholic Schools." Paper presented at the Catholic Education Conference, Canberra.

Hansmann, Henry. 1980. "The Role of Non-Profit Enterprise." *Yale Law Journal* 89:835–98.

Hanushek, Eric. 1986. "The Economics of Schooling: Production and Efficiency in Public Schools." *Journal of Economic Literature* 24:1141–77.

Heller, J. M. 1982. "A History of the Independent Schools Salaries Officer's Association of the Western Australian Industrial Union of Workers, 1960–1976." University of Western Australia. Mimeo.

Hogan, Michael. 1984. *Public Versus Private Schools: Funding and Directions in Australia*. Victoria: Penguin.

James, Estelle. 1988. "Interactions Between Private and Public Provision of Education: The Case of Australia." Paper presented at the American Economic Association meeting.

James, Estelle. 1991. "Public Policies Toward Private Education." *Journal of International Educational Research*.

James, Estelle, ed. 1989. *The Nonprofit Sector in International Perspective: Studies in Comparative Culture and Policy*. New York: Oxford University Press.

James, Estelle, and Susan Rose-Ackerman. 1986. *The Nonprofit Enterprise in Market Economies*. New York: Harwood.

Keeves, J. P. and S. F. Bourke. 1976. *Australian Studies in School Performance*. Vol. 1, *Literacy and Numeracy in Australian Schools: A First Report*. Canberra: Australian Government Publishing Service.

Kemp, D. A. 1978. *Society and Electoral Behavior in Australia*. Brisbane: University of Queensland Press.

Ministry of Education and Youth Affairs. 1984. *Commonwealth School Commission Guidelines, 1985–88*. Canberra.

Praetz, Helen. 1982. *Public Policy and Catholic Schools*. Hawthorn, Victoria: Australian Council for Educational Research.

Praetz, Helen. 1982. *Public Policy and Private Schools*. Hawthorn, Victoria: Australian Council for Educational Research.

Report of the Committee of Review into the Impact of Radford College. 1983. *Schools for the ACT*, vols. 1 and 2. Canberra: Australian Government Publishing Service.

Report of the Interim Committee for the Australian Schools Commission. 1973. *Schools in Australia*. Canberra: Australian Government Publishing Service.

Report of the Panel of Commonwealth School Commissioners. 1985. *Planning and Funding Policies for New Non-Governmental Schools*. Canberra.

Report of the Review Committee. 1985. *Quality of Education in Australia*. Canberra: Australian Government Publishing Service.

Theobald, Marjorie. 1983. "Women Teachers' Quest for Salary Justice in Victoria's Registered Schools, 1915–1946." *Melbourne Studies in Education*.

U.S. Department of Education. 1985. *Digest of Educational Statistics*.

Williams, Ross. 1984. "The Economic Determinants of Private Schooling in Australia." Discussion Paper No. 94, ANU Centre for Economic Policy Research.

Williams, Ross. 1984a. "Interactions Between Government and Private Outlays: Education in Australia, 1949–50 to 1981–82." *Economic Record* 60:317–25.

Williams, Trevor. 1987. *Participation in Education*. Hawthorn, Victoria: Australia Council for Educational Research.

Williams, Trevor, and Margaret Batten. 1981. *The Quality of School Life*. Hawthorn, Victoria: Australian Council for Educational Research.

Williams, Trevor, Margaret Batten, Sue Girling-Butcher, and Jeff Clancy. 1981. *School and Work in Prospect: 14-Year-Olds in Australia*. Hawthorn, Victoria: Australian Council for Educational Research.

Williams, Trevor, and Peter Carpenter. 1991. "Private Schooling and Public Achievement." In *Journal of International Educational Research*. Forthcoming.

Williams, Trevor, Jeff Clancy, Margaret Batten and Sue Girling-Butcher. 1981. *School, Work and Career: 17-Year-Olds in Australia*. Hawthorn, Victoria: Australian Council for Educational Research.

PART 3
HOUSING POLICY

7 *G. Thomas Kingsley*

Housing Vouchers and America's Changing Housing Problems

In the mid-1970s, the United States began to alter fundamentally the way it provides housing assistance to the poor. Before then, almost all assistance was delivered through a production approach, a practice wherein new housing projects were built specifically for low- and moderate-income families with government subsidies bringing rents down to levels they could afford. Since then, consumer-oriented approaches—most notably, the housing voucher program—have become dominant.

With housing vouchers, the beneficiaries do not have to live in specific projects. Like all other renters, they select their own apartments from those available in the private housing market. They then pay a portion of the total rent for the unit—an amount determined by formula to be affordable for them given their income; a subsidy payment makes up the difference. What differentiates this approach from a straight income-transfer program is that recipients must live in units that have passed a housing quality inspection. If they now live in a substandard unit and want to stay, repairs have to be made before voucher payments can start. Alternatively, they can move to another apartment that already meets the standards. If they already live in a standard unit, they can stay and receive payments automatically. Almost all poor families who do live

G. Thomas Kingsley is Director of the Center for Public Finance and Housing at the Urban Institute in Washington, D.C.

in standard housing have to pay an unreasonably large share of their income for rent. In this case the voucher payments do not change their housing conditions but simply relieve the pressure on other components of the family budget.

Clearly, the housing voucher program is a form of privatization. It replaces government supported production with a process in which subsidies facilitate the regular functioning of the private market. In fact, among all recent privatization initiatives it may have achieved the highest level of political acceptance since it, and another program based on the same approach, have become the U.S. government's primary instruments for delivering housing assistance. In one way, though, it does differ from most other privatization initiatives. Normally, such initiatives deal with expanding the private role in fields that have been traditionally regarded as public sector responsibilities. But in the United States, providing housing has always been thought of predominantly as the job of the private sector.

This chapter begins by explaining why government got involved in housing in the first place. This leads into the story of America's experience with housing production programs and what went wrong with them. The chapter then offers a more complete explanation of the housing voucher concept and reviews the results of a major series of experiments with that concept in the 1970s. This is followed by an examination of important changes that have taken place in the nature of U.S. housing problems and the way the voucher approach relates to them. The final sections describe the transition of vouchers into a national program and offer an evaluation of the approach in relation to both the expected benefits and costs of privatization and the challenge of emerging U.S. housing problems.

How Government Became Involved

Through the late nineteenth century, housing was almost solely a private sector operation in America, little influenced by government at any level. By then, however, the industrial revolution had brought the rapid growth of cities and, with them, high-density tenement housing for low-income workers. The congestion and squalor of tenement housing, particularly in New York City, caught the attention of the reform movement around the turn of the century. The response of local governments was regulation consisting of new codes that implied criminal penalties for builders and landlords who broke the rules.[1]

The competition of the marketplace is supposed to prevent the production of shoddy goods. Why did it fail so markedly in this case? The answer is that the housing market has "imperfections" that are more serious than those in the markets for most other commodities. Unlike products such as food or clothing, housing is fixed to one specific location, stays in use for a very long period of time, is purchased very infrequently by the consumer, and has a basic unit of production that is much more expensive in relation to family incomes. This means that producers cannot adapt their product lines to changing demand patterns as easily. Comparison shopping is harder for consumers and once a purchase is made it is not so easy for them to change their minds.

These market imperfections make a generally accepted case for some government involvement in housing, but at the time of the early regulations the goal was only to improve private market behavior, not to replace it in any way. This remained true of the next major housing policy initiatives (the first at the federal level) put in place as a part of the New Deal. As a response to the devastation of housing finance during the depression, the nation established several agencies: 1) the Federal Housing Administration (FHA), which provided insurance for long-term low-down-payment mortgages that significantly reduced the risk of loans for housing; 2) the Federal National Mortgage Association (FNMA), which further reduced that risk by providing a secondary mortgage market; and 3) the Federal Home Loan Bank (FHLB), which regulated the lenders and provided them with a central source of credit. This system is generally regarded as America's greatest success in housing.[2] It promoted mortgage lending that was much more stable and much less expensive than had existed before 1930, and thus laid the base for the post-war boom in home construction.

Still, these changes were not likely to have much direct effect on the housing conditions of the poor, and those conditions had deteriorated substantially during the depression years. The response to this problem was the nation's first production program, public housing, created by the Housing Act of 1937.

The Production Programs

Public housing is planned and built by local public housing authorities (PHAs) throughout the country.[3] The federal government covers the full cost of project development and, at least initially, tenant rent payments covered operating costs. Construction under the program began in earnest shortly after the war but grew fairly modestly thereafter. Annual net additions averaged 27,700 units through the 1950s and 41,500 in the 1960s compared to total annual net additions to the occupied housing stock averaging 1.03 million over those two decades.[4]

A new production approach was started in 1961—publicly assisted housing. Projects were built and operated by private developers who received federal subsidies in return for the commitment to allocate units to low- and moderate-income households at reduced rents. Initially, subsidies were delivered through below-market interest-rate loans although other mechanisms have since been used. Given the low production rates of public housing, the theory suggested that publicly assisted housing would add to the total output of low-rent housing, and serve those whose incomes were inadequate to allow them to pay market rents but higher than those of the target group for public housing.[5]

Momentum for the production programs grew in the Johnson administration when the Kaiser Committee (the President's Committee on Urban Housing, 1969) called for a stronger national commitment to improving the housing conditions of the poor. The establishment of the U.S. Department of Housing and Urban Development (HUD) in 1968 was also a symbol of increased national concern for the issue. Indeed, the production systems responded, expanding to achieve record construction volumes in the early 1970s.

But these programs were already evidencing a series of problems, enough so that President Nixon placed a moratorium on further production in 1973 pending the results of an evaluation. After that evaluation, Congress passed the Housing and Community Development Act of 1974, which created a new form of publicly assisted housing to replace earlier versions. However, by 1980 much of the support for further growth of any production programs had evaporated. What went wrong? There were six basic criticisms:

1. *High Cost.* Most important, it became clear that the production programs were extremely expensive. The annual subsidy cost of publicly assisted housing, including interest rate subsidies and tax benefits, was estimated to range from $4,000 to $6,000 in 1980 dollars (Schnare et al. 1982). For a variety of reasons (e.g., use of more expensive sites, paying high construction wages as mandated by the Davis-Bacon law, delays due to special administrative requirements), units built under government production programs have cost more than those built privately. After adjusting for differences in time and location, Schnare et al. (1982) estimated that the development costs of a typical public housing unit had been 40 percent higher than unsubsidized construction. No more than one-fifth of this gap could be explained by differences in characteristics like unit type and size. The estimated gap for publicly assisted housing was smaller (3–12 percent), but it still existed. Analysis by HUD's Office of Policy Development and Research (1982) also showed that operating costs were higher for publicly assisted than for private market projects.

2. *Financial Instability.* Furthermore, many of the previously built projects had become financially distressed. The rules for public housing had been adjusted to focus more on serving persistently poor families. But with inflation in operating and maintenance costs, such tenants could no longer afford rent payments that would cover even those costs. The only solution was for the federal government to pick up a large part of the bill for operations on top of paying the initial capital costs. Although they rented to somewhat higher income groups, similar problems were affecting publicly assisted housing as operating costs went up. By 1975, it had become necessary to assign about 11 percent of all insured multifamily mortgages to HUD—141,000 units in fore-

closed properties and an additional 282,000 in assigned properties (Struyk, Turner, and Ueno 1988).

3. *Inequity.* The limited availability of subsidy funds coupled with the high cost per unit implied that the number of units constructed under the production programs could serve only a small fraction of those eligible for assistance. It is estimated that by 1974, almost 40 years after the initiation of public housing, only 1.2 million households (15 percent of those eligible for assistance) were being served.[6] The contrast—providing extremely generous benefits to a few while the majority got nothing—was a growing congressional concern in the late 1970s.

4. *Concentration of Poverty and the Lack of Freedom of Choice.* Under the production programs, living in "the projects" was the only choice available to poor families who wanted housing assistance, and many of these projects were very large. With the concentration of so many poor households in any one location a host of social problems was inevitable, including crime and vandalism. With the intense fiscal pressures noted above, few housing authorities could expand their security and repair or maintenance budgets in response. These difficulties received considerable attention from the media in the late 1970s. The nationally televised demolition of the Pruitt-Igoe project in St. Louis was probably the most prominent event. Once considered a model project, severe and apparently insoluble social and physical deterioration led local officials to decide that demolition was the only reasonable course of action. Many public housing authorities around the country operated much smaller projects and managed them effectively. But large project problems created vivid negative images and clouded the reputation of the program as a whole.

5. *The Substitution Issue.* Two studies of the moderate-income production programs (Swan 1973; Murray 1983) concluded that those programs did not actually create a net increase in the housing stock. If the programs had never existed, they argued, private market activity would have expanded leading to the same aggregate growth in the stock. Evidence has also been assembled to show in particular, that in cities where the number of households is declining or growing slowly (cities where subsidized programs have been concentrated for the most part), expanding new construction can lead to more rapid rates of loss from the older stock (Weicher 1982). Some of this work relied on sophisticated analytic techniques not readily intelligible to the average voter, but these conclusions did add to the political doubts about the attractiveness of the production approach.

6. *"Politicizing" Housing Provision.* Finally, there is the view that beneficiaries believe government housing providers will not be as tough as the private sector in enforcing rules and, therefore, will not be as rigorous in meeting their own financial obligations. In a survey of the nation's 29 largest PHAs, Struyk (1980) found that 18.5 percent of all tenants were behind on their rent pay-

ments and the process that PHAs had to go through to evict problem tenants
was extremely cumbersome. There were also some well publicized evidences
of this sort of problem in publicly assisted housing. One example was the
Mitchell-Lama program in New York City where some residents of its subsidized cooperative projects (a vocal group politically) openly reneged on their
debt service payments and the city government long avoided the disciplinary
action that probably would have been automatic from a private mortgagee
(Woodfill 1971). No one has done the careful comparative analysis that would
be required to reliably assess the importance of such behavioral differences.
Again, however, the image of these sorts of problems added to the doubts
about the production approach.

The Housing Voucher Experiments

The voucher concept (initially called *rent certificates*) was in fact considered
as an alternative to the production approach at the time public housing was
enacted in 1937, but it did not develop much support until the mid-1960s when
some of the troubles of the production programs became evident. An adap-
tation of public housing that went part way to a consumer orientation started
on a small scale in 1965;[7] in 1969 the Kaiser Committee recommended a program of experiments to test the voucher approach (at that time, called *housing
allowances*). They felt experiments were needed primarily because they were
concerned that a large-scale program of this type might considerably inflate the
rents of existing housing. Congress mandated the experiments in the Housing
and Community Development Act of 1970 and the experimental design process, which added other research questions, began shortly thereafter. (These
events are described more completely in Struyk and Bendick 1981.)

The resulting HUD-sponsored Experimental Housing Assistance Program
(EHAP) was the largest social experiment ever conducted, giving housing
allowances to 30,000 households in 12 experimental sites. The program had
three components: 1) the Supply Experiment, a full-scale test of the market
impacts of a voucher program in two mid-sized metropolitan areas. All eligible
households could participate and detailed tenant and landlord surveys documented the effects over a five-year period; 2) the Demand Experiment, a test
of the reactions of smaller samples of consumers to varying program formulas
in two other cities; and 3) a small Administrative Agency Experiment that
tested administrative features in eight urban areas.[8] The Supply Experiment
was designed and operated by the Rand Corporation and the others by ABT
Associates, Inc.

In the most prominent program design, tested in the Supply Experiment,
standard rents were estimated for each housing unit size in each locality. These
represented the market rent required locally to secure a modest housing unit

that would meet program quality standards. This is basically the same concept as the Fair Market Rent (FMR) schedules that HUD has since estimated and regularly updated as a basis for similar program operations in most urban areas. Enrollees who secured units of adequate quality then received subsidy payments calculated as the difference between the estimated standard rent and 25 percent of their own adjusted gross incomes. Thus, the higher the income rose, the lower the payment became. Monthly checks went directly to the recipients who were then responsible for making the full rent payment to the landlord. After allowance payments began, household incomes were recertified every six months and housing was reinspected annually.

Results of the experiments have been extensively documented. (See Struyk and Bendick 1981; Lowry 1983.) The principle findings were as follows:

Program Participation Rates Were Lower Than Many Had Anticipated

In welfare (specifically the Aid to Families with Dependent Children program, or AFDC), about 80 percent of all eligible households participate. In the Supply Experiment, 56 percent of all eligible renters enrolled (i.e., applied and were certified as income-eligible) and 75 percent of all enrollees secured certifiable housing and received payments. In all, then, only 42 percent of all eligibles eventually participated. Why the difference? First, housing allowance payments (averaging $85 per month) were modest compared to the average AFDC payment, thus the monetary incentive to participate was not as strong. Second, AFDC recipients do not have to find acceptable housing to receive payments. The 25 percent of allowance program enrollees who never qualified were disproportionately composed of those who found out at enrollment that their monthly payment would be too small to be "worth the trouble"; and those who would have had to make substantial personal changes to qualify (e.g., move out of a substandard unit that required costly repairs and to which, for one of a number of reasons, they had a strong attachment). Of those renters who did qualify, 51 percent already lived in standard units and stayed there; 38 percent persuaded their landlords to make repairs to their present units (or made the repairs themselves) so that the unit met the standards; and 11 percent moved to another unit that met program standards.

Housing Quality Did Improve, But the Effects Were Modest

The figures above show that a fairly small proportion of successful transitions from enrollee to recipient required housing repairs. Payments made to the majority of participants who already lived in standard units and stayed there simply reduced previous constraints on their consumption of other goods. On average, they had been paying 47 percent of their incomes for decent housing beforehand, and the program, as per the formula, reduced that ratio to 25 percent. In most of the transitions that did entail repairs, only inexpensive repairs were required ($38 on average). Apartments with modest defects were much more likely to be upgraded than those with serious deficiencies. Many of the repairs were made by the tenants themselves or by landlords working in concert with the tenants. Still, the Supply Experiment showed that the program did motivate higher rates of subsequent expenditure on maintenance and repairs than was typical (to keep the unit qualified for the program).

The Programs Had Very Little Effect On Household Mobility
Even a smaller proportion of all enrollees moved to qualify for payments, and very few who did move left their previous neighborhoods. Housing vouchers, therefore, are not likely to disrupt neighborhoods or "have much effect on income or racial segregation, the length of the journey to work, neighborhood quality, or on movement between the central city and the suburbs" (Struyk and Bendick 1981).

The Programs Did Not Cause Rent Inflation
Supply Experiment estimates indicate that rent inflation in the program sites while the experiment was underway was about what could have been expected if no program had been implemented. This outcome is not surprising considering the findings above. Only a small percentage of all eligible households participated and most of the subsidy funds allocated to them went to increase nonhousing consumption. The increment to effective demand for housing was small in relation to the size of the local market.

Per Unit Costs in the Housing Allowance Program Were Significantly Below Those of the Production Programs
The most exhaustive analysis of this issue (Mayo et al. 1980) showed that in the Demand Experiment sites the annual subsidy costs of the housing allowance programs ranged from $1,869 to $2,361 in contrast to production program costs ranging from $3,561 to $4,155 in 1975 dollars. (See Table 7.1.) The analysis also estimated annual market rental values for same units based on quality measures and other unit characteristics. The ratio of cost to value is a measure of program efficiency. Costs were higher than market values for all programs but the differences were much greater for production programs than for housing allowances (the difference between market rent and cost for housing allowances was roughly equal to the program's administrative cost). In both sites, public housing was the least efficient program in these terms. Mayo and Barnbrock (1985) concluded, "producer-oriented programs generally provide most or all of their benefits in the form of better housing than tenants otherwise would have consumed . . . consumer-oriented programs such as housing allowances could have served from two to three times as many house-

Table 7.1. Annual Program Costs Relative to Housing Rental
Value, Two-Bedroom Units (in 1975 $)

	Cost	Rental value	Cost/ value
Pittsburgh			
Public housing	4,155	1,888	2.20
Publicly assisted housing[a]	4,136	2,057	2.01
Housing allowances	1,869	1,626	1.15
Phoenix			
Public housing	3,561	1,989	1.79
Publicly assisted housing[a]	3,571	2,429	1.47
Housing allowances	2,361	2,084	1.13

Source: Mayo, Stephen K., et al. 1980.
[a] Section 236 Program.

holds per year per subsidy dollar as could producer-oriented programs of the mid-1970s."

Consumer-Oriented Programs Have Much Simpler Administrative Requirements (Implying Lower Administrative Costs)

Administrative costs in the Supply Experiment averaged $163 per recipient year in 1976 dollars—55 percent of the average administrative cost for AFDC at that time (Kingsley and Schlegel 1982). Consumer-oriented programs require only a few administrative functions—informing eligible households of the availability of the program, performing means tests and housing inspections, and making payments. Administrators do not have to get directly involved in the production process by purchasing, building, leasing, or managing housing, or in supervising or regulating the activity of private builders or landlords.

All in all, the experimental allowance programs were able to keep low-income families in decent housing at reasonable rents and at a very low public cost. However, while they were efficient, they were far from dramatic. They were housing programs that did not have sizable effects on housing. They did not stimulate new construction or even much substantial rehabilitation.

Given these outcomes one might have expected housing advocates to drop the idea. That did not happen because, coincident with (and furthered by) the assimilation of EHAP findings, the policy community realized that the nature of America's housing problems had changed fundamentally since 1937. The allowance programs did not produce a massive housing supply response, but it appeared that a massive supply response was no longer what was needed.

Table 7.2. Changes in the Housing Stock and Housing Quality, 1940–1980

	1940	1950	1960	1970	1980
Total occupied housing units (millions)	34.9	42.8	53.0	63.4	80.4
Percent of units:					
Lacking some or all plumbing	55	34	15	6	3
Overcrowded[a]	9	6	4	2	1

Source: Census data as presented in Struyk, Raymond J., et al. 1988.
[a] Overcrowding defined as more than 1.5 persons per room.

The New View of the Housing Problem

Data that documented the change had been available for some time, but somehow the new view of the housing problem did not sink in (i.e., it did not modify the "conventional wisdom" in the policy community) until the late 1970s. The history of the post-1940 era summarized so far in this chapter has focused on federal subsidy programs. While that history was unfolding, the private sector was playing a much more active role. Benefiting from the New Deal reforms of the housing finance system and responding to the unprecedented growth of household incomes that occurred over this era of consistent economic expansion, private developers built much more new housing between 1940 and 1980 than had existed in total before then. Older units dropped out of the stock and were replaced by new units of higher quality. Local governments furthered quality improvements by raising housing standards and enforcing them more rigorously. Seriously deficient housing declined precipitously as a percentage of the total stock. (See Table 7.2.)

At the same time, housing prices had increased substantially, particularly during the 1970s. (See Table 7.3.) In an era of heavy inflation, the prices of owner-occupied housing grew even faster than the Consumer Price Index. By 1980, it had become much more difficult for young families to afford to purchase a home and renters were having to pay a much larger share of their incomes for rent.

Table 7.4 shows the extent of each type of housing problem for a somewhat later period (1975–1983). The data corroborate the trends cited above (diminishing quality problems and growing affordability problems) and highlight the extent to which housing problems of all types are concentrated among very low-income (VLI) renters. In 1983 the following housing characteristics were observed: 1) 9 percent of all households (but 19 percent of VLI renters) lived in an inadequate unit (as determined by housing quality standards normally used by HUD - Simonson, 1981); 2) 3 percent of all households (but 5 percent of VLI renters) who were not in inadequate units lived in overcrowded conditions (here defined as more than one person per room); and 3) 17 percent of all households (but 56 percent of VLI renters) not in either

Table 7.3. Changes in Housing Costs and Affordability, 1970–1980

	1970	1980
Median value owner occupied housing ($ 000)	$17.1	$51.3
Median value/income ratio	1.7	2.5
Median monthly gross rent, renter occupied housing	$108	$241
Median rent/income ratio	0.20	0.27
Percent renters paying more than 35% of income for rent	25	34

Source: Bureau of the Census 1981.

Table 7.4. Composition of America's Housing Problems, 1975–1983

	Total	Home Owners	Renters VLI[a]	Other
1975				
Households (mill.)	72.5	46.9	10.1	15.5
Percent				
Inadequate Unit	11	8	24	12
Other, Crowded	4	3	6	4
Other, Cost Burden	12	5	49	8
No Housing Problems	73	84	22	76
Total	100	100	100	100
1983				
Households (mill.)	84.8	54.9	17.0	12.9
Percent				
Inadequate Unit	9	6	19	10
Other, Crowded	3	2	5	3
Other, Cost Burden	17	8	56	16
No Housing Problems	71	84	20	71
Total	100	100	100	100

Source: Irby, Iredia. 1986.

[a] VLI = Very Low Income (household income 50 percent of local median or less). See text for definitions of housing problem categories.

of the above categories, had unreasonable cost burdens; i.e., annual housing expenses exceeded 30 percent of incomes (40 percent for homeowners paying into mortgage principal).

For all groups, the percentages living in inadequate housing and crowded conditions declined between 1975 and 1983, and the shares with unreasonable cost burdens increased substantially. To be sure, housing quality problems had not been eliminated by the early 1980s, but they had much diminished. America's most serious housing problem by then had become the inability of many households to afford the decent housing that was available. In this environment, housing vouchers (which, according to the experiments, cost much less and received higher marks for their impact on affordability problems than their impact on housing quality) seemed to be on the right track.

Developing a National Program

We noted earlier that there had been some experience with a limited-scale consumer-oriented program since the late 1960s. Congress accelerated that experience by creating the Existing Housing component of the Section 8 Lower Income Rental Assistance Program in the Housing and Community Development Act of 1974. The EHAP experiments had just begun, but Congress apparently did not want to wait until all the results were in before they gave some boost to a consumer-oriented approach.

Section 8 "certificates" are like housing vouchers with two exceptions. First, with vouchers, beneficiaries always receive payments equal to the difference between the standard rent (FMR) and the fraction of their income deemed to be affordable. They have an important shopping incentive, since if they find a bargain (a standard-quality apartment renting for less than the FMR), they still get the same subsidy payment but do not have to pay out as much for rent. Under Section 8, the payment is calculated as the difference between the actual rent and the affordable fraction of their income, so the shopping incentive does not exist. Second, voucher recipients are able to occupy units that rent for more than the FMR, but consistent with the formula, their assistance payments do not go up if they do so. Section 8 recipients, however, are prohibited from occupying units that rent for more than the FMR, thus the range of choice for them is curtailed.

Under the Carter administration, production programs again expanded and remained the dominant mode of housing assistance but the Section 8 Existing Housing component also grew rapidly. From fiscal years 1977 through 1980, an additional 290,000 households per year on average received assistance, 64 percent of whom were housed in new construction projects. (See Table 7.5.) But by 1980, the high costs of this new wave of production activity, the emerging findings of EHAP, and the recognition of the changing nature of America's housing problems all increased doubts about further reliance on the production approach. A new President's Commission on Housing convened and its report (1982) advocated that the production programs be curtailed and that housing vouchers become the nation's primary vehicle for providing housing assistance.

Table 7.5. Additional Households Receiving HUD
Rental Assistance by Program Type, 1977–1986
(in thousands)

Fiscal Year	Total	New Construction	Other
1977	354.4	226.8	127.6
1978	317.0	190.5	126.5
1979	303.1	200.3	102.8
1980	187.9	129.5	58.4
1981	158.9	75.3	83.6
1982	55.8	17.4	38.4
1983	53.7	6.3	47.4
1984	88.3	9.6	78.7
1985	102.7	16.9	85.8
1986	98.6	13.1	85.5

Source: Congressional Budget Office data as presented
in Struyk, et al. 1988.

The Reagan Administration warmly accepted these proposals. Its budgets
recommended recisions of previously adopted budget authority for the production programs, no additional units under publicly assisted housing, and almost
none for public housing. It strongly supported the voucher concept in principle, but its overall budget goals called for substantial reductions for housing
subsidies. Therefore, while consumer-oriented programs (vouchers and Section 8 existing) got a much larger share of the pot than in the past, the pot
was so much smaller that the actual rate of addition to these programs under
Reagan was not as large as it had been in the Carter years.

Congress fought back, but not very hard. It did not adopt the administration's proposed voucher program officially until 1988, although it had let the
program develop over the preceding five years as a demonstration.[9] It did appropriate more funds for housing than the president recommended (but not
full restoration to previous levels) and it did provide for some more, but not
much, new public housing. The results are shown on Table 7.5. During the
1982–86 period, the number of new households added to the assistance rolls
per year averaged 12,700 for the production programs (7 percent of the 1977–
80 average) and 67,100 for the consumer-oriented programs, mostly Section 8
Existing (64 percent of the 1977–80 average).

Nonetheless, the number of housing program beneficiaries has continued
to grow and a larger share of all eligibles is being served. The Congressional
Budget Office (1988) reports that at the end of Fiscal Year (FY) 1987, 4.30
million households were receiving HUD rental assistance and that sufficient
funds had been appropriated to support 4.65 million by the end of FY 1988. At
that level, they estimated that 34 percent of the eligibles would be served, an

impressive change from the 15 percent in 1974 noted earlier. Only 35 percent of the 1988 beneficiaries (1.64 million) were assisted via vouchers and Section 8 certificates, but that too is impressive considering that those programs did not exist in 1974.

Performance and Prospects

Vouchers and Section 8 certificates have performed pretty much as the experiments suggested they would with no major housing supply impacts but support for continued maintenance and considerable budgetary relief for households in the face of rising housing prices. And the cost advantages remain. Congressional Budget Office (1988) estimates still assume annual costs for the consumer-oriented programs at about half of those for production programs.

There had been a concern that the approach was not working as well as the experimental models. Wallace et al. (1981) found that, as of 1979, the success rate for Section 8 certificates (percent of enrollees finding acceptable housing) was only 46 percent. In a more recent survey, however, Kennedy and Finkel (1987) showed that the average success rate has since increased to 60 percent. Their surveys found that both vouchers and certificates have worked well in a variety of markets. The only notable exceptions in their sample were New York City and Boston, tight markets where those finding certifiable housing ranged from only 30 to 45 percent.

Also, the study found that success rates for vouchers have not differed from those for Section 8 certificates to date. Because they are not bound by the FMR constraint, it had been expected that participation would be higher for vouchers. However, PHAs have been administering certificates for a longer period of time and their greater familiarity with them may have so far offset the greater flexibility built into the voucher approach. The expected advantage of the voucher program may emerge quantitatively as more experience with it is gained.[10]

In the national policy arena, a surprising consensus has been building in support of the voucher concept. While there are still complaints about its limited impacts on supply, groups all across the political spectrum now advocate an expansion of a consumer-oriented approach into an entitlement program— one that would assist all eligibles that choose to participate. Proponents include a prominent housing advocacy group, the National Low-Income Housing Coalition (Zigas 1989); the Heritage Foundation (Butler 1989); and a broad-based task force chaired by James Rouse and David Maxwell to provide inputs for new housing legislation under the sponsorship of senators Cranston and D'Amato (National Housing Task Force 1988). The recommendations by Zigas and the task force call for production assistance to supplement vouchers, but there are no longer any serious recommendations to restore the production approach to primacy. The task force report suggests that production assistance flow through a type of block grant to the states rather than through a federally managed program as in the past.

Assessment

It is hard to find much fault with housing vouchers as a privatization measure. Compared to production subsidies, they win hands down in relation to most of the criteria listed in Chapter 1—particularly efficiency, equity, choice, and empowerment. As a solution to America's housing problems, however, they are not a panacea.

The acceleration of housing costs over incomes has not abated. The affordability problem is much more serious than it was a decade ago, and there are no indications that relief is on the way. Homelessness, a new phenomenon of the 1980s, was started by deinstitutionalization, but there is little doubt that the housing affordability gap has been a major cause of its expansion.

The FMR schedules for vouchers and certificates are regularly adjusted to reflect changes in local rent levels. This means that as the gap between rents and incomes expands, so do federal subsidy outlays. It is hard to imagine Congress buying into a voucher entitlement program with no prospects for cost containment. They could, of course, change the formula and cut back on the average subsidy. In fact they did that in 1981, raising the required tenant contribution in the Section 8 program from 25 percent to 30 percent. If they go too far in this direction, however, and the affordability gap continues to grow, the voucher approach will not work. Success rates will decline as fewer and fewer poor households are able to find housing that they can afford even with some subsidy.

After the experience of the past 20 years, hardly anyone believes it would be feasible to solve the housing problems of America's poor solely through supply-side (production) programs. The growing consensus is that a demand-side (consumer-oriented) approach should be the foundation. But that does not imply that some public intervention on the supply side in addition is not appropriate. There are two possibilities.

The first would be to attack rising housing costs directly. On the surface it seems hard to quarrel with America's relentless drive toward housing quality improvement, but that drive has its pernicious side. Stringent zoning requirements and other regulations in the suburbs prohibit lower-cost housing solutions. Because of strong vested interests, building codes mandate continued reliance on costly and outmoded materials and practices. Well intended efforts to eliminate low quality, single-room-occupancy accommodations in large cities leave the former inhabitants with no housing at all.[11] These problems are not easy to address from Washington, but the growing affordability gap is nationally debilitating. Some action at the federal level seems appropriate.

The second would be to reestablish some form of production assistance. The recent research on vouchers suggests that this is not needed in most cities (i.e., where voucher success rates have been high), but urban areas with more severe supply constraints may want to consider some production support to supplement vouchers. Two observations seem appropriate. First, while a number of creative new production efforts have been attempted of late in various states and localities, a resource-constrained environment implies that the burden of proof should remain on the production program designers. They need to demonstrate how their schemes will avoid the excess cost and other problems that have plagued that approach in the past. Second, if no inroads are made on the cost-control side as discussed above, it is difficult to see how any production approach could be made cost effective in today's environment.

NOTES

1 Both the housing conditions of the period and the nature of the reforms are described in Gallion and Eisner 1975.
2 For full discussions of the evolutions of America's housing finance system, during this period and thereafter, see Tuccillo 1983, and Hendershott and Villani 1977.
3 Most PHAs are autonomous agencies operating outside of local government, although their Boards are normally appointed by elected local officials. In many cases their administrative costs are covered entirely by federal grants, although some also receive municipal funding.
4 These data are calculated from the Bureau of the Census (1975) series, which shows the total stock of low-rent public housing under management (occupied or available for occupancy) increasing from 201,700 units in 1950 to 478,200 units in 1960 and 893,500 units in 1970.
5 More complete examinations of the history of these programs are provided in Struyk, Mayer, and Tuccillo 1983, and Struyk, Turner, and Ueno 1988.
6 Burke (1984) estimated that there were 8.4 million very low-income renter households in 1974, out of which 1.2 million were receiving HUD subsidies. The number of very low-income renter households (those with incomes at or below 50 percent of the median incomes in their communities) is usually considered equivalent to the total number of eligibles.
7 This was the Section 23 program in which PHAs rented units on the private market and made them available to low-income tenants. It goes only part way because, in a truly consumer oriented program, the beneficiaries select the unit and deal directly with the landlord themselves.
8 The Supply Experiment was conducted in Green Bay, Wisconsin, and South Bend, Indiana. The Demand Experiment sites were Phoenix, Arizona and Pittsburgh, Pennsylvania. Administrative Agency Experiments sites included Bismark, North Dakota; Durham, North Carolina; Jacksonville, Florida; Peoria, Illinois; Salem, Oregon; San Bernardino, California; Springfield, Massachusetts; and Tulsa, Oklahoma.
9 This was called the "Freestanding Voucher Demonstration." See discussion in Kennedy and Finkel 1987.
10 See the discussion of this point by Weicher 1988, 15.

11 For a comprehensive examination of the effects of local regulations on housing costs see Seidel 1978.

REFERENCES

Burke, Paul. 1984. "Trends in Subsidized Housing, 1974–81." Unpublished paper. Washington, D.C.: U.S. Department of Housing and Urban Development, Division of Housing and Demographic Analysis, Office of Economic Affairs.

Burt, M. R., and B. E. Cohen. 1988. "Feeding the Homeless: A Manageable Problem and Solution." Backgrounder Update No. 44. Washington, D.C.: Urban Institute.

Butler, Stuart. 1989. "The Federal Role in Low-Income Housing." Paper presented at the Federal National Mortgage Association Conference, Translating Housing Needs into Shelter: Strategies for the 1990s, Washington, January.

Downs, Anthony. 1983. *Rental Housing in the 1980s*. Washington, D.C.: Brookings Institution.

Gallion, Arthur B., and Simon Eisner. 1975. *The Urban Pattern: City Planning and Design*. 3d ed. New York: Van Nostrand.

Hendershott, Patrick H., and Kevin E. Villani. 1977. *Regulation and Reform of the Housing Finance System*, Washington, D.C.: American Enterprise Institute.

Irby, Iredia. 1986. "Attaining the Housing Goal?" Unpublished paper. Washington, D.C.: U.S. Department of Housing and Urban Development, Division of Housing and Demographic Analysis, Office of Economic Affairs.

Kennedy, Stephen, and M. Finkel. 1987. *Report of First Year Findings for the Freestanding Housing Voucher Demonstration*. Washington, D.C.: U.S. Department of Housing and Urban Development, Office of Policy Development and Research.

Kingsley, G. Thomas, Sheila Kirby, and W. Eugene Rizor. 1982. *Housing Allowance Program Administration: Findings from the Supply Experiment*, N-1846-HUD. Santa Monica: Rand Corporation.

Kingsley, G. Thomas, and P. M. Schlegel. 1982. *Housing Allowances and Administrative Efficiency*, N-1741-HUD. Santa Monica: Rand Corporation.

Levine, Martin. 1982. *Housing Assistance Program Options*. Washington, D.C.: Congressional Budget Office.

Lowry, Ira S., ed. 1983. *Experimenting with Housing Allowances: The Final Report of the Housing Assistance Supply Experiment*. Cambridge: Oeleschlager, Gunn and Hain.

Mayo, Stephen K., and J. Barnbrock. 1985. "Rental Housing Subsidy Programs in West Germany and the United States: A Comparative Program Evaluation." In *U.S. and West German Housing Markets*, ed. K. Stahl and R. Struyk. Washington, D.C.: Urban Institute Press.

Mayo, Stephen K., Shirley Mansfield, David Warner, and Richard Zwetchkenbaum. 1980. *Housing Allowances and Other Housing Assistance Programs—A Comparison Based on the Housing Allowance Demand Experiment, Part 2: Cost and Efficiency*. Cambridge, Mass.: Abt Associates.

Murray, Michael P. 1983. "Subsidized and Unsubsidized Housing Starts: 1961–1977." *Review of Economics and Statistics*, 65 (Nov.): 590–97.

National Housing Task Force. 1988. *A Decent Place to Live: The Report of the National Housing Task Force*. Washington.

Newman, Sandra J., and Ann B. Schnare. 1986. *Reassessing Shelter Assistance in America*, Washington, D.C.: Urban Institute Press.

Newman, Sandra J., and Ann B. Schnare. 1988. *Subsidizing Shelter*, 58. Washington, D.C.: Urban Institute Press.

Office of Policy Development and Research. 1982. "Alternative Operating Subsidy Systems for the Public Housing Program." Chapter 10 in *Private Market Operating Cost Data*. Washington, D.C.: U.S. Department of Housing and Urban Development.

Office of Policy Development and Research. 1986. "Housing Vouchers and Rental Housing Markets." Unpublished paper. Washington, D.C.: U.S. Department of Housing and Urban Development.

President's Commission on Housing. 1982. *The Report of the President's Commission on Housing*. Washington, D.C.

Schnare, Ann B., et al. 1982. *The Costs of HUD Multifamily Programs*. Washington, D.C.: Urban Systems Research and Engineering, U.S. Department of Housing and Urban Development.

Seidel, Stephen R. 1978. *Housing Costs and Government Regulations: Confronting the Regulatory Maze*. New Brunswick, N.J.: Center for Urban Policy Research, Rutgers University.

Semer, Milton P., et al. 1976. "Evolution of Federal Legislative Policy in Housing: Housing Credits." In *Housing in the Seventies: Working Papers*. Washington, D.C.: U.S. Department of Housing and Urban Development, National Housing Policy Review.

Simonson, J. 1981. "Measuring Inadequate Housing Through Use of the Annual Housing Survey." Washington, D.C.: U.S. Department of Housing and Urban Development, Office of Policy Development and Research.

Struyk, Raymond J. 1980. *A New System for Public Housing: Salvaging a National Resource*. Washington, D.C.: Urban Institute.

Struyk, Raymond J., and Marc Bendick, Jr. 1981. *Housing Vouchers for the Poor: Lessons from a National Experiment*. Washington, D.C.: Urban Institute Press.

Struyk, Raymond J., Neil Mayer, and John A. Tuccillo. 1983. *Federal Housing Policy at President Reagan's Midterm*. Washington, D.C.: Urban Institute Press.

Struyk, Raymond J., Margery A. Turner, and Makiko Ueno. 1988. *Future U.S. Housing Policy*. Washington, D.C.: Urban Institute Press.

Swan, Craig. 1973. "Housing Subsidies and Housing Starts." *American Real Estate and Urban Economics Association Journal* 1 (Fall): 119–40.

Tuccillo, John A., with John L. Goodman. 1983. *Housing Finance: A Changing System in the Reagan Era*. Washington, D.C.: Urban Institute Press.

U.S. Bureau of the Census. 1975. *Historical Statistics of the United States: Colonial Times to 1970*. Washington, D.C.: U.S. Department of Commerce.

U.S. Bureau of the Census. 1982. *Annual Housing Survey*, 1980, Part A: General Housing Characteristics. Washington, D.C.: U.S. Department of Commerce.

U.S. Congressional Budget Office. 1987. "Net Additional Households Assisted, Level of Funding, and Outlays for Housing Assistance Programs, 1977–1988." Memorandum, Congress of the United States.

U.S. Congressional Budget Office. 1988. *Current Housing Problems and Possible Federal Responses*. Congress of the United States.

Wallace, James E., et al. 1981. *Participation and Benefits in the Urban Section 8 Program: New Construction and Existing Housing*. Cambridge, Mass.: Abt Associates.

Weicher, J. C. 1982. *The Relationship Between Subsidized Housing Production and Loss Rates Within Metropolitan Areas*. Project Report, Contract Number 1481-01, Washington, D.C.: Urban Institute.

Weicher, J. C. 1988. "The Voucher/Production Debate." Unpublished paper for the MIT Housing Policy Project.

Woodfill, Barbara. 1971. *New York City's Mitchell-Lama Program: Middle Income Housing?*. R-786-NYC, New York: Rand Corporation.

Zigas, Barry. 1989. "The Federal Role in Low-Income Housing." Paper presented at the Federal National Mortgage Association Conference, Translating Housing Needs into Shelter: Strategies for the 1990s, Washington, January.

8 *Richard Hula*

Alternative Management Strategies in Public Housing

Since its inception, the U.S. public housing system has been mired in contro-versy. Early criticism was rooted both in ideological objections to government-provided housing, and a more pragmatic concern as to whether government had the expertise to do it. Each strand of this critique survives today, re-inforced by a very widely held view that public housing is little short of a monstrous failure. Such charges come not only from those long hostile to the program, but also from many past supporters. Indeed, some of the program's most vociferous critics are its major beneficiaries, public housing residents.[1] Specific complaints such as substandard construction, physical deterioration, and social disorganization are well known. Drug use, violent crime, and van-dalism are seen as epidemic. In spite of significant federal subsidies, a number of large local housing authorities are essentially bankrupt. Multibillion-dollar modernization programs have failed to arrest physical deterioration of the stock. Perhaps the most dramatic evidence of failure is provided by empty, uninhabitable buildings in cities notoriously short of low-income housing. For example, the Chicago Housing Authority reports that in spite of a waiting list of over 40,000 people, one-sixth of all CHA apartments (6,000 units) are vacant due to deteriorated conditions (Planning 1988).

For some, the best solution to the crisis in public housing is the example of

Richard Hula is Associate Professor at the Institute for Urban Studies at the University of Maryland.

Pruitt Igoe in St. Louis. Here the St. Louis Public Housing Authority deemed a large complex beyond redemption and simply blew it up. There are, however, compelling reasons to reject this view. First, not all public housing is in a state of such extreme crisis. Some local housing authorities do provide decent housing to low-income individuals and families. Second and even more compelling, is the fact that the public housing stock is a genuine social resource. The 1.3 million units of public housing represent a 75-billion-dollar public investment, and make up a significant proportion of the total low-income housing stock (NAHRO 1988). Public housing accounts for between five and 10 percent of all rental housing in some large cities (Ostrowski 1984). Finally, it should be stressed that even with its negative image, demand for public housing generally exceeds available units. It has been estimated that in 1987 more than 800,000 qualified families were on waiting lists for public housing. These families face an average waiting period of 13 months. In a number of cities this waiting period is measured in terms of years (Matuief 1987). To seek to dismantle the public housing system is to ignore both past investment and future potential.

For almost twenty years, policy makers have sought to devise rational policy that could stem the decline of this housing resource. Initially, many saw the problems of public housing as a direct result of insufficient funding, and argued that increased appropriations would lead to dramatic improvements in the system. Congress has approved significant funds to public housing through a system of operating subsidies and modernization programs. The impact of these efforts has convinced most observers that increasing expenditures alone is unlikely to generate long-term, self-sustaining improvement. Although there is little question that any serious effort to upgrade public housing will require increased investment, housing experts are virtually unanimous in the view that if long-term improvement is to occur, significant changes in the organization and management of the system are also required.

Alternative Strategies for Improvement

This chapter explores several strategies that have been put forward to improve public housing management. Common to each is the belief that the private sector is the appropriate source of reform.[2] The specific link between the reform and the private sector varies. It is sometimes indirect, with the market (and market theory) serving primarily as a conceptual framework for governmental solutions. Witness how often policy makers stress market values such as efficiency and incentives for housing managers. We are often told that if only local housing authorities could act more like private business, public management would surely improve. In contrast, other reform proposals call for a fundamental change in the organization of public housing.

Specific reform strategies can be placed on continuum defined by the degree of privatization proposed. One end of this continuum is defined by fairly modest proposals to borrow specific administrative practices from the private sector. For example, computer and information management technology, developed largely in the private sector, has been widely adopted by local housing authorities. Local authorities have relied on private firms for a number of support services, particularly the construction of new housing. Such borrowing, however, does not challenge the formal status of public housing as a public program.

Other reform proposals seek to manipulate incentives facing housing managers. The goal is to create a market-like environment in which housing managers behave as rational economic maximizers rather than public bureaucrats. For example, efforts have been made to use formulas to compute subsidy payments which reward local-level cost-containment. Once again, such innovations do not threaten the public nature of the program.

Some reform proposals do, however, blur the public status of public housing. Policy makers seem increasingly interested in hybrid management strategies which combine elements of public and private control. For example, local authorities have signed contracts with for-profit and nonprofit organizations to manage projects. Of particular interest is the concept of resident or tenant management. In this case, the local housing authority contracts with tenants to manage their own units. Although each of these management forms retains a commitment to public housing, each involves a significant devolution of authority to private hands.

The most extreme form of privatization involves the dismantling of the public housing system by putting the public stock into private hands. This is essentially the British government's policy of selling Council Housing units to tenants. Although actual efforts to privatize public housing in the United States have been quite modest in scope, they have generated a great deal of interest. At the federal level HUD has sought and received limited congressional authority to sell some units. Several local tenant management corporations have expressed a strong desire to purchase their projects.

An Introduction to the Public Housing System

The form and structure of public housing in the United States has undergone a significant transformation in the past 30 years, shifting from a program targeted to moderate income whites to one targeted to low-income minority families.[3] This transformation was in part the result of economic and demographic changes occurring after the Second World War. War-generated restrictions on home construction, which had inflated middle-class demand for public housing, were removed. Many higher income families in public housing sought newer housing in the private sector. Federal housing policy also sought to narrow and target eligibility for public housing to low-income families. The speed of transformation was enhanced by the decision of many nonminority families to leave public housing in the face of increasing social and political change.

The emerging emphasis on housing very low-income families dramatically reduced local authority revenue. Whereas in the early years of the program local authorities had been quite successful in meeting operating expenses through rents, by the late 1960s some authorities reported they were no longer able to do so. In response, federal operating subsidies were targeted to local authorities facing financial difficulties. Through the 1970s, Congress further reduced the power of local authorities to set rents and give preference to any but the lowest income applicants. Although the federal legislation that put these rules into effect also increased subsidy payments, the net revenue effect on authorities was negative.[4] In addition to an overall decline in the economic health of local authorities, these regulations had the effect of substantially reducing local administrative autonomy. Although the resulting pattern of "regulatory federalism" was seen by a number of observers, particularly at the local level, as an overly intrusive federal role, resistance to the new rules was largely ineffective.

Changing federal policies also had a significant impact on the social and political dynamics within local housing authorities. Once again, this effect was often seen as negative since many authorities felt poorly equipped to meet the new demands placed on them. In some cases, even the physical stock was seen as inappropriate. Poorly designed high-rise projects fell into disrepair. Demand for large apartments quickly exceeded supply. Increasingly, exacting regulations limiting local power to deny admission to public housing reduced the ability of local authorities to deny housing to "problem" tenants. As the number of such tenants increased, local managers argued that public housing projects were difficult to manage.

The ability of local authorities to be good managers within the constraints imposed by federal policy has become a matter of some debate. Kuhn (1988) argues, for example, that bad management was actually imposed on local authorities as a matter of public policy. Many observers argue, however, that local authorities had some responsibility for the problems of public housing. Bratt (1985) notes HUD's inspector general reports suggesting that financial management in many PHAs ranged from uninformed to criminally fraudulent.

As problems in the public housing system escalated, federal policy makers sought alternative strategies for providing housing assistance to low-income citizens. Severe limits imposed by the Nixon administration reduced new starts in conventional public housing from 104,000 in 1970 to less than 19,000 in 1974 (Judd 1988). Section 8 housing subsidies, introduced in the Community Development Block Grant of 1974, quickly replaced conventional public housing as a source of new assisted housing. Section 8 programs stressed subsidies to private owners rather than public ownership. By 1979, the Section 8 program was in the aggregate as large as conventional public housing (Struyk 1980:165). Henceforth, the problems of public housing would be the maintenance of existing stock rather than its expansion.

Improving Public Housing Management

In the early 1970s, HUD was under significant pressure to revise its subsidy strategy to encourage local management efficiency, and thus lower overall subsidy payments. The outcome of this effort was the implementation of the Performance Funding System (PFS). The PFS computed operating subsidies as the difference between an authority's approved funding level and its expected level of revenue. Approved funding levels were taken as the financial needs of a well managed project.[5] The subsidy ceiling imposes a direct constraint on public housing authority spending. Such constraints are seen as analogous to market forces which drive efforts to minimize costs. In addition to such limits, PFS also contains positive incentives for good management. Specifically, local authorities are allowed to retain unused operating funds.[6] Thus, it is to the economic advantage of the housing authority to meet its basic management functions at a cost below the level specified in the PFS formula. Some elements of the PFS system have been warmly accepted by local housing managers. The most important of these is the stability that the system brings to the funding process. Since PFS greatly reduced the uncertainty surrounding annual operating subsidies, the ability of housing managers to plan was significantly enhanced. Other aspects of PFS, however, have met with much less enthusiasm. Of foremost concern is the level of funding. A number of large public housing authorities saw a relatively dramatic reduction in the level of subsidies following the implementation of PFS. The emphasis on the base year of 1972 had the effect of locking in subsidies to that level. Ironically, those authorities that minimized costs during the base year continue to receive the lowest subsidy. By providing a single set of subsidy payments, the PFS introduced an inflexible allocation system. Often fairly clear distinctions between the needs of different authorities are not recognized. In addition, changing needs are not anticipated. As an example, Kuhn (1988) cites the failure of PFS to fund project security programs.

Consistent with the underlying logic of PFS, HUD designed and implemented a variety of programs to improve public housing through specific management innovations. Although they varied significantly in structure and scope, they shared a number of important assumptions. Each defined management as infrastructure critical to planned upgrading and physical modernization of the public housing stock. As a result, modernization funds, were sometimes technically a separate allocation, but often were linked to participation in management improvement programs. Each assumed that public housing managers faced similar problems, and that there ought to be generic management strategies applicable to a great number of housing authorities. It was assumed that once developed, management techniques could be used throughout the system. Once again, the private sector was seen primarily as the appropriate model for the design of new management strategies. Thus, the identification and implementation of private sector management techniques became an important goal.

HUD's first management program, the Housing Management Improvement Program (HMIP), was implemented in 1972. This was a small demonstration project involving thirteen local authorities. Each of the participating authorities was expected to produce a comprehensive management plan.[7] Particular emphasis was given to the development of specific management tools which could be utilized by other authorities. In all, 160 documents or "products" were made available to other PHAs by demonstration authorities. Researchers at the Urban Institute suggest that these projects had, at best, a very modest impact; and they were unable to find any significant utilization of results by other authorities. Successor programs emphasized the development of management plans for specific authorities.[8]

The result of these HUD programs is difficult to summarize. Although there is some modest evidence that these programs led to some authority-specific improvement, the search for transferable management technology proved consistently elusive. This suggests that such technology may not exist. As a result, many have sought answers for the ills of public housing that extend beyond traditional approaches to public housing. By and large, these more dramatic proposals have come from those outside the mainstream of public housing administration, and have sought to transfer authority away from such administration. Often they come from the residents of the housing themselves.

Alternative Strategies in St. Louis

While every housing authority has had a unique history, the St. Louis Public Housing Authority exhibits a pattern common to many large authorities (Meehan 1979). Following years of relative prosperity, the authority began to experience significant economic and social stress in the 1960s. Efforts to raise revenue through rent increases touched off a rent strike by public housing residents in February of 1969. By the time the strike was settled in October of that year, the authority was near economic collapse.[9] Under the terms of the settlement, the St. Louis Housing Authority implemented a holding-company philosophy in which the authority acted as an umbrella organization for a set of largely independent operating units. A major transfer of authority to tenants organizations was accomplished through the creation of a Tenant Advisory Board (TAB). Composed of representatives from various tenant organizations, TAB was given seats on the authority board and thus power to make policy. Actual project management was provided under contract by several types of private organizations including for-profit private businesses (usually real estate firms), religious nonprofits, and tenant management corporations.[10]

Private Firms

Although the HUD management programs had long attempted to borrow general techniques from the private sector, contracting with private firms to manage public housing represented a significant extension of efforts to direct private sector expertise to problems of public housing. Such contracting was seen as a way to introduce market discipline to the management of public housing. Competition for management contracts was expected to maximize efficiency and innovation. Obviously such market mechanisms were thought to be most relevant to for-profit private firms but it was hoped that cost discipline would also be introduced by nonprofit organizations.

Only very limited data exist on the impact of private firm management in St. Louis. Meehan (1979) argues that even where data exist, it is almost certainly misleading to compare privately and publicly managed units since particular management forms are associated with particular types of units. Indeed, the critical variable in predicting management efficiency is the nature of the housing being managed:

Very roughly, and to some extent impressionistically, the public-versus-private character of management is far less important to the quality of operations than the amount of resources available, the quality of the initial design and construction, and, of course, the type of tenant occupying the unit—whether elderly or family. Most of the indicators of management performance commonly used in public (and private) housing—occupancy, administrative cost, maintenance effectiveness, collection losses, accounts receivable, tenant complaints, and so on—seem most influenced by the elderly-versus-family character of the occupants. (Meehan 1979:155)

To further support his claim that occupant characteristics overwhelm management characteristics, Meehan cites a HUD performance assessment undertaken in 1975–76. The assessment was based on percentage of rents collected monthly, percentage of units rented, rent roll, number of annual review, the ratio of expenditures for ordinary maintenance to budget amount and proportion of maintenance time spent at productive work. Positive and negative points were allocated on the basis of performance on each indicator. In 1976, HUD published statistics on a sample of fourteen large housing authorities.

Seven had a positive score, seven negative. The average score for elderly units was +82. For family units the average score was −503.

Although the St. Louis experience generated some interest in private management, its use remained very limited. A 1982 HUD evaluation examined in some detail 19 of the 21 sites in which for-profit firms had been granted contracts to manage public housing for a period of at least one year. The privately managed sites were compared to a control group (chosen on the basis of similarity) on 12 cost indicators and 29 performance indicators. Because of widely recognized differences in costs, the analysis was reported separately for rural projects, urban elderly projects, and urban family projects. Few differences in performance or cost indicators were found among rural projects. Costs were reported to be 28 percent higher at privately managed urban elderly units. Performance measures were similar in these units. For family units management, costs were higher in contract projects, although the differences were not nearly as large as those in elderly projects. In the family units, performance indicators were also lower in private contract units. Differences were particularly clear for indicators of rent collection and occupancy rates.[11]

While the major focus of the HUD private contract evaluation was the aggregate impact on local housing authority costs, it also provided insight into the impact of private contracting on the distribution of costs and benefits in the housing projects. Not surprisingly, the increased costs of managing urban units is primarily a function of management fee. For urban family units costs, administrative costs were reported to be $5.00 per unit greater than conventional sites. For elderly sites, this difference was $28.00. In each of the three types of contract sites employee benefits per unit were lower than in similar conventional sites. Thus, private contract management generated a redistribution of benefits toward the managing firm, with little aggregate benefit to the local housing authority or residents.

Tenant Management

A second alternative management strategy, tenant management, was also introduced by the St. Louis Housing Authority. Under tenant management, day-to-day administration of the project was to be the responsibility of managers selected by and responsible to an elected board of resident directors. As with contracts with private firms, tenant management was based on a sharing of power and responsibility with the local authority. However, the local authority continued to retain significant management responsibility. The broad pattern of joint responsibilities in the administration of the projects is presented in Table 8.1. The model outlined in Table 8.1 has been widely cited, and has been used to define tenant management in a number of public housing sites.

The goal of tenant management was strongly supported by most leaders

Table 8.1. Division of Responsibility Under Tenant Management Demonstration Prototype

Tasks	TMC	TMC and PHA	PHA
Tenant selection and screening		X	
Development of annual operating budget		X	
Allocation of operating funds among selected budget line items	X		
Preparation and disbursement of TMC payroll			X
Provision to TMC of incentives to encourage cost savings and discourage overexpenditures			X
Leasing vacant apartments	X		
Institution of eviction proceedings and documentation of relevant information	X		
Processing of evictions, including legal proceedings and physical removal when appropriate			X
Physical collection of rents			X
Follow up on rent delinquencies	X		
Conduct of annual rent reviews	X		
Processing of work orders for maintenance service requests	X		
Inspection and preparation of vacant apartments	X		
Supervision of on-site maintenance personnel	X		
Hiring, firing, and supervision of management personnel	X		

Source: From MDRC, 1981, Table 2-1, p. 24, and used with permission of MDRC.

of the St. Louis rent strike, as well as many other parties in the conflict. Many saw it, not only as an alternative management strategy, but as a process of community empowerment. Kolodny argues, however, that support for the concept was also bred from a sense of desperation:

According to most accounts, management by the tenants was entertained in St. Louis as a gesture to keep the peace and because they were the only potentially legitimate force left. Many informed observers doubted that any conventional public housing approach would be able to reassert order and stability in a situation that had gotten far out of hand. (1983:9)

Like private contracting, it was hoped that tenant management would improve the quality of real estate management by a shifting of incentives facing managers. However, these incentives were not those of the market per se, but did involve a number of market-like mechanisms. This included, for example, efforts to tie self-interest to management outcomes since resident managers were consumers as well as suppliers in public housing. It was also expected that tenant managers would better represent and be more accessible to the larger resident community. This "closeness" would ensure that policy decisions as to the allocation of scarce resources would more likely maximize resident preferences. Thus, tenant managers should be more efficient than conventional managers. Finally, it was thought that TMCs would have a number of strategic advantages over conventional managers, since residents would likely have greater knowledge of the local environment, and thus be better able to implement policy. In particular, tenants ought to be better able to deal with disruptive or noncooperative tenants.

In addition to the traditional management functions, supporters of tenant management saw it as a mechanism for addressing fundamental factors in the decline of public housing. Tenant management was seen as a way to create and sustain economic opportunities for residents. Such opportunities might come from both the management unit itself and other related organizations. Finally, some saw in tenant management a means to social and community mobilization, leading to the development of a wide range of social services within the housing project.

Organization and training of the tenant management corporations began in 1971 with financial support from the Ford Foundation. In 1973, contracts were signed between two tenant management corporations and the St. Louis Housing Authority to assume management responsibility for 1,256 family units. By the end of 1976, three more TMC contracts had been signed, bringing some 3,000 units under tenant management, almost half of the total units in the St. Louis Housing Authority.

The National Tenant Demonstration

Based largely on the perceived promise of tenant management in St. Louis, HUD and the Ford Foundation agreed in 1976 to sponsor a National Tenant Management Demonstration to assess the general applicability of tenant management in public housing.[12] Seven project sites were selected to participate in the demonstration, although one was dropped relatively quickly. The six active sites included A. Harry Moore and Curries Woods (Jersey City), Iroquois Homes (Louisville), Que-View (New Haven), Callipoe (New Orleans), Ashanti (Rochester). At each site, it took significantly longer to recruit and train a cadre of tenant managers than expected. Although tenant management was in place in five of the six sites by the end of the demonstration, two functioned less than a year.

An extensive evaluation effort was built into the design of the demonstration. Obviously, the quality of real estate management under tenant management contracts was an important concern but other potential impacts of tenant management were included, such as the implementation of physical improvement plans, efforts to increase tenant employment, and overall satisfaction. The importance assigned to such factors is revealed by HUD's selection of

Table 8.2. Real Estate Management Indicators for Demonstration Tenant
Management Corporations [a]

	TMC Site					
Indicators	Jersey City (A. Harry Moore)	Jersey City (Curries Wood)	Louisville	New Haven	New Orleans	Rochester
Average rent due						
Entire	+	−	−	+	+	*
Pre/Post	+	NA	−	+	+	*
Average rent collected						
Entire	*	*	*	+	+	+
Pre/Post	*	NA	*	+	+	*
Rent collection rate						
Entire	+	*	+	−	*	*
Pre/Post	*	NA	+	−	*	*
Percent units owing more than one month rent						
Entire	+	*	+	−	*	+
Pre/Post	*	NA	*	−	*	*
Vacancy rate						
Entire	+	+	+	+	+	+
Pre/Post	+	NA	*	+	*	+
Vacant unit preparation rate						
Entire	+	*	+	−	+	+
Pre/Post	+	NA	+	*	*	+
Routine job completion rate						
Entire	−	−	+	NA	−	+
Pre/Post	−	NA	*	NA	−	+

Source: Data from MDRC, 1981, pp. 127–163.
[a] (+) statistically significant improvement (−) statistically significant decline. (*) no change. (NA) not ascertained

the Manpower Demonstration Research Corporation (MDRC) to implement the evaluation. The MDRC was experienced in both demonstrations and manpower programs, but had little expertise in housing or real estate management.

The evaluation of real estate management skills centered on the analysis of a number of specific indicators. An overview of the outcomes is provided in Table 8.2. Although the pattern is clearly mixed, the data show that a statistically significant improvement in management services occurred over the length of the demonstration for 58 percent (23 of 40) of the indicators. In 32 percent of cases (13 of 40), an improvement occurred after a formal management contract was signed. Within this generally positive trend, there was significant variation across sites. A. Harry Moore (Jersey City), Rochester, and Louisville reported improvement on at least five of the seven management indicators. In contrast, New Haven reported a decline in three of the management indicators.[13] The MDRC evaluation concludes:

In comparison with their conventionally managed counterparts, the tenant management sites performed as well in all management areas. In essence, the weight of the evidence seems to indicate that public housing residents are fully capable of performing "hard" management tasks—the nuts and bolts of real estate management—at a level that seems comparable to that of conventional public housing managers. (MDRC 1981:163)

As has been noted, most supporters of tenant management see it as a means to ends beyond narrow real estate management. A key element of these extended goals was the successful implementation of modernization efforts. In addition to funds for management training and support, the demonstration sites received 15 million dollars of modernization funds, and additional support under HUD's Targeted Projects Program. There was widespread consensus among the designers of the demonstration that access to such funds was a means both to generate interest in the tenants and to grant credibility to the tenant management organization.

The impact of these modernization funds was ambiguous, both as an institution building device and as an implementation strategy. Although these expenditures almost certainly increased tenant interest, they also served to create a pattern of tension and conflict between local authorities and the TMC. Professionals in the local authorities sometimes felt under attack by "naive" residents. On the other hand, resident managers sometimes claimed excessive interference on the part of authority employees. Some of this tension was natural given the fact that, although described as a collaborative effort, it was the local authority which retained final authority and responsibility for modernization. The level of successful implementation of modernization projects is equally unclear. Although TMCs reported a fairly high percentage of modernization projects completed by the end of the demonstration, the largest and most important of these often were not. Some had hardly begun.

Tenant management also had an important economic development component. For most demonstration tenant management corporations job creation was limited to the TMC itself. The hope that residents might receive training and employment through modernization efforts was not realized. Obviously the stability of the employment that was created was closely tied to the stability of the TMC itself.

A final outcome measure considered by MDRC was resident response. Using survey data collected by the Urban Institute in 1976 and 1979, an effort was made to identify changes in resident perceptions associated with the ten-

Table 8.3. TMC Tenants' Evaluation of the TMC [a]

Tenant's Evaluation	Average or Percentage of Respondents	Number of Respondents
Overall		
Residents believing that TMC is able to get things done		
Yes	47.0	(62)
No	32.6	(43)
Don't know	20.4	(27)
Total	100.0	(132)
Residents believing that TMC has made things better for		
Most of the tenants	26.5	(35)
Some of the tenants	23.5	(31)
Few of the tenants	23.5	(31)
None of the tenants	9.8	(13)
Don't know	16.7	(22)
Total	100.0	(132)
TMC Versus Old Tenant Organization		
Residents believing that TMC represents tenants		
Better than old tenant organization	28.0	(37)
Same as old tenant organization	27.3	(36)
Worse than old tenant organization	18.1	(24)
Don't know	26.5	(35)
Total	100.0	(132)
Average Score [b]	1.13	(97)
TMC Versus PHA		
Residents who believe TMC is managing project		
Better than PHA	26.5	(35)
Same as PHA	34.1	(45)
Worse than PHA	22.0	(29)
Don't know	17.4	(23)
Total	100.0	(132)
Average Score [b]	1.06	(109)

Source: Adapted from MDRC, 1981, Table 7-18, p. 206. Data obtained from Suzanne B. Loux and Robert Sadacca, 1980, "Analysis of Changes at Tenant Management Demonstration Projects," Working Paper #1335, Washington, D.C.: Urban Institute. Used by permission.

[a]Limited to respondents who knew there was a TMC/tenant organization (N = 132).

[b]2 = better; 1 = same; 0 = worse.

Table 8.4. Estimated and Actual Costs Associated with Tenant Management Demonstration[a]

	Estimated Net Operating Costs	Actual Net Operating Costs	Increase	% Change
	For Entire Demonstration Period			
Jersey City				
A. Harry Moore	$2300	$3493	$1112	32%
Curries Woods	$2280	$3527	$1247	36%
Louisville	na	$1807		
New Haven	$1236	$1657	$421	25%
New Orleans	$1834	$2075	$241	13%
Rochester	$821	$1345	$524	39%
	For Contract Period Only			
Jersey City				
A. Harry Moore	$727	$1010	$283	28%
Curries Woods	na	na		
Louisville	na	na		
New Haven	na	na		
New Orleans	$549	$586	$37	7%
Rochester	$555	$899	$353	39%

Source: Data from MDRC, 1981, pp. 209–238.
[a]Reported in units of $1,000. Net operating costs calculated as total costs minus rents.

ant management experiment.[14] The survey data provide convincing evidence that tenant managers were quite visible to project residents. More than 75 percent of the respondents indicated that they knew of the tenant association. This compares with 32 percent of the residents in the control site claiming knowledge of existing tenant organizations. Moreover, residents see the tenant managers as having an impact on the administration of their housing project. Tenant management is clearly associated with perceived increase in rule enforcement.[15] Overall resident evaluation of tenant management is presented in Table 8.3. In general, residents saw tenant management in positive terms. More than 73 of the residents who knew about the tenant management organization felt that tenant managers had improved conditions for at least some residents. Sixty percent of residents surveyed felt that TMCs were doing as well or better than conventional management. Twenty-eight percent thought TMC did a better job representing their interests than did conventional managers. Finally, 47 percent of those who knew about the TMC thought it was an institution that could "get things done." In those projects having the most viable organizations (A. Harry Moore in Jersey City, Louisville, Rochester, and New Orleans), resident evaluations were much more positive.

In sum, the MDRC evaluation offers a modestly positive view of tenant management. Unfortunately such gains are not without cost. With two sets of data, Table 8.4 estimates these costs. The first compares an estimated total cost

figure if TMC systems had remained under conventional management with
actual costs for the full period of demonstration. The data show tenant management is more expensive than conventional management, sometimes dramatically so. The second set of data gives a similar overview of projected and
actual management costs for the period a TMC contract was in force. These
two sets of data attempt to differentiate start-up costs and recurring costs. If
these data are valid, two points seem clear. First, tenant management is expensive relative to conventional management. Second, tenant management is
likely to generate long-term cost increments, not only one-time start-up costs.

The MDRC concluded that tenant management is a "feasible alternative to
conventional public housing management under certain conditions." (MDRC
1981: 239) However, cost was cited as an important constraint since TMC
was generally seen as equal to but not clearly superior to conventional management. Finally the evaluation concludes that very specific conditions for
successful tenant management are required. These include the need for strong
indigenous leadership and a positive relationship between TMC leaders and
the local authority. The failure of tenant management in Sunrise Acres (Oklahoma City), Que-View (New Haven), and Currie Woods (Jersey City) was
seen largely as a function of these variables.

As the original demonstration was coming to an end, HUD made the decision to extend it an additional two years in the four sites where tenant
management seemed to be taking hold. Following the extension, a second
evaluation was authored by Robert Kolodny for the National Association for
Housing and Redevelopment Officers (NAHRO). This second effort was much
less systematic than that prepared by MDRC since the extension did not fund
the demonstration's large data collection component. This second evaluation,
however, did have the advantage of time whereas the earlier evaluation was
completed after most demonstration TMCs had been functioning for two years
at most, the latter observed the results of four to five operational years' experience. Thus, it was expected that the tenant management corporations ought to
have achieved a degree of maturity.

Consistent with the MDRC evaluation, Kolodny concludes that tenant administrators are capable real estate managers. He does, however, question
MDRC high estimates of both short- and long-term costs of tenant management. (See Table 8.4.) He suggests the MDRC findings are due more to the
availability of the funds than the need for the services they purchased. He notes
that tenant management corporations have been established in St. Louis and
other nondemonstration sites at very modest cost. For example, the Jersey City
Housing Authority introduced an additional tenant management corporation at
Montgomery Gardens using only normal operating funds. Total training costs
were $77,000 over a three-year period.

Kolodny stresses the importance of TMC activities other than real estate

Table 8.5. Summary of Non-real Estate Management
Functions of St. Louis TMC

Social Services
Four daycare centers
Share care center for infants
Social service directors
Comprehensive health center
Community center

Employment
Catering business
Chore services program
Janitorial company

Physical and Economic Development
Modernization of empty buildings in projects
Turnkey development of new housing
Management of new housing
Training for apprentices in building program
Development of local shopping mall
Renovation of local buildings for low income housing

Self-Sufficiency
Purchase $15,000 van
Capitalize janitorial company ($30,000)
Fund youth program ($15,000)
Subsidize daycare ($10,000)
Social service emergency fund ($1,500)
Fan purchase ($2,000)
Housing renovation ($11,000)
Salary supplements for TMC ($6,000)
Summer employment ($7,500)
Annual dinner ($4,000)

Source: Data from Kolodny, Robert, 1983 pp. 76–80.

management. He argues that the MDRC study underestimated the magnitude
of such efforts because the impacts of such activities evolve over a fairly long
period of time and are difficult to quantify. He cites the accomplishments
of the St. Louis tenant management corporations as evidence. These include
successes in the area of social services, employment, physical and economic
development, and self-sufficiency. Table 8.5 presents a description of some of
these activities.

Kolodny's report is significantly more enthusiastic about the prospects of
tenant management than the MDRC evaluation, due in part to the different
time frame of the two reports. The MDRC evaluation focuses on the short-
term impact of tenant management. At the time the MDRC concluded its

work, it was by no means clear that any of the TMCs would be able to be maintained. Kolodny had the advantage of several additional years of observation. More important than this difference, however, is the varying emphasis given to specific outcome measures. Kolodny sees tenant management as primarily a community empowerment program. The MDRC evaluation gives much more emphasis to the more limited conceptualization of tenant management as a real estate management strategy.

Recent evidence provided by Monti (1989) suggests that tenant management may indeed have significant potential as a community development strategy. He argues that two of the St. Louis tenant management corporations have had a significant role in creating the conditions leading to a revival of their neighborhood. However, Monti's work also underscores the difficulty of measuring the impact of tenant management on local economic development. Political and social development are even more elusive.[16]

Public Housing Initiatives in the Reagan Era

The election of Ronald Reagan in 1980 ushered in an intense debate over the future magnitude and strategy of almost all federal social welfare programs. Although the rhetoric of the administration was often more radical than its action, this was not true for housing and community development programs. From 1981 to 1988 overall HUD budget authority was reduced by over 40 percent, dropping from 4.59 percent of all federal spending to 1.31 percent. Assisted housing programs suffered even greater cuts, declining by over 70 percent. The Reagan administration effectively brought to a halt new construction of any type of new subsidized housing. Whereas the 1981 HUD budget called for a total 200,000 new assisted units, the 1988 budget called for only 5,000 new family units of public housing and 9,500 units for the elderly and handicapped.[17]

Reagan administration officials were particularly hostile to the concept of conventional public housing, arguing that the federal government's limited responsibility in the area of low-income housing should be met through a set of user subsidies in the private housing market. Indeed, the site-specific subsidies created by the Section 8 program were also criticized as an inefficient intrusion into the market. In its place, a voucher system in which housing consumers were free to choose their residence was proposed. Such a voucher plan was begun as a demonstration project in 1983, and made permanent in the Housing and Community Development Act of 1987. By the end of the Reagan years significant resources had been shifted from the Section 8 housing to vouchers.

Specific federal policy toward conventional public housing remained relatively unchanged. Modest operating subsidies (approximately $1.5 billion annually) continued to be allocated by a PFS formula. Although the formula was modified somewhat in 1987, there is little evidence of any significant change in the direction or impact of the subsidies. Beginning in 1980, local authorities were required by the Comprehensive Improvement Assistance Program (CAIP) to develop five-year plans for addressing major modernization needs. As part of the CAIP plan, authorities were to outline management strategies to maintain these improvements. Such planning has had relatively little impact, however, since modernization funding remained unpredictable and generally quite low, seldom exceeding more than a billion dollars. As a result, most modernization funds continue to be targeted to emergency repairs rather than comprehensive redevelopment (Ostrowski 1984). Predictably, the declining condition of the public housing stock has continued, with recent estimates of modernization needs exceeding $20 billion (NAHRO 1988).

Federal officials have looked with interest and approval at the British experiment of selling discounted public housing to residents. Although it is obvious that public housing in Great Britain is quite different than in the United States, the British privatization movement has been cited as a model for how the federal government might both arrest the decline of the U.S. public housing stock and free itself from an unwanted responsibility.

Many proponents of privatization have given a particularly strong endorsement to tenant management. Conservative scholars and policy makers see it as a first step toward privatization. Stuart Butler, Director of Domestic Policy at the Heritage Foundation, has made this strategy explicit:

A British style ownership program with tenant management as an intermediate stage, could be an effective method of turning public housing tenants into homeowners. . . . Once several successful demonstration projects have been undertaken and publicized, the administration should be able to count on wider political support, especially near beneficiary groups, for a more extensive program. (Silver, McDonald, and Ortiz 1985:213)

Congressional support for tenant management was made explicit in the Housing and Community Development Act of 1987, which for the first time identified tenant management as a federal policy goal and provided a total of five million dollars for a series of 50 technical assistance grants to tenant council and resident management corporations. The legislation also provided for the purchase of public housing projects by residents.[18]

Although there is little doubt that conservatives are most supportive of tenant management, the concept has also found some favor with liberal politicians. For example, the District of Columbia's congressional delegate Walter Fauntroy cosponsored legislation with then-Representative Jack Kemp to encourage tenant management. In fact, the liberal Fauntroy joined the conservative Kemp in promoting legislation to permit the outright sale of public housing units.

For the most part liberals are significantly less enthusiastic about privatization, stressing instead the community empowerment aspects of tenant management.

Current implementation of tenant management was spurred by a 1.9 million-dollar demonstration grant by the AMOCO foundation to the conservative National Center for Neighborhood Development. The grant supports a tenant management demonstration in twelve public housing projects. Interestingly, about half of the projects included in the first year of the demonstration have a significant history of tenant management. A. Harry Moore (Jersey City), B.W. Cooper (New Orleans), and Iroquois Homes (Louisville) were veterans of the earlier HUD demonstration. Cochran and Carr Square in St. Louis were formed after the public housing rent strike. Bromley Heath in Boston was formed by OEO funds in the early 1970s. More recently formed TMC corporations in the project include Kenilworth-Parkside (Washington D.C.), LeClaire Courts (Chicago), Montgomery Gardens and Booker T. Washington (Jersey City), Lakeview Terrace (Cleveland), St. Barnard and St. Thomas (New Orleans).

The major focus of the AMOCO demonstration is the development of appropriate training materials for resident management corporations in various stages of development. The curriculum is composed of a series of modules which are targeted to organizations at various levels of development. Initial units explore the formation of tenant organizations. Later units review real estate management practices. The curriculum assumes that ownership is a natural step in the evolution of tenant management. In addition to the training program, some energy has been devoted to further evaluation of tenant management outcomes. The NCNE hopes to commission a series of rigorous evaluations of established tenant management sites. To date, however, only one such review has been published, a cost-benefit analysis of Kenilworth-Parkside in Washington D.C.

Kenilworth-Parkside has been widely cited as the premier example of a successful transition to tenant management. This 464-unit project located in southeast Washington implemented tenant management in 1982. There is little dispute about the poor conditions in the project in the years preceding tenant management. Project managers were unable to provide even such basic services as hot water and heat.[19] Numerous reports cite dramatic improvement following the implementation of tenant management. These include not only improved real estate management reflected in rent collection, vacancy rates, and the control of vandalism, but in the development of social and educational services. Successful economic development and employment programs are also reported.

Coopers and Lybrand, under contract to NCNE, prepared a cost-benefit analysis of Kenilworth-Parkside. Unfortunately, much of the expected rigor of the proposed analysis fell victim to a lack of appropriate data.[20] The analysis was limited to specific costs and benefits of tenant management which accrued to the District of Columbia government, and could be quantified in terms of dollars. The report identified five "benefit streams" (NCNE 1986): 1) increased rents (estimated by the difference between average rents at Kenilworth-Parkside and the Authority as a whole); 2) increased rental income due to reduced vacancies (again estimated as the difference between the Kenilworth-Parkside rate and the Authority average); 3) a reduction in resident public assistance through job creation and economic development efforts; 4) an increase in tax revenue from employed residents; and 5) a higher level of service to residents in the project provided by an increased number of persons working there. The report argues that while each of the benefit streams is conceptually distinct, one need estimate only the monetary value of the first and second, since the last three may be seen as the effects of reinvesting this revenue into the project.[21] The total estimated value returned by the tenant management corporation from 1982–1985 was $1,978,669. Projections to 1991 suggest a benefit stream of $5,713,722.

Estimating costs of tenant management proved to be even more problematic than estimating benefits. In fact, necessary data simply did not exist. The Coopers and Lybrand study was forced to use estimates based on average costs reported in the 1976 HUD demonstration. Unfortunately, these data were not at all stable across projects. Therefore, mean values are not likely to be valid estimates. Even more important, however, is the omission of modernization, and other "off budget" funds such as grants in the estimates of cost. The Coopers and Lybrand report justifies this omission by noting that until 1985 the TMC had responsibility only for operating expenses. However, this ignores previous research that the availability of such funds, whoever ultimately controls them, will likely have significant impact on the maintenance and growth of tenant management.

Although the quantitative evidence on the benefits of resident management in Kenilworth-Parkside is certainly open to criticism, it seems difficult to argue with the overall conclusion that there has in fact been a dramatic and positive change in the project. As is often the case, however, a policy success can often raise more questions than it answers. Most obvious is whether this is a success which can be maintained and replicated in other public housing projects. Less obvious issues center on the underlying criteria used to measure success, in particular the vision which drives the implementation of new tenant management corporations.

The Future of Tenant Management and Ownership

Popular accounts continue to provide tantalizing anecdotal evidence that tenant management is a viable alternative to public management. Nevertheless, caution is in order. Although popular reports stress success, it is equally clear that tenant management is quite difficult to implement, and may be even more difficult to maintain. Of the seven original 1976 HUD demonstration sites, only four ever became viable. Two of these have since lost their contract and are presently seeking to regain it through the AMOCO demonstration. While two St. Louis groups are cited as having great success, three other tenant management corporations established in St. Louis have failed (Kolodny 1983; Monti 1988). Echoing the MDRC study, Robert Rigby, director of the Jersey City Public Housing Authority, argues that for tenant management to succeed three fundamental conditions must be met. These include a stable, well-trained leadership; a supportive relationship between the PHA and the tenant association; and sufficient resources for capital improvement.[22] If Rigby is correct, several important conclusions emerge. First, tenant management cannot act as a substitute for investment. Tenant management almost certainly demands an initial increase in necessary resources, although it may lead to a more efficient long-term use of social resources. Unfortunately, there is simply no reliable data which would permit a realistic estimate of either short- or long-term costs of tenant management.

Rigby's observations also raise the possibility that certain elements of successful tenant management, in particular, political leadership are beyond the direct manipulation of policy makers. Reading reports of tenant management, one is struck by the critical importance of indigenous leadership, and the prodigious effort required by that leadership. While some leaders often assert that required skills are common, the evidence on this point is far from convincing.

A related question is whether or not tenant management can survive its original leadership. Once again, there is little relevant data since most successful tenant management corporations continue to be headed by "first-generation" leadership. Note that the issue of continuity is a bit more subtle than simply whether new leaders will emerge as housing managers. Also at stake is whether the community based nature of tenant management can be maintained. As tenants display the ability to manage their own property it is possible that tenant management might evolve into a form of conventional management in which PHA employees are also residents. Kolodny (1986) suggests that such a tendency might exist in maturing tenant management corporations.

Contributing to the confusion surrounding efforts to evaluate tenant management is a fairly muddled conceptual understanding of what it is, and what it is expected to produce. The structural diversity and level of responsibility assigned to tenant management organizations has been noted. For any systematic evaluation of tenant management some measure of definitional order will need to be imposed on the cases being analyzed. Similarly, there is no consensus as to the goals of tenant management. Efforts implemented in the 1970s usually embraced a community empowerment perspective. From this view, public housing remains a collective good, although the collectivity may shift from the broader society to the resident community. More recent converts to tenant management see it as a first step in the process of individual ownership, a bridge leading from public to private housing.

This conceptual ambiguity is more than a simple intellectual distraction for it provides important parameters defining the current debate on public housing reform. For example, it helps to clarify the basis of the widespread political support for tenant management, and predicts when that support might begin to break down. Current support seems clearly to be based more on a shared commitment to a short-term strategy than long-term goals. As such goals become identified, the broad consensus supporting tenant management may not survive. Evidence for just how frail this supporting coalition may be is provided by the controversy generated by HUD's announcement that it was prepared to sign a contract with the Kenilworth-Parkside tenant management corporation committing the agency to sell the project to the residents. Initially, this signing was perceived as a major media event, with perhaps President Reagan himself attending. Several prominent past supporters of the administration's efforts at Kenilworth-Parkside claimed that the signing was staged as a way to mask the lack of a viable federal housing policy. As the signing was taking place, Jessie Jackson and Walter Fauntroy were holding a press conference lambasting administration housing policy.[23]

Perhaps the most interesting aspect of this controversy was the firm commitment of the resident managers at Kenilworth-Parkside to proceed. At one level this decision is hardly surprising since ownership has become a fundamental goal of the corporation's leadership. Nevertheless, it represents a fascinating instance of a low-income group choosing to support a policy position articulated by a conservative Republican administration rather than that offered by traditional liberal allies. To be sure, it would be inappropriate to attempt to infer any long-term political shift on the basis of a single incident. However, observers have noted that the large-scale privatization of public housing in Britain has been quite popular with those able to purchase housing. As a result, it is widely expected that this group is likely to be more sympathetic to conservative politicians than it has in past elections. This possibility has not gone unnoticed by conservatives in the United States.

Even more speculative is the possibility that successful tenant management may shift political priorities within the resident organization itself. Monti notes, for example, that an emphasis on home ownership may have a negative effect on current residents. Indeed, he claims that an effort to remove the poorest residents at Kenilworth-Parkside is already in force:

The removal of poor but otherwise good tenants to make room for new ones with jobs and who can afford to buy their apartment unit has bothered many people at

Kenilworth-Parkside. Still, it has not deterred the site's leader from pursuing plans for home ownership across the site.

Although claims of such displacement policy are controversial, there can be no doubt that resident managers have articulated a number of policy positions quite independent of their "natural" liberal base. The most important of these have been efforts to free themselves from federal regulations requiring union labor for modernization work so as to be able to train and employ their own residents. The political effect has been, of course, to cast tenant management in an increasingly neoconservative framework.

Local Management Initiatives

Although tenant management and tenant ownership are the most widely publicized housing reform efforts of the Reagan administration, some effort has been made to decentralize public housing by strengthening the local housing authority. Particular emphasis was given to increasing local revenue and thus reducing federal liabilities. Early in the Reagan administration, the proportion of tenant income which could be charged in rent was increased from 25 to 30 percent. The administration also proposed a demonstration program which would further relax federal regulations on income and rent limits. In this way, local authorities would be free to attract a more heterogenous population, allowing for more stable resident communities and enhanced revenue opportunities. Local authorities who agreed to participate in the demonstration would be expected to forgo federal operating subsidies within three years.

Local housing authorities have responded to proposed deregulation with some interest. It is, of course, broadly consistent with the view expressed by numerous public housing managers that one of the chief reasons for the decline of public housing was obtrusive federal regulation. A statement adopted in 1987 by the National Association of Housing and Redevelopment Officials calls for federal policy changes to allow public housing authorities to move toward economic self-reliance (NAHRO 1988).

The search for self-reliance has led local public housing authorities to explore techniques to expand assisted housing in ways not dependent on federal funds. Such efforts are perhaps best characterized as a process of public entrepreneurship. Some center on the use of tax exempt financing. Here authorities loan revenue generated by tax-free bonds to private developers. In return for below-market financing, developers agree to set aside some proportion of the newly constructed units for low- and moderate-income individuals and families. Public authorities often cover administrative costs through a variety of management fees associated with the financing.[24] A number of state and local authorities are experimenting with dedicated housing trusts to finance the construction and renovation of assisted housing (Barron 1988). Other authorities are offering valuable land to developers to entice private investment for re-developing current public housing sites.[25]

Prospects for Public Housing Reform

Any discussion of the future of public housing needs to be addressed in the form of two questions. The first centers on how additional publicly assisted housing might be created. Although the future of assisted housing is uncertain, it is reasonable to assume that it will not take the form of conventional public housing. Indeed, conventional public housing has been out of favor for almost twenty years. If there is to be any expansion of the assisted housing stock, it will almost certainly take the form of some sort of market subsidy.

Although there is little likelihood of significant addition to the stock of conventional units, the future of existing units provides a second critical concern of housing specialists. Efforts to reform the management of public housing makes it clear that no single quick fix is likely to be discovered. Problems facing public housing go beyond questions of individual incompetence, specific administrative technique, or even funding levels. The modest impact of HUD administrative reforms, as well as an inability to implement specific technology transfers, reinforce this view. Thus, meaningful reform is likely to involve more fundamental structural change.

Proponents of some form of privatization assert that such change must take the form of a rejection of the principle of public management. Although such an argument is justified by impressive logic, there is little empirical support for it. Specific attempts to use private sector management firms have not had a significant impact on either the quality or cost of management in public housing.

The case of tenant management is more interesting. The debate concerning its potential is, of course, due in part to a lack of empirical evidence. Evaluation research, however, is unlikely in itself to create a consensus as to the merits of tenant management. Central to its evaluation is a clarification of the goals which drive the public housing system itself. Tenant management transforms public housing from a shelter program into a community empowerment effort. It is a transformation which places enormous demands on its supporters. Past efforts at community mobilization have had limited success at best, and the long-term prospects for tenant management are best put in that perspective. It should be noted that where such community mobilization has had some success, outcomes have sometimes been greeted with significant political hostility. Certainly, this was true of OEO community organizations in the 1960s and 1970s.[26] Although the political coalition presently supporting tenant management is more broadly based than that supporting community action in the 1960s, the stability of tenant management is unproven.

Tenant management does serve to remind both policy makers and scholars that too often the current debate on privatization policy in the United States conceptualizes the issue as a simple dichotomy between markets and government. To do so fails to recognize alternative social institutions which might be integrated into efforts to implement collective social preferences. Tenant management may prove to be one such alternative.

Long-range prospects for private ownership of public housing are more problematic than tenant management. Although little empirical evidence on actual sales exists, several facts seem clear. First, relatively few projects seem suitable candidates for ownership programs. If tenant management is to be a prerequisite to ownership, then only fifteen to twenty projects can be considered candidates for ownership programs. Meehan (1988) correctly notes that an ownership program also screens out very low-income individuals and families who will simply be unable to finance such a purchase. Silver, McDonald, and Ortiz (1985) are almost certainly correct when they argue that the number of such sales will remain very limited, having primarily symbolic rather than substantive significance.

Any serious effort to upgrade or even maintain the public housing system will require a comprehensive strategy which extends beyond tenant management and tenant ownership. Where is this strategy to be found? There is no single, simple answer. The experience of the past twenty years does suggest very strongly that a highly centralized bureaucracy is unlikely to succeed. Perhaps increased decentralization within the public housing system could create needed innovation. Certainly, efforts of some local authorities in generating interesting and innovative strategies to provide and maintain housing for moderate- and low-income families suggest the value of increased local autonomy.[27]

Local innovation cannot, however, substitute for federal investment. Local authorities simply do not have the resources to address the long-term capital investment crisis in which they find themselves. The poor and inappropriate design of public housing demands extensive renovation funds. Without such expenditures, a continuing loss of public units is inevitable. Similarly, if public housing is to be available to the very poor, operating subsidies will be required. Although conceptually such funds might be obtained from state and local tax revenues, political reality limits such spending to the federal level. It seems clear that if the public housing system is to remain viable, its public character needs to be maintained.

NOTES

1   Note, however, that this point can be overstated. Available evidence does not show that residents are unanimous in their dislike of public housing. Indeed, there is some evidence that overall resident satisfaction is surprisingly high. See Bratt (1985).

2 For a discussion of the range of privatization strategies see Hula (1988).

3 Other important changes have also occurred. Of particular importance is an emerging emphasis on housing for the elderly. For a more complete discussion of the changing priorities of the public housing system see Meehan (1979) and Struyk (1980).

4 The most important source of these changes was a series of legislative enactments referred to as the Brooke Amendments. These are described, in quite critical terms, by Kuhn (1988).

5 The identification of well-managed projects was based on research undertaken by the Urban Institute. Operational measures of successful management were measures of satisfaction expressed by major sets of actors in local housing authorities. Populations sampled included residents, managers, authority personnel, and HUD Area Office personnel. Several traditional real estate management indicators such as occupancy rates were also used.

6 Note this incentive does not extend to rental income. A local authority's operating subsidy is reduced by an amount equal to any increase in total rental income. This provision is intended to prevent housing authorities from discriminating against the lowest income public housing residents.

7 The HMIP was initially designed as a fairly narrow social experiment to measure the effects of centralization within local authorities and staff versus tenant control of local projects. This goal was abandoned in favor of having PHA's submit proposals for their own management plan.

8 For a summary of these programs see Struyk (1980:135–62).

9 Meehan (1979) argues that it was not the strike per se that did such severe economic harms, but rather the large "freerider" population that paid rent neither to the authority nor to the strike committee. Also, a number of units were severely damaged by vandals during this period.

10 St. Louis was not unique in efforts to develop innovative management strategies. Each of the management strategies implemented by the SLHA has, in fact, been independently developed elsewhere. However, St. Louis is important because of the political visibility of the efforts and later efforts to generalize from the St. Louis experience to other authorities. Such diffusion is much less clear in other cases.

11 For an overview of this evaluation see Miller (1984).

12 There were other experiments with tenant management. For example, in 1971 OEO funded a TMC at Bromley Heath in Boston. However, there is little evidence that these efforts had a significant impact on policy makers.

13 Some face validity for these indicators is obtained from the fact that the New Haven was terminated shortly after the completion of the demonstration. It is, of course unclear whether these indicators show the reason for the failure of the TMC or are a result of it.

14 One hundred and eighty-one randomly selected residents were interviewed at the six tenant management sites. Three hundred and ninety-five residents were interviewed at 18 control sites. See details Loux and Sadacca (1980).

15 This conclusion is based on specific indicators such as increased apartment inspections, as well as general questions relating to "overall strictness" of the tenant management corporation. See MDRC (1981) 196–207.

16   The issue of time frame is particularly relevant. It is reasonable to assume that political and social effects may be measurable only over a much longer time frame than is generally used in the evaluation of social policy. For example, Eisinger (1978) argues that the impact of OEO programs on the development of black political leadership was not clear until some years after the program had largely been dismissed as a failure. It is not unreasonable to assume that the tenant management movement might have a similar effect.

17   For an overview of HUD budget cuts see Nenno (1989).

18   In 1984, HUD established the Public Housing Home Ownership Demonstration Project in which approximately one thousand units were to be sold. See Silver, McDonald, and Ortiz (1985) and U.S. Congress (1985).

19   Prior to tenant management, Kenilworth-Parkside had been managed by a private, for-profit real estate firm under contract to the District authority.

20   Much of the difficulty centered on the lack of project specific data. For a complete discussion see NCNE (1986:8–10).

21   Obviously this is a fairly conservative assumption since it is possible that there might be some sort of multiplier effect on the value of those resources reinvested into the projects. This reflects a consistent effort to use conservative assumptions in estimating benefit streams for the project.

22   Monti (1988) suggests a qualification to this view. He claims that if relations are too cordial the development of tenant management will be retarded. He suggests that the optimal environment is cooperative but "with some distance."

23   Not all liberal supporters refused to participate. District of Columbia mayor Marion Barry was not only present at the signing, but later joined a delegation visiting the White House to thank President Reagan for his efforts in support of tenant management. See Mariano (1988) and "Barry Thanks Reagan" (1988).

24   Tetreault (1989) has identified such programs in Pittsburgh, Fairfax City, Virginia, Montgomery County, Maryland, San Francisco, and Minneapolis.

25   The Boston Public Housing Authority has used such a leveraged strategy. Chicago considered but ultimately rejected a similar strategy. See "Is Public Housing on Its Last Legs?" (1988).

26   For a discussion of the impact of OEO community empowerment efforts see Marris and Rein (1982), Moynihan (1969), and Sundquist (1969).

27   Local autonomy also creates an environment which might generate spectacular failure as well as success. Consider, for example, the judicial receivership of the Boston Housing Authority, and the near takeover of the Chicago PHA by HUD on grounds of administrative incompetence.

REFERENCES

Barron, Myra H. 1988. "New Deals: PHAs as Financiers." *Journal of Housing* 45, no. 1 (March–April): 69–75.

"Barry Thanks Reagan." 1988 *Washington Post*, 30 November D3e.

Bratt, Rachel G. 1985. "Controversy and Contributions: Public Housing Critique." *Journal of Housing* 42, no. 5 (September–October): 165–73.

Bratt, Rachel G. 1986. "Public Housing: The Controversy and Contributions." In *Criti-*

cal Perspectives on Housing, ed. Rachel G. Bratt, Chester Hartman, and Ann Meyer. Philadelphia: Temple University Press.

Eisinger, Peter K. 1978. *Community Action Programs and the Development of Black Leadership*. Madison: Institute for Research on Poverty, University of Wisconsin.

Granville Corporation. 1983. "Public Housing Authority Experience with Private Management: A Comparative Study." Paper prepared for U.S. Department of Housing and Urban Development, Office of Policy Development and Research.

Hula, Richard C., ed. 1988. *Market-Based Public Policy*. London: Macmillan. "Is Public Housing on Its Last Legs?" 1988. *Planning* 54, no. 9 (September): 16–18.

Judd, Dennis R. 1988. *The Politics of American Cities: Private Power and Public Policy*. Boston: Scott, Foresman.

Kolodny, Robert. 1986. "The Emergence of Self-Help as a Housing Strategy for the Urban Poor." In *Critical Perspectives on Housing*, ed. Rachel G. Bratt, Chester Hartman, and Ann Meyer, Philadelphia: Temple University Press.

Kolodny, Robert. 1983. *What Happens When Tenants Manage Their Own Public Housing*. NAHRO report submitted to the Office of Policy Development and Research, U.S. Department of Housing and Urban Development.

Kolodny, Robert. 1981. "Self-Help Can Be an Effective Tool in Housing the Urban Poor." *Journal of Housing* 38, no. 3 (March): 135–42.

Kuhn, A. W. 1988. "PHA Management: Are the Critics Right?" *Journal of Housing* 45, no. 2 (March–April): 67–74.

Lewis, Vincent V. 1984. "Computers and PHA Management: The Consortium Approach." *Journal of Housing* 45, no. 1 (January–February): 7–10.

Loux, Suzanne B., and Robert Sadacca. 1980. *Analysis of Changes at Tenant Management Demonstration Projects*. Working Paper 1335. Washington D.C.: Urban Institute.

Manpower Demonstration Research Corporation. 1981. *Tenant Management: Findings from a Three-Year Experiment in Public Housing*. Cambridge, Mass.: Ballinger.

Mariano, Ann. 1988. "Tenants in D.C. Project Move Toward Ownership." *Washington Post*, 25 October, B:1a

Marris, Peter, and Martin Rein. 1982. *Dilemmas of Social Reform: Poverty and Community Action in the United States*. Chicago: University of Chicago Press.

Matuief, Mark. 1987. "This is Public Housing." *Journal of Housing* 44, no. 5 (September–October): 175–81.

Meehan, Eugene J. 1988. "Low Income Housing: The Ownership Question." *Journal of Housing* 45, no. 3 (May–June): 105–10.

Meehan, Eugene J. 1975. *Public Housing Policy: Convention Versus Reality*. New Brunswick, N.J.: Center for Urban Policy Research, Rutgers University.

Meehan, Eugene J. 1979. *The Quality of Federal Policy Making: Programmed Failure in Public Housing*. Columbia, Mo.: University of Missouri Press.

Miller, Ted, Harvey Dickerson, and Ira Greenstein. 1984. "Private Management: A Comparative Analysis." *Journal of Housing* 41, no. 6 (November–December): 199–204.

Monti, Daniel J. 1988. "Economic Development in Low-Income Neighborhoods: The

Case of Tenant Managed Public Housing Sites in the United States." *Built Environment* 14(3–4): 201–8.

Monti, Daniel J. 1989. "The Organizational Strengths and Weaknesses of Resident Managed Public Housing Sites in the United States." *Journal of Urban Affairs* 11(1): 39–52.

Moynihan, Daniel P. 1969. *Maximum Feasible Misunderstanding*. New York: Free Press.

National Association for Housing and Redevelopment Offices. 1988. "Keeping the Commitment: An Action Plan for Better Housing and Communities for All." *Journal of Housing* 45, no. 1 (January–February): 11–22.

National Center for Neighborhood Enterprise. 1986. *Cost-Benefit Analysis of the Kenilworth-Parkside Public Housing Resident Management Corporation*. Washington D.C.: National Center for Neighborhood Enterprise.

Nenno, Mary K. 1988. "Housing and Community Development: A New Cycle of Policies and Partners." *Journal of Housing* 46, no. 2 (January–February): 75–82.

Ostrowski, Elaine. 1984. "Managing Public Housing: The Impact of the 80s." *Journal of Housing* 41, no. 2 (March–April): 40–43.

Peterman, William A. 1988. "Resident Management: Putting It in Perspective." *Journal of Housing* 45, no. 3 (May–June): 111–15.

Pynoss, Jon. 1986. *Breaking the Rules: Bureaucracy and Reform in Public Housing*. New York: Plenum Press.

Silver, Hilary, Judith McDonald, and Ronald J. Ortiz. 1985. "Selling Public Housing: The Methods and the Motivations." *Journal of Housing* 42, no. 6 (November–December): 213–28.

Struyk, Raymond J. 1980. *A New System for Public Housing*. Washington, D.C.: Urban Institute.

Sundquist, James L. 1969. *On Fighting Poverty: Perspectives from Experience*. New York: Basic Books.

Tetreault, Bernard L. 1989. "New Waters: Creative Roles for PHAs." *Journal of Housing* 45, no. 3 (May–June): 98–102.

U.S. Congress. House 1985. "Homeownership Demonstration Program." Hearings Before a Subcommittee of the Committee on Government Operations. 99th Cong., 1st sess.

U.S. Congress. House 1986. "Tenant Management of Public Housing." Hearings Before the Subcommittee on Housing and Community Development of the Committee on Banking, Finance and Urban Affairs, 99th Cong., 2d sess.

9 *Hilary Silver*

The Privatization of Public Housing in Great Britain

The sale of more than one million British council houses is among the world's most frequently mentioned examples of successful privatization. The "Right-to-Buy," which the Thatcher government bestowed upon sitting council tenants, has inspired such American conservatives as HUD Secretary Jack Kemp who, while still a congressman, helped secure a version of the policy in the 1987 Housing and Community Development Act.

Privatizing public housing has great appeal among the British and American New Right for it seems to achieve a number of goals simultaneously (e.g., Butler 1980; Pirie 1988). On the economic front, it appears to reduce the role of government, in line with monetarist and supply-side objectives of diminishing state expenditures, taxation, and debt. It should return housing production, maintenance, and finance to the more efficient competitive market.

In social terms, the policy is compatible with conservative notions of the welfare state. Government should provide a safety net that guarantees minimum standards for the truly needy without eroding work incentives, rather than redistribute resources and reduce inequality. Privatizing public housing also promotes the libertarian goal of a citizenry composed of consumers freer to choose once released from bureaucratic serfdom. It is part of the decades-old Tory dream of a "property owning democracy."

Hilary Silver is Assistant Professor of Sociology and Urban Studies at Brown University.

Finally, by selling public housing directly to voters, the policy promises to cement political support for the Conservatives. In line with public choice theory, it breaks up local opposition strongholds with vested interests in council housing and creates a counter-group in favor of privatization.

The sheer number of sales under Mrs. Thatcher is usually cited as evidence of the policy's success. In this chapter I question whether the Right-to-Buy has actually achieved all the New Right's economic, social, and political aspirations for it. In the first section, I review the origins and legislative evolution of the Right-to-Buy. I describe trends in sales, the type of houses sold, who bought them, and where. I then evaluate the fiscal, social, and political consequences of the policy in light of the government's professed objectives.

What emerges is a more qualified success than is often claimed. Therefore, I consider whether there are any alternatives to the Right-to-Buy in the housing policies of the opposition parties. However, new Conservative approaches enacted in the 1986 and 1988 Housing Acts suggest the government has tried to preempt these alternatives and reshape them in ways that suit its own purposes.

The Evolution of the Right-to-Buy

Although the Thatcher government's housing policies broke with the past in a number of ways, the sale of British council housing to sitting tenants was hardly new. Indeed, before the 1919 Addison Act established a national public housing subsidy system, local authorities had to sell any houses they built within ten years (Merrett 1979:20). The 1919 Act, encouraging council-built "homes fit for heroes," transformed the *mandatory* sales requirement into *permission* to sell with ministerial approval. This permission remained in force except during World War II and under the postwar Labour government. Yet the number of sales between 1939 and 1952 was negligible, and amounted to a mere 2000 annually during the rest of the 1950s (Merrett 1979; Murie 1975).

As Labour and the Conservatives alternated in office over the years, the conditions of sale frequently changed, reflecting long-standing party differences over housing policy more generally. Partisan disagreements over sales, expressed in numerous administrative circulars, centered on the extent of low-income housing shortages, sales prices, fiscal implications, and the degree of local discretion to be granted in the matter (Burnett 1986; Murie 1975; Cooper 1985; Holmans 1987; Forrest and Murie 1988).

By the late 1960s, the sales issue became increasingly politicized. After Tory victories in local councils which had aggressively sold council housing, voices were raised in the party to advocate unrestricted council house sales and the Right-to-Buy policy as a vote winner. In response, Labour issued a 1968 circular placing a quota on local authority sales in four large conurbations where rental shortages were said to exist. In 1970, the Heath government immediately removed the quotas to give local authorities more autonomy to sell and reinstituted a general consent to sell at discounts of up to 20 percent of value. As inflation accelerated, discounts up to 30 percent were authorized. New 1972 housing finance provisions added purchase incentives by raising council housing rents. Sales did increase substantially in the early 1970s, but for most tenants, prices became increasingly out of reach. Similarly, because local authorities with a fiscal surplus from sales proceeds would lose Exchequer subsidies, councils were discouraged from selling. Finally, the government could not compel local authorities to sell and many, both Labour and Conservative, resisted the policy.

Yet some Tories vigorously pressed for an aggressive policy to encourage council sales. In the 1974 campaign, the Tory manifesto promised a Right-to-Buy on reasonable terms. The Conservative spokesman for the environment, Margaret Thatcher, promised that local authorities would be forced to sell to tenants. Labour opposed this as a transparent attempt to buy votes. The Callahan government maintained the general consent until the late 1970s, when council house sales started rising again. Under party pressure to curtail this, the government restricted sales to occupied houses and to tenants of at least two years standing.

The Conservative call for a statutory Right-to-Buy under more favorable financial arrangements figured prominently in its election campaign of 1979. Immediately upon entering office, Mrs. Thatcher increased discounts so that prices fell below historic costs. Table 9.1 indicates that sales rose continuously during the late 1970s, even before passage of the 1980 Housing Act. This implies that there was already pent-up demand for home ownership in the council sector. One can only speculate whether added incentives were really necessary to stimulate sales.

Viewed historically then, the Right-to-Buy legislation was not as radical a departure as it first appears. Yet it was very popular with the voters. Indeed, after a second defeat in 1983, Labour also accepted it. Over time, a bi-partisan consensus developed in favor of public sector tenants' right to buy their homes. ·

The Right-to-Buy

This right, granted to council tenants of at least three years standing, was the centerpiece of the 1980 Housing Act. As with earlier sales legislation but much more drastically, it altered the financial terms of sale and guaranteed a right to a council mortgage. Discounts rose from 33 percent after three years tenancy by one percent a year up to 50 percent. In the event of a resale before five years, 20 percent of the discount had to be repaid for each year remaining. The 1980 Act also strengthened tenant rights relative to local authority discretion.

Table 9.1 indicates that the Right-to-Buy produced a marked increase in the

Table 9.1. Sales of Local Authority and New Town
Dwellings, England and Wales, 1939–1988

Year	Sales	Year	Sales
1960	3169	1975	2950
1961	4148	1976	5895
1962	5061	1977	13385
1963	4158	1978	30620
1964	4282	1979	42595
1965	4369	1980	85710
1966	5825	1981	106535
1967	5497	1982	207370
1968	10434	1983	146290
1969	9094	1984	107485
1970	7367	1985	95405
1971	20652	1986	91151
1972	61957	1987	108686
1973	41831	Sept. 1988	116408
1974	5372		

Sources: Department of the Environment, *Housing and
Construction Statistics*, HMSO. Figures include leases,
sales to housing associations, and sales of dwellings previously municipalized.

number of council houses sold after 1980. Purchases peaked in 1982 and, under
the particular terms of the 1980 Act, began falling off. In response the government introduced more generous financial conditions and terms of purchase,
lowering the income thresholds sufficiently to permit additional households to
buy. They did little to alter the general trend.

In 1984 the Housing and Building Control Act extended the Right-to-Buy
to sitting tenants of only two years, at a 32 percent discount, and increased
maximum discounts to 60 percent. Housing on leased land and some housing
for the disabled could now be sold, and those not entitled to a full mortgage
received the right to a shared ownership lease. Tenants of charitable housing
associations excluded from the Right-to-Buy became eligible for a grant to
buy a house on the open market on the same terms as council tenants. The
1984 Housing Defects Act protected buyers from purchasing faulty council
properties.

Council apartments, compared to houses, sold poorly. Therefore, the 1986
Housing and Planning Act reduced the prices of flats by 42 percent for tenants
of two years standing up to 70 percent for residents of 15 years or more. It also
lowered resale restrictions from five to three years as a means of encouraging
labor mobility.

The 1986 Act was a watershed. Cognizant of the declines in sales to individual tenants, the government also authorized sales of entire estates to private developers, including housing associations. By 1987, 15,000 units were sold in this way (Forrest and Murie 1988:239) and indeed, Table 9.1 suggests a recent increase in sales figures. If an estate was sold, tenants had to be consulted, could be relocated if they remained, but retained their Right-to-Buy. The 1988 Housing Act extended this new approach to disposing of public housing by granting remaining council tenants the "Right-to-Rent" (i.e., to choose their own private landlord to whom the council would have to sell).

Before evaluating the fiscal, social, and political impact of the Right-to-Buy, it is worthwhile to describe the type and location of council houses sold and the social background of their buyers.

What Was Sold

The quality of British council housing is, on the average, superior to that of American public housing, but the nature and condition of the stock varies considerably. This variation often reflects the period in which localities built any given estate. Better quality housing dates from 1924–35 and 1945–51, while units built as slum clearance replacements in the 1930s or after 1950 tend to be of poorer quality.

Despite this variation, the vast majority of the units sold were single-family houses, often with gardens and other amenities. The more individualized the unit, the more desirable it was. Indeed, sales of houses on the end of a terrace or the edge of an estate were more likely to be sold (Forrest and Murie 1988:174), as were those on more popular estates. But buyers shunned flats, especially those in high-rise buildings. Flats accounted for just five percent of all sales, although they comprise about a third of all council dwelling units. The reasons for this lack of popularity are diverse, and so the effect of the new financial incentives offered in 1986 was trivial.

Sales did alter the public/private mix of types of accommodation. Whereas councils owned three percent of detached houses in 1972, they held only one percent ten years later (Somerville 1986). More generally, the poor condition of the continually aging council house stock limited its desirability for purchase and created further incentives for selling these properties to private developers for renovation.

The quality of the housing sold also interacted with local authority allocation procedures. Households lucky enough to have been allocated better quality houses suitable for owner occupation were also more likely to have the wherewithal to buy them (i.e., relatively large, middle-aged families). The socioeconomic status of tenants was also related to the spatial distribution of council house sales.

Where It Was Sold

Were the geographical pattern of council house sales only a function of the number of public housing units in a locality, one would expect the spatial distribution of sales to be much like that of council property. It is precisely the opposite. Sales were greatest in those areas where home ownership, not council housing, was most common. This is true on a regional basis as well as more locally. Almost one-third of all council dwellings sold since 1979 were located in Southeast England, a region experiencing rapid economic growth and notable housing price inflation. Relatively high sale figures were also recorded in the East Midlands, East Anglia, and Southwest regions. In contrast, few sales, in relative as well as absolute terms, took place in areas with very large council housing stocks: the North, Scotland, and London, especially Inner London (U.K. Department of the Environment, *Local Housing Statistics*, and *Housing and Construction Statistics*). Thus, the recent exacerbation of the long-term North-South economic divide and its consequences for regional housing markets help explain the broad regional pattern of sales.

Examining sales figures at the local level further refines this spatial generalization. Dunn, Forrest, and Murie (1987) report that the local level of council house sales was lower where flats comprised a larger share of the council stock and where male unemployment was greater, confirming the importance of general economic conditions and the suitability of the stock for home ownership. Sales were also more frequent in municipalities that sold more council houses before the Right-to-Buy was passed and in those under Conservative political control. If sales are broken down further to the intra-urban level, similar patterns are observed (Forrest and Murie 1988:139–48).

Who Bought

Surveys of council tenants who exercised their right to buy produce a strikingly consistent profile in which socioeconomic status and life cycle stage are prominent. For example, the 1984 General Household Survey found that among English council tenants who bought their homes since 1981, two-thirds were 45 years old or older and most were married with dependent children. Most heads of buying households were employed full time and were disproportionately in non-manual occupations, although the absolute majority were skilled manual workers, reflecting their larger numbers in the council tenancy. Viewed generationally, buyers came from the cohort that benefited most from the postwar welfare state, including the expansion of council housing. Yet buyers had more experience of owner-occupation as children than did non-buyers. Many bought for family reasons (Stubbs 1988). Conversely, council tenants who never considered buying rejected it because of financial reasons, their age, or the low quality of their homes (Kerr 1988).

The same social profile emerges from a 1985 Building Societies Association study of the 55–60 percent of council house buyers who financed a purchase with private mortgages. Unlike surveys that compare council house tenants who do and do not buy their homes, however, this one indicates how they differ from first-time buyers in general. While the type of housing purchased (terraced and semidetached houses) and the regional distribution of sales (concentrated in the southeast) were similar, council house buyers were considerably older (43 vs. 31 years, on average), paid less for their homes (by almost half), and borrowed a larger proportion of this lower price (95 vs. 85 percent) than all first-time buyers. A study based on Halifax Building Society loans found that, compared with buyers who were private sector tenants, council tenant buyers purchased larger and newer homes and were much less likely to purchase a flat (Nellis and Fleming 1986).

The General Household Survey also asked council tenants whether they had considered buying their homes during the last two years. Contrary to expectation, the proportion held steady at 21 percent between 1981 and 1986. However, those taking active steps to do so fell from ten to six percent. Those considering buying in 1986 were more likely to be skilled and own-account workers, those aged 30–49, those in large adult households, and occupants of houses rather than flats or maisonettes. As in previous years, the most frequent reason for not considering buying was financial, followed by one's age and the quality of the unit inhabited.

A final comparison can be made between those who bought their council houses in the mid-1970s and those who bought under the Right-to-Buy, based on a local survey (Stubbs 1988). One significant difference is that early buyers were less likely to have been through the experience of slum clearance and displacement from private rental accommodation. Early buyers were also more likely than later ones to vote Tory in 1983.

With these facts in mind, it is now possible to assess the Conservatives' claims for council house sales.

Evaluating the Right-to-Buy

Fiscal Objectives

The fiscal impacts of the Right-to-Buy are deeply embedded in the Conservatives' economic policies. Monetarism, already adopted by the Callahan government during the inflationary 1970s, came to dominate public policy in the 1980s. The Thatcher governments concentrated on restricting the money supply and most particularly, the Public Sector Borrowing Requirement (PSBR), an indicator of the difference between public revenues from taxation and from asset sales, and total public expenditures. The PSBR has fallen over the decade and since 1988 budgets are in surplus, with excess revenues devoted to Public Sector Debt Reduction. Privatization in general and housing policy in particular figured prominently in this trend.

If one looks beyond the PSBR, however, the monetarism of the Thatcher governments was far from an unqualified success (Brittan 1984; Robinson 1986; Thompson 1986). Public expenditures continued to rise in real terms. This was particularly true of social security, as a consequence of both high, prolonged unemployment and long-term demographic trends the government could do little about. The government gradually abandoned money supply indicators for expenditure targets as a share of GDP, a statistic that gave the impression of spending reductions as the economic recovery progressed. By 1988, however, Britain had the highest inflation rate in Europe, a large part of which, it may be added, reflects rising house prices. High interest rates, rather than fiscal changes, have been the major response.

Monetarism allowed supply-side economics to dominate taxation policy. The British tax structure, including that for housing, was made more regressive in order to create work and investment incentives. The latter, too, were not always successful (Thompson 1986; Parry 1986).

The decline in Britain's PSBR may appear enviable to Americans who face an unprecedented budget deficit after the Reagan Administration pursued similarly motivated tax and spending cuts. The economic recovery, however, which reduced the public cost of unemployment and raised the tax yield, accounts for only part of Britain's fiscal turnaround. In addition, a peculiar accounting system permits the Exchequer to subtract any receipts from assets sales, namely, *privatization proceeds*, from its capital accounts. Virtually all the reduction in the PSBR results from "selling the family silver," of which Britain has far more than the United States and which, in the early 1980s, was derived largely from council house sales. It is this unconventional practice, rather than fiscal or monetary policy, that is most responsible for balancing the British budget.

Thus, any assessment of the Conservatives' housing policies warrants close attention to accounting procedures since they can be quite misleading. For example, on the revenue side, council house rent hikes and especially the sale of public housing raised massive receipts to help reduce the PSBR. But increasing expenditures for homeowners were not accounted for in the Department of the Environment's (DOE) housing budget. The Government extended tax incentives to private landlords and building societies, kept rates (property taxes) down for the increasing number of homeowners, and compounded its outlays on owner occupation through "invisible" tax allowances for capital gains and mortgage interest payments. Indeed, as house prices soared in the early 1980s, Mrs. Thatcher raised the ceiling on this last item from £25,000 to £30,000.[1]

Similarly, spending on items officially budgeted under DOE housing programs appears to have been cut more than any other major category. Indeed, while spending on social security, education, health, and personal services increased in real terms, housing was the only major welfare state program to suffer real cuts, amounting to 59 percent between 1979 and 1986 (Hoover and Plant 1989:163; Robinson 1986). As a proportion of all government expenditures, housing fell from seven percent in the mid-1970s to only two percent in 1987–88 (Forrest and Murie 1988:87).

Nevertheless, large increases in housing expenditures are hidden away in the voracious social security accounts.[2] If only the increases in social security "housing benefit" and tax relief are taken into account, the apparent halving of housing expenditures disappears (Leather and Murie 1986; Robinson 1986). Table 9.2 confirms this.

Between the last Labour budget of 1979–80 and the most recent Conservative one pertaining to 1988–89, tax expenditures for mortgage interest rose by £4050 million. Capital gains relief increased by at least £1000 million, and the government's planned figure for 1988–89 has jumped to £10000 million. Rent rebates and allowances, excluding those from supplementary benefit, rose from £480 million in 1979–80 to £2516 million in 1983–84 when the integrated housing benefit scheme was implemented.[3] Today this program costs £1300 million more than that. Smaller off-budget items, each of which rose over £100 million under Mrs. Thatcher, are bed and breakfast costs to house the homeless and payment of mortgage interest for homeowners receiving supplementary benefit. Indeed, the number of owner occupiers in receipt of supplementary benefit for housing expenses other than those paid by housing benefit rose from 544,000 to 794,000 between 1981 and 1986, when the government decided to cover only half the interest payments in the first months of unemployment. A conservative estimate of total increases in housing expenditures on these off-housing budget items amounts to over £6000 million.

This figure far exceeds the savings from cutbacks and council sales. Current expenditures in the housing budget fell by £500 million between 1979–80 and 1988–89. Despite the recent decline in the number of council sales, house price inflation helped capital receipts to jump £3000 million in cash terms during the same period, for a total savings of £3500 million. It is easy to conclude that, even with annual fluctuations, considerable public outlays have been necessary for Mrs. Thatcher to favor home ownership and means-tested subsidies over council housing.

Moreover, this accounting excludes trends in capital expenditure. What is notable in this regard is the reorientation of government spending. Whereas in the 1970s, most capital funds went to local authority Housing Investment Programmes (HIPs) for building new council housing, Table 9.2 indicates this item declined in cash terms. Instead, capital spending has gone increasingly

Table 9.2a. Central Government Housing Expenditures (in £ millions)

Fiscal Year	Gross Capital Expenditures	Current Expenditures	Capital Receipts	Total DOE
78/79	2698	1396	− 521	3573
79/80	3148	1834	− 468	4514
80/81	2910	2134	− 587	4457
81/82	2564	1612	−1045	3131
82/83	3313	1259	−1877	2695
83/84	4010	1102	−1958	3154
84/85	3973	1098	−1804	3267
85/86	3573	1176	−1787	2962
86/87	3641	1296	−2132	2805
87/88	3826	1339	−2462	2703
88/89p	4163	1340	−3440	2064
89/90p	4158	1286	−3801	1710
90/91p	4030	1320	−3400	2130

Source: H.M.Treasury. *The Government's Expenditure Plans*, (1987), Table 3.9; 1983–84 to 1985–86, Cmd. 8789 (HMSO, 1983), Tables 2.7; 2.12.2; 1989–90 to 1991–92 (January 1989), Cmd. 609, 615, 621 (for 83/84 on).

Note: Gross Capital Expenditures include renovation and new construction of local authority, New Town, and housing association properties as well as support for private sector homeownership, renovation, and clearance. Capital receipts include those of local authorities, public corporations, new towns, and central government, although the first source accounts for virtually all such revenues. Income Tax relief is for qualifying interest on loans for purchase or improvement of owner-occupied property and exemption of capital gains tax on gains arising on disposals of a person's only or main residence (or a residence provided for a dependent relative until abolished). The letter *p* designates projected figures.

to housing associations for building new rental properties, to private households (including tenants, since 1980) as improvement grants, or to councils for renovating their existing stock.

This is not to say that local authorities willingly accepted the new role assigned them. After all, if 90 percent of British taxes are collected by central government, local councils spend about 25 percent of all public outlays (Glennerster 1985). Rate Support Grant, similar to American revenue-sharing, provides about three-fifths of local expenditure, and rates account for much of the rest. The government reasoned that if local authorities, particularly those under Labour control, had money, political considerations would encourage them to spend it (Hoover and Plant 1989). The Right-to-Buy was particularly worrisome in this regard because councils owned the houses being sold and the proceeds were credited to their HRAs. These accounts are composed of

Table 9.2b. Off-Budget Housing Items

	Housing Benefit	Supplementary Security Interest Payments	Tax Expenditures		Bed and Breakfast for the Homeless
			Mortgage Interest	Capital Gains	
78/79	410		1110	1500	
79/80	480	50	1450	2000	
80/81	630	50	1960	2400	
81/82	930[a]	100	2030	2800	
82/83	1003	150	2150	3000	
83/84	2516	150	2750	2500	
84/85	2839		3500	2500	20
85/86	3136		4750	2500	46
86/87	3373		4500	3000	77
87/88	3585		N.A.		116
88/89p	3817		5500	10000	
89/90p	4611				
90/91p	5000				

Sources: H.M. Treasury, 1983, *The Government's Expenditure Plans 1983–84 to 1985–86*, HMSO, Cmd. 8789 Tables 2.7, 2.12.2; *1989–90 to 1991–92*, 1989, HMSO, Cmd. 609, 615, 621; Board of Inland Revenue, *Inland Revenue Statistics*, 1979 through 1987.

[a] DHSS Housing benefit 1978/79–1981/82 refers to rent rebates and rent allowances not paid with supplementary benefit. Administrative costs not shown.

Exchequer subsidies and local contributions largely from three sources: Rate Fund Contributions, sales receipts, and rents. Thus, to achieve cutbacks in council spending, central government not only reduced its own grants, but also passed a series of bills between 1979 and 1987 that placed strict controls on local government taxation and spending, including the use of sales proceeds.

As housing revenues dried up or were declared off limits, councils' only recourse was to raise public housing rents. The goal was to further privatize housing costs by placing more of the financial burden on tenants. Council rents did rise on average from £5.90 a week in 1978–79 to £18.77 in 1988–89, although they continued to lag behind earnings and registered fair rents in the private sector. Tenants' ability to pay constrained the policy's fiscal impact. Although rent increases and rate limitations provided incentives for tenants ineligible for housing benefit to buy their homes, charging poorer eligible residents higher rents simply passed the cost through to the social security budget (McCulloch 1987).

Central government constraints on local authorities not only created enormous friction over rate-capping and other financial issues. It also engendered "constitutional" conflicts over which level of government had the right to set local housing priorities. The 1980 Housing Act gave the Secretary of State the power to review local progress on council house sales to prevent foot-dragging or obstruction. During the early 1980s, he did so in at least 200 municipalities, which, if not confined to those controlled by Labour, produced the most acrimony in their case. In 1982, local councillors in Labour-dominated Norwich unsuccessfully took the government to court over their right to refuse to implement the Right-to-Buy until other pressing housing needs were met. Future legal challenges were foreclosed when the Court of Appeal ruled that, whatever the relations between central and local government, the Right-to-Buy protected individual residents against abuses of state power (Forrest and Murie 1986).

The irony is that in spite of the acrimony these battles caused, the government was unable to achieve its privatization goals by reducing net spending on housing. Unfortunately, it is much more difficult to assess whether or not the Right-to-Buy per se reduced public expenditure.

There are several reasons for this. First, the policy is deeply enmeshed in virtually every housing item of the budget. As indicated earlier, spending restrictions, subsidy cutbacks, rent hikes, tax relief, rate limits, housing benefit eligibility, and supplementary security payments of mortgage interest all influence the financial attraction of buying beyond the effect of price discounts alone. As inducements to home ownership, one could reasonably count all of these as part of the privatization policy.

This raises a second problem: trying to assess what portion of all the relevant budget items are strictly attributable to the Right-to-Buy. For example, about 40 percent of new homeowners are former council tenants, but they have smaller mortgages and tax liabilities than other new homeowners. Should sales be responsible for 40 percent of the approximately £5000 million increase in mortgage-interest tax relief? Should all housing benefit costs be assigned to council housing, given that most recipients are public tenants, when at the same time, the government insisted on raising their rents? Without trying to resolve these issues, Table 9.3 indicates the types of potential savings and losses associated with council house sales.

With a few exceptions (U.K. DOE 1980; Black and Stafford 1988:108), most analyses indicate the Right-to-Buy costs the central government money (Kilroy 1982; Lansley 1979; Maclennan 1982:276; Balchin 1981:130–35). Tax relief to new homeowners is not only more expensive than public housing subsidies in the early years of a mortgage, but remains in effect longer. Council housing units eventually become debt-free, but each time a former council unit is resold, the cost in mortgage-interest tax relief increases. Even if housing benefit is counted on top of unit subsidy as part of the expense of council housing, the Right-to-Buy would cost the Treasury more in tax allowances for owner-occupiers. Moreover, with public housing cutbacks and rising private

Table 9.3. A Fiscal Balance Sheet on British Housing Privatization

Revenues and Savings
1. Exchequer Subsidy Reductions and Constraints on Local Authority Rate Funds, Capital Expenditures (HIP), and Borrowing for Housing
2. Council House Sales Proceeds and Interest on LA Mortgages
3. Higher Council Housing Rents
4. Reduced Operating, Maintenance, and Rent Rebate Expenditures
5. Possible Inheritance Tax Revenues in Long Term

Expenditures and Costs
1. Means-tested Housing Benefit (Rent Rebates, Allowances, Supplementary Security Mortgage Interest Payments)
2. Tax Deductions: Mortgage Interest, Capital Gains
3. Local Authority Housing Opportunity Costs: Discounts, Foregone rents, Continued Construction Mortgage Debt, Council Mortgages, Bed and Breakfast Costs for the Homeless, Rent Arrears, Deferred Maintenance
4. Capital Expenditures for Private Housing Improvement Grants and Repair of Defective Units Sold
5. Staff and Publicity Costs relative to Sales

house prices, the gap in subsidy between owner-occupied and council units is growing over time.

Indeed, to assess the policy's impact on *local* authority finance, it is necessary to make many assumptions about long-term future trends in a large number of relevant variables (Schifferes 1979; Kilroy 1982; Charles 1982; Foreman-Peck 1982; Posnett and Edwards 1982; Forrest and Murie 1988; Kirwan 1984). The gains—from sales proceeds, reduced housing benefit, Exchequer subsidies, maintenance and administrative costs, interest earned on accounts, and repayments of loans by buyers—must be weighed against losses—in rental income relative to operating costs, and in discounted prices. Whether councils come out ahead or not depends on the assumptions made about future economic conditions, government policies, and the durability of housing, all factors that become increasingly uncertain in the longer term when losses from sales begin to accumulate. Even so, the weight of the evidence suggests local authorities do not come out ahead by selling council housing at a discount, except opportunistically in the short run.

In sum, the successive Thatcher governments have not achieved a reduction in public, social, or housing expenditures. It is virtually impossible to assess definitively the fiscal consequences of council housing sales, because of both the uncertainty of assumptions about future trends in many variables and the difficulty of isolating sales, strictly speaking, from changes in housing policies generally. Nonetheless, it is clear that the Right-to-Buy, although it contributed to reducing the PSBR in the short term, involved long-term public costs as well.

Social Objectives

The redistributive consequences of Mrs. Thatcher's fiscal policies are less in question. In line with conservative conceptions of the welfare state, the reallocation of expenditures among programs and the restructuring of the tax burden reinforced the effects of economic trends in raising income inequality among Britons (Walker and Walker 1987). Although public spending on housing has not declined, changes in housing policies have redistributed those resources towards higher income groups.

The Marginalization of Council Housing

Housing expenditure items that were cut mostly pertained to the council sector, which shrank from 32 to 26 percent of all British housing between 1979 and 1988 (Table 9.4). By 1985, the number of council houses sold exceeded those newly built by seven to one (*Social Trends 1987*:145). Any new council houses constructed may now meet lower standards, through a deregulatory form of privatization, adding to the loss of better units caused by sales.

Instead of new public building, local capital spending has shifted to renovating existing housing stock. Despite local variation reflecting the age and type of properties, the existing council stock is deteriorating. The cost of refurbishing existing council housing has been estimated at £20 billion (Audit Commission 1986). Current funding for renovation and repairs of council housing is woefully inadequate, but more of the meagre capital allocations available are being earmarked for other housing sectors. Although the Housing Corporation budget to support housing associations was also cut, its share of total capital expenditure rose. Moreover, increasing numbers of private individuals received improvement grants, regardless of their ability to pay. Only recently have these regressive measures been recognized; new legislation urges housing associations to use their grants to leverage private funds and targets improvement grants on those unable to finance repairs on their own.

Current expenditure cuts have compounded the operating difficulties in council housing. Even before Mrs. Thatcher became Prime Minister, council housing had "difficult-to-let" estates in which poor management led to frictions with tenants (Power 1987). One indicator of management quality that makes other tasks possible is rent collection. This function is especially crucial in light of recent trends in local authority finance. Yet, as council rent levels have risen, so too have rent arrears. In 1988 alone, rent owed local councils rose 16 percent to £226 million, albeit concentrated in a small number of poorer localities. In theory, housing benefit should have assisted those unable to pay, but in practice, the government progressively disqualified thousands of

Table 9.4. Recent Trends in Housing Tenures, Great Britain
(as a proportion of all dwellings)

	Public Housing	Owner-Occupied	Housing Assns[a]	Private Rentals[a]
1976	31.4	53.7		14.8
1977	31.7	54.1		14.2
1978	31.7	54.7		13.7
1979	31.5	55.3		13.1
1980	31.2	56.2		12.7
1981	30.6	57.1	2.1	10.1
1982	29.5	58.6	2.2	9.6
1983	28.6	59.9	2.3	9.2
1984	27.9	60.9	2.4	8.7
1985	27.3	62.0	2.5	8.3
1986	26.7	62.9	2.5	7.9
March 1987	26.5	63.2	2.5	7.8

Source: U.K. Department of the Environment. 1987. *Housing and Construction Statistics*. London: HMSO. Table 2.2, 4.
[a] Prior to 1981, figures on private rentals include dwellings rented from housing associations. In England alone, where housing association units are concentrated, they rose from 1.6% to 2.2% of the stock between 1976 and 1980.

low-wage households from the program. Indeed, changes in housing benefit "income tapers" introduced new work disincentives for tenants earning just above the thresholds (Esam 1987; Kemp 1985).

The impact of privatization policies on relets in council housing is controversial. On the one hand, with a vacancy rate of four percent a year, only four houses out of any 100 sold would have been available for relets to new council tenants, and perhaps even fewer, given that buyers are still middle-aged (Black and Stafford 1988). Furthermore, transfers of existing council tenants account for about 43 percent of all new council lets, up from 40 percent in 1981, although demand for transfers is more than triple the actual number of relets made (Minford, Peel, and Ashton 1987). Surprisingly, government data indicate that total lettings have, if anything, increased. At the same time, the percentage of new council house lettings going to homeless families has increased from 18 percent in 1981–82 to 31 percent in 1987–88 (Treasury 1987, 1989).

On the other hand, government critics argue that the declining supply of council houses due to sales and reduced building makes it increasingly difficult for councils to meet rising demand for moves within and into the sector. The sale of higher quality units to relatively large families has reduced the possibility of moves by council tenants to a better or larger unit when they need it.

This is viewed as inequitable. The problem multiplies over time, since second and subsequent relet opportunities are lost.

While the supply is decreasing, the demand for council accommodation is growing. It is fueled by economic trends, such as historically high long-term unemployment, falling labor force participation, rising poverty rates and income inequality. It is compounded by demographic trends toward smaller household formation and migration from the North to the South. The continued contraction of Britain's private rental sector, which traditionally housed the nation's poorest households, has also contributed to demand.

Thus, waiting lists for council housing now exceed 1.6 million households, almost 100 times the number of new units being built a year. Homelessness in Britain is soaring for a wide variety of reasons. In 1978, when the new Housing (Homeless Persons) Act went into effect, local authorities officially accepted 60,000 households while today the figure is more than double. About half lose their homes after a period of rent or mortgage arrears, "sometimes because they have bought their council house and find they have bitten off more than they can chew." (*The Economist* 1987:57–58). But the problem seems to result more from curtailed public construction than sales per se, for the homeless are disproportionately found in inner London where council house sales have been slow. Faced with capital spending limits, councils must place the homeless in bed and breakfast hotels at a cost far greater than new construction, public acquisition of private dwellings, or public void rehabilitation would be (Walker 1987). Since 1987, councils with the worst problems were allocated £74 million, with half going to Greater London to make vacant council properties fit for the homeless (*Social Trends* 1989).

This "marginalization" of council housing means not only that it is unfavorably treated by government policies, but that the socioeconomic and political status of its residents is increasingly marginal as well (Forrest and Murie 1988; Hamnett and Randolph 1987). Although the council sector has contracted, the number of tenants receiving supplementary benefit has risen, from 1.3 million in 1979 to 2.0 million in 1986, amounting to over 60 percent of the tenantry (U.K. DOE 1987). Two-thirds of public tenants receive some housing benefit. The proportion of council tenants who are economically inactive continues to grow, including pensioners, single-parent households, and families of the long-term unemployed. Whereas the median household income of council tenants was slightly above the British median from 1953 until the mid-1960s, it has continuously declined at a rate that accelerated in recent years. In 1983, it was only 58 percent of the median for all households (Bentham 1986). Similar trends are true of the educational and occupational characteristics of council tenants (Hamnett 1984; Somerville 1986).

The Diversification of Owner-Occupiers

In contrast to subsidies for council tenants, most observers agree that tax relief for homeowners is regressive, for its value rises with the size of mortgage and thus, in most cases, with tax liability and income. Although tax deductions apply only on mortgages up to £30000 and even though some ministers have suggested lowering this threshold, Mrs. Thatcher opposes such a change. Tax relief also interacts with stage in the life cycle, as the poorer elderly are likely to have paid off their mortgage, while those who have recently bought their homes have higher interest payments (Doling and Stafford 1987). The latter include ex-council tenants and many younger homeowners, of which Britain has a larger share than any other country.

In contrast with the increasingly residual nature of council housing and as a consequence of government encouragement, homeowners have become more socially diverse. Between 1978 and 1983, the proportion of homeowners receiving supplementary benefit rose from 18 to 21 percent. During the same period, the proportion of British households in the lowest income decile who are owner-occupiers has risen from 18 to 27 percent (Somerville 1986). The vast majority of these families have no mortgage and can be assumed to be elderly, although some are new owners of low-quality housing or buyers of cheaper properties in low price areas. And even with mortgage tax relief, ex-council tenants who buy their homes are not exactly rich.

This rise in low-income home ownership has been accompanied by new problems which dispel some myths about the superiority of this tenure. In some cases, home ownership actually impedes labor mobility because of the great price differentials between parts of the country. In other instances, home ownership is no guarantee that property will be kept in good condition. Poor families facing unforeseen catastrophic repair costs must choose between dangerous levels of indebtedness and living with the damage. Indeed, elderly and nonworking homeowners, who are more likely to live in unfit dwellings, usually choose the latter. The cost of repairing the owner-occupied sector in 1981 was estimated at £19.4 billion, similar to the 1986 price tag for rehabilitating the council sector (Karn, Doling, and Stafford 1986). Moreover, risky lending practices, such as variable rate mortgages for up to 100 percent of a property's value, leave households with little equity should interest rates rise beyond what they can afford. Indeed, during the 1980s, mortgage arrears and defaults have multiplied many times over (Building Societies Association 1986).

The Distributive Effects of Council House Sales

I have already indicated a number of ways in which council house sales have exacerbated problems in both the public and owner-occupied sectors, reflecting the complex interaction between housing tenure and socioeconomic status

(Barlow and Duncan 1988). The profile of typical council buyers suggests that sales rob the council sector of its more affluent tenants, but brings more lower-income households into owner-occupation. This is, of course, what the government intended—the creation of a property-owning democracy. The extension of home ownership down the socioeconomic ladder is supposed to equalize the distribution of private wealth.

At the same time, the whole range of housing privatization initiatives was designed to discourage public dependency among working households in favor of targeting resources on the "truly needy." If the redistributive question is whether sales effect a transfer from above-average income households to below-average ones, there is reason to believe they do not. Rather, the nature of the transfer is largely among those at the lower end of the income distribution. Certain council tenants have been receiving less in subsidy and in standards of accommodation in favor of both the more affluent working class who buy and the poorer, government dependent population.

Few dispute that council tenants are better off in terms of government subsidy after they purchase their homes. They receive a discount off the market value of a relatively high quality home, insured against structural defects, without any moving costs. They can resell it in three years at market value with no penalty, except trying to find another one at an affordable price. Resold council houses, though still small in number, tend to go to younger, white-collar households similar to first-time buyers in general. Nor are they the cheapest houses on the market, suggesting that council buyers enjoy appreciable capital gains (Forrest 1980; Crook 1986). If former tenants do not resell, their children may have a sizable inheritance. Buyers also have easy access to credit, including public mortgages and improvement grants, and avoid rising council rents, especially if they do not qualify for housing benefit. Their tax relief on mortgage interest exceeds the sum from which they would benefit as council tenants.

In contrast, council tenants who do not buy are less well off. It will be recalled that many non-buyers feel they are too old or cannot afford to purchase. Others who could afford to buy, but had the bad luck to live in an undesirable unit when granted the Right-to-Buy, are now less likely to be transferred to one deemed worthy of purchase. Government expenditure cuts reduce the funds available for improved management, maintenance, and renovation of their homes. Most significantly, as rents rise, housing benefit is available to an increasingly poorer segment of the council tenantry, putting a squeeze on working tenant households. Uncompensated rent hikes do induce some of these working families to buy, although their incomes may be too precarious to support home ownership in the long run. But many working council tenants, who evaluate their capacity for owner-occupation differently, do not buy.

Ineligible for housing benefit, they face work disincentives as their rent rises. For them, the housing burden increases.

In sum, the social impact of Mrs. Thatcher's housing policies is regressive from the viewpoint of the income distribution as a whole. Rich homeowners as well as buyers of council housing receive more subsidies than council tenants. Thus, as the government intended, the welfare state is getting out of the business of reducing inequality. Rather, through means-tested benefits at mean levels, it sets a minimum standard which is gradually eroding. But what is perhaps most instructive is the penalty in public subsidy paid by working families who exercise their new freedom to choose by remaining council tenants. Economic rationality, taking only housing policies into account, could push them into either precarious home ownership or unemployment.

Political Objectives

Of course, the squeeze on this social stratum has political significance. No assessment of the Right-to-Buy would be complete without considering the evidence for the policy's political success.

Mrs. Thatcher's political goals go far beyond simple reelection. Expressed in countless speeches and party documents, her objectives extend from persuading Britons to adopt her particular ideology to "ridding the country of socialism." In housing as in other policy areas, she seeks to create a political counter-group in opposition to supporters of public intervention. The Right-to-Buy must be assessed at least in terms of its impact on voting, public opinion, and the political potential of organized opposition parties.

The Electoral Impact of the Right-to-Buy

There is considerable evidence to suggest that council house sales have been politically beneficial for the Conservatives. The most obvious reason is that Mrs. Thatcher became the only modern British Prime Minister to win re-election to a third consecutive term. Less apparent is the extent to which her housing policies were responsible for her victories.

The strongest evidence that they were effective comes from studies of voting behavior in the 1979, 1983, and 1987 elections. Homeowners of all classes strongly favored the Tories, just as council tenants voted disproportionately for Labour (Rose and McAllister 1986; Dunleavy 1979; Sarlvik and Crewe 1983; Butler and Kavanaugh 1984, 1988). Mrs. Thatcher received particularly strong support among working class homeowners in Southeast England, where council house sales have been higher and property values have risen most (Johnston 1987; Warde 1986). Indeed, in 1979, the Tories enjoyed exceptionally high voting swings in the New Towns of the South, where large numbers of high-wage manual workers lived in council housing (Crewe 1981:293).

whereas in 1983, Labour fared poorly in a few towns where a large proportion of council stock was sold (Riddell, 1983:156). Finally, the most persuasive evidence of the Right-to-Buy's political payoff was that a majority of council house buyers voted Conservative in 1983 (Riddell 1983:155; Dunleavy and Husbands 1985:137). Similarly, in 1987, 56 percent of new owner-occupiers voted Tory and only 18 percent for Labour (Hoover and Plant 1989:173).

Nevertheless, a closer look at the vote gives rise to reservations about the resounding Tory victory. First, Mrs. Thatcher never won a majority of the electorate. Rather, she obtained a relatively constant plurality of the vote, around 43 percent, which the British electoral system translated into a majority of Parliament seats. This Tory showing was scarcely different than its average share of the vote from 1950 to 1970 when two-party competition was greater. Thus, Mrs. Thatcher benefited from the recent electoral fragmentation of the opposition in which disenchantment with Labour enabled a third party, the Alliance, to run second in a large number of constituencies (Crewe and Searing 1988; Rose 1987).

Second, a social breakdown of the 1987 vote indicates that the constant Tory showing conceals some important party switching. Despite declines in the number of working-class voters and council tenants, Labour has been making inroads among the middle class, especially among highly educated and public sector workers. In the face of losses of middle class support, the Tories' preservation of their constant share of the vote was predicated on winning over more manual workers. Historically, the party has always been relatively successful in courting skilled manual workers, the very group overrepresented among council house buyers. Thus, not only has her party always promoted working class home ownership, but Mrs. Thatcher also made blatant appeals to this group with the Right-to-Buy in all three of her campaigns. Indeed, between 1979 and 1987, support for Labour among skilled manual workers fell from 45 to 36 percent (Butler and Kavanaugh 1988:275).

Does this imply the sales strategy was successful? Cross-sectional voting data alone cannot answer this question for it raises the issue of causality. One must ask whether the same inclination leading to a Tory vote also led to buying one's council house. In fact, council house buyers were already more likely than those remaining tenants to vote Conservative in 1979. Nor did they switch to the Tories more often than non-buying council tenants. Three-quarters of both council tenants and buyers who supported Labour in 1979 remained loyal in 1983 (Heath, Jowell, and Curtice 1985:49–53). Although purchasers did support the Tories more than tenants did, those buyers who defected from Labour preferred the Alliance over the Conservatives in 1979 and 1983 (Williams, Sewel, and Twine 1987). The apparent electoral effect of buying simply reflects the net impact of shrinkage in both public sector housing and the working class, which has kept the share of working-class homeowners in the electorate constant over time.

There is conflicting evidence concerning the impact of being a council house buyer on voting in the 1987 election. Depending on the method and control variables, some report no difference in the voting of comparable council tenants and buyers (Heath, Jones, and Curtice 1989), while others find a small significant effect (McAllister and Studlar 1990; Hoover and Plant 1989). One reason for the contradictory findings may be that housing tenure effects on voting, relative to those of class, attenuated in the socially polarized 1987 election (Crewe 1987), producing a contest of haves and have-nots unlike any in living memory (Butler, 1987).

Impact on Public Opinion

Does the fact that Mrs. Thatcher was thrice elected imply she has convinced her compatriots of the benefits of privatizing public housing? On the one hand, after a decade in office, most of the British public considers the Right-to-Buy to be one of her greatest accomplishments (*The Economist*, 29 April 1989). Indeed, already by 1975, polls suggested that the sale of council houses was among the most important public issues related to housing (Harrop 1980). In 1979, the sales policy had widespread support not only among the electorate at large, but also among council tenants, even those who continued to support Labour (Crewe 1981:293). There was a 35 percent difference in opinion over the Right-to-Buy between stable Labour voters and those switching from Labour to the Conservatives between 1974 and 1979, but even a majority of Labour voters favored the proposal when Mrs. Thatcher was first elected.

Compared with other issues, however, only a minority of council tenants who wanted to buy considered the sales policy very important. Hence this attitude had no significant effect on party choice (Sarlvik and Crewe 1983:102, 262–78). Moreover, even in 1986, after most tenants who could buy had done so, 60 percent of council tenants still supported the Right-to-Buy (Jowell, Witherspoon, and Brook 1986), but this did not prevent Labour from winning their votes by a two-to-one margin the next year.

In fact, Britons did not rank any housing issues as very important in recent elections. In 1979, only five percent of the electorate selected housing as one of the top two issues in the election (Rose 1981); their big concerns were strikes, unemployment, and inflation (Sarlvik and Crewe 1983). In 1987, the major issues were unemployment, the National Health Service, education, and defense (Worcester 1987).

Furthermore, even council tenant purchasers who supported the Tories in 1983 did not do so because of housing policy. Rather, they cited a disillusion with Labour, support of the Falklands war, and Mrs. Thatcher's "strong

leadership" as reasons for their vote. Nonbuying council tenants also swung to
the Tories for these reasons. What did appear absent was "any appreciation of
a continued need for collectivism in housing production, allocation, finance,
or maintenance" (Stubbs 1988:155). While tenure may be statistically associated with people's votes in line with the housing policy positions of the
parties, its effect is not acknowledged by or reflected in the political attitudes
of British voters (Franklin and Page 1984).

Nor were council house buyers consistently favorable on other issues of
privatization (Stubbs 1988). Only manual workers who exercised their right
to buy appear more likely than nonbuyers to hold privatized, individualistic
political opinions (Williams, Sewel, and Twine 1987). Indeed, the British public at large expresses considerable ambivalence about most of Mrs. Thatcher's
welfare and tax policies.[4]

Impact on the Opposition Parties

To rid Britain of socialism, Mrs. Thatcher needs to do more than win office
and exhort public opinion of the correctness of her ideology. This is because
the Labour Party is entrenched in a number of important institutions, including local authorities. As Gamble (1988) notes, the politics of Thatcherism
entails a strong state and a struggle for hegemony. One means to achieve this
was the centralization of power, justified explicitly as a way to curb "loony
left" councils. For example, Mrs. Thatcher doggedly pursued the abolition of
the metropolitan level of government, especially the gadfly Greater London
Council, despite considerable dissension from her own party. The controversial constitutional and democratic issues raised by curbs on local finance have
already been discussed. But there was also a political dividend to implementing public expenditure cuts by squeezing local authorities. Citizens concerned
with declining service quality and public employees receiving pink slips might
more readily blame their councils instead of the government. Not only did
spending cuts result in lay-offs and greater work loads for remaining council employees, but rhetoric about "unresponsive, paternalistic bureaucrats"
provided their disgruntled clients with an accessible target. Indeed, one reason why housing was more vulnerable to cutbacks than other social programs
may be because its defenders (public employees in direct labor organizations
and local councillors) are not well organized on the national level (O'Higgins
1983). In sum, the subordination of local to central government deprived the
Labour Party of powers and resources that could be used to retain and win
support in the next election or pursue new alternative "socialist" policies.

Summary

The fiscal, social, and political evaluations of the Right-to-Buy may be summarized in a number of conclusions. First, the state appears to be no less

involved in the housing market today than it was in 1980. Rather, the nature of that intervention has changed considerably. The government failed to cut not only general spending (except as a proportion of GDP), but housing expenditures as well. Although the fiscal impact of council house sales is open to some dispute, depending on the assumptions made about future economic trends and the items included in the calculus, their redistributive impact is clear.

The middle-aged families in the nonmanual and skilled manual classes who were fortunate to be living in single-family council houses clearly benefited financially from the Right-to-Buy, both because they enjoyed a windfall in discounts and because they avoided the impact of declining housing expenditures by local authorities. Homeowners across the income spectrum continue to enjoy greater public subsidy than tenants, although many may now face heavier housing burdens on their family budgets. In social terms, therefore, the state has eased redistribution, encouraged self-reliance, and increased inequality, in line with New Right doctrine. On the other hand, the safety-net aspect of the welfare state has eroded as well. The minimum standards enjoyed by council tenants, whether through object or subject subsidies, have not kept pace with economic growth. Working poor families, like those in the United States, are bearing the greatest burden of the reorganization of state welfare provision.

Finally, the political success of the Right-to-Buy has been called into question. Mrs. Thatcher was indeed reelected with the help of skilled manual homeowners, many of whom bought their council houses. However, this "counter-group" to prowelfare interests has always had a propensity to vote Conservative and so accounted for few defections to the Tories from the Labour Party. Moreover, as two-thirds of British households achieve owner occupation, homeowners become more heterogeneous. Not only have the Tories ceded middle-class professional votes to Labour, but their working class home owning support appears to be eroding as interest rates rise. While the Right-to-Buy has always been popular, it was not as important as other issues in determining people's votes. Thus, it should come as no surprise that Mrs. Thatcher has increasingly turned her attention to depriving the Labour Party, its institutions, and voting blocs of the political resources to launch effective policy alternatives to privatization.

Alternatives to the Right-to-Buy

The Labour Party opposed the Right-to-Buy in both the 1979 and 1983 campaigns, promising to "end enforced council house sales, empower public landlords to repurchase houses sold under the Tories on first resale and provide that future voluntary agreed sales will be at market value" (Forrest and Murie 1988:63). Yet a year after its second defeat, the party gave qualified endorsement to the Right-to-Buy. Existing tenants would retain this right, but where there was a scarcity of rental housing, they would receive a "portable discount" to purchase a unit on the open market. Any sales proceeds would be released to local authorities for massive new council house building (Labour Party 1987). The 1987 Alliance manifesto was virtually identical on these matters. But Labour went further, trying, one could argue, to outdo the Tories on housing rights. In its housing publications, Labour proposed that private sector tenants of absentee landlords also have the right to buy their homes and that homeowners who cannot find a private buyer would have a "right to sell" their house to the council.

Although the party's main alternative to privatization remained council housing, it also undertook to improve it, in line with a general trend toward decentralization of Labour-led councils designed to increase efficiency, accountability, responsiveness, and citizen participation (Blunkett and Green 1983). One means of pursuing these goals was to encourage housing cooperatives even though the parties have differed since the 1960s on which type of coop they prefer. As one would expect, the division is over ownership.

Labour has traditionally favored rehabilitation, "short life," and tenant management coops (TMCs) with which councils contract for services while retaining title to the property. The first two types evolved from movements of squatters, students, single-member households, and tenants opposed to massive slum clearance and displacement in the late 1960s and who, as voluntary community-based housing associations and coops, improve existing deteriorated housing with public funds (Ospina 1987). Short-life coops now provide temporary shelter for the homeless in once-vacant property (Trott 1987). The last Labour government, which established a Cooperative Housing Agency within the Housing Corporation to advise, administer, and finance coops, passed a 1975 act, based on the American model, permitting tenants to manage their housing cooperatively. It guaranteed continued public subsidies of their units, but the number of TMCs did not take off until Mrs. Thatcher took office (Tinker, et al. 1987).

Nevertheless, Labour remained ambivalent about ownership coops. In the 1970s, TMCs were legally forbidden to buy their housing. During the 1980s, a number of Labour-led councils clashed with local coops over funding and rules (Ospina 1987; Preston 1987; McDonald 1986; Brindley 1988). Currently, Labour proposes giving all tenants the right to take collective control of their homes through TMCs and even offers them cash backing to build new homes if councils prove reluctant to do so. It reasons that "estates pepperpotted with TMCs will look less attractive" to private landlords (Labour Party 1988). Nonetheless, while agreeing to financially assist and advise tenants who want to leave local authority control, Labour continues to warn about the dangers of *ownership* cooperatives:

While this appears democratic, tenants should be aware of the responsibilities involved. Ownership coops, like housing associations, are likely to get less grant in future from central government, making them more reliant on financial institutions which could ultimately call the tune on rent arrears and allocation policies. (Labour Party 1988:13)

One reason for this ambivalence is the Conservatives' perspective on coops. Since the 1960s, when the Tories introduced subsidies for "co-ownership societies," they saw coops as an alternative to home ownership. These societies, placed under the Housing Corporation in 1964, owned equal shares in their properties, which were managed by professionals, not their mostly middle-class residents. They were few in number until 1974, when Housing Corporation Grant became available, but most of them disbanded through individual sales under the Right-to-Buy. The Housing Corporation also subsidizes, advises, and oversees independent voluntary "par-value coops," which are collectively owned by their members and allow no individual capital gains on increased market worth of the property.

When the number of council sales started declining, the Tories took a new approach to privatizing public housing. The government aimed "to encourage local authorities to see themselves as enablers to ensure that everyone is adequately housed, but not necessarily by them" (Treasury, Cmd. 609 1989:5). The 1988 Housing Act gave tenants the right to choose their own "independent sector" landlord (i.e., a for-profit developer/manager, a housing association, *or a cooperative*). If a majority of the sitting tenants do not vote to oppose a bid by one of these entities, the council must sell to it (Kemp 1988; Coleman 1989). Thus the Tories support coops that take over the ownership, not just the management, of council housing. Though subsidized and controlled by the Housing Corporation, these coops become independent of local authorities, i.e., the Labour Party.

The different partisan coop preferences are well illustrated by Glasgow, a Labour bastion with 60 percent of its housing stock in council hands and only a few thousand units sold under the Right-to-Buy. Yet it is an exception in its pioneering, enthusiastic support of cooperatives (Ospina 1987; Ash 1988). The city had 30 tenant rehab coops and 11 TMCs by 1987. Taking a pragmatic approach to its housing problems and with insufficient revenue, the council agreed it had to sell a large proportion of its stock to private developers. But years before the Tories, Glasgow also proposed turning hard-to-let estates over to "community ownership par-value cooperatives," which it hailed as a "collective Right-to-Buy" (Glasgow District Council 1985). As a mutual housing association, tenants would purchase their units, be eligible for off-budget subsidy, and be free of the Conservatives' Right-to-Buy law. If the coop failed, the council would repurchase it.

The Tories blocked this plan, requiring the coops to register with the

Housing Corporation which would supervise them as a nonmutual housing association, with a different subsidy structure and the Right-to-Buy intact. In 1989, the government also approved a pilot scheme to sell Scottish council houses at a price below 20 percent of their value to increase the very low rate of sales there. However, Glasgow council devised a way to avoid central government approval and is now overseeing three coops organized along its original community ownership model.

How viable an alternative are coops? In Glasgow as in British coops generally, tenant participation, knowledge, and interest is low, although residents are satisfied, especially with repairs. Faced with a choice, only one percent of council tenants would opt for a private landlord, while seven percent would accept, respectively, a tenant coop or a housing association. Obviously, most prefer to stay local authority tenants (Bazlington 1988). Despite bi-partisan encouragement, fewer than 1000 housing coops of any kind exist in Britain today, most being small and less than ten years old. While they serve low-income working households, most are found in rehabilitated older housing, which means they do not deal with the supply shortage (Clapham, Kemp, and Kintrea 1987; Tinker, et al. 1987; Underwood 1987). The survivors may be successful, but they tend to form under exceptional circumstances which cannot be easily replicated elsewhere (Harloe 1987; Power 1987).

The National Federation of Housing Cooperatives and advocates of an independent coop movement do not want to be used as a way either to avoid or promote privatization (Ward 1985; Turner 1972; Bibby 1989). However, because low incomes create financial constraints, they almost all need public subsidy and hence, political support. This comes with strings attached, except, perhaps, in the unlikely case of a Social and Liberal Democrat government, which would support a strong, autonomous "third sector" and the decentralization of council housing to ownership coops and neighborhood housing trusts (SLD 1988).

Conclusion

By the mid-1980s, council house sales to tenants were falling off and it became clear what the Right-to-Buy would and would not accomplish. In fiscal terms, public housing sales had provided short-term revenue windfalls to balance off rising expenditures. Hooked on these receipts to reduce the PSBR, the government had a strong incentive to keep selling the quarter of the nation's housing stock still in public hands. The 1988 Housing Act outlined a way to privatize more of it—giving alternative landlords a right to buy council housing.

In social terms, the marginalization of council housing through expenditure cuts and a shift to housing benefit kept the pressure on local authorities to sell an increasingly deteriorating stock. As rents rose, tenants would see in return little improvement in the quality of their housing and might decide to opt for a noncouncil landlord.

In political terms, the electoral payoff to making homeowners of council tenants was largely accomplished, although the number of new Tory votes won by the Right-to-Buy was probably minimal. Now the Conservatives have the problem of keeping their increasingly heterogeneous owner-occupying constituency happy, at a cost in public expenditure more than rivaling that which Labour would spend to subsidize its council-tenant supporters. The Tories' consumerist appeals to voters may eventually backfire, particularly if interest rates rise. Higher mortgage payments produce political dissatisfaction, even as they cost the government more in interest tax relief.

Meanwhile, Labour has been busy recasting itself as a friend of the consumer-citizen. Labour-controlled local authorities have pursued decentralization to improve service delivery, accountability, and responsiveness. They have made creative use of limited funds to serve low-income citizens without succumbing completely to the market. Through cooperatives and other devices, they now portray themselves as defenders of "community."

The 1988 Housing Act, in taking a new tack toward privatization, is the Conservative response to Labour's alternatives. Determined to sell more public housing, the Tories are going where the money and capacity is—to the private sector. Hence, the government has increased tax incentives and decontrolled rents to encourage private rental housing investment. It created four Housing Action Trust public-private partnerships to take over troubled inner-city estates by government fiat. And it has allowed private developers to bid for entire council housing estates in competition with housing associations and tenant cooperatives which themselves depend on the government through Housing Corporation regulation and finance. As Housing Corporation funds are cut back, coops must raise rents and try to leverage private money, thus being forced to privatize further. Since they are at a disadvantage in terms of finance, scale, and experience relative to private developers, they cannot be expected to become a major alternative to public or for-profit housing. The new Tory approach to privatizing public housing coopts and controls, while paying symbolic lip service to one of the few alternatives to council housing proposed by the Opposition. It remains to be seen whether cooperatives will help Labour circumvent the "landlords' right to buy" (Platt 1988) or whether, as some New Right thinkers maintain (Harris and Seldon 1987), direct democracy will prove impractical and inefficient compared to the market.

NOTES

1   There remains some debate over whether tax expenditures ought to be considered a subsidy. New Right economists argue it is not and thereby consider council housing

an unfair tax on homeowners who pay rates and tax on building society interest (Butler 1980; Black and Stafford 1988). However, for most economists, the issue is not whether tax relief is a subsidy, but its nature (Atkinson and King 1980; Balchin 1981; Doling and Stafford 1987; Ermisch 1984).

2 The social security budget consists of two parts: contributory benefits from the National Insurance Fund, and noncontributory benefits. Among the latter are means-tested "supplementary benefit" or income support and means-tested "housing benefit" or housing allowances (For details on housing benefit, see Malpass 1988; Kemp 1985).

3 Prior to the introduction of the housing benefit program, rent allowances were provided from two sources: social security for those receiving supplementary benefit and rent rebates from local authorities for public and private tenants earning below a certain income threshold. These two programs were integrated in 1982 and recipients were gradually shifted, with transitional payments, to the new housing benefit system during the following year.

4 There is disagreement, however, over how to interpret this public ambivalence. See Brook, Jowell, and Witherspoon 1989; Taylor-Gooby 1985; Harris and Seldon 1987; Saunders and Harris, 1987.

REFERENCES

Ash, Joan. 1988. "Glasgow's Housing Achievements." *Housing Review* 37 (January–February): 32–34.

Atkinson, A. B., and M. A. King. 1980. "Housing Policy, Taxation, and Reform." *Midland Bank Review* (Spring): 7–15.

Audit Commission. 1986. *Improving Council House Maintenance*. London: HMSO.

Balchin, Paul N. 1981. *Housing Policy and Housing Needs*. London: Macmillan.

Barlow, James, and Simon Duncan. 1988. "The Use and Abuse of Housing Tenure." *Housing Studies* 3 (4): 219–31.

Bazlington, Chris. 1988. "Council Tenants Back Their Landlords." *Voluntary Housing* 20 (June): 6.

Bentham, Graham. 1986. "Socio-Tenurial Polarization in the United Kingdom, 1953–83: The Income Evidence." *Urban Studies* 23 (April): 157–62.

Bibby, Andrew. 1989. "An Uncertain Life with the Co-op." *The Independent*, 4 March, 36.

Black, John, and David Stafford. 1988. *Housing Policy and Finance*. London: Routledge.

Blunkett, David, and Geoff Green. 1983. *Building from the Bottom: The Sheffield Experience*. London: Fabian Society.

Brindley, Tim. 1988. "The Politics of Popular Planning: Co-operative Housing on London's South Bank." Paper presented at the conference on Housing Policy and Urban Innovation, Amsterdam, June.

Brittan, Samuel. 1984. "The Politics and Economics of Privatization." *Political Quarterly* 55:109–28.

Brook, Lindsay, Roger Jowell, and Sharon Witherspoon. 1989. "Recent Trends in Social Attitudes." In *Social Trends 1988*. London: HMSO, 13–20.

Building Societies Association. 1986. *BSA Bulletin*. no. 47 (July): 30.

Burnett, John. 1986. *A Social History of Housing*, 2d ed. London: Methuen.

Butler, David. 1987. "Election of Haves and Have-Nots." In *The Times Guide to the House of Commons, June 1987*, ed. Alan H. Wood, 32–34. London: Times Books.

Butler, David, and Dennis Kavanaugh. 1984. *The British General Election of 1983*. London: Macmillan.

Butler, David, and Dennis Kavanaugh. 1988. *The British General Election of 1987*. London: Macmillan.

Butler, Stuart M. 1980. *More Effective Than Bombing: Government Intervention in the Housing Market*. London: Adam Smith Institute.

Charles, S. 1982. "The Opportunity Cost of the Sale of Local Authority Rented Accommodation: A Comment." *Urban Studies* 19 (1): 83–84.

Clapham, David and John English, eds. *Public Housing: Current Trends and Future Developments*. London: Croom Helm.

Clapham, David, Peter Kemp, and Keith Kintrea. 1987. "Co-operative Ownership of Former Council Housing." *Policy and Politics* 15 (4): 207–20.

Clapham, David, and Keith Kintrea. 1987. "Importing Housing Policy: Housing Co-operatives in Britain and Scandinavia." *Housing Studies* 2 (3): 157–69.

Clapham, David, and Keith Kintrea. 1987. "Public Housing." In *Regenerating the Inner City: Glasgow's Experience*, ed. David Donnison and Alan Middleton, 93–116. London: Routledge and Kegan Paul.

Coleman, D. A. 1989. "The New Housing Policy: A Critique." *Housing Studies* 4 (1): 44–57.

Cooper, Stephanie. 1985. *Public Housing and Private Property, 1970–1984*. Aldershot: Gower.

Crewe, Ivor. 1987. "A New Class of Politics." *Guardian*, 15 June, 9.

Crewe, Ivor. 1981. "Why the Conservatives Won." In *Britain at the Polls, 1979*, ed. Howard R. Penniman, 262–306. Washington: American Enterprise Institute.

Crewe, Ivor, and Donald D. Searing. 1988. "Mrs. Thatcher's Crusade: Conservatism in Britain, 1972–1986." In *The Resurgence of Conservatism in Anglo-American Democracies*, ed. Barry Cooper, Allan Kornberg, and William Mishler, 258–303. Durham: Duke University Press.

Crook, A. D. H. 1986. "Privatization of Housing and the Impact of the Conservative Government's Initiatives on Low-Cost Homeownership and Private Renting between 1979 and 1984 in England and Wales: 3. Impact and Evaluation of Low-Cost Homeownership Policy." *Environment and Planning A* 18:639–59.

Doling, John, and Bruce Stafford. 1987. "MIRAS—Who Benefits?" *Housing Review* 36 (May–June): 81–2.

Dunleavy, Patrick. 1979. "The Urban Basis of Political Alignment: Social Class, Domestic Property Ownership, and State Intervention in Consumption Processes." *British Journal of Political Science* 9 (October): 409–43.

Dunleavy, Patrick, and Christopher T. Husbands. 1985. *British Democracy at the Crossroads*. London: Allen and Unwin.

Dunn, R., R. Forrest, and A. Murie. 1987. "The Geography of Council House Sales in England—1979–85." *Urban Studies* 24:47–59.

Ermisch, J. 1984. *Housing Finance: Who Gains?* London: Policy Studies Institute.

Esam, Peter. 1987. "The Bottom Line: Has Conservative Social Security Protected the Poor?" In *The Growing Divide: A Social Audit, 1979–1987*, ed. Alan Walker and Carol Walker, 110–19. London: Child Poverty Action Group.

Foreman-Peck, J. 1982. "The Appraisal of Sales of Local Authority Rented Accommodation: A Comment." *Urban Studies* 19 (1): 79–82.

Forrest, Ray. 1980. "The Resale of Former Council Houses in Birmingham." *Policy and Politics* 8 (3): 334–40.

Forrest, Ray, and Alan Murie. 1986. *An Unreasonable Act?* SAUS Study no. 1, University of Bristol.

Forrest, Ray, and Alan Murie. 1988. *Selling the Welfare State: The Privatization of Public Housing*. London: Routledge, Chapman and Hall.

Franklin, Mark N., and Edward C. Page. 1984. "A Critique of the Consumption Cleavage Approach in British Voting Studies." *Political Studies* 32:521–36.

Gamble, Andrew. 1988. *The Free Economy and the Strong State: The Politics of Thatcherism*. London: Macmillan.

Glasgow District Council. 1985. "Community Ownership in Glasgow." Briefing Paper. Glasgow Housing Department, May.

Glennerster, Howard. 1985. *Paying for Welfare*. Oxford: Basil Blackwell.

Hamnett, Chris. 1984. "Housing the Two Nations: Socio-Tenurial Polarization in England and Wales, 1961–81." *Urban Studies* 43:389–405.

Hamnett, Chris, and Bill Randolph. 1987. "The Residualisation of Council Housing in Inner London, 1971–1981." In *Public Housing: Current Trends and Future Developments*, ed. David Clapham and John English, 32–50. London: Croom Helm.

Hands, John. 1978. "The Co-operative Housing Agency: 18 Months On." *Housing Review* 27 (November–December): 148–50.

Harloe, Michael. 1987. "The Declining Fortunes of Social Rented Housing in Europe." In *Public Housing: Current Trends and Future Developments*, ed. David Clapham and John English. London: Croom Helm.

Harris, Ralph, and Arthur Seldon. 1987. *Welfare and the State: A Quarter-Century of Suppressed Public Choice*. London: Institute of Economic Affairs.

Harrop, Martin. 1980. "The Basis of Political Alignment: A Comment." *British Journal of Political Science* 10 (July): 388–98.

Heath, Anthony, Roger Jowell, and John Curtice. 1985. *How Britain Votes*. New York: Pergamon Press.

Heath, Anthony, Roger Jowell, and John Curtice. 1989. *The Extension of Popular Capitalism*. University of Strathclyde Studies in Government and Politics, no. 60 Glasgow.

HMSO [Her Majesty's Stationery Office]. 1988. *Social Trends 1987*. London: HMSO.

Holmans, A. E. 1987. *Housing Policy in Britain*. London: Croom Helm.

Hoover, Kenneth, and Raymond Plant. 1989. *Conservative Capitalism in Britain and the United States*. London: Routledge.

Johnston, R. J. 1987. "A Note on Housing Tenure and Voting in Britain, 1983." *Housing Studies* 2 (2): 112–21.

Jowell, Roger, Sharon Witherspoon, and Lindsay Brook. 1986. *British Social Attitudes: The 1986 Report*. Aldershot: Gower.

Karn, Valerie, John Doling, and Bruce Stafford. 1986. "Growing Crisis and Contradiction in Home Ownership." In *The Housing Crisis*, ed. Peter Malpass, 125–50. London: Croom Helm.

Kemp, Peter. 1985. "The Housing Benefit Scheme." In *The Year Book of Social Policy in Britain 1984–5*. ed. Catherine Jones and Maria Brenton, 30–46. London: Routledge and Kegan Paul.

Kemp, Peter. 1988. "Shifting the Balance Between State and Market: The Reprivatisation of Rental Housing in Britain." Paper presented at the Housing Between State and Market conference, Dubrovnik, September.

Kerr, Marion. 1988. *The Right to Buy*. London: HMSO.

Kerrell-Vaughan, A. R. 1948. "Building Costs, Subsidies, Reconditioning of Rural Houses, and the Sale of Local Authority Houses." In *Housing Topics of 1948*. National Housing and Town Planning Council.

Kilroy, Bernard. 1982. "The Financial and Economic Implications of Council House Sales." In *The Future of Council Housing*, ed. J. English, 52–93. London: Croom Helm.

Kirwan, R. M. 1984. "The Demise of Public Housing?" In *Privatization and the Welfare State*, ed. Julian Le Grand and Ray Robinson, 133–45. London: Allen and Unwin.

Labour Party. 1987. *Britain Will Win*. London: Labour Party.

Labour Party. 1988. *A Guide to the Housing Act 1988*. Information Paper no. 85. London: Labour Party.

Labour Party. 1985. *Homes for the Future: Statement to Annual Conference 1985 by the Labour Party National Executive Committee*. London: Labour Party.

Labour Party. 1987. *Providing Homes for People*. London: Labour Party.

Lansley, Stewart. 1979. *Housing and Public Policy*. London: Croom Helm.

Leather, Phillip, and Allan Murie. 1986. "The Decline in Public Expenditure." In *The Housing Crisis*, ed. Peter Malpass, 24–56. London: Croom Helm.

McAllister, Ian, and Donley T. Studlar. 1990. "Popular versus Elite Views of Privatization: The Case of Britain." *Journal of Public Policy* 9 (2): 157–78.

McCulloch, David. 1987. "The Financial Aspects of Change." In *Public Housing: Current Trends and Future Developments*, ed. David Clapham and John English, 51–66. London: Croom Helm.

McDonald, Alan. 1986. *The Weller Way: The Story of the Weller Streets Housing Cooperative*. London: Faber.

Maclennan, Duncan. 1982. *Housing Economics: An Applied Approach*. London: Longman.

Malpass, Peter, ed. 1986. *The Housing Crisis*. London: Croom Helm.

Malpass, Peter. 1988. "Pricing and Subsidy Systems in British Social Rented Housing: Assessing the Policy Options." *Housing Studies* 3 (January): 31–39.

"Margaret Thatcher's Ten Years." 1989. *The Economist*, 29 April, 57–58.

Mason, Tim. 1987. "The Crisis in Council Housing." *New Society*, 7 August, 9–11.

Merrett, Stephen. 1979. *State Housing in Britain*. London: Routledge and Kegan Paul.

Minford, Patrick, Michael Peel, and Paul Ashton. 1987. *The Housing Morass: Regulation, Immobility and Unemployment*. London: Institute of Economic Affairs.

Ministry of Housing and Local Government. 1960. *Housing Acts: Sale and Leasing of Houses*. Circular no. 5/60. London: Whitehall, 15 February.

Murie, Alan. 1975. *The Sale of Council Houses: A Study in Social Policy*. CURS Occasional Paper no. 35. University of Birmingham.

Nellis, J. G., and M. C. Fleming. 1986. "The Process of Housing Privatization and Tenurial Change in the UK: Some Further Evidence." Paper presented at the International Research Conference on Housing Policy, Gavle, Sweden.

"No Place Like Home." 1987. *The Economist*, 26 December, 57–58.

O'Higgins, Michael. "Rolling Back the Welfare State: The Rhetoric and Reality of Public Expenditure and Social Policy under the Conservative Government." In *The Year Book of Social Policy in Britain 1982*, ed. Catherine Jones and June Stevenson, 153–77. London: Routledge and Kegan Paul.

Ospina, Jose. 1987. *Housing Ourselves*. London: Hilary Shipman.

Parry, Richard. 1986. "United Kingdom." In *Growth to Limits: The Western European Welfare States Since World War II*, vol. 2, ed. Peter Flora, 158–240. Berlin: de Gruyter.

Penniman, Howard, ed. 1981. *Britain at the Polls 1979*. Washington American Enterprise Institute.

Pirie, Madsen. 1988. *Privitization: Theory, Practice, and Choice*. Aldershot: Wildwood House.

Platt, Steve. 1988. "Goodbye Council Housing?" *New Society*, 26 February, 12–14.

Posnett, J., and C. Edwards. 1982. "The Opportunity Cost of the Sales of Local Authority Rented Accommodation: Reply." *Urban Studies* 19 (1): 85–7.

Power, Anne. 1987. *Property Before People: The Management of Twentieth-Century Council Housing*. London: Allen and Unwin.

Preston, Keith. 1987. "Tenant Management Coops: A Local Authority Perspective." *Housing Review* 36 (May–June): 101–3.

Riddell, Peter. 1983. *The Thatcher Government*. Oxford: Martin Robertson.

Robinson, Ray. 1986. "Restructuring the Welfare State: An Analysis of Public Expenditure, 1979/80–1984/85." *Journal of Social Policy* 15 (January): 1–21.

Robinson, Ray, and Tony O'Sullivan. 1983. "Housing Tenure Polarization: Some Empirical Evidence." *Housing Review* 32 (July–August): 116–7.

Rose, Richard. 1987. "Socialism's Slipping Gears." *Times Higher Education Supplement*, 25 September, 13.

Rose, Richard. 1981. "Toward Normality: Public Opinion Polls in the 1979 Election." In *Britain at the Polls 1979*, ed. Howard R. Penniman, 177–209. Washington: American Enterprise Institute.

Rose, Richard, and Ian McAllister. 1986. *Voters Begin to Choose: From Closed-Class to Open Elections in Britain*. London: Sage.

Sarlvik, Bo, and Ivor Crewe. 1983. *Decade of Dealignment: The Conservative Victory of 1979 and Electoral Trends in the 1970's*. Cambridge: Cambridge University Press.

Saunders, Peter, and Colin Harris. 1987. "Biting the Nipple: Consumer Preferences and State Welfare." Paper presented at the Sixth Urban Change and Conflict Conference, University of Kent, September.

Schifferes, S. 1979. *Facts on Council House Sales*. London: Shelter.

Social Democratic Party/Liberal Alliance. 1987. *Britain United: The Time Has Come*. London: SDP/Liberal Alliance.

Social and Liberal Democrats. 1988. *Partnership for Diversity: The Social and Liberal Democrats Approach to Housing*. English Green Paper no. 2. London.

Social Trends 1987. 1988. London: HMSO.

Somerville, Peter. 1986. "Housing Tenure Polarisation." *Housing Review* 35 (November–December): 190–3.

Stubbs, Cherrie. 1988. "Property Rights and Relations: The Purchase of Council Housing." *Housing Studies* 3 (2): 145–58.

Taylor-Gooby, Peter. 1987. "Disquiet and State Welfare: Clinging to Nanny." Paper presented at the Sixth Urban Change and Conflict Conference, University of Kent, September.

Taylor-Gooby, Peter. 1985. "Pleasing Any of the People, Some of the Time: Perceptions of Redistribution and Attitudes to Welfare." *Government and Opposition* 20 (3): 396–406.

Taylor-Gooby, Peter. 1985. "The Politics of Welfare: Public Attitudes and Behavior." In *The Future of Welfare*, ed. Rudolf Klein and Michael O'Higgins, 72–91. Oxford: Blackwell.

Thompson, Grahame. 1986. *The Conservatives Economic Policy*. London: Croom Helm.

Tinker, Anthea, Patricia Dodd, Paul McCafferty, and Simon Dougall. 1987. "Cooperative Housing—Interim Results of a DoE National Study." *Housing Review* 36 (January–February): 14–16.

Trott, Tony. 1987. "Shortlife Co-ops: Mortgage Finance for Housing Co-ops." *Housing Review* 36 (May–June): 103–4.

Turner, J. 1972. *Housing by People: Towards Autonomy in Building Environments*. London: Marion Boyars.

Underwood, Simon. 1987. "Who Lives in Housing Co-ops?" *Housing Review* 36 (May–June): 100–101.

U.K. Department of the Environment. Annually. *Housing and Construction Statistics*. London: HMSO.

U.K. Department of the Environment. *Local Housing Statistics*. London: HMSO.

U.K. Department of the Environment. 1980. *Appraisal of the Financial Aspects of Council House Sales*. London: HMSO.

U.K. Department of the Environment. 1987. *Housing: The Government's Proposals*. White Paper, Cmnd. 214. London: HMSO.

U.K. Treasury. Annually to 1989. *The Government's Expenditure Plans 1989–90 to 1991–92*. Cmd. 601–621, January.

Veljanovski, Cento. 1987. *Selling the State: Privatisation in Britain*. London: Weidenfeld and Nicolson.

Walker, Alan, and Carol Walker. 1987. *The Growing Divide: A Social Audit, 1979–1987*. London: Child Poverty Action Group, June.

Walker, Bruce. 1987. "Public Sector Costs of Board and Lodging Accommodation for Homeless Households in London." *Housing Studies* 2 (4): 261–73.

Ward, Colin. 1974. *Tenants Take Over*. London: Architectural Press.

Ward, Colin. 1985. *When We Build Again*. London: Pluto.

Warde, Alan. 1986. "Electoral Mysteries: Class and Space in the British Election of 1983." *International Journal of Urban and Regional Research* 10 (June): 289–94.

Williams, Nicholas J., John B. Sewel, and Fred E. Twine. 1987. "Council House Sales and the Electorate: Voting Behavior and Ideological Implications." *Housing Studies* 2 (4): 274–82.

Worcester, Robert M. 1987. "What Did the Polls Portend?" In *The Times Guide to the House of Commons, June 1987*, ed. Alan H. Wood. London: Times Books.

PART 4
LAW ENFORCEMENT POLICY

10 *Malcolm M. Feeley*

The Privatization of Punishment in Historical Perspective

This chapter places the contemporary debate over privatization of corrections in historical perspective. In so doing, it shows that the debate ignores a central function of privatization, which is its potential to expand the state's capacity to punish. I demonstrate this in a three-part analysis. The first section traces the recent growth of privatization, examines the current debate over the relative efficiencies of private and public corrections, and then argues that this debate is misdirected. The next part develops this thesis by examining the consequences of earlier efforts at private penal administration. The third section assesses the implications of the current privatization movement in light of the lessons of history.

The Debate over Private Corrections

In recent years, there have been efforts to privatize significant segments of corrections. (Savas 1987:868; Logan 1990; McDonald 1990; Ryan and Ward 1989.) Private entrepreneurs have begun to play a major role in financing and building correctional facilities, in supplying a variety of auxiliary services, and in obtaining contracts to operate and administer prisons and jails. Many

Malcolm M. Feeley is Professor of Law at Boalt Hall of Law School at the University of California at Berkeley.

private for-profit and nonprofit organizations also run programs for offenders who are released into their custody or who must participate as a condition of probation. These programs provide job training, drug treatment, educational services, and the like. The most controversial feature of the recent privatization movement, however, has been private companies assuming responsibilities for operating secure prisons and jails.

As of October 1988, more than twenty-five for-profit companies, many backed by venture capital, were competing for rights to build, own, and operate jails and prisons throughout the United States (*Private Vendors in Corrections* 1988). By most accounts these efforts have been successful, and certainly, they are growing in size and number (Babcock 1985; Savas 1987). In 1986 the state of Tennessee enacted a Private Prison Contracting Act (1986 Tenn. Pub. Acts, chap. 932) which permits private businesses to build and operate prisons (McAfee 1987:851); as of 1989 the Corrections Corporation of America (CCA) was preparing to operate a 144-bed juvenile facility and was negotiating with the state to operate other facilities. The Wackenhut Company and the CCA each have contracted with the state of Texas to build and operate two 500-bed maximum security facilities (Panel on Corrections Policy 1987). Wackenhut, CCA, and other companies operate custodial facilities for the United States Immigration and Naturalization Service (INS). The United States Correction Corporation operates a custody center in San Antonio, Texas (Panel on Corrections Policy 1987). In North Carolina, Tennessee, Florida, and New Mexico, CCA operates county jails (*Private Vendors in Corrections* 1988). Buckingham Security Ltd. operates Pennsylvania's Butler County Jail (*Private Vendors in Corrections* 1988). And U.S. Corrections Corporation operates Kentucky's Marion Adjustment Center (Panel on Corrections Policy 1987). Still other private companies operate correctional facilities scattered across the country. Some of these companies have entered into consulting agreements to plan for privatized prison services in France, Germany, and Great Britain (Panel on Corrections Policy 1987).

Privatization in juvenile corrections has grown at an even faster pace. During the past thirty years, placements in private programs (e.g., training centers, residential treatment and counseling programs, foster care, and diversion programs) in lieu of state-run facilities has become quite common. Indeed, during the past thirty years, the number of private placements has grown at a faster pace than public programs. Currently in the United States, a substantial portion of all juveniles under court supervision are in the custody of privately operated programs. No doubt, this more extensive involvement of the private sector in juvenile corrections is due to the early history of juvenile corrections which initially depended on volunteers, a long-standing preference for noncustodial programs for juveniles, and the decentralized and local administration and financing of juvenile justice programs.

In recent years, jails, prisons, and juvenile facilities have also turned to private vendors to supply a host of services, including food, health, counseling, vocational training, education, and at times, administrative services (Hackett et al. 1987). Currently, there are hundreds of different for-profit and nonprofit contractors providing all sorts of services for adult and juvenile corrections. This trend is continuing unabated (Camp and Camp 1985:14).

In recent years, the private sector has also radically altered the ways correctional facilities are financed and built. Private lease-purchase arrangements increasingly are replacing government-issued bonds. Designed by such investment firms as E. F. Hutton, Merrill Lynch, Morgan Stanley and Company, and Shearson Lehman Brothers, lease-purchase agreements allow governments to make installment purchases of property which were privately financed and built (DeWitt 1987; Chaiken and Mennemeyer 1987). This allows them to make capital purchases without having to commit huge blocks of tax funds and without having to obtain voter-approved bond issues.[1] Since the construction is privately financed, bids can be let faster, contracts negotiated more easily, and construction completed more swiftly. As of 1987, at least $2 billion worth of correctional construction had been financed in this manner (Chaiken and Mennemeyer 1987:23). If one assumes that the same facilities would otherwise have been built with conventional financing, all this translates into huge savings for taxpayers during inflationary periods.

Advocates of these forms of privatization assert that they are efficient and cost-effective. These claims are buttressed by a number of independent studies which conclude that private companies can finance new facilities without the need for voter-approved bond issues, and can construct them more quickly and cheaply than government (Chaiken and Mennemeyer 1987:49). Other studies have found that private contractors, freed from cumbersome public personnel policies and unionized work forces, are able to run correctional institutions and related programs more efficiently and cheaply. Indeed, there is a near consensus that privatization of a number of correctional functions, especially the new forms of financing and the new methods of providing services, is more effective and more efficient than long-standing conventional methods (Mullen 1985).

Despite generally favorable reviews, correctional privatization has its critics who dismiss cost comparisons which show private enterprise to be more cost-effective. They argue that such studies ignore liability issues, do not identify long-term costs, and do not compare institutions which serve identical populations (DiIulio n.d.; Mullen 1985). Some suggest that private providers may be operating loss leaders in order to capture the market. Others are concerned that skimming off the low-security convicts into private facilities will reduce the administrative flexibility of state correctional departments that are left to manage the most intractable group of inmates (Dickey 1987). A few critics base their arguments on the abuses of the convict lease systems and other privately administered corrections schemes of the nineteenth and early twentieth centuries (McAfee 1987).

The most substantial opposition, however, comes from those who raise principled objections to the idea of privatized corrections. Three objections to privatization are often made on constitutional grounds: 1) that the establishment of private prisons violates the constitutional prohibition against delegating governmental responsibilities to private parties; 2) that it reduces state liability and hence raises costs of running prisons; and 3) that it violates the Thirteenth Amendment which prohibits involuntary servitude by private parties.

After an exhaustive analysis of these issues, Ira Robbins (1988) argues that although none of these concerns poses an insurmountable obstacle to private prisons, when the costs of overcoming them are considered, privatized corrections are not likely to be any less expensive than public corrections.

Both federal and state case law permit delegation of a wide variety of functions to private contractors, and pose no insurmountable obstacle to private prisons provided reasonable precautions are taken to avoid conflicts of interest. For instance, reviewing courts must be assured that private contractors do not promulgate disciplinary rules and then interpret them in ways that benefit the company. Despite recent narrow interpretations, Robbins (1988:118) has concluded that state action doctrine will not exempt states with private prisons from liability for violations of prisoners' rights. Finally, in addressing the Thirteenth Amendment issues, he (1988:133) concludes that the prohibition is a bar neither against confining state prisoners in private facilities nor requiring them to work in private-sector jobs so long as they are not exploited.

John DiIulio (1987:79–80) also criticizes privatization on grounds of principle. Drawing on John Locke's *Treatise on Government*, he argues that because punishment is one of the core functions of government, it should be administered by governmental agencies. "To remain legitimate and morally significant," DiIulio asserts, "the authority to govern behind bars, to deprive citizens of their liberty, to coerce (and even kill) them, must remain in the hands of government authorities." He (1987:81) concedes that "farming out" corrections to private contractors might be economically efficient, but asserts that doing so "undermines the moral writ of the community." Although he purports to have put forward a moral argument against private prisons, he does not categorically oppose privatization. His concern is that private prisons may weaken the legitimacy of government. Thus, he does not so much offer a moral objection as a prediction: if government delegates too many responsibilities to the private sector it jeopardizes popular support and its own credibility. It remains to be seen if there is evidence to support this claim.

As important as this debate over the efficiency and economy of privatized corrections is, it ignores other and, I believe, more important questions. For the most part, the debate assumes comparability of activities and asks simply, which sector—public or private—can perform them most efficiently? Even vigorous critics tend to frame issues this way. John DiIulio assumes that the central question is, Who should administer the prisons—the public or private sector? His purpose is to expand the relevant range of consideration to include selected externalities of private administration that tend to be ignored by proponents.

To frame issues of privatization solely in terms of the substitution (of private for public functions) ignores another, more significant question: To what extent does privatization expand and transform the state's capacity to punish? This chapter argues that the most significant consequence of privatization historically has been the generation of new and expanded sanctions and forms of social control.

If I am correct, then the privatization movement should be assessed from a dynamic and historical perspective, one that can determine if and how privatization expands the sanctioning capacity of the state and how this expanded array of punishments is distributed across different sectors of society. These are obvious and important questions, but ones that are largely ignored in discussions of correctional privatization.

The limits of assessing privatization solely in terms of efficiency and effectiveness are suggested by Shearing and Stenning's (1983) work on private police. They found that private security guards are much more than merely privately paid enforcers of public laws. "Private security," they observe (1983: 53), ". . . has introduced the control and supervision of policing into places traditionally beyond the scope of public policing." Officials of Disneyland, for example, can impose restrictions that authorities at the Bronx Zoo cannot. Private police have different orientations, enforce different norms, and draw on a wider variety of sanctions. Private police blur the distinction between private and public, and as a consequence, "more of our activities are coming under the supervision, and often control, of some form of police (Shearing and Stenning 1983:53)." As new forms of social organization permit ownership of "mass private property" with concomitant growth of private security, traditional forms of both private property and law enforcement are called into question. In sum, Stenning and Shearing argue that as private organizations have grown, private police have radically transformed the policing function.

Private corrections must also be understood as a complement to and an expansion of public correctional programs.[2] This perspective is supported by a review of earlier efforts which relied on private entrepreneurs. Such an inquiry reveals that private entrepreneurs have generated new sanctions, which have been applied to those who otherwise would not have been sanctioned. The new sanctioning and social control is both broader and deeper than what preceded it.

In advancing this thesis, I must issue a caution. Throughout history there has not always been a clear distinction between public and private realms. The early modern state depended on a host of institutions which we might regard as private but which were clearly invested with public responsibilities. Indeed, some public offices were hereditary and others were bought and sold. And some private businesses, such as those of publicans, were generally understood to be public services operated for the general benefit of society. The aim of this chapter is not to trace the shifting contours of the public-private distinction, but more generally, to show that with respect to criminal justice administration, the state has a long history of reliance upon entrepreneurs to provide innovative responses to new problems.

Private Corrections in History

The history of the development of the modern criminal justice system in Great Britain and the United States is a succession of piecemeal reforms brought about by pressures to expand the capacity and effectiveness of the criminal law. Many of the reforms were initiated by entrepreneurs who sought to accomplish what government could not or would not. Often, however, the two have gone hand in hand as entrepreneurs developed successful innovations that later were incorporated into the machinery of government.

Involvement of the private sector is found in all segments of the criminal process. No doubt, it stems in some part from the Anglo-American political culture which is skeptical of governmental authority and which promotes voluntary associations and private initiatives.[3] Whatever the precise reasons, it is clear the private initiatives have played an important role in shaping the modern criminal justice system. In England, privately run "prosecution societies" were the precursors of the modern, state-funded system of prosecution, and the modern police system has its origins in voluntary and private law enforcement schemes. Gaols in smaller communities throughout England, for centuries, were run as businesses by ale house keepers, whose cellars doubled as gaols. From the Elizabethan era to the early twentieth century, English and American courts depended upon a type of private probation system to monitor petty offenders (Samaha 1974).

The continued need to rely on the bail bondsmen is a modern example of this entrepreneurial heritage but so too is the private corrections system. The private sector has played a crucial and innovative role in responding to demands to increase and expand sanctions in the face of rising crime and declining confidence in government. Current developments parallel earlier efforts, and so it is to this history that I now turn.

Transportation

Shortly after the first colonists arrived in Virginia in 1607, they were followed by a handful of convicted felons, transported there as a condition of pardon to be sold into servitude. Thus was set into motion a new penal system, a system that operated successfully for nearly 250 years. For half of that period it constituted England's dominant mode of punishment for serious felons.

Emerging as a response to what was widely perceived as an ineffectual criminal justice system, transportation to the New World was a marriage of efficiency and effectiveness. It was efficient in that its costs were borne by profit-seeking merchants selling their human cargo and by planters who purchased it. It was effective in that it sanctioned thousands of offenders who otherwise would have gone unpunished.

One estimate is that fully one-half of the immigrants to the Americas during the eighteenth century were transported convicts and indentured servants (Smith [1947] 1965). Following the American Revolution, transportation shifted to Australia, where convicts constituted the initial wave of settlers.

During the long North American phase of transportation, some 50,000 convicts were shipped across the Atlantic, most notably to Virginia, the Carolinas, and Maryland where they were sold as agricultural laborers (Ekirch 1987). Between the time the first convict ship sailed into Botany Bay in 1789 and the time transportation ended in 1868, over 100,000 convicts were put to work in Australia as agricultural workers, sheepherders, and manual laborers.

Why one form of punishment loses favor and another is instituted is not readily answerable. At any period, a number of alternatives may simultaneously be employed, and one may emerge to push others into the recesses. Banishment and forced labor, for instance, have been used as forms of punishment in diverse societies throughout history. Whatever the precise reasons for its emergence in seventeenth-century England, transportation cannot be divorced from the rise of mercantilism and the British colonial experience.[4] It began, as I have suggested, with the first settlement in North America and grew in rough proportion to the flow of English settlers to the Americas.

What underlay the entire administrative and economic structure of transportation was reliance upon private enterprise to effect the public policy. More precisely, transportation was an innovation promoted by mercantile interests which was only reluctantly embraced by public officials as they slowly came to appreciate its cost effectiveness.

It began as an outgrowth of the trade in indentured servants but the same social and economic conditions that induced people to settle in the New World also generated indentured servitude.

In his monumental book on the subject, *Colonists in Bondage*, Abbot Emerson Smith writes of the economic forces that gave rise to and sustained this process:

From the complex pattern of forces producing emigration to the American colonies one stands out clearly as most powerful in causing the movement of servants. This was the pecuniary profit to be made by shipping them. Labor was one of the few European importations which even the earliest colonists would sacrifice much to procure, and the system of indentured servitude was the most convenient system next to slavery by which labor became a commodity to be bought and sold. ([1947] 1965:4–5)

These observations about the trade in indentured servants apply equally well to the trade in convicts. Smith writes: "Even the convicts were handed over to private individuals. They shipped them to Maryland and Virginia and sold them at an excellent profit to the same planters who denounced the English government for allowing them to come at all." ([1947] 1965:6) Indeed the two groups, indentured servants and convicts, were often merged; the public was likely to see both groups as scoundrels and ne'er-do-wells. Intellectuals and public officials, concerned with Malthus's predictions of escalating populations, roving mobs, and unemployment, also lumped them together, regarding both groups as part of the surplus underclass for whom the colonies served as an overflow valve. Colonial landowners viewed both servants and convicts as sources of cheap but inefficient labor. And merchants saw them as cargo to be comingled in the holds of their ships and sold to the highest bidders on the other side of the Atlantic.

As it emerged in North America, transportation developed from a simple ad hoc arrangement to a sophisticated market which allowed the state to sanction thousands of felons at little or no public cost, and which provided handsome returns to entrepreneurs. In the early days, arrangements for transportation were left to the offender, his or her family, or the county. If they were unable to raise money for passage, convicts might languish in dockside gaols for months or years. Some were able to negotiate free passage in exchange for allowing the captain to sell them into bondage. Having gained considerable experience in the lucrative trade in indentured servants, shippers eventually sensed the vast potential of this new market and pressed the government for subsidies and exclusive contracts to transport all convicts from selected counties. This generated a steady supply of convicts, which in turn stimulated still greater demand for their labor in the colonies. As business arrangements developed, shippers were guaranteed a steady supply of convicts and built specially designed ships to pack their human cargo tightly. Without government contracts, shippers had been able to make profits transporting healthy male convicts. But when they agreed to take women, children, and the aged, as well as convicts, they were able to obtain guaranteed quantities and subsidies, and make even more handsome profits. Their successes in expanding the market in convict trade are reflected in a series of commissions of the privy council which expanded authorization for transportation and granted exclusive charters for transportation to selected shippers (Ekirch 1987:97–111). Indeed, in 1763 the British government was able to negotiate contracts with shippers that did not provide for subsidies. The shippers could make sufficient profits without the subsidies.

The American Revolution called an abrupt halt to this lucrative and efficient regime of sanctioning, but not before convicts constituted a substantial portion of all immigrants to North America.[5] After prolonged consideration, Australia was selected as the site for a renewed policy of transportation.

British officials had become enchanted with the idea of establishing an English beachhead on the new continent, especially in the face of what they thought was a growing French presence in the South Pacific. Convict colonization in Australia would serve a multiplicity of purposes: it would offset the growing French naval presence in the region and thus protect shipping lanes for British merchants; it would generate new markets; it would provide a solution for relieving population pressures at home; and of course, it would provide an answer to the pressing question of what to do with the thousands of convicts crammed into the rotting hulks in the Thames and stashed in the crumbling gaols throughout the kingdom. It would even provide a solution to the growing Irish question; political agitators could be removed to Australia. With these arguments, British shippers and naval officials were able to persuade the Privy Council to adopt a policy which required the use of convict labor to establish a British presence in Australia.

Thus in 1783, the first English settlers to land in Australia were a handful of naval officers and sailors with a cargo of convicted felons. What began as a trickle in the 1780s and '90s, turned into a torrent that lasted for fifty years.

The economy and administration of transportation to Australia differed substantially from the earlier American experience. The American operation had been a wholly private operation once the government relinquished control over the convicts at the gates of the county gaols or on the London docks. Contractors in turn amassed their human cargoes and transported and sold them at auction on the decks of their ships up and down the American seaboard. In contrast, in Australia the government played a central role in every stage of the process. In a land unpopulated but for the aborigines, there was no preexisting demand for labor, no market for convicts. The government first had to create this demand; thus, the convicts were the settlers. Relying on convict labor colonial officials established the first settlements and the first economy. Every step of the process was government financed and government administered, so that the economies of privatization that earlier had kept the costs of British penal policy to a minimum were not repeated in Australia. Following as it did on the heels of the nearly free transportation to the American colonies, this new policy engendered considerable opposition from a variety of quarters.[6]

Despite occasional setbacks, the Australian experiment continued apace.

The defense of the costly investment was a traditional defense of mercantilism: by establishing an English presence in Australia, British markets and British naval power in the region would expand. Earlier, in the Americas, India, and Africa, British merchants had established themselves in ways that had forced the government to follow. In Australia the logic was the same, but the situation was reversed: government investment was needed to protect and promote British trade and industry. Here the government simply had to make a greater initial investment.

This reasoning proved to be sound. For the first few decades, Australian transportation was an especially costly operation since the government had to bear the full costs of moving the convicts 15,000 miles and establishing brand new communities. As the settlements flourished and vast new markets opened, however, the free population grew and generated its own demand for convict labor. With this, some of the cost of transportation shifted away from the government.

The very success of the experiment in transportation was eventually its downfall. As the free population in Australia grew, facilitated in large part by the availability of the cheap convict labor, so too did the resentment among a segment of the free settlers who began to object to the fact that Australia was England's dumping ground (Neal 1987; Hughes 1987). By the 1860s, this feeling was strong enough to put an end to transportation. By that time, more than 100,000 English, Scottish, and Irish convicts had been sent to the "fatal shore."

Despite its demise, the policy of transportation had more than justified the vision of its early supporters. Initially entrepreneurs had devised a low- to no-cost penal policy. And with the end of transportation to North America, they took the lead in devising the plan for redirecting convicts to Australia in a way that coupled the solution to the penal problem with plans for expanding their markets and sphere of influence.

It is impossible to know who first seized upon the idea of transportation. Was it the entrepreneurs, experienced in the profitable trade in indentured servants and anxious to expand their markets? Or was it government officials desperate to find cheap ways to cope with the crisis of law and order? Whatever the precise history of its early years, transportation was an overwhelmingly successful innovation. In an era when strong government, and particularly a strong criminal justice apparatus, was anathema to large segments of the English population, the strategy of a decentralized, privately administered, low-cost penal system was a brilliant way to expand the state's capacity to sanction without having to expand its administrative structure. The policy of transportation multiplied many times over the state's penal capacity and at low cost to the government. It expanded the reach and efficacy of the criminal sanction without the need for a centralized bureaucracy. From the vantage point of those who established it, the marriage of efficiency and economy, of penal policy and mercantilism, must be judged an enormous success.

The genius of this privately administered system of control may more fully be appreciated when one realizes that it was put into place and fully functioning one hundred years before the English Parliament first authorized the appointment of a full-time, paid judge, and nearly two hundred years before it established the first professional police force in London. When they eventually came, both these developments were fiercely resisted by a combination of the working class, which feared the repressiveness of a stronger central government, and the aristocracy, which viewed strong government and a centralized legal system as encroachments on their traditional domains. Transportation as penal policy represented one of the first victories of the ascending middle class, which eventually came to dominate English government and to secure a stronger central government and effect major changes in the police and courts. It was able to effect changes in the penal capacity of the state precisely because it could do so without the need to increase directly the size and the strength of the central government. As an innovative policy, transportation combined the quest for greater law and order with reliance on the market—more particularly with the quest for personal profit.

The significance of transportation as a powerful penal policy should not be underestimated. It was not simply a substitute for the gallows; it was more. It was an innovation of gigantic proportions. It radically transformed the administration of criminal justice.[7] Although it was a merciful alternative to those few who otherwise would have been hanged, in terms of numbers it had its greatest impact on those who ran no risk of death. Those guilty of the worst offenses continued to be hanged, so that transportation to North America had little or no impact on the use of capital punishment.[8] Rather, the new alternative swept up those who would have claimed benefit of clergy and escaped punishment altogether and those who otherwise would have received an unconditional pardon, a whipping, or a small fine. For still others, it increased the likelihood of prosecution, conviction, and punishment since victims were more willing to prosecute and juries more willing to convict if they knew the offenders would not be hanged.

Transportation expanded the sanctioning power of the state enormously which was precisely its intended effect. Unlike the quest of some contemporary reformers who seek alternatives that reduce reliance on the criminal sanction, transportation was designed as a sanction that would deter crime more efficiently than the threat of death and remove the criminal from society. It was motivated by a desire for more not less repression and it was successful.

The genius of this regime of sanctioning in an era when central government was weak and fiercely resisted was that responsibility for its administration and financing was wholly in the hands of entrepreneurs who operated it as a highly profitable business. In doing so, they succeeded beyond the wildest dreams of those who first embraced the idea.

Private Prisons

Contemporary historians of the development of the modern prison in the eighteenth and early nineteenth centuries have emphasized theories of social control and reform that guided the early reformers. They have been intrigued with the theories of rehabilitation in the regime of solitary confinement in Philadelphia's Walnut Street Jail, and the system of silence in New York's Auburn Prison, as well as the importance these two institutions had in shaping American penal policy. By focusing on the theories of correction and discipline, and treating deviating practices as unintended consequences, these historians have ignored the economic factors that shaped early prisons.[9] From this perspective many of the early practices that appear to be failures in light of the idealists' theories can be reassessed more positively.[10] While they did not rehabilitate, some of these systems of punishment came close to paying for themselves. And certainly, one of their appeals was the claim of entrepreneurs that they could pay, at least partially, for themselves.

This section, then, argues that one of the reasons that the modern prison emerged as a viable alternative to transportation and the death penalty was that entrepreneurs successfully argued that it would increase the law's effectiveness at low or no cost to the state. I do not mean to argue that the idealism of early reformers who advocated imprisonment as an effective and more humane means of dealing with criminals was unimportant. Clearly it was.

Indeed, the idealists and entrepreneurs were often one and the same, as will be seen in the discussion of Jeremy Bentham's involvement in English prison policy. To wrench David Rothman's (1980) phrase out of context, prison policy in both England and the United States was, from the outset, a marriage of "conscience and convenience." Entrepreneurial reformers promised a modern form of punishment that was at once more humane and cost-effective. Private contractors could manage prisons and employ convicts in labor which would be both morally uplifting and rehabilitative as well as financially rewarding. Plans took various forms: locating private businesses in public prisons, privately operating prisons, locating state-run businesses within the institutions, leasing convicts to private contractors, or using convicts on public works projects in lieu of contract labor.

The particular forms that prison development took in England and the United States are the result of three interrelated factors: 1) the meager capacity of the state to provide public services itself and the general reliance on private contractors to supply all sorts of public services; 2) the earlier success of private schemes in criminal justice, particularly transportation, the administration of gaols, the hulks, and in Europe, forced labor; and 3) the growth of the factory, which served as a model for prison design, discipline, and productivity, and which fits nicely with emerging theories of the causes of crime.

Private Contractors and State Capacity

Prior to the dawn of the modern state, governments—and particularly the British and early American governments—lacked even rudimentary administrative capacities. As demands on the central government to expand services increased, they far outstripped the ability of the puny bureaucracy to handle them. Until government itself could grow, it had to rely upon administrative forms designed for an earlier era, which meant dependence on volunteers and private contractors.[11] Dependence on private initiative and volunteer services to provide education, fire protection, toll roads, and even judging, policing, and prosecution was common and well established prior to the growth of bureaucracies. As officials began to search for an alternative to the largely privately administered system of transportation, it was only natural to consider private-sector alternatives.

Earlier Successes with Privatization

The idea of private prisons or prisons depending on private contractors to exploit the labor of convicts to offset the cost of running prisons was a natural outgrowth of the criminal justice administration of the time. For centuries many gaols in England, especially in small communities, had been run by contractors, typically alehouse keepers who housed just a few prisoners in their basement stock-rooms.

Profit was made by charging prisoners for room, board, and drink, and from reimbursement by the county for maintenance of those prisoners who could not pay. By the end of the eighteenth century gaols had taken on some of the features of prisons as they began to hold convicted inmates pending their appeals for pardons or as they awaited transportation. Many of the early advocates of expanded imprisonment had in mind the expansion of this system of privately administered gaols.

With the advent of the American Revolution the English government had to move quickly to find an alternative to transportation. With a minimum investment, contractors purchased and transformed surplus naval vessels into floating prisons where they then stuffed hundreds of convicts in a single hold. The hulks, as these prison ships were called, were moored in the Thames in London and in ports throughout England; they were used for more than fifty years to house short-term prisoners and those scheduled to be transported to Australia. Some of the hulk contractors attempted to turn their temporary business into something more permanent, and promoted the hulks as a permanent alternative to transportation. They proposed to house and care for convicts on the hulks in exchange for the right to exploit their labor in the building and repair of harbors, levies, docks, and highways. Although most of these plans never came to fruition, a few hulk contractors were able to obtain public works contracts and use convict labor.[12] Perhaps it was this experience that later led the government to commit itself to a policy of low-cost imprisonment based on the exploitation of convict labor.

The Factory as a Model for Prisons

A third factor that shaped the debate about English penal policy was the prevailing criminology of the day. It linked crime with lack of discipline and unemployment. Transportation was one curative for this diagnosis—sell convicts in the labor market so that they might learn discipline and a skill. But if crime was the result of the lack of disciplined work habits, what could be better than a factory-like prison to instill discipline? And how better to accomplish this goal than to model the prison after the factory? As Melossi and Pavarini (1981) and others have demonstrated, the factory served as an important image in shaping the notion of prison. It encouraged the notion of efficient management and the productive use of labor, and it invited private participation in its management. Indeed Foucault (1979) sees the institution of both prison and factory as a much more general effort to impose discipline throughout society.

Throughout the late eighteenth century in Great Britain, there was widespread debate about criminal law and penal reform.[14] The efforts of John Howard, William Eden, Samuel Romilly, William Wilberforce, and others, had led Parliament to consider a host of reforms in the administration of criminal justice. Among them was the replacement of capital punishment with domestic imprisonment, which the reformers argued was a more efficacious deterrent because victims would be more willing to prosecute and juries more willing to convict if a person's life was not at stake. One such reform, Jeremy Bentham's inspiration, in fact, was the Criminal Justice Act of 1779, 19 Geo. III, c. 74, which authorized the acquisition of sites for two prisons near London and specified a plan for managing them.

Jeremy Bentham seized upon this act to promote his own ideas about prison reform. Working with his brother, Samuel, he designed and aggressively promoted his design for the Panopticon, a prison of efficient design that would allow maximum surveillance at minimum cost. Well known for his efforts to rationalize and codify the criminal law and for his design of the Panopticon, Bentham also developed detailed plans for a private contractor to run the Panopticon once it was built. From the early 1780s until the early 1800s, Bentham was obsessed with this idea and enlisted a long list of influential men in his effort to obtain an exclusive contract to build and operate the nation's prisons. These prisons, he argued, should be managed by a private contractor whose income would be derived from small fees paid by the government and the productive labor he could extract from the convicts. He, of course, was that person (1834, IV). To this end he invested thousands of pounds of his own money in efforts to acquire a site and to develop a prototype of the Panopticon. His voluminous correspondence on this matter reveals that he was active in seeking support from well-placed officials and well-respected reformers. It also reveals that he believed that he would become a very wealthy man if he obtained the exclusive contract to run the prisons (Himmlefarb 1968:33).

Bentham lost his bid to build and manage English prisons, and eventually he turned to pursue other interests. But his plans were published and widely circulated and continued to influence the development of the prisons. Throughout the nineteenth century in both France and the United States his ideas for delegating prison services to private contractors were put into effect.

In the United States a version of Bentham's plans was promoted by one of his great admirers, Edward Livingston of Louisiana. In his proposed "Code of Reform and Prison Discipline," Livingston (1873:590–94) covered in Bentham-like detail every minute facet of prison design and management, including a provision that the warden's pay was to be determined in part by a "percent of the gross amount of sales . . . of the articles manufactured in their prisons . . . and also [a] percent on the amount of sums paid for the labour of the convicts by manufacturers." In France the government also came to rely on private contractors to operate prisons (O'Brien 1982).

Contemporary historians have tended to dismiss as naive the plans of officials for economic viability of prisons during the early years of their development. But in so doing they have ignored the importance of labor and private contractors in the early prisons. Even the celebrated "reformatories" in Pennsylvania and New York, although built, owned, and operated by government, originally relied on private contractors to use convict labor to offset a large share of the costs. The importance of such ideas, as we have seen, is suggested by Livingston's elaborate plans which, among other things, linked the income of the warden to the productivity of prison labor. In a number of states contractors paid the prison a fee or a percentage of their profits for the right to employ convicts. The precise forms of prison labor varied considerably from institution to institution and from state to state, but it is clear that during this formative period policy makers hoped that by running them like private businesses, prisons could begin to pay for themselves.

Although many quickly came to find that a prison could not be run as a business and that it was likely to be a drain on the state, some states, particularly those with limited resources and rapidly growing populations, came to depend heavily on private contractors.

Although all the early prisons sought to exploit the labor of convicts, the first state to rely upon a private contractor to run the entire prison system as a business was Kentucky. Frustrated by the high cost of running an inefficient and costly prison, in 1825 the legislature leased the entire prison and its population to an enterprising businessman (Lewis 1922:257). The agreement called for the contractor, Joel Scott, to clothe, house, and feed the prisoners, maintain the buildings, and pay the state $1000 plus one-half his net profits. In return he could employ the convicts at hard labor, and in lieu of salary keep the other half of the net profits from their labor. By several accounts Scott was successful in running the operation. Orlando Lewis (1922:258) reports that there are no records of allegations that the prisoners were ill-treated during the years Scott operated the prison, and that the state made money. Indeed when Scott retired, there was intense competition among those who sought to succeed him. Kentucky's leasing system continued for some years, and came to an end in the 1880s when workers succeeded in getting the legislature to pass a law restricting the "unfair competition" of prison labor.

Kentucky's lease system, one of the earliest to depend upon private contractors, became a model for western and other southern states. In Tennessee and some other states, contractors used convict labor in coal mines. Elsewhere convicts were employed in small-scale manufacturing. And in the late nineteenth century, the convict lease system provided labor for road and railway construction (Lewis 1922; McKelvey 1961; Wines 1880:106–16, 161–211; Cable 1883:296).

In its own way, the southern convict lease system was highly successful. Despite their relative lack of wealth and the economic dislocations of the Civil War, southern states were able to accommodate the increased number of criminal offenders that resulted from the shattered economy and the abolition of slavery. And widespread reliance on the criminal sanction and convict labor served as a means to control the black population. Indeed, by relying on convict lease systems, the southern states were more efficient than the more wealthy states in the northeast; they were able to incarcerate a higher proportion of offenders and impose longer average sentences than states in other regions of the country (Cable 1883:297). Furthermore, they were able to accomplish all this at a cost well below that of other states (Cable 1883:297; Martin and Ekland-Olson 1987). In short, reliance on private contractors facilitated the expansion of the capacity of the criminal justice system at a time when state governments could not easily afford to provide such services themselves.

After the war the western states experienced rapid growth and increased demands for services which outstripped administrative capacity and the tax base (McKelvey 1977:61, 94). Privatization again proved to be an efficient solution. Nebraska, Kansas, Oklahoma, and Oregon leased their prisons and prisoners to contractors who, for a small fee and the right to use convict labor, agreed to assume responsibility for them. In Utah convicts were farmed out to enterprising individuals who agreed to watch over them in exchange for the right to their labor (McKelvey 1977:227).

California had embraced private prisons much earlier but for the same reasons, as a response to the dramatic increase in demand for services brought about by the rapid influx of people at the outset of the gold rush. Here too, demand outstripped the capacity of the fledgling state government, and in the first decade after statehood, it had to turn to private contractors to house convicts in surplus ships in San Francisco Bay and to build and operate the prison at San Quentin.

From the outset there was strong opposition to the contract and convict lease systems, and by the middle of the twentieth century, it was strong enough to end them. Several factors led to their demise: 1) the success of a coalition of labor, manufacturers, and farmers who opposed unfair competition and pressed for legislation restricting the use of convict labor and the sale of convict made goods; 2) the efforts of reformers who mobilized public opposition to the scandalous conditions in many of the privately run facilities and lease systems; and 3) the growth of the modern welfare state, which increased the capacity of governments to manage large-scale institutions.[15]

This brief history of the earlier experience with privatization in prisons reveals just how intimately the origins of the modern prison are bound up with the efforts of private entrepreneurs. To a considerable extent the modern prison is an invention of private entrepreneurs who convinced government officials that they could create and maintain an extensive penal system at little or no cost when the state lacked the administrative capacity. Although the entrepreneurs may have been wrong, they nevertheless were convincing enough at the time to have played an important role in formulating a policy of heavy reliance on imprisonment and to have created the expectation that its costs could be offset by running prisons according to business principles.

More generally, this brief history suggests that when the state is faced with demands it cannot meet, entrepreneurs can and do help develop a response, ultimately enlarging the state's capacities. As with transportation, early private prison contractors responded to a widely felt crisis, developed innovative solutions and quickly implemented them. That their inventions were later modified or absorbed by the state does not indicate failure but success. Merchants responded to the crisis of law and order in the eighteenth century by developing a market in convict labor and a system of transportation. When this policy faced problems, shrewd businessmen saw the value of putting surplus naval vessels to good use. As transportation waned and the United States grew, enterprising businessmen and planters responded to the crisis of law and order by exploiting convict labor in the American South and West. Each of these policies represents an extension of and an expansion of penal policy—entrepreneurs providing new forms to respond to immediate crises which, in turn, were incorporated into the fabric of an expanded and more effective criminal justice system.

The Lessons of History

Like their earlier counterparts, contemporary entrepreneurs are responding to a perceived crisis of corrections and demands for an expanded repertoire of sanctions by facilitating new forms of punishment and control. Although this movement is at times characterized as a quest for substitutes for punishment considered ineffective or inappropriate, the net result is to expand the range and variety of sanctioning in ways that bring an increasing number of offenders under state-directed supervision.

Even something as simple as lease-back financing must be seen in this light. In recent years, voters have rejected around half of all bond issues for jail and prison construction, so an innovation that avoids the need for voter approval significantly affects the correctional capacity and penal policies.

More important, however, is the role of the private sector in expanding new forms of punishments and control. At the outset of this paper I provided an overview of the debate over privatization. Much of the controversy focuses on a handful of efforts by for-profit companies to take over the management of existing custodial facilities and to build and operate new ones. As important as these issues are, they are not the most significant features of the privatization movement. The area where privatization has made its greatest impact is in the development of new forms of intermediate punishments and controls.

Despite its awesome powers the modern criminal justice system remains something of a clumsy giant; it can impose terror through the death penalty and lengthy prison terms, and it can slap offenders on the wrist with fines and suspended sentences. But it has limited capacity to do much in between. In the twentieth century probation and parole emerged as such intermediate forms of sentencing and control. They are important additions to the state's capacity to sanction, and have grown rapidly. For years, the total number of offenders on probation and parole has vastly exceeded the total numbers of offenders sentenced to jail and prison. Although conditions for probation and parole vary, often they are much more than perfunctory. Technical violations of either can trigger administrative hearings that can result in a quick decision to return to custody. Still, it is the sense that such intermediate forms of punishment are underdeveloped that has led contemporary entrepreneurs to search for new and expanded conditions for parole and probation.

The private sector has taken the lead in developing innovative ways to fill this gap. Just as entrepreneurs in the eighteenth century pioneered in the development of transportation as intermediate punishment, entrepreneurs today have pioneered in the development of three new forms of intermediate penalties. Most of them involve expanding the functions of probation and creating new conditions to be imposed. They include: 1) treatment programs; 2) supervised release for parolees and "pre-parolees" employing new forms of low security custody; and 3) sophisticated technologies for surveillance of probationers. Each of these new forms merges rehabilitative and punitive philosophies, just as the concepts of surveillance and custody, incarceration and liberty begin to merge at times. It is the involvement of private contractors with these forms of intermediate punishments, and not the operation of private high security custodial facilities, that constitute the greatest growth area of private corrections.[16]

Private Sector Treatment Programs

Supervised treatment programs, usually imposed as a condition of probation, include drug treatment, alcohol abuse, and job training programs. Virtually nonexistent thirty years ago, they are now commonplace in the criminal justice system. Almost all are private and many are run for profit, deriving both their clients and their income from contracts with local governments. Some are designed as long-term, residential facilities and others as out-patient clinics. Program philosophies vary widely; some are organized with strict, military-like discipline; others are based upon religious beliefs; some are devoted to group therapy; others stress rugged individualism and self-reliance.

Many of these private programs were developed in the late 1960s and early 1970s, stimulated in part by the President's Crime Commission and the Law Enforcement Assistance Administration (LEAA) (Feeley and Sarat 1980). Although many were eliminated in the federal cutbacks of the late 1970s and 1980s, they did establish and expand private sector involvement in the correctional process. The growing desire to respond to the widespread use of drugs has rekindled interest in these types of programs, and we can expect their numbers to increase.

These programs handle a large number of criminal offenders. For every offender housed in a privately managed jail or prison, there are several in privately operated noncustodial treatment programs operating on contracts with state and local governments. Despite their numbers and importance, these private programs are largely ignored in discussions of privatization in corrections. This may be because such programs are regarded as merely service providers rather than penal programs. Or it may be because their role as agents of state control is obscured because participation is voluntary. But if we broaden our frame of reference and consider them as forms of punishment (or substitutes for incarceration) we must realize that these new treatment programs are also integral components of the penal system that extend the reach of the criminal sanction and expand the array of penalties the state can impose. As such, they are part of a much expanded repertoire of punishments which can be used in concert with each other. In the aggregate they also constitute an impressive extension of state control which is often exempted from due process standards required of public agencies.

Low Security Custodial Programs

Another important development in corrections in recent years has been the growth of low-security custodial facilities. Many of the most innovative types of low-security custody have been developed by advocates of privatization, and many of the most successful such institutions are operated by private contractors. Today this form of custody constitutes one of the fastest growing areas of corrections and the most important segment of the business of private, for-profit contractors.

The juvenile justice system, in particular, has come to rely on private contractors to provide such low-security custodial facilities (Cohen 1985:64). This in turn has increased its flexibility in dealing with juveniles and expanded its capacity to commit them into custody. California, Florida, Massachusetts, Michigan, Pennsylvania, Rhode Island, and Washington, among others, rely extensively on private contractors to care for their wards. In a number of states placement in private out-of-home settings constitutes a major component of the state's juvenile corrections policy; in some, private placements outnumber placements in public facilities. As of November 1987, 53 percent of California's adjudicated delinquents who were in custody were placed in private facilities (Farbstein and Associates 1988:61–63). This may be linked to that state's willingness to place juveniles in custody, since next to Washington, D.C., it also has the highest juvenile confinement rate in the nation. As of February 1985, California confined 430 per 100,000 juveniles in the population, up ten percent from the year before and more than twice the nation's average of 185 per 100,000 (Flanagan and Jamieson 1988:477).

In recent years, Massachusetts also has come to rely extensively on private custodial placements for juveniles (Krisberg 1989). Although its rate of custodial placements is much lower than California's, Massachusetts has radically changed the way state officials employ custodial sanctions. Under the earlier regime of custody in strictly run, but poorly managed state facilities, only a handful of hard core youths were committed. Under a regime of more benign private placements, the state is now much more willing to impose short-term custodial sanctions as "shock" therapy, using them intermittently in conjunction with probation. Thus private placement has permitted development of an expanded and more flexible custody policy. As such, it has extended considerably the reach of the sanctions at the disposal of juvenile authorities in that state.

It must be stressed that these private custodial placements in California, Massachusetts, and elsewhere, are not simply more efficient versions of state-run programs. Although they have redirected some juveniles who otherwise would have been detained in secure public institutions, they also target groups that once would not have been placed in custody at all. In short, they add a new intermediate level of sanctioning to the state's repertoire.

Private contractors have played a similar role in developing low-security facilities for adult offenders and there is a growing differentiation between what the private and public sector facilities offer. The private sector is developing more facilities at the low end of the security spectrum, while corrections departments cope with the growing numbers of offenders sent to more secure facilities. Although there is no comprehensive list of the low-security custodial facilities operated by private contractors, for the most part they are community work-release centers, work camps, pre-release centers, short-term detention facilities, restitution centers, return-to-custody facilities, residential treatment programs, and the like.

Many of the facilities are developed under the banner of community corrections. Although it is an ambiguous term, there is general agreement that community corrections refers to the development of locally administered, intermediate or mid-level penal policies in order to redirect some portion of the prison-bound population to less restrictive and less expensive alternatives nearer home.

Community corrections clearly has had the effect of expanding penal options through the involvement of the private sector. Connecticut law, for example, provides for a network of public and private agencies to offer services—including custody at the local level—for offenders who otherwise would be imprisoned. Colorado has come to depend on an extensive network of private vendors to provide minimum security facilities. Maryland law provides state funding for local community corrections centers, which, in some locations, are run by private contractors. Still other forms of privately administered sanctioning permitted under the rubric of community corrections include pre-release centers for offenders about to complete prison terms, restitution centers which require community service or work release, residential substance abuse programs, and in California and Texas, "return to custody" centers, special low-security institutions for parole violators.

Private sector involvement in community corrections is increasing, and there are indications that it will continue to grow especially as prison populations exceed capacity and pressures mount to increase alternatives that are more flexible and less costly.

New Technologies for Surveillance and Control

New technologies are still another response to the growing concern with crime. Only a few years ago, for example, chemical testing was performed by state laboratories in a costly and time-consuming manner. Now private drug testing companies can offer fast, cheap, and reliable tests to detect a large variety of illegal substances,but expanded use of cheap and reliable drug tests has increased the likelihood of detection, which in turn has raised the number of parole and probation violations. This has transformed probation and parole officers from social workers to law enforcement officials. The upsurge in the numbers returned to custody has in turn generated demands for specialized low-security custodial facilities and new forms of confinement. In short, new technology has placed burdens on the correctional system and affected traditional rules.

Private contractors have also introduced a variety of electronic devices which monitor the movement of people. These devices can be used as surveillance and offer the possibility of confinement without custody. Developed by specialized security firms and still in its infancy, electronic monitoring has a vast potential as an effective and inexpensive intermediate form of punishment. For instance, it can easily replace work-release facilities and be used to confine drunk drivers to their homes or places of work.

Conclusion

Let me return to the question posed at the outset: Are private prisons more efficient and effective than public prisons? I have argued that this is not the most important question to ask. My excursion into the history of privatization suggests that the most significant feature of private involvement in corrections is the capacity of the private sector to promote new forms of penality which expand the capacity of the state to apply the criminal sanction.

Similarly, current privatization efforts may be producing equally significant changes. In recent years the private sector has played a major role in promoting new forms of intermediate level control and new technologies for surveillance and control. In so doing it has helped to expand the reach of the criminal sanction. Indeed, these developments suggest that traditional categories and concepts of punishment are insufficient to describe new forms that blur the distinction between law enforcement and corrections, punishment and surveillance, custody and liberty.

NOTES

In preparing this paper I have benefited from discussions with and comments from a number of colleagues, including Leo d'Anjou, David Garland, Bill Gormley, Bob Kagan, John Langbein, David Lieberman, John Lowman, Jutta Lungwitz, Charles McClain, John P. S. McClaren, Shelly Messinger, David Nelken, Stuart Scheingold, Ira Sharkansky, Jerry Skolnick, and David Sugarman. An earlier version of this paper was presented at the Symposium on Law, Legal Theory, and Social Policy sponsored by the West Coast Law and Society Group in Vancouver, British Columbia, March 1989. I benefited greatly from the discussion generated at this presentation. I am also indebted to the Daniel and Florence Guggenheim Foundation whose generous grant to the Center for the Study of Law and Society has supported this and related crime policy research efforts.

1   Chaiken and Mennemeyer (1987:2) report that "in recent years under half of the jail construction bond issues have been approved nationwide."

2   Most of the literature and debate about privatization is framed in terms of whether privatized correcions is marginally more efficient than publicly managed corrections.

3   This tendency is a distinguishing feature of American government, and has been commented on frequently since Tocqueville published his celebrated *Democracy in America* ([1836] 1961). See, for example, Walter Dickey (1987).

4   For an excellent overview of the rise of this form of punishment and a description of how it fit within the larger system of punishments of the times, see John M. Beattie (1986:445–519).

5   Smith ([1947] 1965:336) estimates that, excluding the Puritan migrations of the 1630s, as many as one-half to two-thirds of all immigrants to the American colonies were indentured servants or transported convicts.

6   Jeremy Bentham, for one, vigorously opposed transportation to Australia, arguing that it was more efficient to build domestic prisons. For a period of twenty years, he campaigned vigorously to build prisons and, in fact, hoped to become the sole contractor for all English prisoners.

7   In making the claim that transportation expanded the power of the state before it possessed a large administrative apparatus of its own, I do not wish to enter into the controversy over the origins of the modern administrative state. See, for example, G. R. Elton (1957) who argues that the Tudors developed a relatively sophisticated governmental administration, and Sidney and Beatrice Webb (1922; 1927; 1929), who argue that the administrative state was a product of the nineteenth century. In contrast I simply want to emphasize that with the institution of transportation the state expanded significantly its capacity to punish, and this development in the seventeenth century preceded by many years the expansion of the state's judicial and policing capacities. Although not quite expressed this way, this is one of the main themes of John M. Beattie's (1986) monumental study of English criminal courts in the seventeenth and eighteenth centuries.

8   John Howard ([1792] 1929:289–90) reports the following figures on executions and transportation ordered at London's Old Bailey: 1749–55: 306 executions; 1756–63 (wartime): 139 executions; 1764–71: 233. During this same period, the court ordered over 5600 offenders to be transported. Howard attributes the decline in capital punishment during this middle period to war, which redirected some offenders who otherwise might have been hanged into naval service. Even though transportation came to be used more frequently towards the end of this period, there was no corresponding decrease in executions. Nor was the level of executions prior to the introduction of transportation anywhere near the level that it was once transportation was embraced. In short, transportation did much more than provide an alternative for capital punishment; it significantly expanded the repertoire of sanctions available to the government. See Howard ([1792] 1929: 289–90).

9   There are notable exceptions. See, for example, Melossi and Pavarini (1981); Ignatieff (1978); Rusche and Kirchheimer ([1939] 1968); and Spierenburg (1987).

10   History is, of course, usually written from a winner's perspective. This may
     account for the fact that contemporary historians have taken the rehabilitative ideal
     of the early reformers so seriously. However, with the loss of salience of the reha-
     bilitative ideal, if not its demise, and the recent increase of interest in privatization,
     it is possible to reassess the early experience with prisons. Those early prison
     policies which contemporary historians have judged failures for their inability to
     rehabilitate may yet be seen more positively, as successful efforts to design and
     administer cost-effective institutions.

11   In contrast to the Continent, England has a long history of depending upon private
     contractors to provide public services. Private toll roads and ferries were oper-
     ated for centuries. For centuries—and even today—England has depended heavily
     upon a volunteer lay judiciary. Indeed, as all American schoolchildren know from
     learning about the use of Hessian troops in the Revolutionary War, the government
     even contracted with foreign mercenaries for military services.

12   A definitive study of the hulks has yet to be written. For the best available treat-
     ments of the subject, see McConville (1981); Oldham (1933); Branch-Johnson
     (1957); and *Reports on the General Treatment and Conditions of Convicts in the
     Hulks at Woolwich with Minutes of Evidence Appendices and Index* ([1847] 1970).

13   Indeed, this was the formative period for the modern criminal justice system. It
     was at this time that the first paid judges were appointed, proposals for a pro-
     fessional police force were first developed, public support to offset the costs of
     private prosecution was introduced, and the first mass-administered forms of pun-
     ishment of ordinary offenders were developed. For an overview of criminal justice
     reform efforts during the period, see Radzinowitz (1968).

14   For a sustained discussion of Bentham's plans for Panopticon, see Himmelfarb's
     chapter entitled "The Haunted House of Jeremy Bentham" (1968); and L. J. Hume
     (1973:703–21).

15   For an interesting study which shows the intimate connection between the rise of
     the modern welfare system and the rise of modern penal policies, see Garland
     (1985).

16   Camp and Camp (1985) identify only a handful of private companies running
     institutions. In contrast they identify hundreds of private vendors who contract to
     provide treatment programs for offenders.

REFERENCES

Babcock, William. 1985. "Corrections and Privatization: An Overview." *Prison Jour-
     nal* 65 (2).
Beattie, John M. 1986. *Crime and Courts in England: 1660–1800*. Princeton: Princeton
     University Press.
Bentham, Jeremy. 1843. *Works*. ed., John Bowring. London: Russell and Russell.
Branch-Johnson, W. 1957. *The English Prison Hulks*. London: Christopher Johnson.
Cable, George W. 1883. "The Convict Lease System in the Southern United States."
     Proceedings of the Tenth Annual Conference of Charities and Corrections, 296–
     97.
Camp, Camille, and George Camp. 1985. "Correctional Privatization in Perspective."
     Prison Journal 65:14–31.

Chaiken, Jan, and Stephen Mennemeyer. 1987. *Lease-Purchase Financing of Prison and Jail Construction*. Washington, D.C.: National Institute of Justice and U.S. Department of Justice, November.

Cohen, Stanley. 1985. *Visions of Social Control: Crime, Punishment and Classification*. Oxford: Polity Press.

DeWitt, Charles B. 1987. *Building on Experience: A Case Study of Advanced Construction and Financing Methods for Corrections*. Washington, D.C.: National Institute for Corrections and National Institute of Justice, U.S. Department of Justice, June.

Dickey, Walter. 1987. Panel on Corrections Policy. La Follette Institute Conference on Privatization in a Federal System. Racine, Wisconsin, 5–7 November.

DiIulio, John J. n.d. "Private Prisons." *Crime File*. Washington, D.C.: National Institute of Justice and U.S. Department of Justice.

DiIulio, John J. 1988. "What's Wrong with Private Prisons." *Public Interest*, 92:66–83.

Ekirch, A. Roger. 1987. *Bound for America: The Transportation of British Convicts to the Colonies, 1718–1775*. Oxford: Clarendon Press.

Elton, G. R. 1953. *The Tudor Revolution*. Cambridge: Cambridge University Press.

Farbstein, Jay, and Associates. 1988. *Statewide Needs Assessment of County Juvenile Facilities: Final Report*. Sacramento, Calif.: Department of Youth Authority, 30 June.

Feeley, Malcolm M., and Austin Sarat. 1980. *The Policy Dilemma*. Minneapolis, Minn.: University of Minnesota Press.

Flanagan, Timothy J., and Katherine M. Jamieson, eds. 1988. *Sourcebook of Criminal Justice Statistics—1987*. Washington, D.C.: U.S. Department of Justice.

Foucault, Michel. 1979. *Discipline and Punish*. New York: Vintage Books.

Garland, David. 1985. *Punishment and Welfare*. London: Gower.

Hackett, Judith, et al. 1987. *Issues in Contracting for the Private Operation of Prisons and Jails*. Washington, D.C.: National Institute of Justice and U.S. Department of Justice, October.

Himmlefarb, Gertrude. 1968. "The Haunted House of Jeremy Bentham." Chap. in *Victorian Minds*. New York: Knopf.

Howard, John. [1792] 1929. *The State of Prisons*. London: J. M. Dent.

Hughes, Robert. 1987. *The Fatal Shore: The Epic of Australia's Founding*. New York: Knopf.

Hume, L. J. 1973. "Bentham's Panopticon: An Administrative History—I." *Historical Studies* 15:703–21.

Ignatieff, Michael. 1978. *A Just Measure of Pain*. London: Macmillan.

Krisberg, Barry. 1989. Presentation at the Center for the Study of Law and Society, University of California, Berkeley, 17 April.

Lewis, Orlando. 1922. *The Development of American Prisons and Prison Customs: 1779–1845*. Albany, N.Y.: Prison Association of New York.

Livingston, Edward. 1873. "A Code of Reform and Prison Discipline." Title 5. In *The Complete Works of Edward Livingston on Criminal Jurisprudence*, vol. 2, 590–94. New York: National Prison Association.

Logan, Charles H. 1990. *Private Prisons: Cons and Pros*. New York: Oxford University Press.

McAfee, Ward M. 1987. "Tennessee's Private Prison Act of 1986: An Historical Perspective with Special Attention to California's Experience." *Vanderbilt Law Review* 40:851–65.

McConville, Sean. 1981. *A History of Prison Administration*. Vol. 1, *1750–1877*. London: Routledge and Kegan Paul.

McDonald, Douglas. Forthcoming. *Prisons for Profits: The Privatization of Corrections*.

McKelvey, Blake. 1977. *American Prisons: A History of Good Intentions*. Montclair, N.J.: Patterson Smith.

Martin, Steve, and Sheldon Ekland-Olson. 1987. *The Walls Came Tumbling Down*. Austin, Tex.: Texas Monthly Press.

Melossi, Dario, and Massimo Pavarini. 1981. *The Prison and the Factory: Origins of the Penitentiary System*. New York: Barnes and Noble.

Mullen, Joan. 1985. *Corrections and the Private Sector*. Washington, D.C.: National Institute of Justice, SNI 191.

Neal, David John. 1987. "The Rule of Law in a Penal Colony: Law and Politics in New South Wales." Ph.D. diss., University of California, Berkeley.

O'Brien, Patricia. 1982. *The Promise of Punishment: Prisons in Nineteenth-Century France*. Princeton: Princeton University Press.

Oldham, Wilfred. 1933. "The Administration of the System of Transportation of British Convicts, 1763–93." Ph.D. Thesis, University of London.

Panel on Corrections Policy. 1987. La Follette Institute Conference on Privatization in a Federal System at Racine, Wisconsin, 5–7 November.

Private Vendors in Corrections. 1988. National Criminal Justice Reference Service, 6 October.

Radzinowitz, Sir Leon. 1968. *A History of English Criminal Law and Its Administration from 1750*. London: Stevens and Sons.

Reports on the General Treatment and Conditions of Convicts in the Hulks at Woolwich with Minutes of Evidence Appendices and Index. [1847] 1970. Shannon, Ireland: Irish University Press.

Robbins, Ira P. 1988. *The Legal Dimensions of Private Incarceration*. Washington, D.C.: Criminal Justice Section, American Bar Association.

Rothman, David. 1980. *Conscience and Convenience: The Asylum and Its Alternatives in Progressive America*. Boston: Little, Brown.

Rusche, George, and Otto Kirchheimer. [1939] 1968. *Punishment and Social Structure*. New York: Russell and Russell.

Ryan, M., and T. Ward. 1989. *Privatization and the Penal System*. Open University Press.

Samaha, Joel. 1974. *Law and Order in Historical Perspective: The Case of Elizabethean England*. New York: Academic Press.

Savas, E. S. 1987. "Privatization and Prisons." *Vanderbilt Law Review* 40:868–99.

Shearing, C. D., and P. C. Stenning. 1983. *Private Security and Private Justice*. Montreal: Institute for Research on Public Policy.

Smith, Abbott Emerson. [1947] 1965. *Colonists in Bondage: White Servitude and Convict Labor in America, 1607–1776.* Gloucester, Mass.: Peter Smith.

Spierenburg, P. 1987. "From Amsterdam to Auburn: An Explanation for the Rise of the Prison in Seventeenth-Century Holland and Nineteenth-Century America." *Journal of Social History* 20:439–61.

Tocqueville, Alexis de. [1836] 1945. *Democracy in America.* New York: Vintage Books.

Webb, Sidney, and Beatrice Webb. 1922. *English Prisons Under Local Government.* London: Longman's Green.

Webb, Sidney, and Beatrice Webb. 1927. *English Poor Law History, Part I: The Old Poor Law.* London: Longman's Green.

Webb, Sidney, and Beatrice Webb. 1929. *English Poor Law History, Part II.* London: Longman's Green.

Wines, E. C. 1880. *The State of Prisons and Child Saving Institutions.* Cambridge: Cambridge University Press.

11 *Albert J. Reiss, Jr.*

Private Employment of Public Police

Following a brief examination of the historical growth of public and private policing in the United States, this chapter examines some new hybrid forms of public and private policing. Specifically we examine ways that police resources, functions, and employees are contracted to private employers. Three major forms of contract policing between public police officers and private employers are examined: Office Contract, Union Brokerage, and Department Contract. These hybrid forms of policing raise special policy issues regarding legal liability of departments for officer conduct, conflicts of public with private interests in private employment of public police officers, and the competition of public with private organizations in meeting demands for private protection.

Public and private employers in the United States have long shared law enforcement functions. Historically, there have been major shifts from private to public as well as from public to private agencies in the policing of a particular activity.

The late nineteenth and early twentieth century brought a major shift from private to public policing. These decades witnessed the dissolution of many company police systems, especially for extractive industries such as mining, for steel manufacturing, and for railroads.[1] Apart from company police forces,

Albert J. Reiss, Jr., is William Graham Sumner Professor of Sociology at Yale University.

there were many private detective organizations, such as the Pinkertons, who were employed by various companies. As public dissatisfaction with company policing of the strife between workers and their employers grew, the franchising of company police declined, and their functions returned to the public police. Legislation creating the first state police system in the United States, the Pennsylvania State Police, in fact grew from a recommendation of President Theodore Roosevelt's Anthracite Strike Commission following their investigation of the protracted strife of miners, who were pitted against the anthracite coal producers, and their Coal and Iron Police in Pennsylvania in 1902–03 (Mayo 1917).

Despite the shift from company to public policing, private policing in the twentieth century has grown into a major private security industry that fills a niche left vacant by the transformation of the public police from a client-centered to a bureaucratic police organization. The size and financial cost of that private security industry now exceeds that of public policing (Manieson and Flanagan 1986). Private security officers, for the most part, lack the sworn coercive authority to enforce the criminal law held by the public police. Ordinarily they can exercise only private powers to maintain order and protect private interests. They cannot fulfill any private demands left unmet by the near monopoly of the public police service on the domestic use of force.

Even that public police monopoly is changing. Legislatures have increasingly permitted the arming of private security and the creation of privately paid police forces who derive their police powers from a public authority. Some private universities have obtained legislative authority to enforce criminal laws and arm their police under supernumerary powers of a public police agency. A growing number of private security agencies obtain permits to arm their guards in banks and late-night retail businesses (Sherman 1986:373). Despite their limited authority to enforce the criminal law by arrest, local police departments often expect private security officers to respond to minor criminal incidents that occur on the property they protect, mobilizing a public police agency only for formal processing of offenders (Cunningham and Taylor 1984:4).[2] They also expect private security agencies to do routine patrol, to control access to private places, and to maintain public order (Sherman 1986:372).[3]

Contract Hybrids in Policing

Although there has been less of a shift from private to public policing in the twentieth century, some recent developments signal the emergence of new hybrids of public and private policing. They emerge primarily through the institution of contract.

One newly developed hybrid is a resource contract partnership between a private corporation and a government body. An interesting example is the private sector resource enhancement program for policing the central area of Oakland, California. Rather than increase its commitment to private security for which most businesses already contracted, private developers and property owners in downtown Oakland have agreed—for a period of 10 years—to provide financial support to a corporation, The Central Business District Security Association, which in turn contracts with the City of Oakland to provide additional police services for the central area. The additional resources include foot, mounted, and Yamaha bike patrol officers. The private corporation has no control over how these resources will be allocated in downtown Oakland but by agreement the additional officers will attend to soft as well as more serious crimes.[4]

Police departments perform a large number of tasks, many of which do not require the powers of sworn authority and which have increasingly been performed by civilian employees of the department. But public bureaucracies often are more expensive than private ones so government contracts with private organizations to perform some police functions. A growing number of police departments, for example, contract with a private organization to perform even such sensitive tasks as investigation of applicants for police employment, clearance of requests for the criminal history of applicants to other government or private employers, polygraph testing, and the development and maintenance of information systems.

The substantial rise in crime since World War II has profoundly affected both private organizational demand for protection of persons and property and the capacity of public police organizations to meet that demand. This demand has largely been met in two ways. The first, as already noted, is by the rapid expansion of private security agencies who contract with public and private organizations to provide protection and security. The second is for private organizations to contract with public police officers who may exercise their sworn authority in off-duty employment.[5]

The three major models that have developed to organize and contract for the services of public police officers are the officer contract, union brokerage, and department contract models (Reiss 1988). Ordinarily the officer is fully uniformed, armed, and has radio contact with department communications, although most departments permit off-duty plainclothes employment.

Under the *officer contract* model, each officer independently searches for and contracts with an employer regarding conditions of work, hours of employment, and rate of pay for a specific form of police service. Typically the employer pays the officer in cash without any withholding for taxes or benefits; thus, it is commonly known as a "cash detail." The main role of the police department in this independent contractor model is to set rules and regulations for off-duty employment, review officer applications for particular jobs, and issue an employment permit if the job meets minimum standards. The department bears the cost of issuing off-duty work permits and any investigations related to off-duty employment.

A variation on the officer contract model is an *officer brokerage* model where one or several officers act as brokers for an employer, hiring other officers to perform a particular duty. These officers typically pay each officer in cash for their work and they receive a broker's fee. Police departments ordinarily do not issue formal permits to officer brokers; a permit is issued only to the individual officers for a particular job that is brokered.[6] Officer broker models are fairly common where large numbers of officers must be employed for a particular job such as policing public events for private sponsors.

Where departments are organized into a collective bargaining unit, occasionally one finds a *union brokerage* model. The fraternal order, police guild, or union becomes a third party to broker the independent contracts between officers and a private employer. The union broker searches for paid details, assigns officers who volunteer for jobs, and sets rates of pay. Each officer ordinarily is paid as a cash detail. The union typically bargains with the department over rates of pay for off-duty work as part of its regular collective bargaining; the department bears the cost of the time of officers assigned to arrange for off-duty employment. Although the department issues off-duty work permits, under this model the union representatives commonly assume responsibility for determining that a job meets the minimum standards set by the department.

The *department contract* model is the most recently developed for off-duty employment. The department (or municipality) contracts with private employers for paid details, assigns officers who register for off-duty employment, and pays officers from the reimbursements by employers. It collects a charge for overhead from employers. The municipal disbursing officer follows the usual procedures for withholding monies for taxes and benefits. Wages for off-duty employment are usually set as part of collective bargaining if the department is organized; otherwise the department establishes off-duty employment rates.

The demand for extra-duty employment, the supply of officers seeking such work, and the range of duties performed varies widely from city to city. Although much off-duty employment is for traffic control, pedestrian safety, and private security, a substantial minority of jobs are for crowd control and the protection of life and property where the officer is at risk of bodily injury and able to exercise powers of arrest.

Departments vary in the kinds of work they allow police officers to perform off duty. The restrictions are greater for employment as a sworn employee than as an employee in civilian jobs, although major prohibitions apply to all off-duty employment. There are three general types of prohibitions on off-duty employment of uniformed officers.[7] Sworn police officers are prohibited from holding jobs when there is: potential conflict of interest between their duties as a police officer and their work for the outside employer; threat to the status or dignity of the police profession; or unacceptable risk of temporary or disabling injury. These prohibitions relate closely to major policy and management issues in secondary employment, issues important to both private and public employers. They are especially germane to police department management.

Policy Issues in Off-Duty Employment

Both police departments and private employers assume a greater risk of civil suit, given the growth of tort liability claims against police departments and their officers. Police departments are potentially liable for actions their officers take while in private employment. Even when claims for damages are dismissed, the department incurs both litigation and opportunity costs. A growing body of tort actions in state courts on the status of police officer arrests when working off duty makes it a matter for managerial concern, especially when they work as private security officers or for private security firms.[8] Although no civil actions for personal liability can be taken against police officers in off-duty employment under Section 1983 of the Federal Code, the scope of Section 1983 invites litigation since the U.S. Supreme Court has implied that liability under Section 1983 need not be limited by state statutory principles of causation. Moreover, Section 1983 may be a remedy for official negligence as well as for intentional harms.[9]

Recent cases in New Orleans (Civil District Court for the Parish of New Orleans 1987) and some other jurisdictions demonstrate that a police department, a private employer, and a police officer may be held jointly and severally liable if the officer is found to have behaved negligently in the exercise of police powers performed while in off-duty employment. A determination of departmental and officer liability when the uniformed officer is employed off duty for a private employer is no simple matter because much depends upon the employment contract and the permit from the police department. It may well make a difference in laying claim to a qualified immunity whether the officer is an independent contractor with a permit from the department or the department has contracted for the employment. Under departmental contract systems, the department clearly assumes a liability for officers in private employment. While department liability is less clear under the permit system, it would seem that the department assumes liability for at least some actions under permit employment where the private employer also assumes liability.

Lines are even more blurred when the off-duty employment involves private security as well as off-duty police officers (which is often the case in policing public events sponsored by private employers). Rarely are lines of authority and responsibility clear in situations such as a professional sports event or a rock concert, making it difficult to determine the liability of the department and its officers and seemingly more difficult, also, to lay claim to qualified immunity.

Many private employers of public police officers fail to indemnify themselves against actions taken by public police officers in their employ, especially when those actions are ones that are taken as a public police officer (e.g., to arrest). Similarly, police departments often fail to consider whether and how they will shift indemnification to private or other agency employers for an officer's actions on off-duty assignment. Given the substantial settlements against police departments, it may be difficult for them to indemnify losses through insurance coverage. At the same time a private employer may be unable to bear the cost or find it difficult to secure explicit coverage for a police officer's actions while in their employ. Most certainly, where there is joint and several liability, both will be sued as responsible parties. Under the department contract system, the police department may require the private employer to waive all claims for injury or damage to the corporation and its employees and to indemnify the public employer against all such claims.

Necessarily there are difficulties in enforcing the law impartially when a police officer serves both public and private interests. Some even conclude that when a police officer works for a private employer, public interest, on occasion, is subservient to private interest. Yet, the public-private distinction may be misleading since police officers at all times have enormous discretionary powers to enforce the law. There is ample evidence that some of the dilemmas and conflicts of interest that arise in off-duty policing also arise in everyday policing on regular-duty assignments. In everyday policing, officers can be faced with dilemmas of whether they are serving private rather than the obligatory public interest. Is it advisable, for example, for a foot patrol officer to give special attention to businesses by dispersing "undesirables" in the neighborhood? Should police departments provide businesses with the criminal record of a prospective employee?

In permitting private employment of uniformed officers it may be difficult for departments to establish clear rules to minimize conflicts of interest. Two principles seem useful, however, in setting rules. The first is that no officer should be employed where an illegal business or activity is operated. The second is that police departments should prohibit officers from working when their public authority can be regarded as coercion for a private interest. They should not be bill collectors or repossessors, for example. Yet it is no simple matter to determine the margin for this rule. The public ordinarily cannot distinguish who is the employer of a uniformed officer. Whether an officer is in- or out-of-uniform or on or off duty when employed is not determinative at law, however. What is determinative is the nature of an officer's action—whether the officer "acted under the color of law" (Brophy 1982).

Arguably one of the most troublesome conflict of interest issues is whether officers enforce the law against their private employers and their employees. While prohibiting employment in places where such conflicts may arise is a partial solution, the problem may be more difficult to control when there is continuing employment for the same employer.

The private employment of police officers with full police powers does not negate the fact that officers are responsible for at least some of their actions to the police employers. This immediately raises the problem of supervision of police officers in off-duty employment by their private and public employers.[10] From the perspective of a police administrator, the department has a responsibility to ensure that police authority is not misused, that the public interest is not compromised in serving a private interest, and that the officer does not engage in misconduct in the dual performance of job and duty. Correlatively, the private employer has a responsibility to supervise and ensure that the private interests are served in a way that is worthy of compensation.

At issue for the police department is how it can supervise or ensure appropriate conduct for officers who are widely dispersed in private settings. Should the department subject them to the dual supervision of the police and the private employer or leave departmental supervision to that which an officer requests by radio? Where the officer is employed under a department contract system, it would seem that the department has a special responsibility to supervise the officer and ensure that the employment is carried out in fulfillment of its contract with the private employer. The police department always retains responsibility for an officer's use of sworn authority.

Little is known about the rate at which officers are injured on off-duty employment and the extent of those injuries. Few injuries appear to be disabling; most involve lost time from regular duty and compensation for the injury. Inasmuch as few departments allocate injury status to on- and off-duty employment, it is difficult to assess the magnitude and cost of off-duty injury and compensation.

Whether and how a department compensates for injuries in off-duty employment depends on its legal obligations as an employer and the contractual obligations the department assumes for off-duty work. Under worker's compensation statutes, employers have obligations to compensate for work-related injury and disability. Because off-duty employment involves a second employer, what costs the department assumes depends upon the status it assumes for secondary employment. Under the department contract system, it assumes such costs unless it makes specific contractual agreements with private employers for them to do so.

Regardless of who bears the immediate costs of injury, the question of who compensates the officer or the department for lost time is an issue. Workers' compensation for private employment provides less compensation than the department ordinarily provides. A department also has additional costs when a police officer is injured since it loses the services of the officer for a period of time. Even if the department were compensated for that lost time at some rate of pay to the officer plus some calculable costs to the department, such compensation cannot replace an injured officer with another trained officer except by forgoing his or her service in another position within the department.

Not uncommonly, it is argued that police officers will perform at lower levels of quality and efficiency if they hold off-duty employment, especially when the officer works more than eight hours in a day.[11] Many police departments, consequently, limit the number of hours that an officer may work in any twenty-four hour period and within a given week. There are no obvious standards for judging just how much off-duty employment should be permitted for a given officer in a given period of time. Certainly, an officer's alertness, accuracy, and reasoning are subject to fatigue from overwork but they also are affected by a host of factors that induce stress. Setting standards for off-duty employment remains problematic for most police administrators.

A closely related question is what pay scale shall apply to off-duty employment, particularly that undertaken on regular assignment days. Under the Fair Labor and Employment Standards code, an officer presumably is entitled to time and one-half for extra-duty employment after regular working hours. Where the department contract system is followed, the department may well be underpaying the officers for off-duty assignments on their regular work days. Such practices can make departments vulnerable to wage recovery suits.

Competition of Off-Duty Employment with Private Security

The *Hallcrest Report: Private Security and Police in America* (Cunningham & Taylor 1985, chap. 12) emphasized the major sources of conflict between the interests of law enforcement and private security agencies. It focused primarily on the unfair competition uniformed contract policing gives private security firms. Two aspects of that competition regarded as particularly unfair were the use of department uniforms and equipment and an officer's use of sworn authority. The authors contended these give an unfair advantage to the police officers in competition for jobs with private employers. Also considered unfair was the option some police departments give officers to own private security firms and employ fellow uniformed officers. This was regarded as a misuse of their official position that enables them to recruit and market police service in direct competition with private security firms. A seemingly less compelling complaint was unrelated to unfair competition—that police officers should not be paid for off-duty work since they were employed for twenty-four-hour duty

year round. The effect of this restriction would be to deny all outside employment to police officers, not just that which is in direct competition with private
security.

Quite clearly off-duty employment of public police officers is in direct competition with the provision of protection and security by private corporations.
It is unclear just how widespread is the competition from officer-held corporations, however. The largest police department in the United States, New
York City, although not permitting off-duty uniformed employment, permits
officers to be employed as security guards for a private employer and allows
police officers who receive a Watchguard License from the New York Secretary of State to employ guards in a security related field (New York City Police
Department 1989). Yet most departments that permit off-duty employment of
uniformed officers do not permit officer-held security corporations and none
of the department contract systems apparently does so.[12]

The department contract system for off-duty employment of police officers is often regarded as competing with private security firms. It is unclear
in what sense the competition is deemed unfair, however, since normally the
cost of that police service is well above that charged by competing private
security firms (even allowing for profit by the private firm) and the off-duty
employment service provides a more highly trained and equipped officer. The
unfairness would seem to derive primarily from the fact that the police officer
wears a public police uniform and has the sworn authority not normally held
by private security officers.

The issue of whether or not the entrance of public police officers into the protection and security labor market is unfair revolves around three main issues:
1) whether and to what extent private security officers or police should be
granted police powers and what, if any, limits should be placed on their exercise; 2) whether the public should bear any of the cost of police when they
serve private interests in off-duty employment; and 3) what are the limits on
claims by private organizations for public police service or, correlatively, to
what extent should private or profit-making organizations absorb the costs of
a public police service that is primarily in their private interest?

The major powers of the public police are granted on the condition that they
be exercised impartially for public rather than private interests. Such powers
are not extended to private agents, although some jurisdictions grant private
agents limited licenses to carry and use arms. A problem arises for the public
police when, as already noted, the employment situation requires serving both
public and private interests. For some situations the work can be divided in
such a way that the public police can carry out their duty as public employees on the public payroll and private security employees handle the other job
requirements. Yet, when it is difficult or impractical to make such a division

of labor in private settings, the market advantage would appear to fall to the public police officer if the decision is based on the preference for a uniformed officer who can exercise police powers. That may not always be the case, however, particularly where the private employer seeks the subordination of public to private interests. In those cases, the market advantage may fall to the private security agency. There may be more in the nature of dual security markets for private firms than a single market.

The private employment of a uniformed public police confers several advantages over private security. Because the officers wear an identifiable public police uniform, citizens accord them full police status since they rarely can determine the employer status of the officer. Studies comparing public police and private security officers suggest there are several other advantages for the private employment of off-duty officers.

The public perceives private security officers as serving only private interests whereas the public police are regarded as their moral protectors (Shearing & Addario 1985:225–53). Thus they can lay claim to moral as well as to legal authority for their behavior. Moreover, the public regards security officers as "low level inept persons" in contrast to public police officers for whom they have higher regard in those same settings (Shearing & Addario 1985:250–53). There is also reason to conclude that the public accords privately employed off-duty police officers higher prestige and as providing greater protection. Hence, they may give an advantage to their private employers, especially if the employers are risk averse.

The advantages to private employers of employing off-duty public police officers, on the whole, appear to derive from their police powers and the public compliance accorded the uniformed police officer with sworn authority. Moreover, the public is mindful that these officers stand for a criminal law enforcement and justice system, a perception that appears still lacking for armed private security officers. Simply arming private security officers, then, would not confer an equal advantage. That the public police generally have more training and experience than private security officers and receive greater compensation may also enter public and private evaluations of their desirability. Just how competitive a private security system can be if they were to invest more in training and compensate their security officers at wages comparable to those for the public police is difficult to judge.

The issue of whether the public should bear any of the cost of providing off-duty police service to private employers is somewhat complex. The public investment in officer training is not prorated as a cost to private employers. Whether and at what rate it should be is unclear. Officers must be trained and equipped regardless of whether or not they work off duty and their rates of off-duty employment are highly variable, making career estimates of training costs difficult. Moreover, inasmuch as fewer than one-half, on the average, of all trained officers ever work off duty and many trained officers have short careers, cost calculations are more problematic.

What seems more germane is that no police department appears to recover the full costs of administering off-duty employment, regardless of the model followed by the department. Although department contract systems ordinarily charge some overhead for administering their off-duty employment program, like almost all departments, they fail to recover all of the costs of issuing permits, lost supervisory time, use of equipment, and injury compensation payments.[13] It seems evident that were police departments to be compensated for their costs of providing trained officers to private employers, either the cost to the private employer would increase or the officers would have to compensate the department for their placement costs.

The question of whether the public should bear these costs of providing police for off-duty employment is not easily answered for there appear to be gains for the department as well as for the private employer. Indeed, many police departments have been able to reallocate manpower to regular duty by transferring the demand for police service to private organizations. Many departments, for example, have withdrawn police service for mass public events that they formerly provided and transferred the cost of providing that service to private entrepreneurs who employ off-duty police and private security officers for those events.

Quite apart from the fact that public police departments have transferred some of the cost of police service to private interests by permitting their employees uniformed work, departments may have less tangible or calculable gains as well. When uniformed police officers are employed off duty, they increase the total police manpower that is visible to the public at a given time. Inasmuch as those times ordinarily coincide with peak demands for regularly assigned police manpower, they provide a critical additional resource. Indeed, they can be mobilized for emergencies under those conditions. Off-duty uniformed officers thus may be an additional deterrent as well as a more rapidly mobilized resource.

The issue of whether the public police force should meet private organizational demands for protection and security is also complicated and admits of no simple resolution. Although the police have enormous discretion to enforce the law, they are obliged to enforce it impartially. The police cannot be expected to give priority to one set of demands over another unless there are clear law enforcement bases for doing so. Private security organizations arise to meet private person or organizational demands for protection and security when they demand that their interests have priority over those of other persons or organizations. Private security organizations are able to meet demands for preferential treatment for protection when the public police cannot do so. Yet it is precisely because of that demand for preferential treatment that a uniformed public police performs off duty. But a public police officer cannot provide preferential treatment in all of the ways open to a private organization. In providing preferential treatment, an officer cannot subvert public purpose and departmental standards. Officers must enforce the law against their employers as well as for them and they must enforce the law impartially. This gives rise to the conflicts of interest previously noted, conflicts that do not necessarily arise for private organization security officers providing preferential treatment.

This preferential advantage of the public police currently comes at a higher cost than private security; private security may well be chosen by a private organization because it opts for lesser priced protection.

Contracting for the off-duty employment of uniformed police and contracting with private security companies also may be seen as meeting complementary rather than competing demands. That complementary relationship is based on a division of labor wherein private security performs routine order maintenance and protective functions and the off-duty police officers enforce the law, induce compliance with it, and handle public order crises. Such a division of labor now often characterizes the policing of mass audience or spectator events. Other complementary arrangements are possible in providing policing and security for large private shopping malls and premises, wherein private security agents provide more routine law enforcement.[14]

It perhaps is mistaken then to assume that the public police and private security are inherently competitive in the service provided private companies. There are times when, as just noted, their relationship can be complementary. And there are times when they will be competing. Understanding the nature of the service sought and the nature of the service delivered by each undoubtedly will tip the scale for the employment of one or the other.

Conclusion

The private security industry regards off-duty employment of police officers as unfair competition, especially when police officers establish private companies that sell private security services with off-duty officers as employees. This form of competition may well be declining. In any event, it constitutes only a very small proportion of the private security business.[15]

From the standpoint of private security, a more ominous form of competition has emerged with the development of the hybrid contract models of public policing. Of special significance is department contract policing wherein departments provide fee-for-service uniformed policing to private organizations. This hybrid model of public policing can be expected to expand in the future. But the clear limit to its expansion or growth is the size of police manpower available for off-duty uniformed employment. Given the demand for private security services, public police departments could not meet that demand without substantial expansion of existing police manpower. Such is unlikely to be the case, given the resources that must be invested in training, maintaining, and retiring a public police officer.

One can expect, therefore, that the off-duty uniformed public police will continue to occupy a significant niche in the provision of private protection and security in one contract form or another. Although they will not be easily dislodged from that niche by competition from private security companies or replaced by a private service with full policing powers, it is doubtful whether they will grow at the substantial expense of the private security industry.

The hybrid models of contract policing have the advantage that they can provide public police service with preferential treatment of private interests. That preferential treatment, whether by private interests augmenting the resources of the regular police service or the regular police service contracting for off-duty employment of its uniformed officers, creates a policy dilemma for public police managers and those to whom they are accountable.

NOTES

1 Accounts of private police systems can be found in the *Report of the Committee on Education and Labor, Private Police Systems*.

2 This RIB summarizes *The Hallcrest Report*, a 30-month study undertaken by Hallcrest Systems, Inc. (Cunningham and Taylor 1985) for the National Institute of Justice.

3 Private security is not limited to private employers. The federal government, for example, employs many private security guards to protect public property when it is regarded under the law as a private place.

4 For a detailed description of this program, see Albert J. Reiss, Jr., *Policing a City's Central District: The Oakland Story*.

5 Off-duty employment of police officers is quite common for municipal, county, and state police. Not all departments, however, permit their police officers to be employed in positions where they are expected to exercise their sworn authority for a private employer. Below we deal only with the off-duty employment of officers in their sworn capacity.

6 Some departments permit police officers to found security corporations that are licensed by state authority and which can employ police officers. New York City permits such corporate holdings by sworn officers. See New York City Police Department, Procedure No. 120-14. This option seems to be declining because of conflicts of interest.

7 For examples of these restrictions on kind of employment in a number of U.S. police departments, see Albert J. Reiss, Jr., *Private Employment of Public Police*.

8 *The Hallcrest Report*, 1985, on private security presents examples (Table 12-1 and pp. 205–06) of tort cases brought in state courts that deal with arrests made by police officers as private security employees.

9 See Peter H. Schuck, *Suing Government: Citizen Remedies for Official Wrongs* for a more general treatment of the allocation of absolute and qualified immunity.

10 For purposes of this essay, the off-duty employer is regarded as a private employer since we are concerned with the privatization of public services. Nonetheless, a public police officer may be employed off-duty by other public agencies as well as by for-profit and nonprofit private organizations.

11 Some officers, such as detectives or special details, often work more than eight hours at a time for the department and regular patrol officers often have to work more than eight hours when policing crisis events or dealing with a special crime problem in an area of the city. Arguments about quality and efficiency are generally not advanced under these circumstances.

12 The officer brokerage model while not formally approved by departments, operates in only a limited sense in direct competition with private security firms inasmuch as most of these private employers would independently contract with the officers for their services. The broker simplifies the employment and payment of those officers and perhaps their recruitment as well.

13 An exploratory study of 13 police departments concluded that no department fully recovered their administrative and compensation costs for their off-duty program. Departments with an independent contractor system recovered none of those costs as they made no charge to the officer for issuing a permit. This was the case for all secondary employment where permits must issue as well as those involving uniformed employment. (See Reiss 1988.)

14 The Edmonton, Alberta Police Department in Canada, for example, has developed standard reporting forms for arrest in shoplifting and other cases where a warrant suffices. These forms are completed by private security agents and need only be reviewed by the arresting officer, thereby reducing considerably the time that the arresting officer must spend in handling cases brought to them by private security agents. This requires the time of fewer on-duty officers assigned to such locations.

15 This conjecture rests on a projection of the relative growth of public and private policing in the past thirty years. Private sector security employment has grown at a far greater rate than public sector policing.

REFERENCES

Brophy, Karen Hayes. 1982. "Department Civil Liability for Officers' Off-Duty Acts." *The Police Chief*, 16.

Civil District Court for the Parish of New Orleans, State of Louisiana, *Merlin Beale, Jr. v. Melius, Inc., William Steele, and the City of New Orleans*, No. 85-8714, February 17, 1987.

Cunningham, William C., and Todd Taylor. 1984. "The Growing Role of Private Security." *Research in Brief*. Washington, D.C.: National Institute of Justice.

Cunningham, William C., and Todd H. Taylor. 1985. *The Hallcrest Report: Private Security and Police in America*. Portland, Oreg.: Chancellor Press.

Manieson, Katherine M., and Timothy J. Flanagan, eds. 1986. Table 1.1 in *Sourcebook of Criminal Justice Statistics—1986*. Washington, D.C.: U.S. Department of Justice, Bureau of Justice Statistics.

Mayo, Katherine. [1917] 1971. *Justice to All: The Story of the Pennsylvania State Police*. New York: G. P. Putnam's Sons; New York: Arno Press and *New York Times*.

New York City Police Department, Procedure No. 120-14, "Off-Duty Employment," Revision No. 89-4, Effective 5-19-89.

Reiss, Albert J., Jr. 1985. *Policing a City's Central District: The Oakland Story*. Washington, D.C.: National Institute of Justice.

Reiss, Albert J., Jr. 1988. *Private Employment of Public Police*. Washington, D.C.: National Institute of Justice, 43–47.

Schuck, Peter H. 1983. *Suing Government: Citizen Remedies for Official Wrongs*. New Haven: Yale University Press.

Shalloo, J. P. 1933. *Private Police: With Special Reference to Pennsylvania*. Philadelphia: American Academy of Political and Social Science.

Shearing, Clifford D., and Susan M. Addario. 1985. "Public Perceptions of Private Security." *Canadian Police College Journal*, 9:225–53.

Sherman, Lawrence W. 1986. "Policing Communities: What Works?" In *Communities and Crime*, ed. Albert J. Reiss, Jr., and Michael Tonry, 373. Chicago: University of Chicago Press.

U.S. Congress. *Report of the Committee on Education and Labor, Private Police Systems*. 76th Cong., 1st sess., 1939, Report 6, Part 2.

12 *Setsuo Miyazawa*

The Private Sector and Law Enforcement in Japan

Introduction

The private sector has long played an important role in law enforcement in Japan, and recent developments have pulled the private sector even further into law enforcement. In this paper, I analyze two longstanding private sector activities—part-time voluntary probation officers and privately managed halfway houses—and two more recent private sector activities—private security services and privately funded prison factories. I begin by tracing the history of the private sector's involvement in each area. Then I ask whether these private sector activities contribute either to efficiency or to effectiveness of law enforcement in Japan.

Although all four cases examined in this paper illustrate private sector activity in law enforcement, it would be a mistake to think of all four cases as illustrating privatization. The first two cases have been in private hands so long that they illustrate a continuing role for the private sector, not a recent transfer of responsibility. The last two cases more clearly illustrate privatization. However, as we shall see, the growing role of the private sector in providing security services has triggered growth in governmental regulation. Also, while the organization responsible for managing prison services is nominally a private entity, its relationship to the government is so close that it is best regarded

Setsuo Miyazawa is Professor of Law at Kobe University in Kobe, Japan.

as a semi-private organization. In all four cases, both the government and the private sector play important roles.

Before proceeding to the case studies, I would like to make three points. First, the Japanese law enforcement system does not have any equivalents of state and local systems in the United States. Everything is under the control of the central government. Prosecution and correction are carried out solely by the Justice Ministry of the central government. Policing is slightly different and police forces are organized at the level of 47 prefectures which divide the country. However, executive officers of these prefectural police forces are employees of the National Police Agency of the central government, and the prefectural police forces are required to follow the standards and policies made by the Agency (Ames 1981, chap. 10). Therefore, there is no need for us to look at the prefectural and local levels with regard to the subject of this paper. Readers may assume that the following discussion applies to the entire country.

Second, Japan has a long history of public participation in law enforcement. As Clifford (1976, chap. 9) has noted, "Japan has never lost its firm grasp of an eternal verity: crime is a community phenomenon." He further notes that "it is traditional to take an interest in one's neighbor and to share in the public control of behavior." One example of this is the system of almost fifty thousand *hogoshi* or voluntary part-time probation officers, which is certainly "[the] most widely publicized and most generally known program in Japan" (Clifford, 1976:106). Since Japan has less than one thousand professional full-time probation officers, the voluntary probation officers are major providers of probation services. Another example is the system of *kosei hogo kai* or rehabilitation aid organizations, which run hostels for probationers and released prisoners. As Clifford correctly notes (1976:107), the government does not have any such facilities; these organizations are sole providers of them.

Third, Japan continues to maintain a crime rate at the lowest level among industrialized countries. Naturally, one wonders whether Japan's considerable reliance on the private sector in law enforcement accounts in any way for this remarkable achievement. As we shall see, there are many positive aspects to the private sector's role in law enforcement in Japan but that does not necessarily mean that the private sector is responsible for Japan's low crime rate. In fact, as I have argued elsewhere (Miyazawa 1988), there is no reason to believe that Japan's crime rate has been affected by the mix of public and private responsibilities. The private sector's role must be evaluated with other, broader criteria in mind.

Voluntary Probation Officers

Probationers and parolees in Japan are supervised and assisted by a two-tiered system of probation officers. The higher tier consists of approximately

900 *hogo kansatsu kan* or full-time probation officers who are stationed at the 50 probation offices and who regularly rotate from one place to another. The lower tier consists of approximately 48,000 *hogoshi* or part-time voluntary officers who stay in their community. Full-time officers are recruited and trained as professionals in counseling, but with approximately 100,000 new probationers and parolees each year, their number is too small to counsel clients individually. Their real work is to assign cases to part-time officers and monitor their activities. Excluding higher-ranking full-time officers in administrative positions, one full-time officer supervises approximately 80 part-time officers, on the average.

The Act of Crime Prevention and Rehabilitation recognizes part-time probation officers as part of the national correctional system, workers who supplement activities of full-time officers. The Justice Minister appoints them upon recommendation from the heads of the probation offices. Their term is for two years, but reappointment is permitted. The authorized maximum number of voluntary officers has been 52,500 since 1950. The country is divided into 884 probation districts and each district has its authorized maximum number of part-time officers. One part-time officer supervises two clients, on the average. In terms of their legal status, part-time officers are an institutionalized part of the public correctional system in Japan. If they are injured or otherwise suffer in the course of their work, they receive compensation as government employees.

Voluntary officers do not receive regular salaries but they do receive reimbursement for actual expenses. In reality, this reimbursement is calculated by very low, fixed standards, and their compensation is more symbolic than real. One estimate of the average annual compensation for 1987 (Ura 1988:17) was merely 51,000 yen, or $360. Financially, therefore, they are truly volunteers.

The history of voluntary officers could go as far back as one hundred years (Segawa 1982; Tsunekawa 1981). Until that time, the government operated a public system of jails for released prisoners who had nowhere to return. This system was abolished in 1889, however, because the number of released prisoners increased and jails became unbearable to the prefectural governments that financed the system at that time. Therefore, the historical background of the system of voluntary probation officers was in effect load-shedding by the government.

The government encouraged private organizations to provide similar services and such organizations gradually appeared. The large-scale amnesty following the deaths of the Meiji Emperor and Empress further accelerated this movement between 1910 and 1920. Some of these organizations started to commission local leaders to provide assistance to released prisoners in their community around that time, and something similar to voluntary probation officers appeared, though they were not yet made part of the public correctional system.

The direct predecessors of the present voluntary officers appeared in 1923 when the Juvenile Law was enacted and the government turned to enclose private efforts under its supervision. This law introduced the system of commissioned juvenile probation officers who were totally unpaid. This system was expanded to include adults in 1936 when the Act of Probation of Ideological Criminals was enacted. Finally, in 1939, the Act of Judicial Probation was enacted, and the prewar probation system was established. Like the present system, the country was divided into probation districts, and the Justice Minister appointed part-time *shiho hogo iin*, or judicial probation commissioners. The authorized maximum number of commissioners was 35,000 in 1941. This process of legal recognition and governmental enclosure should be understood as part of a larger governmental effort to unite and mobilize the whole country for the war, which met enthusiastic responses from private organizations that had sought formal recognition of their activities by the government.

After Japan was defeated in the war, the General Headquarters (GHQ) of the occupation force first tried to abolish the whole system and start a new system staffed completely with full-time probation officers. Probably because of the financial difficulty of immediately employing a large number of full-time probation officers, however, the GHQ eventually changed its policy. Like many other areas of the pre-war governmental system, the system of part-time probation officers was preserved under a new name of *hogoshi* by the Act of Voluntary Probation Officers of 1950. The authorized maximum number of officers was set at 52,500 at that time, and it has remained the same ever since in spite of the country's population and economic growth.

Fortunately for the government, a sufficient number of people have found nonmaterial rewards as part-time probation officers. The attitudes and behavior of part-time probation officers express their dual status as volunteers and governmental agents. On the one hand, in a survey conducted in 1979, more than two-thirds of part-time officers responded negatively to the idea of receiving regular salaries (Segawa 1982:359), suggesting pride in their voluntary status. On the other hand, the average age of voluntary officers rose from 53 in 1953 to 61 in 1987 (Ura 1988:8), a major reason for which is their interest in decoration and other awards. Older officers with more experience have better chances of decoration and other higher-order awards, and commentators warn that "no reform plans of aging voluntary officers will get smooth implementation without consideration of this point" (Segawa 1982:364) and recommend expanding chances for younger officers to receive higher-order awards in order to keep up their morale (Ura 1988:20).

How efficient is the current system? An average part-time officer handles two cases at once for annual compensation of only 50,000 yen or so. Compared to it, the annual salary of a full-time probation officer may easily reach five million yen, one hundred times the compensation for a part-time officer. We cannot realistically expect a full-time officer to handle 200 cases at once. Therefore a part-time officer is definitely cheaper per case than a full-time officer.

Next, the dimensions of effectiveness and quality come together here. It is tempting to assume that a professionally trained, full-time officer can provide services with higher quality and is more effective in rehabilitation of the client. Particularly when the client is a juvenile or a young adult, as is often the case, the generational gap between a part-time officer and client might also inhibit rapport between them.

The Research Division of the Research and Training Institute of the Justice Ministry conducted an experimental study of the relative effectiveness of full-time and part-time probation officers in 1961 (Iwai et al. 1974). Four full-time probation officers at the Tokyo and Yokohama probation offices engaged in direct supervision for one year beginning in October 1961, and 92 probationers supervised by them for at least six months were followed for the next 11 years. The control group was 144 probationers randomly selected from among those supervised by part-time probation officers of the same probation offices during the same period of time. The arrest rate was lower for the experimental group while they were supervised. The difference disappeared, however, soon after they left supervision, and the overall arrest rate of the experimental group after 11 years was 62 percent, higher than 54 percent for the control group. It is possible that the two groups were not matched carefully and the experimental group included more difficult cases. It is also very likely that during the 11 years after supervision, various factors beyond the control of full-time officers intervened and wiped out any positive impacts they had made. It is nonetheless clear that full-time probation officers failed to prove their higher effectiveness. Moreover, contact with the client was much more difficult for full-time probation officers because they commuted from outside the community, and they had to spend far more time than part-time officers per case. Part-time officers were clearly more efficient in this regard, too.

After this and similar attempts produced disappointing or inconclusive results, the Justice Ministry apparently lost its interest in direct supervision by full-time professional officers. While academic commentators still propose a drastic increase of full-time officers, those inside the ministry do not see any such possibility, but rather fear possible cutbacks in the present system (Ura 1988:12), given the austere fiscal policy of the moment.

It must be surprising to foreign observers that the probation and parole system in Japan has remained virtually the same since 1950, in spite of the tremendous economic expansion and societal changes in these four decades. Not only has the personnel structure of the system remained the same, but also the size of the system has not changed much. The fact that the crime rate has remained low and stable and crime has not become a major political issue explains this stability. While there is no scientific basis to claim causal impact of the present system of probation and parole on the crime rate, advocates of the present system can nonetheless cite the low crime rate as proof of the effectiveness of the present system.

If anything, change in law enforcement is likely to be a result of changing demographics. The present system of voluntary probation officers relies heavily on those people who do not need to work for a living and who stay in their community for many years. In fact (Ura 1988:10), in 1987, 24 percent of part-time officers did not have any job, and 19 percent were in the fields of agriculture, forestry, or fishery. Since the majority of the latter group is likely to be retired farmers or fishermen living with their sons, the system is dominated by unemployed people who live in the same community for a long period of time without a need to have regular employment. Only such people can have time to spare for clients.

It is becoming increasingly difficult to find such people in urban settings where probation officers are most needed because mobility has become higher, older people have moved to suburban areas, and the farming and fishing population has been shrinking. One possible source of new part-time officers is housewives, and indeed (Ura 1988:10), the percentage of women rose from seven percent in 1953 to 20 percent in 1987. However, the increasingly higher mobility of the urban population and the increasing participation of women in the work force could still pose a serious problem if, by any chance, the crime rate jumped.

Such a scenario is very unlikely, however. The Japanese system of probation and parole will not change much for the foreseeable future.

Private Half-Way Houses

I have written that the government abolished shelters for released prisoners in 1889 and private organizations then took over that function. The situation has not changed at all in the past century. The government operates no such shelters even today. Private organizations called *kosei hogo kai* or rehabilitation aid organizations provide such services. They are direct descendants of those early organizations and celebrated their centennial in 1988 (Zadankai 1988). Lacking public half-way houses, they are the only Japanese equivalents of those that exist in other countries.

Established with approval by the Justice Minister, there were 100 such rehabilitation aid organizations as of April 1988, with a total capacity of 2,313 men and 120 women (Homu Sogo Kenkyujo 1988:185–87). On the average,

60 percent of the capacity is filled. Nearly 90 percent of residents are probationers and released prisoners who are entrusted to those organizations by the heads of the probation offices; the rest are admitted by the organizations.

This system of privately run half-way houses is another, more extreme example of enclosure of private resources by a government that does not want to take financial responsibility for the rehabilitation of criminals. There is an interesting report on the financial situation of a relatively large rehabilitation aid organization in Osaka with 100 beds (Hayashi 1988). It renovated the building in 1986 for a total cost of 439 million yen (approximately $3 million); the government subsidized with only 3 million yen. The largest contributor was the national cycle racing organization, which donated 275 million yen. The rest was borrowed from banks and other organizations, except the aid organization's own fund of 26 million yen. While contributing less than one percent of the renovation cost, the government can use almost the entire facility for its purpose.

On the other hand, these organizations depend heavily on the government for operating costs. The annual revenue of the same organization in Osaka was 64 million yen in 1987, of which 55 million yen was a governmental subsidy for the entrusted residents. The total number of resident-days was 20,814, and the daily subsidy from the government per resident was approximately 2,600 yen (approximately $18). Fifty-seven people stayed daily, on the average, and they were supervised and assisted by nine staff members.

Since the governmental fund is the most stable source of revenue, these organizations now prefer not to admit clients on their own authority and have thus lost much of their private nature. The close supervision by the government has also contributed to this process. From their establishment, facilities, programs for residents, qualification of managers, to forms of financial reports, they are required to follow standards set by the government. The government treats them virtually as part of public programs, while funding only a portion of their financial needs. Yet, unlike voluntary probation officers, staff members of aid organizations cannot receive compensation as government employees even when they suffer in the course of their activities. Therefore, they often become voluntary officers in addition to their daily activities at these organizations.

Ironically, this almost total control by the government has not been much help to these aid organizations. In 1959 there were 172 aid organizations, with the total capacity of 4,200 beds (Segawa 1982:367). Seventy-two organizations have been closed since then, and almost 1800 beds have been lost. The major reason is, of course, their financial difficulty. While they are heavily regulated by the government, the government does not provide them with adequate funds.

This financial difficulty has caused problems in staffing, which has resulted in a further loss of their private nature. Since these organizations cannot pay competitive salaries, they now rely heavily on retired correctional officers, who often bring bureaucratic attitudes with them.

Unlike full-time probation officers for voluntary probation officers, we have no alternative to this system of private half-way houses, and there is no way to compare their efficiency and effectiveness with alternatives. One simple research strategy regarding effectiveness may be to compare probationers and parolees who stayed in those aid organizations with other probationers and parolees for recidivism. No such research has so far been conducted.

In addition to their financial problems, these aid organizations now face increasingly hostile community responses (Fujimoto 1988). Unlike part-time probation officers who work on an individual basis from their own house, aid organizations need a fairly large physical facility and are quite conspicuous in the community. Typically, when an aid organization tries to renovate or expand the building, local residents oppose, and the plan is often amended as a compromise so that a male facility is changed to a female facility or the size of the facility is reduced.

Unless the government moves to establish a public system of half-way houses, financial difficulty coupled with this community rejection could lead to extinction of the remaining aid organizations. It must again be surprising to foreign observers that in spite of tremendous economic growth, the Japanese government has so far failed to introduce a public system of half-way houses. Because the crime rate has been stable at a very low level, such a program could not be too costly given the size of the Japanese economy. Ironically, however, this very favorable crime situation has failed to make correctional policies a social and political issue and has allowed the government to continue its irresponsible policies.

Private Security Business

There was something that might be called load-shedding by the government in the case of voluntary probation officers and private half-way houses, at least in the earliest days of modern government in Japan. Private security business has not experienced any such process. This industry appeared totally at the initiative of the private sector. However, its recent situation again indicates a pattern that resembles enclosure of private resources by the government.

The first private security companies were established in 1962 when the Japanese economy was starting to grow and, under an increasing manpower shortage, major companies were looking for contractors who would provide marginal functions such as guarding the company building, a function once handled by their own employees. The Olympic Games in Tokyo in 1964 boosted this new industry by hiring a large number of private guards. Various expositions and other major events provided additional opportunities to expand the market and promote public acceptance. From 1962 to 1972, the industry grew to 775 companies with a total work force of 41,146 (Keisatsucho 1974:71). Until that time, no law directly regulated this industry, though the National Police Agency favored a legal basis to extend its control to this industry.

This young industry had many problems (Sato 1971). Of the 321 companies that existed in March 1971, 20 presidents were convicted criminals, including two members of organized crime. While private guards assisted police in 72 cases in 1970, they also committed 95 Criminal Code offenses (comparable to felonies in the United States), including 47 crimes committed during their work time. Some private security companies illegally worked as employment agents. They were employed to physically suppress farmers and radical students opposing the construction of the Narita Airport, minority shareholders at shareholder meetings, or union members during strikes. In short, membership and activities of this industry indicated elements of organized crime (Ames 1981, chap. 6).

The Act of Security Business was adopted in 1972, finally giving police the legal basis to regulate the industry directly. The law required a newly established company to report to the relevant prefectural public safety commission, the supervisory body of the prefectural police force (Ames 1981:12–13). The Act also prohibited certain convicted criminals from starting business or being employed in this industry; provided that private security companies may not interfere in legal exercise of rights and liberties of other people; and gave the prefectural public safety commissions the authority to take disciplinary actions, including suspension of business. The National Police Agency took a basically negative attitude to the development of this industry around this time. *White Paper on Police* of 1974 (Keisatsucho 1974:72) stated, for instance, that while private guards assisted police in apprehension of criminals in 2,164 cases in 1973, 43 companies received disciplinary actions and private guards committed 57 Criminal Code offenses in one year since the law had become effective. The report concluded its section on private security business with the statement that "there is need for the police to strengthen guidance over private security companies in the future."

In spite of this negative attitude of police, the industry continued to grow, more than fourfold in the ten years following the enactment of the Act. In 1982 there were 3,546 companies with 133,946 employees (Keisatsucho 1983:134). Services provided by these companies were also diversified. Larger companies started electronic security systems in which men were dispatched only upon alarm, while other companies started transportation security services.

Familiar problems continued to appear, however. In 1981 there were 1,513 cases of violation of the Act and disciplinary action was taken in 55 cases

(Kobayashi 1982). The largest group of those violations was failure of training and supervision of employees, which accounted for 546 cases. They included cases in which many people were injured during crowd control due to wrong judgments or accidents caused by faulty traffic control. Approximately 200 companies had corporate officers who had spent time in prison, while private guards committed 362 major Criminal Code offenses and 371 other offenses in 1981, including a murder by a person with a history of alcoholism and a series of 38 thefts from work places. Electronic security systems were not totally reliable, either. There were some cases of failure to respond immediately, while other cases involved false alarms to which police responded unnecessarily.

The Act was thus amended in 1982 to expand the regulatory power of police. Under the new act, a new private security company can be established only upon approval by the prefectural public security commission, and must be reapproved every five years after that. Conditions to disqualify officers and employees are expanded; the prefectural public security commissions are given authority to examine the knowledge and skills of employees; companies are required to appoint persons responsible for training for each office from those who were qualified by the public security commissions; and companies providing electronic security systems are required to satisfy standards set by the public security commissions.

In short, the new Act strengthened police power at the start of business and extended its authority to daily operations. Firmly enclosing the industry in its jurisdiction, the National Police Agency now indicated a subtle change in its attitude towards it. *White Paper on Police* of 1983 (Keisatsucho 1983:134) stated that "upon this amendment, we intend not only to strengthen guidance and supervision over private security business, but also to try healthy development of the industry." Indeed, the industry grew to 4,586 companies and 202,611 employees in 1987 (Keisatsucho 1988:152). Police campaigned to organize this large number of companies under a single industrial association in each prefecture, to encourage incorporation of these associations, and to promote qualifying examinations of special skills in airport security and other areas.

Though the relationship between the governmental agency and private organizations is clearly more indirect in this case than in the case of voluntary probation officers and private half-way houses, this case represents another example of governmental effort to enclose private resources under its control. The private security industry now provides police with an enormous network of cooperating private persons which is better trained, organized, and equipped than any neighborhood citizen group and is almost as large as the police force itself.

With regard to the issue of effectiveness, we could ask how much the growth of private security industry has contributed to the stable crime rate. No one has ever done such an empirical analysis, however, and we cannot know the answer to this question.

From the perspective of efficiency, we may ask whether the growth of this industry has saved the growth of public police and, hence, public spending in the maintenance of security. The answer is that the growth rate of police has gone down, but the number of police is still increasing. In the 18 years between 1973 and 1985, the authorized number of sworn officers grew from 186,288 (Keisatsucho, 1974:379) to 217,023 (Keisatsucho 1986:271), with an annual growth rate of 2,561. In the two years between 1985 and 1987, the authorized number grew only 2,923 (Keisatsucho 1988:302), with an annual growth rate of 1,462. Given the present austere fiscal policy and stable crime rate, however, it is remarkable that police still enjoy a positive growth rate. This pattern provides a sharp contrast to the lack of growth of correctional services under the jurisdiction of the Justice Ministry as illustrated by the preceding cases of probation and half-way houses and, particularly, by the following case of prison industry.

Prison Industry Operated by Outside Funds

A prison industry operated by outside funds is the most recent development in law enforcement in Japan. This involves the transfer of public responsibility to the nonprofit sector and is closer to the concept of privatization than the cases of probation services and half-way houses. However, this transfer was not intended to promote effectiveness or efficiency, but took place due to outside pressure totally unrelated to such considerations. Moreover, responsibility was not transferred to purely private organizations, but to a closely related nonprofit organization.

According to the former Justice Ministry officers interviewed for this case study, the government decided in March 1982 to impose an across-the-board budget reduction of 1.4 percent on all governmental agencies, including the Justice Ministry. The annual budget of the Justice Ministry in 1983 was approximately 400 billion yen (approximately $2.8 billion) and the 1.4 percent reduction meant a loss of approximately five billion yen. Unlike such ministries as the Ministry of International Trade and Industry, or the Ministry of Construction, with a large amount of flexible funds to implement various policies, the Justice Ministry had no fund that was not earmarked for salaries of employees or purchasing of office equipment, materials for prison industry, and other items. The Justice Ministry did not want to reduce salaries, which accounted for approximately 90 percent of the budget; the only possibility was to make cutbacks in purchasing.

The head of the accounting department, a prosecutor, first cut one billion yen by returning the Department of Registration of Governmental Properties to the Finance Ministry on the grounds that it should be the function of Finance. He then looked at the budget to operate prison industry. Activities in prison industry can be divided into three groups: production upon orders from private businesses with materials supplied by them, production with materials purchased by governmental budget, and accounting and other support functions. Production by governmental budget accounted for approximately 20 percent of the prison industry, and approximately four billion yen were spent annually to purchase materials. The accounting department head thought that if they found an outside source to provide this four billion yen, the Ministry would satisfy the imposed requirement of budget reduction and change this portion of prison industry into a profit-making operation.

The accounting department head assembled chief wardens and explained his idea. The idea was not to transfer responsibility to purely private organizations, but to establish a nonprofit organization with a subsidy from the investment and loan accounting of the national budget, which was separate from the general budget and was not subject to the across-the-board reduction. This way, prison industry would still receive governmental funds, while at the same time the Justice Ministry would satisfy the requirement of budget reduction.

This nonprofit organization would operate like a trading company which works as an intermediary between prisons and their customers. The accounting rule of the general budget required all profits to go directly into it, and prisons were not allowed to reinvest their profits in their own operation. The new nonprofit organization would not be bound by this rule. Since it would be able to reinvest its profits, the subsidy from the investment and loan budget would be necessary only for the first few years.

The Justice Ministry asked the Japanese Correctional Association to establish such a nonprofit organization. This association was originally established in 1888 as a nonprofit organization called the Great Japan Prison Association which was closely related to the Interior Ministry in charge of the correctional system in those days, as an effort to convince foreign countries that Japan was already a modernized country so that unequal treaties signed earlier should be repealed (Tokubetsu Teidan 1988). The earliest activities of this association included training of prison wardens (including many illiterates) and promotion of the idea that corrections should be a responsibility of the government. Now, with a former prosecutor general as its president and the present head of the Bureau of Corrections of the Justice Ministry as its chairman of the board, the majority of members of the Japanese Correctional Society are present and former correctional officers. The association gives correctional officers travel grants to study abroad, awards for long service, education in foreign languages, and insurance and pension plans. Leaders of the association are proud of its status as the only association of governmental employees for which the Emperor sees recipients of higher-order awards (Tokubetsu Teidan 1988:64–65). Though legally a separate entity, the association functions virtually as part of the Justice Ministry, and it was natural for the Ministry to ask this organization to undertake the new program.

The Prison Industry Cooperation Division (the PIC Division) of the Correctional Association was thus established in July of 1983. Though the PIC Division was to take over a prison industry with an annual budget of four billion yen, the Finance Ministry did not give the division a subsidy of the same amount. The Finance Ministry argued that since the division would be able to reinvest profits, a subsidy of two billion yen would be enough as the starting capital and that amount would be terminated after five years. The division borrowed an additional 550 million yen from banks, and personnel from the existing part of the Correctional Association, and started its operation. Government funding of prison industry through the general budget thus disappeared.

In 1987 (Mizushima 1989), four years after its establishment, the PIC Division provided jobs to 14 percent of inmates, and accounted for 28 percent of the revenue of prison industry. This means that work provided through the division was more profitable per inmate than other work. According to managers of the PIC Division whom I interviewed, its capital has also grown to 3.3 billion yen, accumulating 1.3 billion yen in six years. The division borrowed 1.1 billion yen from banks, but it has already paid back 0.9 billion yen. The unusual aspect of this borrowing is that it has been made under the individual name of the division head who was a former chief warden of a prison in Tokyo. They estimate that 22 billion yen of the general budget has been saved.

The management of the PIC Division is supervised by the committee, including the head and other higher-ranking officers of the Bureau of Corrections, which meets once every month to approve decisions of the division. The division does not really operate with flexibility like a private trading company.

The division has proved to be more effective, however, than the old system of prison industry, in which each prison received orders for its products. The division has been forced to be more effective in finding customers for more profitable products because it was required to become self-sustaining in five years. By necessity, it has become more aggressive in marketing. This higher capability in marketing has a significant benefit for inmates. In Japan, most prison terms carry forced labor and the government has responsibility to provide jobs to inmates. The division has made it easier for the government to carry out this responsibility. Moreover, because the division receives more orders for more marketable products, inmates working for the division can also learn better skills.

The creation of the PIC Division has also made prison industry more efficient in terms of the size of revenue relative to the size of public spending.

In 1982, before the division was established, revenue of prison industry was 18.9 billion yen for the governmental budget of 5.6 billion yen, while in 1987 revenue was 15.7 billion yen for the budget of 2.3 billion yen (Mizushima 1989:154–155). The return rate of 1987 was twice that of 1982 simply because the governmental spending was cut by more than half. These figures hide the initial subsidy, but the PIC Division has become self-sustaining, and the higher efficiency of prison industry is now genuine.

In order to improve public recognition of prison products, the division now uses the same brand name "CAPIC" for all the products. The division has also contracted the Japan Productivity Center, a think tank, to draw plans for future development. Plans include a computerized central inventory system, standardized products, a centralized distribution system, and a research and development department. It is uncertain, however, how many of the plans will actually be implemented. A key factor may be how much the Justice Ministry is willing to allow the PIC Division to operate like a real private company and adjust the related portion of prison industry according to its business decision. Since doing so will inevitably mean that a sizeable portion of the public correctional system is managed virtually by a private organization, the Ministry will not easily move in that direction. It is clear, however, that while the PIC Division was created as a response to pressure from outside the correctional system, it is nonetheless making positive contributions to the system.

Conclusions

A review of the four areas of private sector participation in law enforcement in Japan leads to different conclusions for each area.

Voluntary Probation Officers

In terms of personnel cost per client, part-time officers cost less than full-time professional officers. The ultimate efficiency cannot be evaluated until we take account the social cost caused by recidivism. However, there is no empirical basis for the belief that full-time officers are more effective than part-time officers in the prevention of recidivism. It may be desirable to increase full-time officers even for the limited purpose of training and supervising part-time officers. Part-time officers have their own problems, including their aging and shrinking pool of new recruits. However, given the present austere fiscal policy and stable crime trend, the Justice Ministry is not likely to increase the number of full-time officers in the near future. We have to maintain the present system of probation which relies heavily on part-time officers, and we may expect, at least, that that will not worsen the crime situation for the moment. Clifford (1976:107) stated that "the system has stood the test of time, and even the surge of affluence that would have permitted the appointment of far more full-time staff did not induce the government to change its probation officer system." I do not think that there is any empirical basis to claim the higher degree of effectiveness of part-time officers which Clifford seems to imply, but it is probable that the system will remain the same for the foreseeable future.

Private Half-Way Houses

If the present system continues, halfway-houses in Japan will eventually disappear, so the government should assume a larger responsibility. On the other hand, it is essential to have locally recruited staff to serve clients effectively in the community. Therefore, one possibility may be a combination of full financial responsibility by the government and management by locally recruited staff. Indeed, Japanese prisons are partly operated under such a system, in which only executives move from one institution to another, while most staff remain in the same institution. Clifford (1976:107) stated that the Japanese hostel scheme has proved remarkably resilient since the Meiji era [1868–1912] and represents a very significant involvement of voluntary effort in the endeavor to rehabilitate offenders," and "if the half-way-in-house concept really develops, Japan has a ready-made pattern of hostels well able to move into this new era." I believe that if the present situation continues, this "new era" will never come in Japan.

Private Security Services

This area requires evaluation from at least two perspectives. One is the need for effective governmental regulation because of the criminal acts by persons associated with this industry. Given the division of functions among governmental agencies in Japan, it is inevitable that the National Police Agency would perform that function.

From the perspective of the appropriate size of police forces in Japan, however, we should not too easily accept the enclosure of the private security industry under the control of the police organization. Using statistics published by the National Police Agency, I once estimated (forthcoming 1990, chap. 2) that in 1985, the number of reported Criminal Code offenses (excluding traffic-related offenses) per police officer in Japan was 7.4, while the number of reported crimes per police officer in the United States was 18.7. In other words, the Japanese police forces are more than twice as large as the United States forces relative to the need for criminal investigation. One may argue that the relatively large police forces have deterred crime in Japan, but no such empirical study has taken place (Miyazawa 1988) and experimental police studies in the United States have cast serious doubts on such a hypothesis. Therefore, the closer control of private security services by the police may simply mean the expansion of the police network of public surveillance and of potential employers of retired police officers. It is clear at this moment, at least, that the national association of the private security industry is staffed with many retired police officers and its money provides the police with a large amount of discretionary funds.

Prison Industry Operated by Outside Funds

Excluding accounting and other support functions, the prison industry in Japan now has two components: the older and larger portion which is operated with materials provided by individual business customers to individual prisons, and the newer and smaller portion operated with materials provided by the PIC Division of the Correctional Association. The older system has the problem of unpredictability in both demand and production, a problem from which both prisons and customers suffer. The PIC system reduces this problem because it provides a catalog of standardized products, consolidates orders from various customers, and places orders to individual prisons according to their production capacities. Because Japanese prisons are required to provide virtually all inmates with some job, the increased stability in demand is particularly important. On the other hand, we may expect that the increased predictability of production and the improved quality of products will lead to increased public support of the correctional system. The PIC system has benefits in these senses.

However, we should not forget the more problematic aspect. Each prison is now operated under specific targets of production. The emphasis on marketability of products introduced by the PIC system will certainly increase pressures on productivity, which might eventually collide with the goal of rehabilitation. Occupational training and educational programs do not play an important role in the Japanese correctional system. In 1988 (Homu Sogo Kenkyujo 1989:139), for instance, only 2.6 percent of the inmates were classified for occupational training, and only 1.1 percent were classified for educational programs. The increased emphasis on the productivity and profitability might jeopardize the expansion of these programs. Moreover, financial compensation for prison labor is not considered a salary, and the average monthly compensation in 1988 was only 3,102 yen (approximately $22) (Homu Sogo Kenkyujo 1989:148). We should take care that the saving of a miniscule portion of the national budget not result in the increased exploitation of captive labor forces.

To conclude, privatization of law enforcement in Japan takes two forms: load-shedding by the government or enclosure by the government. In load-shedding, the government continues to maintain control over the operation of programs. In enclosure, the government acquires control over the operation of programs. Since a stable crime trend is likely to keep law enforcement (probably excluding police) a low priority issue for the government, this situation will probably continue for the foreseeable future.

REFERENCES

I gratefully acknowledge that Mr. Takehiko Fujii and Mr. Seizo Yamasaki, the director and deputy director of the Prison Industry Cooperation Division of the Correctional Association, kindly provided much information about their division through an interview. I also acknowledge the encouragement and editorial assistance provided by William Gormley and Alice Honeywell.

Titles of Japanese-language articles are translated into English. Book and journal titles have not been translated.

Ames, Walter F. 1981. *Police and Community in Japan.* Berkeley: University of California Press.

Clifford, William. 1976. *Crime Control in Japan.* Lexington, Mass.: Lexington Press.

Fujimoto, Seiji. 1988. "Rehabilitation Aid Associations and Local Community" (in Japanese). *Kosei Hogo to Hanzai Yobo* 91:9–33.

Hayashi, Nobuaki. 1988. "Treatment and Management of a Large-Scale Rehabilitation Aid Association" (in Japanese). *Kosei Hogo to Hanzai Yobo* 91:93–112.

Homu Sogo Kenkyujo, ed. 1988. *Hanzai Hakusho, 1988.* Tokyo: Okurasho Insatsukyoku.

Homu Sogo Kenkyujo, ed. 1989. *Hanzai Hakusho, 1989.* Tokyo: Okurasho Insatsukyoku.

Iwai, Keisuke, et al. 1974. "A Study on the Direct Supervision by Probation Officers" (in Japanese). *Homu Sogo Kenkyujo Kenkyubu Kiyo* 17:287–304.

Keisatsucho, ed. 1974. *Keisatsu Hakusho, 1974.* Tokyo: Okurasho Insatsukyoku.

Keisatsucho, ed. 1983. *Keisatsu Hakusho, 1983.* Tokyo: Okurasho Insatsukyoku.

Keisatsucho, ed. 1986. *Keisatsu Hakusho, 1986.* Tokyo: Okurasho Insatsukyoku.

Keisatsucho, ed. 1988. *Keisatsu Hakusho, 1988.* Tokyo: Okurasho Insatsukyoku.

Kobayashi, Koji. 1982. "Partial Amendment of the Act of Security Business" (in Japanese). *Keisatsugaku Ronshu* 35 (9): 128–45.

Miyazawa, Setsuo. Forthcoming. *Policing in Japan.* Albany: SUNY Press.

Miyazawa, Setsuo. 1988. "Learning Lessons from Japanese Experience." Paper presented at the U.S.–Japan Bilateral Session: A New Era in Legal and Economic Relations at Tokyo, 29–31, August.

Mizushima, Yoshio. 1989. "Present and Prospect of Prison Industry" (in Japanese). *Keisei* 100 (1): 148–63.

Sato, Masayoshi. 1971. "Problems of Private Security Business" (in Japanese). *Keisatsugaku Ronshu* 24 (8): 107–16.

Segawa, Akira. 1982. "Probation and the Roles of Private Volunteers" (in Japanese). In *Gendai Keibatsu Ho Taikei* ed. Kazuhiko Ishihara et al., 7:353–88.

Tokubetsu Teidan. 1988. "Centennial of the Correctional Association" (in Japanese). *Keisei* 99 (3): 44–72.

Tsunekawa, Kyoko. 1981. "On the System of Voluntary Probation Officers" (in Japanese). In *Nihon no Kyosei to Hogo* vol. 3, ed. Kyoichi Asakura et al., 249–63.

Ura, Toru. 1988. "Present and Prospect of the System of Voluntary Probation Officers" (in Japanese). *Kosei Hogo to Hanzai Yobo*, 89: 1–25.

Zadankai. 1988. "Centennial of Rehabilitation Aid Associations" (in Japanese). *Kosei Hogo to Hanzai Yobo* 91: 34–92.

PART 5
PRIVATIZATION IN PRACTICE

13 *Carl E. Van Horn*

The Myths and Realities of Privatization

Debates over the privatization of governmental services are hampered by confusion as ideologues on the left and right hurl political slogans back and forth. Advocates of more *or* less privatization frequently talk past one another because they are talking about different phenomena. (Kolderie 1984) Unfortunately, consideration of privatization alternatives often proceeds without a clear understanding of the concept under scrutiny or any evidence upon which proponents and opponents base their conclusions. (Pack 1987) The comprehensive survey of state and local officials discussed in this chapter provides evidence about privatization as it is practiced in one large state. By examining the reality of privatization, one can begin to expose some of the myths that inhibit a more reasoned discussion of its advantages and disadvantages.

The term privatization has two distinct meanings. As an ideological principle, privatization equals smaller government, lower taxes, and less government intervention in public affairs. The concept of privatization as a strategy for shrinking government, not surprisingly, evokes great controversy. (Butler 1985) According to conservative theorists, government produces more regulation and services than it should. Individuals, families, and private organizations should provide regulation and services according to the demands of

Carl Van Horn is Professor at the Eagleton Institute of Politics at Rutgers University and Director of Policy, Office of the Governor of New Jersey.

the private market. Publicly held assets—land, mineral assets, public transit systems, space satellites—should be sold to the highest bidder. Potentially profit-making enterprises would then be managed more effectively and the public would pay less for the services received.

There is another, less controversial, meaning of privatization—the use of private organizations to manage and deliver public programs. The central question is not *whether* governments *provide* a given service, but rather *how* they *deliver* it. From this perspective, the issue is not the size of government, but governmental performance.

Privatization as a management strategy, rather than as a public philosophy, is the primary concern of this chapter. The use of private firms to carry out public purposes has important political, economic, and administrative implications that should be evaluated. Will such strategies promote important public policy values? How does the reality of privatization compare with the rhetoric of reform? Which forms of privatization are most promising and which ones are most worrisome?

Debates about the merits of privatization usually focus exclusively on the question of efficiency: is it cheaper to deliver a public service through a private vendor as opposed to a government agency? (Linowes 1988) If efficiency was the only goal maximized by government, then government would not only be much smaller than it is, but also distributed differently. Clearly, governments foster several values—effectiveness, accountability, equity, continuity—in addition to the efficient delivery of programs.

Champions of privatization often make broad claims, arguing that enlarging private sector delivery of public programs will achieve cost savings. They assume that private firms will do a better job of handling services because of management know how and the profit incentive, qualities lacking in public sector organizations. Presumably, consumer choice and competition can be achieved through voucher systems, whereby consumers of education, or housing, or day care receive vouchers that are redeemable for a specific service at a variety of participating agencies and firms. (See Chaps. 4 and 7 in this volume.)

Privatization advocates also argue for greater private sector involvement in governmental decision making. Even if private firms are not responsible for delivering a program, governmental performance can be enhanced by private sector oversight. A public-private partnership frequently cited as a model are the Private Industry Councils under the Job Training Partnership Act. Federally funded programs are governed at the local level by private volunteers who have significant control over program operations. (Baumer 1985)

States and local governments have relied upon private, for-profit and private, nonprofit firms to deliver public programs for decades. Attention to the cost and effectiveness of government programs experienced a renaissance during the 1970s and 1980s. In the wake of tax- and budget-cutting policies at the federal and state levels, public officials began searching for alternative delivery mechanisms that might allow government to achieve more with less money. (Van Horn 1989)

Pressure to trim state and local budgets diminished somewhat in the late 1980s. As the economy rebounded, many governments experienced a surge in revenues. Most states have adjusted to the sharp reductions in federal aid that occurred in the mid-1980s. Nevertheless, the demand for rethinking government service delivery continues and may experience renewed vigor during the next round of budget reductions in the 1990s.

A careful assessment of privatization alternatives should consider several criteria for judging management reforms and bring relevant empirical evidence to bear. (Hatry 1985) Many discussions of privatization suffer from one of two limitations. In some cases, only the efficiency criterion of governmental performance is considered. Such one-eyed analysis can result only in misleading conclusions. In others, the debate is carried on in metaphysical terms, without reference to what governments are actually doing and why.

This chapter attempts to avoid those pitfalls by considering a range of opportunities and constraints that occur with government reform through privatization. The trade-offs involved in privatization of government service delivery may then become clearer so that future analysis can move beyond the hurling of political slogans.

The New Jersey Study

Many of the observations and conclusions in this chapter are drawn from a study of state and local government programs in New Jersey conducted by the Eagleton Institute of Politics at Rutgers University in 1986 and 1987. Commissioned by the New Jersey State and Local Expenditure and Revenue Policy Commission, the study inventoried and weighed the advantages and disadvantages of public and private delivery of public services.

Senior professional administrators or chief financial officers were contacted in all of New Jersey's 21 counties and in 88 municipalities chosen at random from the 567 in the state.[1] Respondents described and assessed methods employed in the delivery of a broad array of governmental services in their community. These included public works such as garbage disposal and road construction, public safety efforts such as police patrol and building inspection, health and social services such as clinics and day care, and such support services as legal help and vehicle maintenance.[2]

State government's experience with privatization was examined through interviews with forty senior personnel from state departments, usually the deputy commissioner or the assistant commissioner responsible for budget, planning, and administration. These managers discussed the nature and extent of contracting for the delivery of state services, their department's use of voucher systems, and the advantages and disadvantages of various approaches to delivering services.

Patterns of Privatization

Municipal and County Governments

Private sector delivery and management of public programs is an important feature of county and municipal government in New Jersey. As revealed in Table 13.1, the typical New Jersey community delivers services in about six of the 31 major categories listed through contracts with private organizations. On average, about three of the services are delivered through agreements with other levels of government and another two services are handled by volunteer groups. Only two of the 88 municipalities used voucher systems to deliver government sponsored programs.

Private contracts are common for the delivery of "public works" services. (Savas 1984) Over half of the municipalities contract for refuse collection; nearly as many arrange to have road construction and maintenance and solid waste disposal services provided in this fashion. Significant numbers also provide towing, parking enforcement, and water supply treatment through contracts. Private contracts are also the preferred method of securing specialized assistance in such services as engineering, legal aid, and planning.

New Jersey's counties employ similar strategies for delivering public services. The average county contracts for about seven of the 25 major service categories listed in Table 13.2, while providing just under two services through agreements with other governments or volunteer groups. Contracting out is a popular method for road and bridge construction and maintenance and for support services. Vouchers systems are again conspicuous by their absence.

Unlike municipalities, counties have greater responsibility for health and social services where they rely heavily on private contractors. (De Hoog 1986) For six of the nine services in this category, the typical county does not use its own employees to carry out programs. Several counties use volunteers or other levels of government to provide drug treatment, day care, mental health services, and aid to the elderly.

When counties and municipalities use private contracts, they usually rely entirely on one or more private firms rather than split the responsibility between government and the private sector. Overall, private contracts command the entire budget in nearly two out of three municipal services and nearly half of county services that are contracted out. The significance of this finding is that governments are establishing monopolies for government service delivery, where only private sector firms compete to deliver the service. The competi-

Table 13.1. Methods of Government Service Delivery in New Jersey Municipalities (n = 88)[a]

	Totally In House	Any Alter- native Method	Not Provided	Total	Contract	Inter- Govern- mental Agree- ments	Other
Public Works							
Refuse Collection	27%	60%	12%	99%	56%	0%	5%
Solid Waste Disposal	18	65	17	100	46	16	2
Recycling	53	21	26	100	13	6	3
Street Lighting	31	65	4	100	52	6	6
Water Supply Treatment	33	43	24	100	21	16	7
Sewage Disposal	34	52	14	100	8	39	6
Road Construction/ Maintenance	49	50	1	100	49	3	0
Parks/Recreation Facilities	87	7	6	100	5	1	1
Towing/Parking Enforcement	33	42	24	99	33	2	8
Other Public Works	39	6	56	101	5	1	0
Public Safety							
Police Patrol	94	1	5	100	1	0	0
Fire	61	34	5	100	0	6	27
Police/Fire Training	32	56	12	100	6	50	1
Ambulances/Rescue Squads	36	51	13	100	9	2	40
Communications/ Dispatching	82	10	8	100	0	10	0
Building Inspection/Code Enforcement	86	12	2	100	11	1	0
Other Public Safety	54	4	42	100	0	4	0
Health/Social Services							
Public Health Clinics/ Services	43	31	26	100	10	22	2
Alcohol/Drug Treatment	10	24	66	100	7	11	7
Mental Health Services	10	28	61	99	9	13	7
Social Services for the Elderly	41	24	35	100	6	13	6
Day Care	9	15	76	100	7	2	6
Temporary Shelter/ Homeless	17	12	70	99	2	7	5
Services for the Disabled	23	9	68	100	2	5	2
Other Social Services	21	7	73	101	0	7	0

Table 13.1. Methods of Government Service Delivery in New Jersey Municipalities (n = 88)[a]

	Totally In House	Any Alternative Method	Not Provided	Total	Contract	Inter-Governmental Agreements	Other
Support Services							
Legal	52	48	0	100	47	0	1
Engineering	42	58	0	100	56	2	1
Planning	57	41	2	100	39	1	1
Vehicle Maintenance	72	28	0	100	23	2	4
Maintenance of Public							
Buildings/Grounds	89	10	1	100	8	2	1
Payroll/Accounting	63	36	1	100	30	5	1

Source: Eagleton Institute of Politics.

[a] Figures in the left hand column show the percentage of municipalities reporting they: (a) deliver each service entirely in-house, (b) deliver all or part of the service through an alternative method, or (c) do not provide the service.

Figures in the right hand column show the percentage delivering each service entirely or partially through: (a) contracts (b) inter-governmental agreements, or (c) some other method. Percentages may total to over 100% as some municipalities deliver a single service through two or more alternative methods.

tion within the private sector may often be quite limited. Competition between public and private organizations is even more unusual.

The identity of the service deliverer varies considerably by the method of delivery, type of service, and level of government (see Table 13.3). Four out of every five municipal contracts are let to private, for-profit firms. Ninety-three percent of contracts are for public works services, 53 percent of those are for public safety, and only 19 percent are for social services. In contrast, county governments allocate only one in three contracts to private, for-profit firms. Instead, they lean heavily on nonprofit organizations for social and health services.

Private sector delivery of government services is neither a new nor a growing phenomenon in New Jersey. Despite substantial budgetary pressures on local governments in the Garden State during the 1970s and 1980s, there was little movement toward or away from private, for-profit contracts for service delivery. Municipal service patterns have been settled for more than a decade with less than one in four initiated since the mid-1970s. Of the 450 municipal services investigated, only 13 percent were privatized within the last five years. In so far as any growth in private contracting has occurred, most has come through contracts with private nonprofit agencies to handle social services.

Table 13.2. Methods of Government Service Delivery in New Jersey Counties (n = 21)[a]

	Totally In House	Any Alter- native Method	Not Provided	Total	Contract	Inter- Govern- mental Agree- ments	Other
Public Works							
Road Construction/ Maintenance	7	14	0	21	12	2	0
Bridge Construction/ Maintenance	6	15	0	21	13	2	0
Parks & Recreation Facilities	12	6	3	21	4	2	0
Flood Control Facilities	10	6	5	21	2	2	1
Public Safety							
Police Patrol	10	0	11	21	0	0	0
Police/Fire Training	15	5	1	21	2	1	2
Ambulance/Rescue Squads	1	8	12	21	2	1	5
Communications/ Dispatching	12	4	5	21	0	3	2
Adult Correction/Detention	18	2	1	21	0	2	1
Juvenile Detention/Shelter	10	8	3	21	4	4	0
Health/Social Services							
Public Health Clinics/ Services	8	7	6	21	4	1	2
Hospitals	7	3	11	21	2	0	1
Alcohol/Drug Treatment	6	14	1	21	10	3	2
Mental Health Services	8	11	2	21	8	3	2
Nursing Homes	16	1	4	21	0	0	1
Social Services for the Elderly	8	12	1	21	6	3	3
Day Care	2	10	9	21	5	0	5
Temporary Shelter/ Homeless	6	11	4	21	9	1	1
Services for the Disabled	7	10	4	21	7	1	2
Support Services							
Legal	11	10	0	21	10	0	0
Engineering	11	10	0	21	10	0	0
Planning	16	5	0	21	5	0	0
Maintenance of Public Buildings/Grounds	15	6	0	21	6	0	0
Vehicle Maintenance	15	6	0	21	5	0	1
Payroll/Accounting	21	0	0	21	0	0	0

Source: Eagleton Institute of Politics.

[a] Figures in the left hand column show the number of counties reporting they: (a) deliver each service *entirely* in-house, (b) deliver all or part of the service through an alternative method, or (c) do not provide the service.

Figures in the right hand column show the number delivering each service entirely or partially through: (a) contracts (b) inter-governmental agreements, or (c) some other method.

Table 13.3. Identity of Service Providers for Contracts

Contracts	Private Firms	Non-Profit	Both	Don't Know	Total	(n)
Municipality Total	79%	16%	4%	1%	100%	(197)
By Service:						
Public Works	93	5	2	1	101	(151)
Public Safety	53	32	5	10	100	(19)
Social Services	19	69	12	0	100	(26)
County Total	27	60	10	3	100	(95)

Source: Eagleton Institute of Politics.

State Government

New Jersey state government also counts on private organizations to conduct many state responsibilities (see Table 13.4). Unlike counties and municipalities, which have a long tradition of privatization, state agencies are relative newcomers to privatization alternatives for some interesting reasons. (Chi 1985) The inability to meet rising demands for services, rather than the fear of budget cutbacks or the desire for efficiency, has goaded several large and rapidly growing departments into using private contractors.

Thus, for example, the Departments of Transportation, Environment, and Human Services found that they could not hire and maintain a work force large enough to meet the demand for services. They contracted with private firms to design and build roads, clean up toxic waste sites, and deliver medical and child care to the indigent population.

Those state agencies not facing rising demands for services have also sought private sector assistance. Many departments purchase highly specialized skills from the private sector that are rarely available within state government. Government agencies have trouble hiring and retaining computer programmers, evaluators, public relations experts, and test development specialists because of the high salaries commanded by skilled practitioners. Other private contracts go for activities purchased that occur only intermittently, such as program evaluations. A few departments deliver routine support services, such as data management and building maintenance, through contracts with private firms.

Private contracts consume large budget shares in some departments and are nonexistent in others. The Department of Transportation estimates that three-quarters of its budget consists of contracts with private businesses to design, build, and maintain roads and bridges. Commerce and Economic Development allocates half of its budget to a tourism promotional campaign that is designed and managed by private businesses. Private, for-profit firms and private, nonprofit organizations expend about half of the Health Department's total operating budget. The Departments of Agriculture, Energy, and Environmental Protection allocate nearly a quarter of their budgets to private firms.

Table 13.4. Summary of Major Program and Support Services Contracted Out in
New Jersey State Departments

Department	Programs and Activities	Support Services
Agriculture	Inspections	Building Maintenance
	Advertising	Administrative Support
	Testing	Data Management
Agriculture	Fish Farm Management	Accounting
Banking	None	None
Civil Service	Testing	Building Maintenance
	Training	Printing
	Arbitration	Data Management
Commerce	Advertising	Printing
		Data Management
Community Affairs	Telephone Hotline	Technical Consultants
Corrections	Medical Services	Data Management
	Drug Treatment	
	Halfway Houses	
Defense	None	Building Maintenance
		Building Security
Education	Testing	Technical Consultants
	Regional Libraries	Printing
	Bibliographic Services	Administrative Support
Energy	Recycling Campaign	Technical Consultants
	Education Programs	Conserv. Retrofitting
Environmental	Hazardous Waste Clean-up	Technical Consultants
Protection	Water Treatment	Laboratory Analysis
	Waste Water Treatment	Research
	Shore Protection	
	Construction	
Health	Family Planning	None Identified
(selective list)	Drug/Alcohol Abuse	
	AIDS Program	
	Environmental Health	
	Lead Poisoning	
	Research And Development	
	Refugee Health Programs	
Higher Education	Academic Grant Programs	Data Management
	Educational Opportunity Grants	Loan Management
	Educational Conferences	Program Evaluations
Human Services	Mental Health Programs	Data Management
(selective list)	Medical Assistance	Audits
	Health Facilities	Disbursements
	Services for Disabled	Claims Processing
Human Services	Welfare Services	Enforcement
	Youth/Family Services	
Insurance	None	Actuarial Reviews
Labor	Vocational Training	Medical Consultants
	On-the-Job Training	
	Professional Development	

Table 13.4. Summary of Major Program and Support Services Contracted Out in New Jersey State Departments

Department	Programs and Activities	Support Services
Law/Public Safety	Police Training	Data Management
	Expert Witnesses	Vehicle Maintenance
	Motor Vehicle Agencies	Micro-filming
	Inspection Stations	Technical Consultants
Public Advocate	Expert Witnesses	Court Reporters
	Attorneys	Administrative Support
	Program Evaluation	
State	None	Micro-filming
Transportation	Construction	Technical Consultants
	Design/Planning	Research
	Inspection	
	Road Maintenance	
Treasury	Advertising/Lottery	Data Management
		Technical Consultants
		Building Maintenance
		Property Management

Source: Eagleton Institute of Politics.

In contrast, less than five percent of the budgets of Banking, Civil Service, Community Affairs, Corrections, Education, Labor, State, and Treasury are contracted out. Human Services delivers about five percent of its budget through hundreds of contracts with private nonprofit firms.

Voucher systems have not been embraced on any wide scale in New Jersey state departments. Only two voucher programs were identified: a day-care voucher program in the Department of Human Services and a Distinguished Scholars program sponsored by the Department of Higher Education that provides an incentive for outstanding New Jersey high school graduates to attend colleges or universities in the Garden State.

Assessing Privatization

Most New Jersey government officials expressed satisfaction with the performance of private contractors. Positive assessments were given by municipal and county officials to approximately two out of three private contracting arrangements, yet substantial numbers of officials expressed serious reservations about the cost, quality, accountability, and reliability of private contract arrangements. A host of constraints, from the influence of private contractors on elected officials to the resistance of public employee unions combine to thwart substantial reassessment or change in the contemporary array of government service delivery.

Efficiency

The desire to save government resources was frequently mentioned by municipal and county officials as the rationale for privatizing government services, as shown in Tables 13.5 and 13.6. Cost savings were a more important factor in the privatization of public works functions than in the private delivery of social services. Cost savings, while still the most prominent reason for privatization of public works, was mentioned by 43 percent of the municipal respondents and 35 percent of the county respondents. Other factors, such as in-house staff limitations, quality of service delivery, and convenience were also important. In fact, limitations of staff and expertise were the most important reasons for contracting with private firms for the delivery of social services.

These findings are important because the principal argument for privatization is that government-run programs are more costly than privately managed programs. According to New Jersey officials, private contracts for service delivery in many cases are not justified exclusively or even primarily on efficiency grounds. State agencies were even less inclined to cite cost savings as the justification for privatization (Dudek 1987).

When pressed, few officials could supply any hard evidence to support their claim that private contracting was cheaper than government service delivery. If cost comparisons were ever made they were forgotten. Without any pressure to change, most local officials had long since decided that they would rely on private firms to perform a range of local, county, and state government services.

Interestingly, three state government departments reported that feasibility studies on the relative costs of providing services through private contracts versus public means revealed negligible or no savings to the government. One department concluded that in-house data-processing services were less costly than similar services provided in the private sector. The Department of Higher Education canceled a private contract for data processing after comparing costs of private and public services. Treasury determined that building maintenance through private contracts would yield only modest savings and therefore decided against changing existing practice.

Concerns about "unreasonable cost increases" were raised with respect to nearly half of the municipal contracts. County officials complained about cost increases involving one out of every three private contracts. In many instances, government officials were powerless to control prices of private, for-profit firms. Pricing practices by private firms operating within various sectors made it difficult for government agencies to obtain competitive bids on many large contracts.

Problems at the county government level were not as severe because counties rely more heavily on private nonprofit contractors. Private nonprofits are

Table 13.5. Most Important Reason for Using an Alternative Method of Service Delivery for Municipalities

	Cost Savings	In-House Limitations	Service Delivery	Administrative Management	Mandate	Convenience/ Other	Total	(n)
Total	36%	22%	7%	5%	11%	18%	99%	(409)
By Service for								
All Methods								
Public Works	37	26	4	3	17	12	99	(193)
Public Safety	41	15	12	5	3	24	100	(121)
Social Services	25	23	8	11	10	23	100	(83)
By Method for								
All Services								
Contracts	41	30	4	6	9	10	100	(185)
Inter-								
governmental	30	17	12	5	19	17	100	(138)
Other	35	12	7	4	3	39	100	(85)
Services Delivered								
by Contracts								
Public Works	43	31	4	4	12	6	100	(134)
Public Safety	53	21	5	5	5	11	100	(19)
Social Services	20	36	4	20	0	20	100	(25)

Source: Eagleton Institute of Politics.

Table 13.6. Most Important Reason for Using an Alternative Method of Service Delivery for Counties

	Cost Savings	In-House Limitations	Service Delivery	Administrative Management	Convenience/ Other	Total	(n)
Total	30%	24%	16%	11%	19%	100%	(89)
By Services for							
All Methods							
Public Works	35	27	12	9	17	100	(34)
Social Services	28	21	19	13	19	100	(53)
By Method for							
All Services							
Contracts	36	30	13	7	14	100	(56)
Inter-governmental	20	7	20	13	40	100	(15)
Other	23	18	24	23	12	100	(17)

Source: Eagleton Institute of Politics.

more easily controlled by county governments because they are not involved in supporting office holders through campaign contributions. In addition, there is often more competition to deliver such programs as job training and social services. Thus, the counties may replace one nonprofit with another without suffering serious political or operational costs.

Effectiveness

If efficiency is not an overwhelming argument for privatization, then one might expect public officials to justify private contracts on the basis of improved management or services to citizens (see Tables 13.5 and 13.6). In fact, quality of service delivery was cited as the principal rationale for privatization in only four percent of the municipal contracts and 13 percent of the county contracts examined in the study. Only six percent of municipal contracts and seven percent of county contracts were given to private firms in order to improve the administration and management of programs, according to the study's respondents.

State and local officials frequently complained that there were not enough qualified private firms to handle the tasks. Thus, even when they wanted to contract for the delivery of government functions, sufficient private sector resources often were not available. Such capacity could be developed, but usually at a high expense to the taxpayer. As an example, Department of Environmental Protection officials complained about their problems in finding private firms with sufficient technical skills to design, construct, and manage toxic waste clean-up projects.

The traditional trio of cost savings, service quality, and better management do not explain entirely the reliance on private contractors for the delivery of public services. Many government agencies employ private contractors because they have no viable alternatives. There are limitations on the size and capacity of government to perform the tasks assigned to it. Private firms provide a means for getting the job done.

Most government agencies have not considered changing the mix of service delivery for quite some time. Capital and personnel resources required to carry out refuse collection or road maintenance were lost long ago from government. For government to regain these lost resources would require a massive financial and time investment; moreover, firms now holding the contracts would strenuously resist.

Thus, many governments are captives of the private contractors providing services to their communities. Their own in-house limitations are an obstacle to change. Indeed, the fear of losing government capacity to deliver a given service and the subsequent loss of control over pricing structures is the most frequently heard argument against turning government services over to private firms.

The perception that specialized talent in the law, engineering, planning, and accounting is best obtained from private firms helps explain why a substantial percentage of these services are delivered through private contracts. According to respondents, nearly one in three private contracts were let due to the lack of expertise or specialized skills within local government. The need to obtain specialized expertise outside government was mentioned by 12 of 20 departments of state government.

In comparison with county and municipal governments, state agencies are more likely to use private firms to fill in gaps in service delivery or to supplement state personnel on a short-term or limited basis. With the exception of the Departments of Energy, Health, Transportation, and Environmental Protection, most departments are willing and able to deliver core department services without the aid of private firms.

Political Considerations

Whatever the original justification for contracting with private for profit firms, continuation of this practice is strongly shaped by contractor contributions to political campaigns. In many jurisdictions, the armies of workers who kept their jobs at city hall or in county government by providing steady campaign contributions and loyal support to their candidates on election day have been joined by platoons of private firms who owe their contracts for legal services, financial advice, and refuse collection to members of council, mayors, and county executives. Communities that never had anything resembling a classic political machine find that private contractors play significant roles in ensuring the election of favorable governing bodies (American Federation of State, County, and Municipal Employees 1987).

Existing contracts are supported by a network of private contractors who contributed to political officials who in turn awarded contracts to those supporters. Several factors foster an environment in which private contractors may influence government decisions affecting their interests.

The stakes involved in many government contracts are substantial indeed. State and local governments in New Jersey spent approximately $17 billion in 1988. A conservative estimate provided by the Office of Legislative Services is that 50 percent of the state's $12 billion budget is contracted out to private firms. Within the last five years, New Jerseyans have authorized the issuance of more than $6 billion in bonds for everything from shore protection to prisons. Within the next three years, county officials will issue more than $4 billion in bonds to build resource recovery facilities. Firms assigned responsibility for acting as bond counsel, financial advisers, or investment bankers for large public projects stand to collect millions of dollars in fees. Individuals appointed to serve as counsel to special authorities or city agencies and boards can earn thousands of dollars.

The practice of soliciting campaign funds from contractors politicizes privatization. Candidates for mayor, council, freeholder, and county executive in New Jersey raise money from those who deliver contracts for the government. With major financial investments at stake, these contractors provide a reliable and growing resource upon which local officials can call. The chief political adviser to a county executive in one of New Jersey's largest counties made this assessment of contractor campaign contributions: "Seventy-five percent of our campaign funds come from contractors or employees of county government. The other 25 percent come from people who want contracts or jobs with county government. Who else would be interested in contributing money?" Indeed, law firms, financial institutions, insurance brokers, paving contractors, waste haulers, and others who are dependent on government contracts for much of their business frequently compete for the opportunity to host important fund-raising events.

The custom of no-bid contracts cements the linkage between government officials, campaign contributors, and government contractors. According to state statute, New Jersey state and local officials may award contracts "at their convenience" for dozens of government services. Government officials are clearly in a position to reward their friends or withhold business from their enemies. Conflict of interest and bidding ordinances for New Jersey government entities are so full of loopholes that a governing board or department can justify virtually any decision. Bidding procedures are relatively stringent for tangible items that can be purchased—paper, tires, cars and trucks—but procedures for obtaining services are much less demanding. Often local governments are not even required to solicit bids, let alone award the contract to the lowest bidder.

Many state and local government officials join private firms doing business with their former employers as soon as they leave government service. The revolving door between government and the private sector insures that private firms have access to critical government clients and, without doubt, influences the decisions of some officials while they are in public office. This widespread and accepted practice was justified by one local official who chose not to be identified, in blunt terms: "Unless you can eventually make money in the private sector no one would want to get into government in the first place."

Some jurisdictions allow city councilmen and county freeholders to award contracts to firms in which they or their families have a direct financial interest. Thus, if a freeholder in Essex county is an insurance agent, the contract for obtaining insurance for county government and its employees could be awarded to the freeholder's firm without violating the county's conflict of interest ordinance. Under the guidelines of the following county ethics code, practically anything is possible:

When awarding a contract exempted from the New Jersey public bidding statutes, a Freeholder or public officials shall not authorize the letting of such contract with any business entity in which he or she own property interests or which employs him or her. . . . This section shall not preclude the authorization of such a contract where the product or service is unique or difficult or unreasonable efforts would be required to obtain a replacement. This section shall be construed to reflect the presumption that the Freeholder acted reasonably.

Responsibility for developing and policing conflict of interest standards for state government employees are decentralized to the twenty department heads. Since most of these individuals are close political allies of the governor, they often use their positions to reward campaign supporters. The connection between campaign contributions and state government contract decisions was revealed in a highly publicized episode near the end of the Governor Kean's first term in 1985. A multi-million dollar data processing contract for the Division of Motor Vehicles was awarded to the accounting firm of Price Waterhouse. The firm did not submit the low bid, but they had regularly and generously contributed to the governor's campaign coffers. What brought this house of cards down was the firm's failure to get the Division's computer to operate effectively. Thousands of motorists received incorrect automobile registrations and licenses. Price Waterhouse was ousted, the Division took back control of data processing, but system-wide reforms to prohibit reoccurrences were not adopted.

Fraudulent and illegal activities are also part of the privatization environment. Dozens of county and municipal officials have been indicted and convicted of taking kickbacks in return for contracts. Announcing a spate of indictments, the U.S. Attorney for northern New Jersey, Samuel A. Alito, Jr. remarked that "bribery-for-business" deals in New Jersey municipal public works departments are "systemic" in some parts of the state. Another prosecutor commented, "It became apparent that relatively honest people had absolutely no qualms in taking kickbacks" (Rudolph 1989).

Accountability

The absence of regular, systematic procedures for evaluating contractor performance and the political influence wielded by those seeking to obtain and hold contracts raises serious questions about the accountability of private firms. In some communities, it appears that the government and its governing body are more accountable to the private firm than the other way around.

Officials complained about the performance of private contractors, but were unwilling or unable to do much about it. Public complaints about the quality of services, flaws in government monitoring of contractors, unreliable firms, insurance and legal problems, and lack of responsiveness to government officials were cited as major concerns in more than 40 percent of the contracts examined. The difficulty of supervising contractors and bidding procedures was noted by state officials from the departments of Education, Energy, Environmental Protection, and Treasury. Serious mismanagement by private firms was mentioned by senior personnel in the Department of Health and the Division of Motor Vehicles, where scandal rocked the Division.

Fears about the lack of accountability for service delivery is a principal impediment to new privatization ventures. For example, the Civil Service Department rejected private contracts for test administration, and the Division of Motor Vehicles eschewed driver testing by private firms due to concerns about possible fraud. Environmental Protection considered hiring private contractors to administer its air pollution enforcement program, but pulled back when staff and industrial firms objected to nongovernment investigations of sensitive matters. Corrections entertained the idea of contracting out for prison facilities in order to relieve overcrowding, but dismissed this approach because of problems with monitoring security. Treasury contemplated contracting for data processing for the Taxation Division, but chose not to do so because of security problems and the need to maintain the confidentiality of records on private citizens and firms.

Conclusions

There is a wide gap between the rhetoric and the reality of privatization as it is commonly practiced in one large state. The theorists who promote privatization conjure up private contracts as a potential saviour for incompetent state and local officials. Cheaper services and high quality are promised. The experience in New Jersey casts serious doubts on the validity of these claims.

The delivery of public services through private contracts is far from a revolutionary idea in the Garden State. The survey of state and local officials reveals an established pattern of contracting with private firms to carry out much of the public's business. Having relied on private contracts for years, local and county governments display little interest in changing the status quo. Despite periods of sharp decline and rapid growth in government spending, and support for privatization from Republican Governor Thomas Kean since 1982, state and local officials made few alterations in traditional service delivery methods. Scant attention has been paid to assessing the performance of ongoing private contracts. Few officials have conducted a careful analysis of privatization alternatives on those rare occasions when traditional government delivery approaches are reconsidered.

Is New Jersey representative of national trends? Without systematic evidence from other states and localities, it is impossible to provide a satisfactory answer to this question. However, there is no reason to believe that New Jersey's practices are radically different from the rest of the nation. Therefore, the implications that can be drawn from these findings are potentially applicable to many other states and communities.

Unfortunately, privatization is not likely to foster significant improvements in governmental performance. In fact, significant economic, administrative, and political constraints will limit any reshaping of current practices for service delivery. (Starr 1987) Changes in methods of government service delivery are going to occur at the margins.

Given the limitations on the scope and impact of privatization, public officials and policy analysts should spend less time worrying about whether to privatize and turn to more important questions such as how well contemporary arrangements for service delivery are working. Government policy makers should improve their ability to acquire and oversee services provided through private contracts. Wishful thinking and ideology are no substitute for careful analysis of alternatives on a case-by-case basis.

Greater effort must be placed into insuring competition and integrity in government contracting procedures. The practice of awarding contracts without an open-bidding procedure should be sharply reduced. At a minimum, contracts in excess of a modest size, say $50,000, should be subject to a competitive, public bidding process. Exemptions that allow governments to make decisions for the sake of convenience, while well intentioned, have clearly been abused by many officials. In most cases, no-bid contracts are nothing more than a license to reward political allies and contributors.

Political calculations and corruption thwart efforts to improve government contracting and inhibit substantial decreases in the extent of private contracts. Conflict of interest standards must be significantly strengthened. Contract awards and the performance of private firms should be periodically reviewed by independent boards. Independent ethics commissions should be established to conduct these reviews and disseminate their findings.

The revolving door must not swing so freely. A one-year ban on post-government employment with private contractors should be imposed on senior government officials. Officials with direct financial interests in projects must not participate in decisions affecting their business.

Clearly, many of the concerns about political influence and even corruption are less applicable to contracts with private, non-profit organizations. Indeed, such firms deliver vital social and health services: two out of every three county contracts are given to non-profit organizations. Nevertheless, private non-profit firms, like any other organization, should be closely monitored by the government agencies that provide funding. Without continued oversight, the energy and innovation initially gained by delivering services through nonprofits may evaporate.

When considering privatization, public officials should look beyond the potential short-term savings and consider the consequence of establishing private sector monopolies for service delivery. The approach in Phoenix, whereby government refuse collection competes with private, for-profit firms, seems to have created a healthy competition that benefits the taxpayers. Unfortunately, analyses are rarely conducted. In addition to short- and long-term efficiency, government officials must weigh other values, such as accountability, service quality, and equity in the equation.

Privatization is neither a panacea nor an abomination. Within limitations, private contracts for public service could be a helpful management tool to lower the cost of government services or to create program innovation. Private contracts for a portion of service delivery may be especially helpful in testing new approaches without committing the entire government apparatus to an unproven method. Private nonprofit firms may be capable of delivering services to hard-to-reach populations, such as the homeless or AIDS victims.

But privatization as it is often practiced suffers from the same weaknesses often attributed to government-run programs. There are no inherent reasons why a program run by a privately controlled entity will be any less expensive, or better managed than a publicly run program. Based on the evidence to date, there is every reason to be highly skeptical of claims that privatization will magically overcome the mundane, but common problems of poor management and greed.

NOTES

The research project was designed and conducted by Cliff Zukin and Carl Van Horn of the Eagleton faculty and graduate students at Rutgers University in consultation with staff from New Jersey State and Local Expenditure and Revenue Policy Commission. I particularly wish to acknowledge the assistance of Robert Goertz and Frank Haines of the Commission staff.

1 A stratified random sample was employed to select the municipalities included in the study. The sample was stratified first by county according to population size. Thus, if a particular county made up ten percent of the state's population it would also represent ten percent of the sample points chosen. The sample was further stratified by population size within counties. Municipalities within counties were divided into groups of under 20,000, between 20,000 and 50,000 and over 50,000. Targets were set so that each group would be represented in the sample proportional to the distribution of the groups within the county. Municipalities were then randomly chosen within these categories.

Almost all (86) of the 90 municipalities selected through this process agreed to cooperate. Two of the four declining to do so were replaced by municipalities in the same county with similar attributes. The sampling error associated with this size sample drawn from the total population of New Jersey's 567 municipalities is approximately plus or minus seven percent, at a confidence interval of 90 percent.

2 In conducting the inventory, Eagleton used the following definitions:

Government Service: Delivered entirely by a government agency with its own employees.

Contract or purchase of services: Government arranges to have service delivered entirely or partially by private firm or nonprofit agency.

Intergovernmental Agreement: Government arranges to have service delivered entirely or partially by another governmental unit through a formal agreement. One government pays to have another governmental unit deliver the service.

Vouchers: Government arranges to have services delivered entirely or partially by private firms or public organizations by designating acceptable service producers and by giving consumers/clients coupons or checks that may be redeemed at the producer of their choice.

REFERENCES

American Federation of State, County, and Municipal Employees. 1987. *When Public Services Go Private: Not Always Better, Not Always Honest, There May be a Better Way.* Washington, D.C.: AFSCME.

Baumer, Donald C., and Carl E. Van Horn. 1985. *The Politics of Unemployment.* Washington, D.C.: CQ Press.

Butler, Stuart. 1985. *Privatizing Federal Spending: A Strategy to Eliminate the Deficit.* New York: Universe Books.

Chi, Keon. 1985. "Privatization: A Public Option?" *State Government News* 9 (June): 4–10.

De Hoog, Ruth. 1986. *Contracting Out for Human Services.* Albany: State University of New York Press.

Dudek, Donna. 1987. "Going Private: Paying Less?" *State Legislatures* 13 (March): 26–29.

Hatry, Harry. 1985. "Privatization Pros and Cons—and Ways to Make Government Agencies more Competitive." *Urban Resources,* 4 (September): 15–17.

Kolderie, Ted. 1984. "The Two Different Concepts of Privatization." *Public Administration Review* 46 (July–August): 1–6.

Linowes, David F. 1988. *Privatization: Toward More Effective Government.* Champaign, Ill.: University of Illinois Press.

Pack, Janet Rothenberg. 1987. "Privatization of Public-Sector Services in Theory and Practice." *Journal of Policy Analysis and Management.* 6 (Summer): 523–40.

Rudolph, Robert. 1989. "Authorities Widen Probe of Graft in Jersey Public Works Departments." *Newark Star-Ledger,* 14 March, 14.

Savas, E. S. 1982. *Privatizating the Public Sector: How to Shrink Government.* Chatham, N.J.: Chatham House.

Starr, Paul. 1987. "The Limits of Privatization." In *Prospects for Privatization,* ed. Steve Hanke, 124–37. New York: Proceedings of the Academy of Political Science.

Stevens, Barbara. 1984. "Comparative Study of Municipal Service Delivery." Unpublished paper. New York: Ecodata.

Van Horn, Carl E. 1989. *The State of the States.* Washington, D.C.: CQ Press.

14 *Janet Rothenberg Pack*

The Opportunities and Constraints of Privatization

Introduction

The privatization movement is about large issues. Shrinking the size of government is the principal goal. To this end load shedding and asset sales are advocated. Neither one has been widely implemented. After two decades of heightened interest in privatization in the United States, efforts consist largely of contracting with private firms for goods and services traditionally financed and produced directly by government agencies. The principal question this chapter explores is why so wide a gap exists between the alleged potential for privatization in the United States and its realization. Several factors may explain the slow pace of implementation.

First, advocates of privatization almost exclusively use an efficiency argument, giving insufficient weight to the extensive distributional implications of their proposals. They also fail to appreciate the complex notions of equity and entitlement associated with many programs that involve subsidies to the middle class. Also, proponents emphasize government failures and minimize the market failures from which so many public interventions derive. In many cases they ignore the social benefits associated with public provision—real benefits whose omission makes public agencies look inefficient when only financial flows are considered or when compared to private production of a more limited service.

Many advocates of load shedding, in particular, have inferred incorrectly

Janet Rothenberg Pack is Professor of Public Policy and Management, Wharton School, University of Pennsylvania.

from the tax limitation movements of the 1970s that the public was demanding major government cutbacks. Maybe the public wants what is produced to be continued, even if it appears inefficient. Proposals for divestiture often fail to distinguish the inefficiencies stemming from *what* is produced (allocative inefficiency) from those resulting from *how* it is produced (technical inefficiency).

Among advocates of privatization, process is ignored almost entirely. If the production process is as important as output, if indeed the two are inseparable, as is probably the case for many social services, the public may not be indifferent to the choice of provider, or may not permit unregulated private provision. Sufficiently stringent regulation may make public and private provision nearly indistinguishable.

Finally, proponents of privatization often assume unquestioningly that competitive private firms will replace monopolistic public producers, and, therefore, consistent with theoretical expectations, more efficient outcomes will follow.

The discussion of privatization may be thought of as the other side of the discussion of the role of the public sector in a mixed economy. Following Musgrave, two of the principal objectives of the public economy are to "secure adjustments in the allocation of resources [and to] secure adjustments in the distribution of income and wealth. . . ." (Musgrave 1959: 5). In the first instance, it is the inefficiencies of market failures that provide the rationale for public interventions. These include barriers to free entry, decreasing cost production processes, external economies or diseconomies, and what Musgrave calls "social wants" (i.e., demands for public goods). A second reason for public intervention is dissatisfaction with the distributional outcomes of market processes.

As the range and size of government programs have expanded, questions have increasingly been raised about whether public production enhances efficiency or is so inherently inefficient that it results in even greater resource misallocation than do the market failures it aims to correct; whether regulation is even more costly to society than the initial resource misallocations. Simply put, the argument goes, the existence of market failure does not mean that a public response will necessarily improve matters. A body of literature on government failure has developed that challenges the efficacy of public intervention and, by implication, calls into question market failure as a sufficient rationale for public intervention (Wolf 1979).

Some claim that privatization can improve resource allocation because the government has become involved in the production of goods and services that do not meet the market failure tests; these goods and services can be and, in fact often are, efficiently produced by private firms. There is no reason, therefore, for public production. Many of the functions of the Coast Guard or of the Post Office, for example, involve the provision of purely private services that are at least as efficiently produced by private firms. Even where public financing is appropriate, public production need not necessarily follow. Public financing of trash collection may be justified on health externality grounds, but collection by private firms under contract or franchise to the government may be more efficient. The argument has even more force in the case of the many inputs used by the government.

Regarding income distribution, the question has long been whether redistribution should be achieved through taxes and income transfers or by the direct transfer of goods and services. The adoption of a negative income tax and cashing out of all other benefits (e.g., health care, food stamps, housing) has been debated for decades without resolution. Privatization of redistributive activities would be consistent with a negative income tax, or other pure cash transfer system, with all purchases of goods and services made directly by consumers from private providers. This would increase consumer sovereignty and improve the efficiency of production.[1]

Among the most frequently debated forms of privatization are load shedding, asset sales, contracting, and vouchers. *Load shedding* eliminates government financing and production of a particular service and lets the private sector take over the function, if a private market develops. The basis for load shedding should be either that the good or service in question is a purely private one and, therefore, is appropriately financed and produced privately, or that the inefficiencies of public production exceed the inefficiencies associated with the market failures of private production. Some argue that if provision is based upon equity rather than efficiency grounds, subsidies (e.g., housing vouchers) are appropriate.

Asset sales transfer ownership and responsibility to the private sector. Here, too, the justification must be that the goods or services are essentially private, or that public production is more inefficient than private. If production also generates externalities, proponents argue that these can be adequately dealt with through production or consumption subsidies or taxes. In many cases, asset sales are proposed for activities unlikely to attract competitors (e.g., electric utilities) and, therefore, require public regulation.

Contracting retains the activity in the public budget but transfers production to the private sector. It is used most often for the procurement of intermediate goods inputs but is being advocated for and extended to a wider range of service inputs as well as to a growing number of final public services (e.g., trash collection). The case for extending contracting rests on efficiency grounds.

The use of *vouchers* keeps financing in the public sector, partly transfers production to the private sector, and increases the scope for private choice of the service package. Here too the argument is that the good or service is essentially a private one, that it can be purchased privately, and that redistributional goals or externalities can be more efficiently achieved via consumption subsidies.

We shall argue below that support for contracting is grounded in public agreement concerning the technical efficiencies likely to be realized. The lack of support for asset sales and load shedding stems from disagreement concerning the existence of allocative inefficiency and differing perceptions of the centrality of distributional issues to many proposals argued purely on efficiency grounds. Where advocates of privatization see allocative inefficiency (i.e., government providing services better left to the private sector entirely or provided in too great a quantity, as a result of subsidies, for example), opponents see valued public outputs that would not be forthcoming from the private sector or would not be produced in sufficient quantities. For example, positive externalities would be ignored. In many of these cases, technical inefficiency in the public sector is overstated because inadequate account is taken of these valued public outputs and externalities in the cost comparisons between public and private producers.

It is neither surprising nor contradictory that contracting with private firms for the production of intermediate inputs or of final services is more common than are asset sales or load shedding. For contracting proposals, technical efficiency is most likely the principal concern; the public sector defines the quantity and quality of what is to be produced and allocative inefficiency is not at issue. However, even in the case of contracting, as proposals move further into the realms in which process and distributional concerns dominate (i.e., final services), technical efficiency is both more difficult to define and less likely to be the main concern.

Goals of Privatization and the Instruments Used to Achieve Them

In order to evaluate the progress of privatization, it is important to look at the proposals that have been made to increase the role of the private sector in the public economy and to consider the expected outcomes of these changes. Three related but not identical goals of privatization dominate the discussion: to reduce the size of the government sector (i.e., the ratio of government expenditures to GNP), to reduce the federal budget deficit (to reduce government expenditures minus government revenues in the short term), and to increase the efficiency of public service delivery (i.e., increase the real output for a given level of government expenditure).

Reduce the Size of Government

The principal goal of the most vigorous proponents of increased privatization is reduction in the size of the public sector. In March 1988, The President's Commission on Privatization issued its report, *Privatization: Towards*

More Effective Government. The opening paragraph of the introductory chapter establishes its orientation:

> . . . the federal government has become too large, too expensive, and too intrusive in our lives. . . . The President's Commission on Privatization was created to assess the range of activities that might properly be transferred to the private sector. . . . (1988:1)

The dominant theme of the report is a long-term reduction in the size of the public sector. The contrast drawn between contracting and other forms of privatization reinforces the emphasis.

> Unlike most forms of privatization, contracting out does not necessarily have as a direct goal the reduction of the ultimate scope of government responsibility. . . . Contracting, nevertheless, can still be linked to the broader aims of the privatization movement. . . . Although the absolute scope of government service responsibility may not decline, the actual size of government—the number of government employees and the extent of government owned resources—will diminish. Reducing the size of government may be an important goal in itself. . . . (1988:244)

The Commission has not misread the aims of what it calls the "privatization movement." The central purpose, to diminish the size of the public sector, is abundantly clear in the statements of its most persistent boosters. The title of E. S. Savas' 1982 book is explicit: *Privatizing the Public Sector: How to Shrink Government*. The title of Stuart Butler's 1985 book, *Privatizing Federal Spending: A Strategy to Eliminate the Deficit*, suggests that eliminating the federal deficit is the purpose of privatization, but the solution is not sought on the revenue side of the ledger. The emphasis throughout the volume is on reducing the expenditure side of the budget, the size of the public sector: "The privatization technique offers an opportunity to outflank the supporters of bigger government. . . ." (1985:4).

The reasons for reducing the size of the public sector are many. The dangers of concentration of economic power are amplified when that economic power resides in the government—when access to employment, to vital goods and services, to supplies of critical materials is combined with political preferences and political control. There are also efficiency grounds. On the demand side, the imperfect ways in which demands for public goods and services are articulated, interpreted, and implemented, make it likely that at least some of the goods and services being produced by the public sector do not comport very well with public preferences. For example, if many of these activities have only limited public characteristics, load shedding or the introduction of user fees could appropriately reduce demand for some services, and vouchers could increase consumer sovereignty. On the supply side, public financing does not necessarily require public production.

Each of the instruments of privatization described earlier might help to reduce the size of the public sector; used in concert, substantial reduction might be achieved. Although load shedding and asset sales remove items from the budget directly, the size of the public sector will decrease only if other expenditures do not fill the gaps. Contracting with private firms for production has not been the favored instrument for shrinking the size of the public sector, although potential efficiency gains are allegedly substantial. One widely accepted explanation of growth in public expenditures is that government bureaucrats have far more incentive to increase their budgets and staff than to achieve greater efficiency. Shifting the locus of production from the public agency to the private sector, some say, would shift the emphasis from budget expansion to cost reduction. Steven Smith (1987), however, finds that contracting for social services increases the constituency in favor of public expenditure as contractors make efforts "to develop a stable financial base and influential political support (Smith 1987:43)." Given the history of Defense Department contracting, this outcome should surprise no one. It is fear of such private sector lobbying that mutes support for contracting as an instrument of privatization (Butler 1985:56).

Reduce The Deficit

If privatization efforts succeed in decreasing expenditures through divestiture or by achieving greater efficiency through contracting, they may be successful as well in reducing the deficit if they can discourage the growth of non-privatized expenditures.

The interest in privatization for deficit reduction has grown along with the size of the deficit. Early in the Reagan administration, the President's Private Sector Survey on Cost Control (the PPSSCC, often referred to as the Grace Commission) was authorized "to identify opportunities for increased efficiency and reduced costs in federal government operations." (U.S. GAO 1985, vol. 1:1). "Since the report's issuance in January 1984, the PPSSCC's work has been repeatedly cited by the President as a major component in his strategy to reduce the deficit." (U.S. GAO 1985, vol. 1:2) Congress also views many of the suggestions of the Grace Commission as important instruments of deficit reduction and accordingly has written into the Deficit Reduction Act a requirement for "the President to report on progress in implementing the PPSSCC recommendations . . ." (U.S. GAO 1985, vol. 1:2) and for congressional committees to propose legislative changes to implement the Commission's recommendations.

Proposals for asset sales are often tied to concern for deficit reduction. The recent report of the President's Commission on Privatization recognizes this but takes a cautious view of deficit reduction as a central purpose of privatizing efforts and of the potential effects of asset sales on the deficit. Contrary to some assertions, the President's Commission also argues that loan sales will not significantly reduce the federal budget deficit (1988:49). As Commission members see the matter,

> to many people, the term "privatization" is synonymous with the sale of government assets, [and] pressure to reduce the federal deficit has led many policymakers to view asset sales as a convenient means of raising revenues. As a result, the benefits of asset sales other than the short-term infusion of cash into the federal Treasury have often been overlooked, and privatization has been transformed from a resource management issue into a budget issue. (p. 162)

Sustained deficit reduction can result from: 1) privatization that reduces the expenditure side of the budget, whether by load shedding, asset sales, or contracting, without similarly affecting revenues; or 2) increased revenues (e.g., through greater reliance on user fees). One-period deficit reduction can be achieved by asset sales, but can only be sustained if the maintenance and operation of the asset would have required substantial current expenditure in the future. If the sale of assets means foregone future revenues, the deficit reducing effects are ambiguous. For this reason, according to the commission report, "in September 1987 an amendment was attached to the Debt Extension Act forbidding Congress from counting the revenues from loan sales as deficit reduction for the purpose of reaching Gramm-Rudman-Hollings deficit reduction targets" (President's Commission 1988:49).

Increase Efficiency

If reducing the size of the public sector is the dominant theme in the work of privatization advocates, enhancing the efficiency of the economy as a whole and the public sector in particular is their *leitmotif*. Supporters of public divestiture and asset sales argue that economic efficiency will be enhanced both by increased consumer sovereignty that will ultimately determine what is to be produced and by the competitive pressures on private producers to minimize costs of production. A less radical way of increasing productive efficiency is to shift public production to private firms through contracting.

The theoretical argument for privatization rests on a competitive model to demonstrate the efficiency of private production, and a public choice-government failure model wherein the public sector does too much and does it inefficiently. One way to reduce costs is to alter production techniques—to be innovative. Given the general assumption that private firms have greater incentives to be more efficient, it follows that they also have greater incentives to be innovative, to search for and to develop new, less costly production processes. They may also be more capable of implementing innovations since they are less constrained by public bureaucratic processes and by inflexible work rules.

Critics of privatization argue that the models are far too simple, that the complexity of implementation may make the promise of private production difficult and costly to achieve (Sappington and Stiglitz 1987). Advocates recognize many of these complications but often dismiss them or make cavalier suggestions for how they can be overcome. Similarly, opponents often simply state the problems and point out their potential costs without providing any evidence concerning the actual importance or frequency of these difficulties or their real costs relative to potential benefits.

The Realization of Privatization

Privatization has not had much effect on the size of government or on the government deficit. There have been few asset sales and little load shedding. Although contracts with private firms may have improved efficiency (*by reducing costs*), government agencies—federal, state, or local—have not moved very speedily to extend private contracting. Moreover, it is more likely that any savings achieved have been used to support other activities rather than to reduce total expenditures. Consistent with such an outcome, a bill has been introduced in Congress requiring that savings realized from contracting be returned to the Treasury (U.S. CBO 1987:15). The following examples illustrate the meagre potential of privatization to reduce government spending, whether national, state, or local. First we consider load shedding and asset sales, then contracting.

Load Shedding and Asset Sales

Suggestions that the federal government divest itself in whole or in part of its public housing, of Amtrak, public lands, the National Space Transportation System, air traffic control, the social security system, many Coast Guard functions, or naval petroleum reserves, to name just a few, have appeared in both government reports and academic literature. At the local government level, recommendations for divestiture are equally numerous and include public transit, airports, sports arenas, day care centers, and many other functions.

The Federal Government

Despite the many proposals over the years for major asset sales, Conrail is the only large sale to have been accomplished. Indeed, opposition to asset sales has been formally embodied in congressional legislation. Public Law 99-349 prohibits "the executive branch . . . from using any federal funds to study or propose PMA [Power Marketing Administration] divestiture, with the exception of the Alaska PMA. . . . The Department of Energy is prohibited from using federal funds to privatize the Naval Petroleum Reserves" (P.L. 99-500 and P.L. 99-591), and under P.L. 100-71, "The Department of Transportation is prohibited from using federal funds for a commission to study the privatization of Amtrak" (President's Commission 1988:164–65). The President's Commission recommends repeal of this legislation and that "the federal government . . . forcefully pursue the divestiture of capital assets . . ." on efficiency grounds.

Important interests are clearly protecting public ownership of major assets. However, some of the proposed asset sales are unrealistic in their disregard for the public values served (or thought to be served) by government expenditures. They ignore important externalities and redistributional goals.

Public Housing. Proposals for selling public housing units to tenants are a case in point. The President's Commission on Privatization recommends selling "public housing in good condition and consisting of detached one-family houses, duplexes and row houses . . . to tenants at a discounted price, with no further government expenditures for upkeep or debt service, while providing vouchers to tenants that freely elect to vacate" (i.e., those tenants who cannot afford even the discounted purchase price) (President's Commission 1988:17–18).

The Commission is not the first to advocate such sales; similar proposals have been made repeatedly despite the substantial constraints on both the demand and the supply side of the public housing market. Demand is limited because only ". . . 9 percent of all public housing households might have sufficient income to purchase public housing without excessive financial strain," (President's Commission 1988:17, citing a study of the Congressional Research Service).[2] And on the supply side, only a very small fraction of the existing public housing units fit the description. A high percentage are in large apartment complexes and are poor in quality.

With respect to the larger multifamily housing projects, it is recommended that where the units are "in satisfactory physical condition and . . . under successful tenant management, sale to tenant cooperatives at a discount should be encouraged, but only with the clear understanding that no operating subsidy will be provided and no further capital investment, not even for debt service on the original construction, will be made by the government after the sale" (President's Commission 1988:20).

In 1987 Congress passed enabling legislation for the sale of public housing units. The limited incomes of public housing residents, the generally poor condition of the housing, and the very small numbers of projects managed by tenant councils (3.2 percent overall and 25 percent of the fourteen largest projects, according to the Commission) suggest little potential for reducing the size of the public sector through such sales. President Bush's first housing proposals include $1.074 billion for tenants to convert and rehabilitate federally subsidized housing into resident-owned coops (*New York Times*, 11 November 89:13). This will not carry privatization of public housing very far forward in light of estimates of $9.5 billion needed simply for "necessary repairs," and $21.5 billion required "for other important work" in public housing projects (President's Commission 1988:22).

Since public housing programs exist largely to serve redistributional goals, it is also unlikely that the withdrawal of government expenditures could be sustained in the event of a failure of tenant ownership. With nearly all public housing tenants' incomes at 50 percent or less of regional median incomes (Savas, 1987, cites an average of 28 percent of the national median), it is unlikely that even far more efficient management of public housing projects can bring independent, nonsubsidized ownership within reach of all but a few. Substantial capital expenditures and continued public subsidy for operating would be required, as would continued oversight of public housing management.

Given the very low incomes and multiple problems of public housing residents, and the substantial proportion of public housing units in large rundown developments, it is unrealistic to propose the sale of public housing to its occupants as a way either to improve housing for the poor or for the federal government to leave the low-income housing business.

Power Marketing Administrations. Still other proposals for divestiture of function and asset sales may have ignored the positive externalities or the public purposes served by various "inefficient" operations. An alternative view is that the positive externalities are small and the public purposes non-existent but that well-entrenched private interests have succeeded in benefiting at public expense. The PMA case illustrates all sides of the discussion.

The Grace Commission recommended that "the federal government begin immediately an orderly process of disengagement from participating in the generation and transmission of electric power through its Power Marketing Administrations." (U.S. GAO 1985, vol. 2:657). As pointed out above, Congress has forbidden the use of funds even to study this subject. The President's Commission on Privatization urges the repeal of the congressional restrictions and recommends that "the federal government should forcefully pursue the divestiture of capital assets" (President's Commission 1988:165).

PMA sales are vigorously opposed by interested parties, in particular, "public bodies and electric cooperatives who would stand to lose their preference rights to purchase relatively inexpensive power which is provided for by current law," (U.S. GAO 1985, vol. 2:658). The strength of the opposition to rate restructuring is embodied in the legislation barring study of PMA sale to the private sector and in "the current prohibition, contained in the PMA's appropriation legislation, against using any funds to study changing their electricity rate structure to reflect 'market' prices for electricity provided" (U.S. GAO 1985, vol. 2:662).

There are other factors beside special interest opposition, however, that weigh against privatization. In this example, and as we will see also in the case

of Conrail and Amtrak, at least part of the estimated saving from privatization stems not from differences in productive efficiency but from requirements
placed on the public operation that either reduce revenues (e.g., rate subsidies)
or increase costs (e.g., by maintaining unprofitable rail routes). If there is a
public purpose served by the subsidized power rates of the PMAs (or the maintenance of unprofitable train routes), that is, if the social benefits exceed the
private benefits, then the government might be expected to make their continu-
ance a condition of sale, either by providing explicit subsidies or by requiring
private producers to make the same low rates available to a preferred class of
customers. In either case, the estimated cost savings from privatization will
need adjustment. If there is no public purpose served, then the elimination of
these subsidies would increase public revenues and consequently reduce the
estimated savings from privatization.

In many of the proposals for asset sales, it is assumed that there are no social
benefits beyond the private benefits and that the only way to limit subsidies
for powerful private interests is through privatization. The result of asset sales
under these conditions is not necessarily more efficient private management
but rather the elimination by the government of costly, inefficient input or
output requirements that affect the operations of both the public and private
sectors.

There are still other reasons for questioning the assertion of the President's
Commission that "assets are generally more efficiently managed by private
owners. . . ." (President's Commission 1988:165). The GAO points out that
the Power Marketing Administration facilities are operated for other purposes
in addition to the provision of power; for "purposes such as irrigation, navi-
gation, flood control, fish and wildlife protection, and power used at the
facility. . . ." (U.S. GAO 1985, vol. 2:657).[3] Thus, comparisons that assume
the only output of the system is power overstate the private production cost
advantage. Although power generation is a private good, many of the other
outputs of the system are more like public goods, unlikely to be efficiently
produced by the private sector without substantial regulation or even to be
produced at all. The GAO argues that before privatization of the PMAs
can occur, "detailed negotiations and comprehensive agreements would be
required to ensure that all interests are adequately protected" (U.S. GAO
1985, vol. 2:657). Building in such protection would, of course, increase
private costs.

Thus the debate about selling off the PMAs is only in part about whether
power can be produced more cheaply by a private than by a public enterprise.
It is, in large measure, a question of whether some users of power should be
subsidized and of taking account of the many other outputs of the PMAs.

Conrail. In 1981, federal legislation was passed explicitly for the purpose of
helping Conrail to become profitable so that it could be sold in the private

sector. It provided relief from state taxes and labor requirements and allowed abandonment of unprofitable lines. Under public management, Conrail, became a profitable enterprise, earning $400–500 million in each of the three years prior to its sale. In 1987, Conrail was sold through a public stock offering for about $1.6 billion.[4]

That Conrail became profitable before being sold to the private sector is noteworthy. If the public sector is held to different requirements than the private sector, cost comparisons are not meaningful. Like PMA, the Conrail example suggests that unfavorable cost comparisons between public and private production can result from different output or input requirements demanded from the public sector, in this case the maintenance of unprofitable routes and various provisions to protect labor. The publicly operated Conrail became profitable when these requirements were removed. If privatized activities are subject to similar standards, they too may be unprofitable, as the regulated private freight lines were before Conrail was created.

The challenge is to account correctly for what is being produced. If Conrail can move from losing money to making profits by dropping unprofitable routes, the question is, why maintain unprofitable routes, not, why is public production more inefficient than private production. Unprofitable routes are maintained either because well-organized, politically effective interest groups are able to protect the benefits they receive at the expense of the rest of the population or because, in fact, they serve important social values not captured in the cost accounting. If the former is the case, and if it is only by joining the elimination of unprofitable routes to privatization that special interests can be overcome, then privatization may yield efficiency benefits quite apart from gains in productive efficiency. If privatization is necessary to enable Congress to relinquish control so that unprofitable activities can be abandoned, then privatization can be beneficial in ways that continued public operation cannot.[5]

Not all regulatory requirements produce inefficiencies, however. Many are designed specifically to deal with market failures, that is, with inefficiencies inherent in private transactions. They may serve public purposes that must be taken into account in considering the relative efficiency of public and private production.

Amtrak. Regarding Amtrak, the President's Commission called for increased contracting out and competition on intercity passenger rail service. It also recommended that "the federal government . . . adopt a multiyear plan to move Amtrak or major portions of its operations to the private sector. . . ." (President's Commission 1988:172). This proposal would "free the railroad from political controversy, preserve passenger rail service, and relieve taxpayers of the burden of federal subsidies." Similar proposals by the Office of Management and Budget since the early 1980s have been rejected by Congress. Even if adopted, it is unlikely that the outcomes envisioned would be realized. Indeed, Congress may continue to subsidize Amtrak precisely because rail passenger service cannot be maintained without help.

Unlike Conrail, which operated both profitable and unprofitable routes, none of Amtrak's routes, even those in the dense Northeast corridor, is profitable (although some do cover variable costs). Despite the achievement of substantial economies and increases in ridership, the 1988 federal subsidy to Amtrak still amounted to 30 percent of operating revenues (compared with 52 percent in 1981), or $574 million (compared with $777 in 1981) (*New York Times*, 13 March 1989: B7; Gomez-Ibanez and Clippinger 1987).[6]

Among the justifications for continued subsidy of passenger rail service are assertions about positive environmental externalities—energy conservation and the reduction of congestion on other types of transportation. Jose Gomez-Ibanez doubts that rail travel, which comprises "less than 1 percent of all intercity passenger miles" could generate substantial externalities. However, this fraction may significantly understate the effects in the most densely travelled areas. It is possible that in the southern Connecticut–New York City–northern New Jersey corridor the transfer of current rail passengers to automobiles might have a decided effect on pollution and congestion. How much of a subsidy would be warranted to avoid these negative externalities is an empirical question. The extensive and costly air quality plan recently adopted by the South Coast Air Quality Management District for the Los Angeles basin suggests that, at least in the Los Angeles area, pollution costs are assumed to be very large (*New York Times*, 26 March 1989: 3: 2.).

For the less dense rail links, it is unlikely that the positive externalities of reduced air pollution, or congestion, or diminution in energy dependence could justify the substantial subsidies that are currently provided. Nor does it appear that the economies possible from rationalizing operations and reducing costs can make these routes profitable, whether privately or publicly run.

The political forces keeping the passenger rail system in place allege that other positive social externalities justify continued subsidies. Usually framed in terms of accessibility, the case is weak, given the availability of other modes of transportation. It seems more likely that the subsidies are maintained to serve a narrow but well-organized set of private interests. One of the factors that may work against continued subsidy is resistance to the large capital expenditure necessary in the near future to replace aging equipment. The president of Amtrak has requested an increase of the annual subsidy to $656 million (from $574 in 1988) to modernize the fleet, meet increased demand, and prevent further deterioration of service.

Whether Amtrak will or should be sold to private investors depends upon two factors that are often confused. The first concerns whether Amtrak should continue to provide the present level, type, and diversity of service. Specifically, are routes that cannot operate without subsidy to be maintained? If not required to maintain such routes, a private organization will surely abandon them. The government-run railroad might find the political pressures to continue service difficult to resist even if it wanted to give up the routes. It may turn out to be more feasible to sell Amtrak simply to achieve route rationalization.

The second factor concerns the relative productive efficiency of the public compared with the private firm, holding the product the same. If bus, automobile, and air transport provide sufficient competition for the railroad, then the private firm may be expected to achieve greater economies of production than the publicly run railroad, insulated as it is from the normal effects of competition.

If there is sufficient resistance to continued subsidy of the passenger railroad or if the required subsidy continues to increase as the need to replace capital equipment becomes more urgent, the privatization of Amtrak may result. In order to have a chance of providing efficient, unsubsidized passenger rail service, Amtrak will have to be permitted to cut routes substantially. If the public wishes to maintain a large part of the existing system, subsidies will have to continue, despite the productive efficiencies a private organization is likely to be able to realize. Only in the most densely traveled corridors is it possible that positive externalities—congestion and pollution reduction, in particular—are great enough to justify subsidized rail passenger service.

Thus, the questions to be dealt with in evaluating the sale of Amtrak are whether substantial allocational inefficiencies exist; if so, whether privatization will correct them; and whether substantial technical efficiencies can be expected with privatization. Although the case for allocative inefficiencies appears sound, the positive effects of privatization on allocative and technical efficiency are only hypothetical. Generalization from Conrail to Amtrak, with respect to the elimination of routes, is tempting but imperfect at best since far more drastic route cutting would be required and the pressures for maintaining passenger trains may be greater than for maintaining freight lines. It should also be remembered that in the Conrail case, commuter routes were shifted to local authorities. Expectations concerning technical efficiency gains are unclear in light of the Conrail experience, in which increased profitability is most closely linked to route rationalization, and in light of the Gomez-Ibanez estimates showing that even an enormously rationalized rail system would be substantially more expensive than alternative forms of passenger travel. If allocational inefficiency is important, and if privatization can substantially reduce it and increase technical efficiency, a strong case for privatization can be made. Even so, it is unrealistic to expect that passenger rail service, in anything like its present form, will be preserved.

State and Local Governments

Proposals for asset sales and divestiture of function are not limited to the federal government. A 1987 survey of city managers in jurisdictions of 5,000 or more people and county executives in counties with 25,000 or more identified three forms of privatization: contracting, asset sales, and privatizing facilities, in which "a private-sector organization builds or acquires a facility, such as a sewage-treatment plant, and then owns and operates the facility for the government." (Touche Ross 1987:1) About one-third of the respondents said they had privatized facilities in the past five years and intended to continue to do so in the next two years; one-quarter indicated they had sold assets in the past five years; one-fifth planned asset sales in the next two years.

Upon closer inspection, the asset sales turned out to have very little to do with privatization. Seventy percent of the cases were land sales and most of the remaining instances were sales of buildings. "The predominant reason for selling assets . . . is that the assets are obsolete and no longer needed by the government. . . . [A]ssets are usually sold not for privatization purposes, but to raise revenue or to get the asset off the government's books. Eighteen percent of the respondents say they sold assets to balance the budget. Only 15 percent say their principal reason for selling assets was to improve services." (Touche Ross 1987:20).

The privatization of facilities, however, does involve private firms in the ownership and operation of infrastructure more commonly owned and operated by governments. According to the survey, the most frequently privatized functions were roads, bridges, or tunnels (34%), solid-waste and resource-recovery facilities (22%, with 32% having plans for such privatization), street lights (30%), sewers or treatment plants (30%), and water mains or treatment facilities (22%). Without additional data and analysis, it is not clear what to conclude. Many of these local examples probably involved neither an asset sale nor the divestiture of an existing local function. Rather, private entrepreneurs assumed responsibility when new facilities were to be developed; there was no obvious displacement of an existing labor force or government bureaucracy. On the margin, however, this may represent a substantial increase in private involvement over what has been almost entirely public.

The privatized facilities consist principally of infrastructure. They do not involve the direct delivery of personal services that would be more likely to elicit opposition from specific facility clientele and public interest groups, as in the cases of public housing, transit, health facilities, or prisons. The transfer of prisons to the private sector is frequently proposed but vigorously opposed with the result that only 5 percent of correctional facilities, 11 percent of housing, 9 percent of mass transportation or transit, and 4 percent of hospitals or extended-care facilities have been privatized (Touche Ross 1987). In these cases distributional and output quality concerns mute the importance of efficiency in production.

Contracting

Contracting is a very different, and more common, form of privatization than either load shedding or asset sales. The public sector remains the provider, the financier, but not the producer. Government agencies regularly purchase a wide variety of goods and services from private firms (e.g., stationery, office furniture, computers, park benches, automobiles). In general, most goods inputs have not been produced by the government itself because it is obviously inefficient to do so. Proposals have increased in recent years to purchase service inputs that have traditionally been produced by government employees—laundry services, vehicle maintenance, computer services, cafeterias, and building maintenance, for example. Even more a departure from past practice are proposals to privatize delivery of final services—transportation, trash collection, social services, public housing, prisons.

The Federal Government and OMB Circular A-76

The oldest major instrument of privatization at the federal level remains OMB Circular A-76 (revised August 1983) first issued by the Bureau of the Budget in 1966, but having its origins in the Eisenhower administration. The circular "requires agencies, with some major exceptions, to use contractors for commercial services if such an approach is less expensive [than public production of these services by more than 10%]" (U.S. CBO 1987:1).

Substantial savings have been realized through the implementation of this circular, although there are large differences among estimates. The Congressional Budget Office (June 1987) estimates current annual savings at $200 million on a cash basis, $325 million on an accrual basis (U.S. CBO 1987:23). The cash figure includes only the reduction in current wage costs but accruals include reductions in future associated expenditures like pension liabilities. These figures are far lower than the estimated $2.8 billion for the period 1981–1987, about $467 million per year, cited by the President's Commission on Privatization (President's Commission 1988:133).

It would be difficult to argue that these savings have been translated into reductions in total expenditure. As we have seen, contracting out is the least favored tool of the most vigorous promoters of privatization, precisely because there are no guarantees that total expenditures will be reduced. Quite the contrary, it is expected that expenditures will be maintained by self-aggrandizing bureaucrats, by a Congress whose members and constituents focus on their own net benefit (income or services from particular expenditure programs minus the shared costs), and an expanding group of contractors who can be expected to lobby for increased expenditures (Butler 1985:56).

Legislation has been introduced that would require savings achieved under A-76 contracting not to be diverted to other uses but to be applied to budget reductions (U.S. CBO 1987:15). However, this might reduce the incentive to conduct A-76 reviews. The President's Commission on Privatization points out that until 1981, A-76 savings were required to be turned back to the Treasury and recommends against reinstituting such a requirement:

Competition and contracting may reduce budget demands, but they are primarily means to improve the efficiency and effectiveness of government services. Savings generated by this program [Circular A-76] should be eligible to be used as incentives to pursue competition and contracting. (President's Commission 1988:138)

Despite the fact that contracting is not likely to result in a smaller public sector or in reducing the deficit, it is considered an important means for improving public sector efficiency. Both the Grace Commission and the President's Commission on Privatization make numerous proposals for broadening its use.

Just as there are large differences in estimates of realized savings, so too are there disparities in the estimates of potential savings. The differences are accounted for largely by whether the estimate is based upon the assumption of full implementation of A-76 requirements or on expanded but still partial implementation. Full implementation refers to an extension of A-76 review to all potential commercial-type activities covered by the circular. Estimates for full implementation range from $1.1 (U.S. CBO as cited in U.S. GAO 1985, vol. 2:230) to $1.4 billion per year (Grace Commission as cited in GAO Vol. II, 1985:230). Recent CBO estimates of the savings that might be realized from doubling the rate of A-76 reviews, an expansion that is far below full implementation, put the average annual savings to be achieved over the 1988–92 period at $400 million on a cash basis and $650 million on an accrual basis (U.S. CBO 1987:23).

An assumption of only partial implementation is justified by the slow rate of compliance with A-76 review requirements to date. According to the CBO, current contract reviews cover the equivalent of about 10,000 jobs per year, compared with approximately 1.4 million persons in "full-time civilian employment in occupations likely to be engaged in providing commercial services" in the federal government in 1985 (U.S. CBO 1987:8).[7] Two of the most important reasons for the difference between the actual and potential number of reviews are the exemption of numerous agencies from A-76 review requirements and resistance of government employees. Employees fear losing control of their agency's performance, not to mention their own jobs. Given the current rate of A-76 reviews and the opposition to its extension, full implementation is unlikely in the near future, even if required legislative changes are made and all the recommendations of the President's Commission for "aggressive promotion" are adopted.

In general, the estimates of potential and of realized savings made by the groups most vigorously advocating the extension of government contracting with the private sector appear to be higher than warranted. Moreover, none of the estimates of savings, whether based upon full or partial implementation, can change total federal expenditures or the deficit by much. Nonetheless, and despite differences in estimates, greater efficiency in the use of public resources is an appropriate end in itself and there are still substantial economies to be realized from more diligent application of Circular A-76.

State and Local Governments
Contracted Activities, 1982 and 1987. Two surveys of city and county governments identify contracting as the most pervasive form of privatization (ICMA 1984 and Touche Ross 1987). Although contracting is widespread, what is surprising, given the enormous attention devoted to the subject in recent years, is that the number of places using contracting for various purposes appears to have expanded very little in the five years between the two surveys, and may even have declined for several service types.[8] What cannot be determined from the data is whether governments using private contracts have increased the number and the size of their contracts.

Responses to the two surveys on the extent of contracting are compared in Table 14.1. Despite the fact that only gross comparisons of the figures are possible, it appears that in only three or four of the sixteen categories—buildings and grounds maintenance, solid waste collection or disposal, data processing, and perhaps transportation and transit—has the proportion of governments that contract for the service increased.

Of the sixteen service categories, four can be classified as intermediate inputs and twelve as final services. Of the latter, seven involve personal services, and five various forms of physical service. The patterns of change over the period among these groups differ in ways that are consistent with expectations. It is easiest to extend contracting to intermediate service inputs. The logic of their production by private firms may be viewed as an extension of procurement, which is common for goods inputs. Resistance may be expected from workers whose jobs may be displaced, although often the contracts include various forms of job protection. With intermediate inputs, there is no client group to add resistance. Two of the four intermediate service categories appear to have experienced a major expansion in the proportion of places acquiring these services under contract: 100 percent in buildings and grounds maintenance, 50 percent for data processing. In the other two cases decreases are observed: about 20 percent for administrative services (probably not statistically significant) and 28 percent in fleet and vehicle maintenance.

Although contracting for final outputs of physical and infrastructure services represents more of a break with past practice, expectations are somewhat simi-

Table 14.1. Contracting Out by Cities and Counties (percentage of cities or counties with activity)

Activity	1982	1987
Buildings & grounds	21–23	46
Data processing	23–25	38
Administrative services	49–51	40
Fleet & vehicle maintenance	32	23
Solid waste—Collection & disposal	44	77
Streets & roads	27–28	32
Traffic signals & street lighting	39–41	36
Parking lots & garages	12–14	16
Utilities, meter reading	13–14	14
Recreation, parks, etc.	13–22	22
Transportation	23–46	55
Public safety	5–11	07
Housing & shelters	18–32	15
Hospitals & health services	27–42	21
Elderly & handicapped services	29–37	18
Child and day care	37–78	16

Notes. The 1982 figures are based upon data taken from the ICMA survey and the 1987 figures come from the Touche Ross survey. The figures presented in the two studies are not directly comparable and several adjustments have been made to take account of the differences.

1. The Touche Ross figures were computed as a percentage of all respondents and the ICMA data were presented as percentages of respondents providing the service in question (which in many cases is less than 100 percent of respondents). Therefore, the Touche Ross figures have been recomputed as a percentage of places providing the service (using the ICMA figures for this percentage).

2. The ICMA data have been adjusted to exclude intergovernmental agreements and other noncontract forms of provision. The ranges arise because contracts are indicated in three categories and any one city may have contracts of all three types. Therefore the lower bound estimate assumes there is overlap among the categories and the upper estimate assumes there is none.

3. The activity categories in the table are taken from the Touche Ross disaggregation. The ICMA data have been roughly aggregated to similar groupings.

lar to those for intermediate service inputs. In this group, solid waste collection and disposal, contracting is up by about 75 percent. The four other activities in this group—streets and road maintenance, traffic signals and street lights, parking lots and garages, and utilities and meter reading—show no change in the proportion of governments contracting over the five years.

Personal services present a very different pattern. Although there is substantial contracting out, particularly with nonprofit organizations, several factors might complicate matters. The output of a social service (e.g., a health center) is more difficult to define than that of a physical service (e.g., trash collection). Social services are disproportionately labor intensive and therefore worker resistance is likely to play an important role. Finally, personal services engage recipients directly, and recipients also may oppose change. The data suggest that large decreases in the extent of contracting are concentrated in the social services. In two of the seven personal service categories—elderly and handicapped services, and child and day care—very large decreases in the proportion of governments contracting for these services are observed. In housing and shelter and hospitals and health care, decreases also appear to have occurred, although given the range in the estimates for 1982, this is a weaker inference. Only in transportation does an increase in contracting appear to have taken place.

Contracts with private firms appear to be undertaken primarily to increase technical efficiency. In fifteen case studies of contracting reported by the ICMA in 1984 and in follow-up work for those cases in 1987, cost reduction was by far the principal reason for shifting the locus of production from the public sector to private firms (ICMA 1984 and Pack 1989). The 1987 Touche Ross survey shows cost reduction to be the most frequently cited advantage of privatization, and of contracting in particular. The experience has generally been consistent with the expectation. In both the Touche Ross survey and the ICMA case studies, reported savings are substantial—from 5 percent to more than 40 percent, with nearly two-thirds of the Touche Ross respondents indicating savings in the range of 10 to 29 percent.

In contracting, as in load shedding and asset sales, privatization is more likely where technical efficiency is the major issue. In the social services, allocation issues as well as process concerns assume great importance. Technical efficiency may be difficult to define and measure; perhaps even more critical, it may be virtually impossible to separate the way in which the social service is produced from the quality of what is produced.

Cost Reduction Over Time. Critics of privatization allege that cost savings will not be sustained, that bidders will offer low prices in order to win contracts and then increase prices once their relationship with the agency has been established. The literature has not usually been concerned with the longer term evolution of contracting relationships. For the most part, it concentrates on comparisons of private and public production costs at a moment in time.

One study that does take up the question of how contracting arrangements develop over time examines a small, diverse group of contracts, including intermediate service inputs like vehicle maintenance, data processing, and housekeeping functions, as well as final service outputs like street cleaning, trash pickup, and fire and ambulance services (Pack 1989). It provides some evidence that initial savings are not indicative of longer term outcomes. Of twelve agencies for which a comparison of costs in 1987 and 1983 was made, only half claimed that their private contracts continued to provide services at lower cost. In most of these cases estimated savings had substantially decreased over the four years. Two agencies still contracting with private firms believed that their own costs would have been lower than current contracts, but cited political obstacles to reversing the contracting decision. In three other cases, production had reverted to the public agency. In one a contractor's poor performance in vehicle maintenance was the reason given; in another, the city's sanitation department had made the lowest bid in the last three rounds of contract bidding; and in a third, the reasons were unrelated to contractor performance.

In these examples, competition appears to be a major element influencing the persistence of savings: there had been fewer bids on average for those contracts for which savings were not sustained than there had been in the places in which savings continue. An additional element is the initial magnitude of savings realized through contracting. The greater the initial savings, the more likely savings to have continued, although not at the initial high level. Where initial savings were very small, they disappeared over the period. These cases do not provide sufficient evidence to determine whether this is due to the private providers underestimating costs initially, either knowingly or inadvertently, or to the public agency redefining the terms of the contract, making it more costly.

Two recent studies yield useful insights into the ways in which contracting for social services develops to limit the realization of desired outcomes, including cost reduction and innovation. Mark Schlesinger, Robert Dortward, and Richard Pulice (1986) examine purchase of service contracts between the State of Massachusetts and private firms for mental health care, and Steven Rathgeb Smith (1987) looks at social service contracts with private nonprofit agencies, also in the State of Massachusetts.

At the time of the Schlesinger study, "the Massachusetts Department of Mental Health maintain[ed] over 2000 separate contracts . . . with over 500 vendors," (Schlesinger, Dortward, and Pulice 1986:249). Three improvements were hoped for from these contracting arrangements: more flexibility, as administrative rigidities of state bureaucracy were avoided; lower costs, from bypassing both civil service and union wage and hiring regulations; and greater responsiveness to local needs, as a result of greater decentralization.

What has been accomplished? The Department of Mental Health's need for monitoring and oversight, as well as "the legislature's desire to maintain accountability . . ." have led to a lengthy and complex contract review process which adds to the costs of administration and to the use of line-item budgets, both of which inhibit innovation and flexibility. Wage costs have declined; "employees in contract agencies receive wages 18% below comparably trained employees in the public sector" (Schlesinger, Dortward, and Pulice 1986:250). However, labor turnover has increased, with detrimental consequences for the quality of care. This implies that the initial public sector wage premium may have been efficient. In addition, the labor cost savings are expected to be transitory. Contractors themselves have successfully urged the legislature to increase the allowed wage rates, unionization of workers is increasing, and an ethics commission has defined the contractors' employees as "state employees."

Still another factor that will affect future costs is the evolution of the system from one explicitly designed to promote competition among private contractors to one that substantially inhibits competition. The authors estimate that one-third to one-half of contracts each year should be subject to competitive bidding (renewal contracts need to be bid competitively only every third year), but in fact only 20 percent of contracts are competitively bid. In addition, the extent of competition is more limited than anticipated—about 1.7 responses per solicitation. Several evolutionary factors have limited and will further limit competition. The "goal of maintaining continuity of care," economies of scale, and the difficulties associated with evaluating providers without a "track record" have led to an increasing concentration of contracts with large organizations. "Between 1984 and 1985, the portion of contracts going to [the] largest vendors grew by about 15%" (Schlesinger, Dortward, and Pulice 1986:252).

Thus, there are many forces working against sustained cost reduction from purchase of service contracts in mental health provision. The need for the government to specify closely and to oversee the delivery of such sensitive services, the increased pressures for wage parity, and the inhibitions on competition all imply that the change in the locus of production will not be accompanied by substantial change in the incentives for or the constraints on efficiency. Without these, the performance of the private nonprofit organizations may be expected to differ little from that of the public agencies.

Smith's study, "Privatization and the Politics of Social Welfare Spending" in Massachusetts (1987), reaches similar conclusions. Although he does not consider costs explicitly, many factors are identified that interfere with the achievement of cost reduction. In 1986, Massachusetts had $600 million of contracts with nonprofit agencies. In the Department of Social Services, 1,700 such contracts constituted 70 percent of the budget. Smith describes a system in which the government departments became increasingly dependent on private agencies to deliver basic social services. The new nonprofit organizations that form the majority of contractors, in contrast with the older nonprofits, have no existence apart from government programs. The government's dependence upon these groups has led, according to Smith, to the propping up of inefficient or mismanaged enterprises in order to maintain continuity and long-term relationships. In addition, given the sensitive nature of the social services—childcare, care of the elderly and infirm—and the enormous sums of money being spent, regulation of the sector has had to expand enormously. Increased regulation has several important consequences: it encumbers, it reduces flexibility in providing services in innovative ways, and it increases administrative costs. As a result, it inhibits precisely those outcomes that private providers seek.

The extensive regulation of the terms and implementation of contracts with private providers of social services identified by Schlesinger and Smith may be expected to carry over to other types of services, in particular, to the diverse personal services discussed earlier for which the production process is critical. The survey comparisons described above, in which decreases in contracting are concentrated almost exclusively in social services, are consistent with the development of social service contracting described by Schlesinger, Dortward, and Pulice and by Smith.

Thus, it appears that initial savings from private contracting overstate the savings to be realized over the longer period. In the case of social services, Schlesinger and Smith argue persuasively that this is closely linked to the increasingly regulated terms on which the contracts are let and to the related decrease in competition. The maintenance of competition is also central to the magnitude and persistence of savings in the cases considered by Pack.

The Future of Privatization: Opportunities and Constraints

This look at how major proposals for privatization have fared in the United States can help us to assess its future. At least over the near term, the types of privatization implemented and the effect on the public sector's size, budget deficits, and efficiency will not be very different from past experience.

Demand for privatization will come either from widely shared perceptions that the government is providing some services better left to the private sector, or from a belief that private production is more efficient even when public provision is otherwise justified. Where public provision is deemed to be unwarranted (e.g., in freight transportation), asset sales and divestiture are appropriate. Contracting with private firms will be the more likely instrument of privatization where the government is believed to be a less efficient producer (e.g., local trash collection) than the private sector.

If the past is a guide, the extension of privatization will continue to be tied more closely to demands for improving technical efficiency than for elimination of allocational inefficiency. Major constraints on privatization derive from the power of groups that benefit from the inefficiencies of public provision such as labor unions, or public production that protects their interests as with low density passenger train routes. However, the extent of privatization in the United States has often fallen short of its advocates' expectations because many of their proposals have been based upon beliefs regarding the inappropriateness of public provision that are not widely shared.

In the case of public provision of goods or services that could better be provided by private markets, comparisons of the public and private product must account for real or perceived externalities conferred by the government provision. The case of Amtrak demonstrated this. Joint products produced in the public sector but not likely to be produced by private firms (the PMAs) must also be considered. And, consideration must be given to the social goals, particularly distributional ones, served by seemingly inefficient public providers. Such factors appear to explain the failure to adopt major privatization proposals.

The overlap between distributional goals and public provision is also too frequently ignored. For example, the recommendations concerning public housing suffer from overstatement. The proposal to sell public housing to its occupants has such limited potential, it hardly seems worth pursuing and proposals to replace public housing with a voucher system are likely to work for only a very small subset of public housing occupants, in those areas with adequate low-rent housing supplies. This is not an argument against using these instruments; rather, a careful analysis suggests that they are unrealistic proposals for solutions to the question of how to provide housing for low-income households, a widely accepted social goal.

There has been less divergence between implementation and the alleged potential for increasing efficiency of public production through contracting with private firms. This is the most extensive form of privatization in the United States. In many cases, however, the conclusion that private producers must be more efficient than government is based upon a theoretical abstraction, not empirical evidence. As contracting moves further from procurement of intermediate goods and service inputs and toward final outputs, in particular, social services, the complications of the simple competitive model and the violations of its fundamental assumptions become more important; the standard implication of the theory, that private production is generally more efficient, may not always follow. Moreover, the extension of contracting to final service outputs raises larger issues than the improvement of technical efficiency.

Advocates of broad brush privatization should be chastened by the results of the Reagan administration's supply side economics. Tax reductions were to yield greater labor intensity, higher investment levels, and better allocation of investment, all leading to a surge in productive capacity. Little of this agenda had a firm base in empirical evidence about labor and investment decisions. The experiment is widely interpreted as having failed. While there are many merits in the arguments for privatization, neither theoretical arguments nor empirical evidence presently provide a compelling basis for urging full speed ahead. The current signals are blinking yellow.

NOTES

1 An intermediate form of privatization would be to distribute vouchers, as in the case of food stamps, and leave production to private firms. This increases consumer sovereignty and takes the government out of the production of the particular good or service, but continues its public financing. Technically, the negative income tax shifts the budget line, whereas vouchers pivot it. In general, the former is preferable on efficiency grounds.

2 It is interesting to contrast the conclusions on this subject of two of the principal champions of privatization. Recognizing the same basic set of facts, Savas concludes that "it is unlikely that more than 2 percent of public housing units could be sold to tenants. . ." (Savas 1987:201) but Butler contends that such sales "offer the chance to relieve the pressure on operating subsidies and social costs in public projects by shifting demand entirely out of the public sector, to the benefit of taxpayer and resident alike" (Butler 1985:75).

3 Indeed, some of the earliest benefit-cost studies were undertaken partly to analyze the value of benefits from such activities. (For example, see Eckstein 1958 and Krutilla and Eckstein 1958.)

4 I rely for the facts, although not for my interpretation, on the account in the report of the President's Commission on Privatization.

5 Any evaluation of the Conrail privatization is complicated by the fact that as a public entity Conrail was responsible for numerous commuter rail routes that subsequently became the responsibility of local authorities. It may be that the economies achieved by Conrail as a result simply shifted the inefficient activities to other public entities.

6 Gomez-Ibanez has estimated the savings to be achieved from rationalizing passenger rail operations and finds that even under the most favorable assumptions, ". . . conventional rail costs are usually substantially higher than bus and auto costs . . . both of which are above ordinary bus or low-cost airline operations. . . ." (Gomez-Ibanez 1987:232). Nor would the introduction of high-speed trains change the picture (Gomez-Ibanez and Clippinger 1987:169).

7 For various reasons they believe this "overstate[s] the size of the commercial work force that agencies will consider for contracting out," but it gives some idea of the order of magnitude.

8 The ICMA data were collected in 1982.

REFERENCES

Butler, Stuart M. 1985. *Privatizing Federal Spending: A Strategy to Eliminate the Deficit*. New York: Universe Books.

Eckstein, Otto. 1958. *Water Resource Development: The Economics of Project Evaluation*. Cambridge, Mass.: Harvard University Press.

Gomez-Ibanez, Jose A. 1987. "Costs of the Various Intercity Modes." In *Deregulation and the Future of Intercity Passenger Transportation*, ed. John R. Meyer and Clinton V. Oster, Jr., 225–48. Cambridge, Mass.: MIT Press.

Gomez-Ibanez, Jose A., and Marni Clippinger. 1987. "The Other Modes: Rail, Bus, and Auto." In *Deregulation and the Future of Intercity Passenger Transportation*, ed. John R. Meyer and Clinton V. Oster, Jr., 161–83. Cambridge, Mass.: MIT Press.

Krutilla, John V., and Otto Eckstein. 1958. *Multiple Purpose River Development*. Baltimore: Johns Hopkins Press.

Musgrave, Richard A. 1959. *The Theory of Public Finance: A Study in Public Economy*. New York: McGraw-Hill.

Pack, Janet Rothenberg. 1989. "Privatization and Cost Reduction." *Policy Sciences* 22:1–25.

Pack, Janet Rothenberg. 1987. "Privatization of Public-Sector Services in Theory and Practice." *Journal of Policy Analysis and Management*, 4:523–40.

President's Commission on Privatization. 1988. *Privatization: Towards More Effective Government* Washington: GPO.

Sappington, David E. M., and Joseph E. Stiglitz. "Privatization, Information and Incentives." *Journal of Policy Analysis and Management* 4:567–81.

Savas, E. S. 1987. *Privatization: The Key to Better Government*. Chatham, N.J.: Chatham House.

Savas, E. S. 1982. *Privatizing the Public Sector: How to Shrink Government*. Chatham, N.J.: Chatham House.

Schlesinger, Mark, Robert A. Dortward, and Richard T. Pulice. 1986. "Competitive Bidding and States' Purchase of Services: The Case of Mental Health Care in Massachusetts," *Journal of Policy Analysis and Management* 5 (2): 245–63.

Smith, Steven Rathgeb. 1987. "Privatization and the Politics of Social Welfare Spending." Paper presented at the Ninth Annual Research Conference of the Association of Public Policy Analysis and Management, Bethesda, October 1987.

Touche Ross. 1987. "Privatization in America: An Opinion Survey of City and County Governments on Their Use of Privatization and Their Infrastructure Needs." Washington, D.C.: Touche Ross.

U.S. Congressional Budget Office 1987. *Contracting Out: Potential for Reducing Federal Costs*, June.

U.S. General Accounting Office. 1985. *Compendium of GAO's Views on the Cost Saving Proposals of the Grace Commission*, vol. 1, "Summary of Findings," and vol. 2, "Individual Issue Analyses."

Valente, Carl F., and Lydia D. Manchester. 1984. *Rethinking Local Services: Examining Alternative Delivery Approaches*. Washington, D.C.: International City Management Association, Management Information Service Special Report No. 12.

Wolf, Charles, Jr., 1979. "A Theory of Non-market Failures," In *Public Expenditure and Policy Analysis*. 3d ed., ed. Robert H. Haveman and Julius Margolis, ston: Houghton Mifflin. 515–34.

15 *William T. Gormley, Jr.*

Two Cheers for Privatization

The privatization debate raises several important questions. Where do we draw the line between the responsibilities of government and the responsibilities of the marketplace? If both the government and the market have a role to play, what is the proper relationship between the two in a specific setting? What values does privatization promote and what values does it threaten? As we redesign our mechanisms for delivering vital social services, what forms of privatization are most promising? What can we learn from the experiences of other countries? What can we learn from the empirical evidence to date?

In more concrete terms, we may pose the following questions: 1) What are the advantages and disadvantages of privatization? 2) Is there a stronger case to be made for privatization in some issue areas than others? 3) *If* we privatize, *how* should we privatize? and 4) If we do not privatize, what alternatives should we pursue?

Advantages and Disadvantages

The case for privatization rests primarily, though not exclusively, on the proposition that privatization promotes economic efficiency. In theory, there are reasons to expect that privatization will result in cost savings, improved performance or both. Private schools, which must compete for students, have greater incentives to perform well than public schools, whose students are assigned to them by law. Private prisons, which must earn a profit or go out of business, have greater incentives to cut the costs of services through better management than public prisons, which may draw upon the public treasury if poor management results in higher costs.

When we shift our focus from theory to practice, however, the picture is mixed. In support of privatization, Kingsley finds that a housing voucher program is considerably more efficient than public housing. If we wish to cut the costs of federal housing programs for the poor, housing vouchers enable us to do that without necessarily reducing the total number of clients served. Similarly, Feeley notes that the private sector has saved taxpayers money by financing and constructing prisons which are then sold or leased to the government. The private sector's ability to move quickly to secure capital investment is a striking advantage, especially when inflation is high and delay can be costly to taxpayers.

On the other hand, housing vouchers do not help in cities where there is an acute shortage of affordable housing for the poor, such as Boston and New York. Indeed, according to HUD, 39 percent of families with vouchers were unable to find suitable housing within four months; and one fourth of those who found housing had to pay more than 40 percent of their income for rent (Cohn 1989:19). Unless the supply of housing for the poor improves, vouchers will be an efficient but only partly effective solution to the poor's housing problems. As for the privatization of prisons, we have no data on the efficiency of privately-run maximum-security prisons, which do not yet exist. Nor is it clear that privately run minimum-security prisons will continue to be profitable if lawsuits successfully challenge the authority of private prison guards.

In education, we suffer from a lack of good evidence on the effects of privatization. The Alum Rock voucher experiment, cited by Lee, included so many protections for public schools and public school teachers that it offers little guidance to policy makers (except that it confirms the political difficulties of institutionalizing a pure education voucher system). Comparisons of public and private schools, such as those conducted by Coleman et al. (1982), are suggestive but flawed (Goldberger and Cain 1982; Willms 1983). Private schools do seem to achieve more at lower cost but they benefit from cheap labor in some instances and their students may be more highly motivated than students who attend public schools.

If we look beyond education, housing, and law enforcement, the evidence is also mixed. As Van Horn notes, local government officials often cite expected cost savings as a reason for privatization, but this is less true of social services than of public works. Also, when asked to cite specific examples of actual cost savings, few local officials are able to do so. Pack, who studied 12 agencies that privatized over a period of four years, found that initial cost savings dissipated over time, especially where there had been limited competitive bidding in the first place. Thus, initial efficiency gains from privatization may not persist over time.

A stronger argument in favor of privatization can be made if one focuses on the concept of choice. Privatization does enable individual consumers to pursue their private choices more freely. Even if government subsidies continue, as in a voucher system, individuals have a wider range of options than they otherwise would. Thus, housing vouchers enable poor people to choose their neighborhood and their home, subject to cost constraints. Similarly, education vouchers permit parents to choose from a wide range of schools, both public and private, with the option of sending their children to a more costly school if they are interested and financially able.

Choice is a popular value, for both proponents and opponents of privatization. Ironically, however, an expansion of consumer choice through vouchers could result in greater government regulation of the private sector and a blurring of the distinction between the public and private sectors. In education, for example, James notes that greater regulation often accompanies increased government subsidies to the private sector. Levin (1989) has argued that this is precisely what would happen in the United States if we were to move towards an education voucher system. This would not only undermine choice (by homogenizing school systems) but it would also increase costs by requiring an expansion of state education bureaucracies.

Even if pressure for greater government regulation is resisted, there are other reasons to be wary of privatization. Like most reforms, privatization involves winners and losers. By all accounts, the sale of Council Housing in Great Britain has been a boon to those who were able to purchase their own home or flat. However, as Silver notes, conditions have worsened for those left behind. The quality of their housing stock has deteriorated, rent fees have increased, and rent defaults have become more common. A similar possibility exists in education. If all parents were issued education vouchers, wealthier families might switch to private schools in even greater numbers, leaving the public schools to cope with a less motivated and less manageable cohort of students. Voucher plans that ensure racial balance would not ensure social class balance and public schools could become less heterogeneous than they are today.

Another argument against privatization is that the quality of social services may deteriorate as private entrepreneurs seek to lower costs and increase profits. It is difficult to evaluate this argument, because the quality of services, especially social services, is exceedingly difficult to measure. Yet while generalizations remain elusive, it is quite clear that privatization can transform public services—in some instances, dramatically. That is precisely the point of Feeley's article on the privatization of prisons and other custodial institutions. Historically, the British government was able to extend the scope and severity of its criminal sanctions through privatization. By transporting prisoners to the colonies and, later, by exploiting convict labor, private entrepreneurs were able to make a living for themselves. More significantly, the state was able to punish larger numbers of criminals at a much lower cost. Shifting to modern times, Feeley argues that the private sector has expanded the range of criminal sanctions available to state and local governments. By developing treatment programs as conditions for probation and by developing sophisticated new monitoring devices to keep track of probationers, private industry has increased the range of punishments available to state and local governments. Thus, in evaluating privatization proposals, we need to consider not only how the inputs would change but how the outputs would change as well.

Conditions for Privatization

Like deregulation, decentralization, and other reforms, privatization is not a plan for all seasons. It is more or less appropriate in different settings or contexts. Contributors to this volume, whose views on privatization are diverse, will not readily agree on a set of principles to guide policy makers trying to decide whether to privatize. Starr opposes privatization across the board and several other contributors are deeply skeptical. Nevertheless, let me attempt to specify several propositions which are at least roughly consistent with the evidence produced for this book.

First of all, privatization is less appropriate for regulation (of firms or individuals) than for the distribution of services. When the state deprives a private party of his or her life, liberty, or property, the state's moral authority and responsibility should be as unambiguous as possible. For this reason, privatization is less appropriate in law enforcement, which includes a strong regulatory component, than in education or housing, where regulation, though present, is less central.

Actually, the distinction between regulation and service delivery is not crystal clear. For example, Feeley cites drug treatment programs for probationers, many of which are run by private organizations. These programs are part of the state's law enforcement apparatus, broadly defined. At the same time, they clearly involve the distribution of social services. Thus, for such programs the propriety of privatization will depend on how one views the mix of functions. More broadly, it seems, the question is not so much whether the program in question includes a regulatory component but rather the scope and severity of the regulations. In law enforcement, we are more squeamish about privatizing a maximum-security prison than we are about privatizing a half-way house for juvenile delinquents. For good reason, the former is quite rare, while the latter is quite common. In some states, group day care centers are tightly regulated by state officials, while child care providers who care for one or two children at home are loosely regulated by nonprofit organizations, under contract to state or local governments. This is perfectly understandable, given differences in the degree of regulation involved.

Second, privatization is less appropriate when social services are involved than when physical services are involved. The outputs of social services are more difficult to measure, the risks of failure are more serious, and the need for accountability is greater. At first glance, housing, education, and law enforcement may be thought of as human services and hence poor candidates for privatization. On the other hand, each of these issue areas, when dissected into its component parts, reveals a more complicated mixture of human and physical services. Thus food services and laundry services, provided by a private firm to prison inmates, are physical or commercial services. The privatization of food services and laundry services within a state prison may be judged purely on the basis of efficiency; the privatization of prison guards raises questions of equity, legitimacy, and accountability. The former is a better candidate for privatization than the latter.

Third, privatization is less appropriate for core services than for auxiliary services. The heart of a government program may be too vital to society to run the risk of lapses of quality or interruptions in service that may accompany delegation to the private sector. Law enforcement and education have some of these characteristics, which helps to explain why the public sector guards its prerogatives so jealously (there are, to be sure, other less noble motivations as well). However, there is no reason why the private sector cannot provide auxiliary services in both of these areas. Neighborhood Watch programs, operated by citizen volunteers with some supervision by public police officers, can play a constructive role in extending the protection and especially the information provided by public law enforcement officials. Private security guards and burglar alarms enable private citizens and firms to purchase greater physical security in order to meet special needs or problems that they face. Although the latter form of privatization raises some equity questions (the rich are better able to purchase auxiliary services than the poor), such concerns can be better addressed through a more equitable income maintenance policy than through restrictions on private purchases of auxiliary law enforcement services. Similarly, there are good reasons for local public school districts to contract out to for-profit or nonprofit firms to purchase supplementary educational services for gifted or disabled students. As Elmore notes, the private sector in the state of Washington has provided valuable services to high school dropouts that public school systems were ill equipped to provide themselves.

Privatization Techniques

Two of the most widely discussed privatization techniques in the United States are vouchers and contracting out. Vouchers are widely discussed because they seem to epitomize privatization, with its emphasis on a minimal role for government and a substantial role for private citizens. Contracting out is widely discussed because it is extensively utilized. Both contracts and vouchers are especially important in the human services area because of the limited appeal of load-shedding (most Americans continue to favor a welfare state) and because of the limited pertinence of asset sales (which apply more to physical services than to human services).

Scholars and practitioners disagree sharply on the merits of contracting out. From the vantage point of practitioners, this is the most convenient and the most popular form of privatization. As Touche Ross (1987) has shown, contracting out is extensively used by local governments throughout the United States, and its popularity continues to grow. In contrast, scholars are deeply skeptical of contracting out. Indeed, this is one of the few points on which contributors to this volume agree.

As Butler points out, government contracts to the private sector create a vested interest in favor of continued government spending. A pro-spending lobby of private contractors, he fears, will make it difficult to arrest the upward spiral in government spending. Van Horn voices a different concern—namely, that private contractors will corrupt the contracting process by offering generous campaign contributions to helpful politicians and attractive jobs to helpful administrators. Thus, he warns that contracting out may corrupt both public administration and the electoral process. As Pack notes, contracting out seldom works as intended. Competitive bidding is the exception rather than the rule. Moreover, even when competitive bidding is required, the number of competitive bids may be so small as to make a mockery of the competitive process. A final problem with contracting out is the difficulty of monitoring quality, especially in the social services area. This may encourage private contractors to cut costs and dilute the quality of the services they deliver in order to maintain comfortable profit margins.

Some of these problems may be avoided by contracting out to nonprofit organizations. Unlike for-profit firms, nonprofits may not contribute to political campaigns, thus reducing opportunities for corruption. Also unlike for-profit firms, nonprofits have limited incentives to deceive consumers about the quality of their services, due to legal restrictions on the distribution of profits to employees. Their commitment to quality may also be stronger than that of for-profit firms, if studies in the health care field are any indication (Weisbrod 1989). Most of these studies (e.g., of nursing homes) reveal that the quality of services provided by nonprofit organizations is superior to that of for-profit firms when appropriate controls are applied. There are, to be sure, problems with contracts to nonprofit firms, as Pack and others have noted. Nonprofit firms also have a vested interest in government spending, and they have fewer incentives to be efficient than for-profit firms. Nevertheless, contracting out to nonprofit firms may be an appealing option, especially in the social services area, where service quality is so difficult to measure and where trust is so important.

In contrast to contracts, which are problematic at best, vouchers have considerable appeal to those who seek to maximize both efficiency and consumer choice. In a sense, vouchers institutionalize a much more rigorous form of competition than competitive bidding. By providing for more or less continuous opportunities for consumer monitoring and consumer choice, vouchers enlist thousands of consumers in the task of scrutinizing and evaluating service-deliverers. If a service provider stints on quality, consumers may vote with their feet.

Like privatization generally, vouchers are more promising in some issue areas than others. Vouchers are especially appropriate under the following conditions: 1) when there is considerable product differentiation and when consensus on product or program quality is elusive; 2) when consumers have the capacity and the inclination to inform themselves; and 3) when extensive consumer choice need not be accompanied by an equally extensive scheme of government regulation.

Day care provides a good illustration of a policy context where these conditions apply. There is considerable variety in the array of private day care services available and there is considerable variety in the day care preferences of parents. Some parents prefer group day care while others prefer family day care; some parents prefer day care near their home, while others prefer day care near their job; some parents prefer to leave their child with someone they know and trust while others prefer to leave their child with someone who is more likely to promote the child's cognitive development. Information about day care options is generally, though not universally, available, and the information obtained is not so complicated that ordinary persons cannot understand it. Interestingly enough, low-income parents seem to devote no less time to the search for suitable day care than more affluent parents (Mathematica 1989:135–37). Observers will disagree on the need for stringent day care regulations. Clearly, children cannot protect themselves. On the other hand, parents often take a keen interest in the quality of day care their children receive, which reduces the need for government monitoring and surveillance.

There is also much to be said for housing vouchers. The housing preferences of the poor, like those of the middle class, vary widely and reflect differences in circumstance and in taste. Whether the poor invest as much time in the search for housing as the middle class is unclear. However, it would appear that the need for government regulation has declined, as the quality of our housing stock has improved considerably over the past 40 years. As Kingsley notes, housing vouchers have enabled us to provide housing to the poor at a relatively low cost and with a relatively high degree of consumer discretion. Vouchers are clearly more efficient than other approaches that have been tried.

The fact that our housing problems have worsened in recent years as voucher experiments have been tried should not be attributed to vouchers themselves. Dramatic reductions in the federal housing budget account for the decline of affordable housing for the poor. In housing, as in other areas, demand-side strategies, such as vouchers, must be accompanied by supply-side strategies.

The case for education vouchers is much more problematic, at least in the United States. First of all, education vouchers raise church-state questions that housing vouchers do not. When a consumer supports a church-sponsored school with public funds, this undermines the religious convictions of tax-payers who do not share that particular faith. Second, education vouchers are likely to require a huge government bureaucracy to ensure high quality in both private and public schools and to ensure that racial balance is maintained. In the United States, any education voucher experiment that embraces both private and public schools is bound to encounter both legal and political difficulties.

Hybrids and Alternatives

Some of the more intriguing reforms discussed in this book maintain a vital role for both the public and private sectors. Tenant management, discussed by Hula, illustrates the potential for creative partnerships between the public and private sectors. Instead of abandoning public housing for the poor, tenant management harnesses the creative energies of housing project tenants who are trained to manage their own project. This approach is at once radical and incremental. It is incremental in that it attempts to make public housing work by ameliorating conditions there. It is radical in that it transfers important decisions from government bureaucrats to poor people.

Studies of tenant management have concluded that it is more effective than efficient. The Kenilworth-Parkside project in northeast Washington, D.C. has been hailed as a spectacular success but that success was fueled by generous government subsidies. On the other hand, demonstration projects are often more costly than full-fledged programs. Thanks to its success, Kenilworth-Parkside stands at the brink of a quantum leap forward for tenants—the transition to home ownership (Osborne, 1989). Given Silver's findings on the sale of Council Housing in Great Britain, one must regard this as an exciting prospect for Kenilworth-Parkside residents. But what about those who remain behind in increasingly less desirable public housing units? The British experience is instructive in this regard. As Silver notes, the disastrous consequences of home ownership in Great Britain for those left behind in Council Housing were due not to home ownership per se but rather to other government policies—reduced subsidies to Council Housing, higher rents, fewer repairs, etc. Above all, the government's failure to create new housing combined with its home ownership policy severely to restrict the mobility of many Council Housing tenants. If the United States experiments widely with tenant management and the eventual sale of public housing units, the British experience should not be forgotten. The privatization of public housing can be good for those who become homeowners and those who do not but only if the government maintains an adequate supply of affordable housing for those who are unable to buy their own housing unit.

Moonlighting by public police officers is another good example of what can be accomplished when public and private roles are combined in new and creative ways. As Reiss shows, this growing trend enables us to improve our collective security at little additional public cost. By relying on off-duty public police officers to provide auxiliary services for special occasions or in designated areas (e.g., an urban shopping mall), private entrepreneurs can protect their property while at the same time ensuring the safety of shoppers and residents in the protected area. Moonlighting is not without its drawbacks. In effect, it provides greater police protection to those who are able to purchase additional police services. In some sense, that would seem to violate our commitment to equal protection under the law. However, in legal terms, we are in effect talking about protection outside the law, even though the officers in question are in fact public employees. Moreover, no one has demonstrated that moonlighting by police has any adverse effects on police budgets. Unless these supplementary services reduce public expenditures for all citizens, moonlighting would seem to improve security for some without diminishing security for others. If so, it is a classic Pareto-optimal solution.

Although contributors to this book have emphasized reforms that redefine public and private roles, meaningful reform is possible without ceding important government functions to the private sector. Recent experiments in community-oriented policing in Houston, Texas, Madison, Wisconsin, and other cities, illustrate the potential for successful policy innovation within the public sector. By assigning police officers to local neighborhoods and by shifting the emphasis of policing from the apprehension of criminals to an attack on the causes of crime, community-oriented policing has institutionalized a new strategy for dealing with crime. It combines decentralization with a pro-active, anticipatory crime-prevention approach. Although further research needs to be conducted, preliminary reports on community-oriented policing have been decidedly positive (Wilson and Kelling 1989).

In education, as in law enforcement, it is also possible to achieve significant progress without abandoning our historic commitment to a strong public sector. A wide range of experiments in choice in public education have been successful or partially successful, as Elmore reports. Minnesota's program allowing high school juniors and seniors to enroll in colleges for high school degree credit has attracted a substantial number of participants and has generated considerable satisfaction among participants. Washington's program of remedial education for high school dropouts, which allows parents to purchase services from a variety of suppliers, has proven much less costly than conventional dropout programs delivered by government itself. Harlem's experiments in choice in public school education have resulted in remarkable progress in the reading skills of disadvantaged youths. Given these success stories, there is much to be said for additional experiments in public school choice, such as Minnesota's open enrollment program, which allows students to transfer from one school district to another, with public funds accompanying the students who switch to their newly chosen school district. Public choice experiments empower parents, discourage flight from inner-city neighborhoods, and apply much-needed competitive pressure to public schools. Moreover, as Boston has demonstrated, public school choice experiments can be designed in such a way that racial balance is not undermined (Steinbach and Peirce 1989:1695).

The broader point is that we can revitalize the public sector without resorting to privatization. At the federal level, environmental impact statements have sensitized a wide variety of agencies to the need for environmental protection, while inspectors general have helped cabinet-level departments to achieve greater efficiency by ferreting out waste, fraud, and abuse. At the state level, proxy advocates have effectively represented consumers in public utility commission proceedings, while nursing home ombudsmen have effectively represented the interests of nursing home residents in dealings with both public and private officials. At the local level, experiments in "quality improvement" have enabled some cities to deliver public services more efficiently by harvesting the insights and creative ideas of public employees. Privatization is not the only path that leads to efficiency, nor is it the only way to guarantee certain rights for consumers.

Conclusion

Throughout this essay I have implicitly accepted the argument that privatization choices should be approached pragmatically, with due attention to particular circumstances and contexts. Clearly, Starr objects to that perspective, on the grounds that a bundle of privatization decisions may be unfortunate even if individual privatization decisions can be justified. From Starr's perspective, privatization cramps our public discourse by accepting private ends as givens. In contrast, service delivery by the public sector presupposes that personal preferences will be reshaped and transformed through public debate, elections, and legislative deliberation.

There is something to be said for Starr's argument, especially in the human services area. We needn't fret a great deal about the values at stake when we choose one method of picking up garbage rather than another. On the other hand, when education, housing, and law enforcement are at stake, we ought to examine critically our own predispositions and challenge the predispositions of others in order to root out prejudices, misconceptions, and misunderstandings. To the extent that privatization curtails such public debate, by substituting private preferences for collective choices, it robs us of the advantages of public deliberation and discussion.

Yet if privatization involves risks, it also involves opportunities. Experiments in privatization and proposals for sweeping privatization have actually triggered a healthy public debate and generated considerable support for public school choice proposals that in effect mimic privatization in a public school setting. Without the privatization debate and without serious arguments in favor of education vouchers and tuition tax credits, it is unlikely that public school choice would have advanced so far. Oftentimes proposals for privatization stimulate creative counter-proposals that enable us to promote choice without abandoning our historic commitment to a strong public sector.

In other issue areas, privatization, depending on its form, may strengthen democratic government rather than undermine it. Which is more democratic—a public housing project managed by government bureaucrats, or a project managed by tenants? Which is more democratic—a highly centralized police department that responds to reports of crimes in progress, or a decentralized department that works closely with citizens in an effort to prevent crimes from occurring in the first place? Which is more democratic—a centralized school board that makes decisions with only token parental involvement, or decentralized educational governance that empowers teachers and parents alike?

Privatization must be unbundled because the concept encompasses techniques that both strengthen and weaken democratic government. Some forms of privatization (e.g., contracting without competition) merely substitute a private monopoly for a public monopoly. Other forms of privatization, especially those that empower consumers or poor people, substitute downward accountability for upward accountability. In some instances, privatization reduces the power of bureaucrats (and their overseers), while increasing the power of citizens. It is difficult to regard this form of privatization as a threat to democratic government.

REFERENCES

Cohn, Bob. 1989. "Looking Beyond the HUD Scandal." *Newsweek*, 21 August, 19.

Coleman, James, et al. 1982. *High School Achievement: Public, Catholic, and Private Schools Compared.* New York: Basic Books.

Goldberger, Arthur, and Glen Cain. 1982. "The Causal Analysis of Outcomes in the Coleman, Hoffer, and Kilgore Report." *Sociology of Education* 55:103–22.

Levin, Henry. 1989, "The Theory of Choice Applied to Education." Paper presented at La Follette Institute Conference on Choice and Control in American Education at Madison, Wisconsin, 17–19 May.

Mathematica Policy Research. 1989. "The Child Care Challenge: What Parents Need and What Is Available in Three Metropolitan Areas." Report Prepared for the U.S. Department of Health and Human Services. Princeton, N.J.: Mathematica Policy Research.

Osborne, David. 1989. "Irresistible Force: Kimi Gray and the Miracle of Kenilworth-Parkside." *Washington Post Magazine*, 30 July, 12–31.

Steinbach, Caroi, and Neil Peirce. 1989. "Multiple Choice." *National Journal*, 1 July, 1692–95.

Touche Ross. 1987. "Privatization in America: An Opinion Survey of City and County Governments on Their Use of Privatization and Their Infrastructure Needs." Washington, D.C.: Touche Ross.

Weisbrod, Burton. 1989. "Rewarding Performance That is Hard to Measure: The Private Nonprofit Sector." *Science*, 5 May, 541–46.

Willms, J. Douglas. 1983. "Do Private Schools Produce Higher Levels of Academic Achievement?" In *Public Dollars for Private Schools* ed. T. James and H. Levin, 223–34. Philadelphia: Temple University Press.

Wilson, James Q., and George Kelling. 1989. "Making Neighborhoods Safe." *The Atlantic Monthly*, 7 February, 46–52.

INDEX

Index